"*Just A Sailor* is the story of a young man's 13 years as an underwater photographer in the U.S. Navy, including a tour in Vietnam with UDT-13. When I first picked up a copy of this book I was not sure if I would enjoy reading it or not-after all, how exciting can underwater photography be? However, it didn't take me long to realize that I was mistaken, and instead of being bored I was in for a real treat. Steve Waterman's story of his time in the Navy is as interesting as it is humorous. The author has a penchant for detail, which enables you to get in to the story in a way that few books permit. Here's a guy whose primary training after enlisting in the Navy in 1964 is photography-not much to inspire excitement at first glance, but as the story unfolds Waterman himself decides that he needs more juice in his career. He decides to take up scuba diving as a hobby, likes it and volunteers to become a Navy diver. He completes that course and moves his career underwater. During the course of his 13 years in the service, the young Photographer's Mate goes through Scuba training, attends Airborne school, completes HALO training, serves a combat tour in Vietnam, and becomes a first class diver. At that time, he was one of only four or five Photographer's Mates in the entire U.S. Navy who held this rating. I can assure you that his story is anything but boring.

"Written in the indisputable style of *Combat Weatherman*, *Just a Sailor* is an enjoyable read. Although every chapter is not a page-turner, Waterman's career in the Navy was anything but routine. Seldom will you read such a complete and graphic description of U.S. Navy divers going about their everyday life.

"An added bonus is the outstanding photographs in the centerfold section of the book. It's easy to understand why the author's services as an underwater photographer were in such high demand. The superb quality of the photos and their subject matter justify the publisher's decision to use 55 of them in the book. Believe me, this is almost unheard of in mass-market paperbacks.[†]

"Steve Waterman is truly a remarkable man. He has enjoyed his life immensely, doing and accomplishing things that most can only dream about. Yet, to Waterman, it was no big deal. His almost cavalier attitude about it all is refreshingly entertaining. Not one to follow blindly where others may lead, the author's shenanigans often got him in trouble with his superiors. That old "devil may care" mind set, characteristic of many in his dangerous profession, always managed to surface at the wrong-and sometimes the right-time. In spite of his occasional irreverence for authority, Steve Waterman was a good sailor. He never let his viewpoint interfere with his sense of duty or his performance. I felt like this guy enjoyed himself and what he did, even though he did it "his" way whenever he could get away with it.

"So read this one. I'm a big fan of the SEALs, and this is as close as it gets without going through Hell Week. As a matter of fact, the author works with SEALs on several occasions during his 13 years in the Navy, some of whom I have known. Great book, great read."

—*Dennis Cummings*
Author of *Men Behind the Trident*

† The first publication of *Just a Sailor* had fifty-five photos. This publication has eighty photos, fifty-two of which were not in the first publication.

"… an excellent autobiography of an ordinary person living an extraordinary life. …His narration is casual, informative, and easy to understand. …Expect to laugh, learn, and ponder upon the passages from *Just A Sailor*. Believe me, Steve Waterman is far more than meets the eye!"

—*Katherine A. Skopik*,
I/O Psychology Student, Middle Tennessee State University

"If you love adventure, the Navy, photography, and diving, *Just A Sailor*, by former Navy photographer/diver Steve Waterman is a must read! *Just A Sailor* is a no non-sense account of what it is like to serve as an enlisted man in the U.S. Navy with the elitist of the elite.

"It's a story that any Sailor, particularly enlisted people, will be able to relate to; of hardship, travel, low pay, dangerous work environments, and combat. …It is one of the best books I've ever read dealing with the pre-PC Navy. Waterman has painted a vivid picture of what Navy life "used" to be like."

—*Art Giberson*
Author of *Photojournalist*,
Blue Ghost: The Ship That Couldn't Be Sunk,
Eyes of the Fleet: A History of Naval Photography

"I found *Just A Sailor* to be a fast-paced, interesting book that was hard to put down. … a good picture of part of our military not usually seen. I write from a background of two years service in an Air Force Special Forces unit.

—*Stephen Bennett*
MSGT USAF Retired, Saint George, Maine

"As a veteran myself, including a tour in Vietnam, I have avoided reading a lot of books just because of the memories they may stir up. … [This book] is an extremely well-written book… with self-confidence, humor, and honesty about himself and his short comings. I was impressed by his intelligent writings and his ability to make the military as understandable as possible. I recommend this book if, for nothing, else the enjoyment of reading a well-written book, but also to give you an insight into the world of a Navy combat photographer."

—*Gary L. Thompson*
Eugene, Oregon

"*Just A Sailor*… NOT!!!!! From the brown water of Vietnam to the blue of the Caribbean and the cold water off New England, Waterman's adventures both entertain and educate us about the "other" Navy, the Navy of Special Warfare, salvage divers, and the underwater photographer. This book is definitely a page turner!"

—*Robert J. Skinner*
"midsouth_books" Memphis, TN

"Waterman tells his autobiographical story in such a modest manner, it is easy to forget how brave he is. …he did things few in the world can claim. …a tale of his experiences as an underwater cameraman, salvage operator, and commercial diver. …Highly recommend!"

—*MicroJoe*

"I give this book five stars because it's one of a kind and no other book can compare to it. Steve Waterman tells his story with pure, unadulterated honesty. ...His prose is straightforward and conversational.

"...He became one of only 15 Navy combat photographers. (There are only 15 of these guys at any one time in the Navy.)

"...Steve's recollection of his service in the Navy is remarkably honest and telling."

—*Robert Bernstein*
St. George, Maine

"Steven Waterman's *Just A Sailor* has taken me to a world within the Navy that I previously didn't know existed. The trip is adventurous, dangerous, and almost always humorous. Waterman's refreshing style of writing is a splash of cold water in the face of this reader of military history. I highly recommend that you read this book if you enjoy reading: about the military life, about combat, about UDT / SEALs, about the Navy, or you just want to read something that is a diversion from the typical military nonfiction. I hope Waterman continues to write as I always need/enjoy a splash of cold water."

—*Bob Taylor*
Houston/Galveston Area, TX

"Steve's words paint a thousand pictures. ...this book does not alienate you through miles of military mumble or intricate technicalities, but rather it draws you into each intriguing page as though you were present through it all.

"...I was truly disappointed when I ran out of pages. Steve's genuineness and candor will cause you to feel as though you've known him for years as he escorts you through his personal and professional world, successes and regrets, triumphs and trials.

"A delightful journey it is. This book should come with a warning: 'May Cause Late Night Reading Addiction.'"

—*Beth Botsis*
Northern Virginia

"As a former Navy Photographer (a PH—before Waterman's time), I thoroughly enjoyed his wandering through his Navy life. I remember the A and C schools being much the same as he described, and got the "feel" of his underwater training and activities just if I had been there. Steve has grasped the real feeling of his Navy life, and demonstrates it quite well to the reader. If you are offended by a few "blue" words, this may not be your reading delight, but if you want to see the world through a Navy Photographer/Divers eyes, this is one to read!"

—*K. Estes "Old Sgt"*
Washington State

"To be selected Chief in 11 years in the Navy is pretty remarkable. And to be a combat photographer/diver is pretty rare. And then to remember almost every name of every person you ever served with is downright documentary. Narrate them all in genuine, salty, sailor talk and publish it in book form and you have *Just A Sailor*. A historical artifact. A war diary. A tribute to those who served."

—*Paul Dietz "Nissantwa"*
Oakhurst, CA

"I just completed reading Steven Waterman's *Just A Sailor* and would like to strongly recommend it to everyone interested in the Navy's Underwater Demolition Teams (UDT), Combat Camera, and Naval Special Warfare during the Vietnam era. ... this book exemplifies "quiet professionalism."

"I would also recommend this book to young men and women interested in joining the service. Waterman ably describes both the positives and negatives of service in the U.S. military and provides some valuable lessons learned for what one may expect to encounter during time spent in the military.

"UDT and SEAL veterans will likely find it entertaining as well, as Waterman is able to recall places and events that occurred during his time in Vietnam, as well as at Little Creek, Norfolk, and Virginia Beach, with remarkable detail.

"I thoroughly enjoyed this book and it provided me with a great personal perspective on what it was like to serve our country during those dangerous times."

—*Tom Hunter*
Norfolk, VA

"There are some authors who seem to make themselves out as bigger-than-life heroes and embellish their memoirs in order to make a good tale. However, author Steven Waterman understates his experiences with humor, honesty, and an almost conversational style of writing in his autobiography *Just A Sailor*. His story is about his experiences as a Navy underwater photographer. He also engages in underwater salvage, and even combat in Vietnam.

"The way the book starts off with the young Waterman getting arrested for underage drinking and then almost dropping out of school, shows that the author was willing to share his personal experiences—blemishes and all! He does a great job of taking the reader though his boot camp training and all the way through the end of his enlistment. Having been in the Army, I found his story to be very interesting, as I had no idea what life in the Navy was like and certainly not the kind of stuff for what he was trained for.

"This book is very funny at times, as the author does not take his life or the Navy, all that seriously. The reader will enjoy the story and find Waterman's personality endearing. You will get to like this guy as you follow him through his Navy career. The book itself is very readable. It is a good tale and it is told well.

—*W. H. McDonald, Jr.*
The American Author Association
Elk Grove, CA

"...In *Just A Sailor*, I enjoyed the Vietnam narration but, surprisingly, found the "civilian aspects" and the diving and photography just as interesting. ...This was an excellent book, and I look forward to the author's next!"

—*G. Kennedy*
Survival Ranger, Fort Bragg

JUST A SAILOR

A Navy Diver's Story of
Photography, Salvage, and Combat

Steven L. Waterman

FindTech, Ltd
P. O. Box 43698
Cleveland, OH 44143
(877) 882-6124 • *www.find-tech.biz*

Published by:
FindTech, Ltd
P. O. Box 43698
Cleveland, OH 44143
(877) 882-6124
www.find-tech.biz

Printed and bound in the United States of America.

ISBN: 0-8041-1037-6
       978-9787637-8-7

First publication: October, 2000
  by The Ballantine Publishing Group, a division of Random House, Inc.

Republished: December 2008
  by FindTech, Ltd

10 9 8 7 6 5 4 3 2 1

Library of Congress Catalog Card Number: 00-105352

Cover design: Penelope Stetz
Cover Photographs: Copyright © Steven L. Waterman 2008

Unless otherwise noted, all photographs in this book were taken by, and are the copyright of, Steven L. Waterman © 2008.

Front cover: A member of AFCCG's Underwater Photo Team
             approaching the Zodiac.
Back cover: Top, Steven L. Waterman home on leave, August 1970 (the
             Navy allowed beards then). *Photo by Norma Drinkwater.*
             Bottom: Steven L. Waterman on his BMW R-60 motorcycle
             with a Steib sidecar. *Photo by Frank Genovese*

Dedication

This book is dedicated to all the men and women who have served our country. Without their sacrifices, we couldn't appreciate the quality of life we experience in America today. I also want to express my sincere thanks to Commander Gerry Pulley, USN (Ret.), who gave me every opportunity to further my career as a Navy diver and photographer; and to my great friend Captain George W. Kittredge, USN (Ret.), who remains my constant mentor.

In Memoriam

My wife,
Mary J. Waterman
May 28, 1947 – January 17, 2006

My mother,
Norma Drinkwater,
March 26, 1926 – April 9, 2008

Contents

Introduction

This is the second publication of *Just a Sailor*. I have updated it with some corrections that were missed the first time around, and have also added some photos (fifty-two of eighty) and omitted others (twenty-seven of fifty-five).

Most of my life, I wondered what it would take to have a book published. I have always felt that those who could accomplish this were far above my level of abilities. After attending a writing workshop some years back, I developed an attitude that being published was hopeless, something akin to winning the lottery.

One feminist New York editor stated, "You have to pay your dues and run the gauntlet of New York's young, male editors." According to her, a writer has to look forward to being rejected many times and one would have to make the rounds and talk the talk, taking full advantage of the old-boy network as much as possible. This attitude sank in and caused me to doubt myself and the very worth of what I had to say. Some of my articles had been published in magazines, but I never felt that I would be published in the way I had envisioned. I made my thoughts clear on this to my wife, Mary, on many occasions. She encouraged me to "just sit down and start writing."

Denny Davis, my cousin, childhood playmate and classmate, and longtime lobster fisherman, said to me one day, "Most of us lead relatively boring lives, Steve. You have done things that others can only read about."

Now, people *can* read about them. It appears to only take three things to get a book published: You need to have something to say, be able to say it, and have a publisher who believes that there are people who want to pay to read it. My first publisher, Random House/Ballantine Books. proved that I did have something to say, but elected not to reprint *Just a Sailor*. I have faith that there are still people who would like to have a copy and arranged for this second publishing.

Chapter 1

Why Not Join the Navy?

It was New Year's Eve, 1963. I was seventeen years old, and Bill Swanson, a high school classmate, and I were out roaming the streets of Rockland, Maine, trying to find somebody who would buy two underage boys some alcohol. Our goal was Gluek Stite, a rank but strong malt liquor that came in small six ounce cans. The stuff would gag a maggot, but it would get you drunk in minimum time. All of us who drank for the sole purpose of getting hammered used it.

Earlier in the evening, as I left my house in Spruce Head, I had asked my mother for some money so I could go to the movies and get something to eat. I did neither that night.

Bill knew a Coast Guard sailor by the name of Reb who would buy beer for kids. We found him in his room above the Oasis Lounge in Rockland. This was a sleazy bar and not a place where "nice" people hung out. We walked up the outside stairs to Reb's room and gave him the money. He went to the market across Park Street to make our purchase.

Reb came back to the room with the malt liquor and handed the brown sack to us. We drank down the nasty, bitter liquid and waited for the buzz that would signify we were attaining the first stages of adolescent intoxication. Reb was lying on his bed reading a girlie magazine, looking at us every once in a while with a big grin as we drank the malt liquor.

A few minutes after having downed our six-packs, we left Reb's room for our first stop, the barroom downstairs. The operators of the place didn't question our ages. I proposed to a woman that she might dance with me. She gave me a quizzical look and impolitely declined the offer.

We then strode valiantly, however unsteadily, out into the street. I was walking up toward Park Street along Main when I was overcome by nausea. Right in front of Phil's Corner, a small luncheonette, I felt the immediate urge to puke. To steady myself, I grabbed firmly onto a parking meter (a long since discarded fixture on Rockland's Main Street) and proceeded to spray yellow Gluek Stite all over my shoes and the surrounding concrete of the sidewalk. Just then, a Rockland cop, Officer Hanley, walked up and asked if I was all right. I replied, of course I was. I had eaten some greasy French fries and they had made me sick, I told him. Bill had seen Hanley walking down the street and had put some distance between us. He shouted at me to run. So, in an alcohol-induced haze, I ran as fast as I could down Main Street toward the South. Figuring Hanley was hot on my ass, I ducked behind Phil's and then went out onto Park Street.

Keep in mind that Phil's Corner was only about fifty feet square and there were no buildings around it. As I ran around the building, I was trying to look back and see if Hanley was following me. I blasted around the building and ran directly into him. He hadn't moved an inch.

"Better come with me, son," were his next words.

I climbed into the cruiser and he drove me to the Rockland Police Department where I was placed in a cell painted therapeutic green, complete with a hole in the floor and no mattress on the bed. My mother's cousin, Officer Bruce Gamage, was on duty that night and he saw some degree of humor in my situation. I KNEW he had done more bad shit than I ever had when he was young, so I was quite sure I was not the first adolescent to have this experience.

As I walked into the station, I shouted, "Go ahead and break out the rubber hoses and beat me. I'll never talk."

I can still remember the grins on the faces of the cops. Most of them were much older than I and probably had lived this very experience and more. "I've had it now," I thought. They will call my mother or father who will have to leave whatever party they are attending to come and get me. I was sure that would mean a slow, and probably painful, death for me.

My father, Bob, and Sonny Drinkwater, a lobsterman friend of my father's, came to bail me out of jail. It required some surety to obtain my release. Sonny put up his house for bond. In those days, drinking as a minor was quite a serious offense. Nowadays, you can kill your grandmother with a tire tool and receive less of a penalty, as long as you felt she really needed killing.

I was unceremoniously dumped into the back seat of Sonny's car. He drove to Spruce Head where I lived with my mother, stepfather, and my two sisters, Heather and Cheryl, in a rented house. I made some comment to my father about never being thought of by anybody as much more than a wasted fuck. That drew a hard slap across the face. That was the last time I ever gave him reason to hit me.

My parents divorced when I was ten years old. They both still lived in the same town, and I had lived with each of them for a while as it didn't require having to change schools.

My father shoved me through the door of our house with a comment to my mother that he had brought "her little boy" home. I went to bed with thoughts of impending death running through my mind. The next day, I got up early and my mother ordered me to saw a cord of firewood into stove lengths, and then split and stack it.

It is important to realize that the legal system in those days was not as understanding as it is now. I was fined thirty-five dollars, given a suspended fifteen-day jail sentence, and placed on one year's probation for this heinous crime. I had visions of never being able to get a job or vote or do any of the other things people take for granted. This labeled me as a convict in my mind. There is a good possibility that one or the other of my parents had pissed off this judge, Galen Legassey, in some way or another. The other possibility was that my stepfather was a simple lobster fisherman and not part of the clique in Rockland. It never entered my mind that I wouldn't be a part of the social scene of Rockland. At that time in my life, I thought that all men were created equal. I was wrong!

When I returned to school after the holidays, the word had spread about my run-in with the law. The Key Club (junior version of Kiwanis) had taken a vote and expelled me. I had to visit my probation officer once a week. His name was McCauliffe. I walked downtown to the Post Office Building and told him I had been a good boy. (As I remember, some years later he became the Postmaster in Rockland, and resigned after being accused of embezzling money from the government.)

To get to McCauliffe's office, I had to pass by the military recruiters' offices. Most of the time the recruiters were not there and a sign on the door announced when they would be in. One afternoon a few months later, when I made my foray into the guts of this bureaucracy, the Navy Recruiter happened to be in. I looked in and there was a first class boatswain's mate sitting at his desk wearing his blue uniform, bedecked with ribbons and gold hash marks. A sign on the desk read "BM1 Allen, USN." I liked that. A title in front of your name, a uniform, and that look in your eye that told others you had seen things they could only dream about or see in movies. I walked in. He looked up from filling out some forms and asked if he could help me. I told him I was considering joining the service and wanted to see what the Navy had to offer. He asked me if I was still in high school. I said I was for the moment, but that it might not last much longer. He pointed to a chair and said he would be right with me.

I looked around the room. There were posters all over the walls from the World War II era. One was a drawing of an attractive girl; another with a girl in dress blues saying her man was in the Navy—that sort of thing. I didn't know if this was an offer to other sailors who weren't at sea, or something to coerce dumb high school kids like me into signing on the dotted line. Somehow, there is always the attraction you are going to have more fun, get laid more, and see more exciting things in the military. They always seem to leave out the part about fighting wars and getting your ass shot off, scrubbing pots and pans, and cleaning heads.

After a few minutes, Boatswain's Mate First Class Allen looked up from his paperwork. He stood up and, with a smile, he reached out and shook my hand as we introduced ourselves. He asked me what I meant about not being in high school for long. I told him I was fed up with the place and was going to quit. He told me that wasn't a good idea because he couldn't guarantee me a school if I did that. He said he would enlist me if I passed the test, but it would be much better if I didn't quit school. Also, the Navy would give me E-2 (Airman Apprentice) right out of boot camp if I had a high school diploma. I didn't know what that meant, but I figured it translated into more money somehow.

I looked over the brochures and told him I would like to be a Photographer's Mate. I was interested in photography and diving, but I understood the Navy didn't enlist you and send you directly to diving school.

Allen told me to discuss it with my parents and see what they thought, then return to his office in a couple of days. Even though I would be eighteen when I joined, it was always good to have the approval of the parents. I knew my chances of going to college were just short of nonexistent. Even if I had the financial means, I hated school with a passion and would never make it. I wouldn't have been able to bring myself to go merely to keep from being drafted. The draft was in full swing now and many of my schoolmates were discussing ways to avoid serving their country in the military.

The next time I went to sign in with my probation officer, I stopped by the Navy recruiter's office. BM1 Allen had some papers laid out on the desk. He asked me to fill in the blanks so he could start the paperwork rolling. He explained that I would not be obligated to join, but he wanted to have things ready if I enlisted. Then he gave me the AFQT, (Armed Forces Qualification Test). The test was multiple-choice and made up of questions about mechanical things, electricity, math, language comprehension, abstract thinking, etc. I finished it in rapid fashion and was told I had scored a 94% out of a possible 99, which impressed the recruiter, as I believe a person had to acquire a score of 40 to join the Navy. He told me I could go to any school I could physically qualify for, once I got in. He then asked if I was on probation or anything like that. I told him I was, for drinking under age. He smiled and said that wouldn't be a problem. He would get the judge to erase my record and it would be as though it had never existed. That happened a lot in those days. Many young men joined the service who may otherwise have ended up in jail. The vast majority of them never had trouble with the law again.

The next day in school, I went to the guidance office and asked to see the catalogs on Navy training. In Maine at that time, the military was still an honorable profession and was not looked down upon as a place where people served who couldn't make it anywhere else. The guidance counselor gave me the books I asked for and I sat down at a desk in his office and looked them over.

That evening, I went to visit my girlfriend, Mary, at her house. Her father, Roland, was always glad to see me and would drop whatever he was doing to sit and talk with me. For some reason, I seemed to spend as much time talking to him as I did trying to get into Mary's pants. I imagine the conversations probably did me more good. I couldn't figure out why a man of his stature would want to sit and talk with me. I was the son of a chicken farmer and the stepson of a lobster fisherman, neither one very successful, and came from a broken home, as they call it now. At that time, I owned exactly four changes of clothes and two pairs of shoes, not counting my rubber boots. Roland always gave good advice. He was well thought of in the community and had started and continued to operate a local petroleum products distribution company, Maritime Oil Company.

Roland said he thought it might be a good thing to go into the Navy. I explained that I thought I could get some good training in photography, travel a little, and possibly learn enough so I could make a living when I got out. He agreed that, for a young man, it was not the worst of options.

My next stop was to get the probation officer to expunge my record of all criminal activity. That was not a problem. It lightened his workload and would get another "troublemaker" out of town.

On June 11, 1964, I graduated from Rockland District High School number eighty in my class of one-hundred-forty. It was not a momentous occasion to me, but I felt many of my classmates thought this would be the apex of their careers. I couldn't wait to get the hell out of this little seacoast community and get on with my life. Rockland and its surroundings had very little to offer, and I would just as soon see it in the rear view mirror for the last time.

I had to take a physical exam and this required me to go to Bangor, Maine to the military medical facility there where Army and Navy medical personnel gave the pre-induction physicals to draftees and volunteers. Volunteers were quickly becoming the minority as the draft was beginning to crank up for the Vietnam War.

The recruiter provided a Greyhound Bus ticket to Bangor and handed me an envelope with some papers in it. He told me to answer "no" to anything I didn't understand. During my childhood and up into my teens, I had been bothered with asthma on frequent occasions. There were times it was so bad that I couldn't go to school. He said it sounded like hay fever to him and that's what I probably should answer on the sheet when they asked me. I took his advice.

The physical exam was typical. They noted that I had slightly flat feet and blue eyes and that was about it. One potential recruit had a big scar on his chest where he'd had open-heart surgery. The corpsmen asked him some questions and then told him he was okay. Another kid wanted to join the Marines. He had high blood pressure and they rejected him. I passed with flying colors and went home on the next bus. It was almost like a dream. I signed my name on some papers and all these things started to happen to me. Somebody wanted to hire me and was willing to pay me work for them. They would give me clothes, fly me around, educate me, and even let me eat all I wanted. Christ, what a deal!

The day before I was to hop the "many windows" to Portland where I would be sworn in, I ran across Mike McNeil and David Cooper. They were friends of mine from high school. They proposed that we get some Gluek Stite and go over to Samoset Resort Road† to slam down a few as a going away party for me. Sounded like a good idea. The

† Samoset Road let to the Samoset Resort, an old hotel that later burned to the ground as the victim of arson.

usual formalities of obtaining the nasty brew were quickly dispensed with and we were on our way to getting drunk. We drove back into Rockland and had parked on Main Street near the Central Maine Power Company building. There was an alley running between the CMP and the building next to it. This alley was a favorite place to take a leak. As I stood there writing my name on the wall getting ready to cross the 't," I felt a tap on my shoulder. I looked quickly around and there was Bert Snow,[†] a Rockland cop.

"Oh Christ," I thought, "here I go again." The recruiter had told me to stay out of trouble and not go screwing around before I got to boot camp. He got all of us down to the jail in various automobiles. I told him I was going into the Navy the next day. The mother of one of the other guys was sick and not likely to live much longer. I can't remember the other bad things we told the officers, but they let us go. David Cooper's mother, Winola, came for us and drove me home. She had been my music teacher my entire time in school and I was quite embarrassed to have her come and take us away in that shape. She didn't have much to say to me on the ride to my house.

At this time, I was living with my stepfather, "Tint" Drinkwater, my mother, and two sisters. We lived in a Cellotex hunting camp that measured about eight feet by twelve feet. Winter had started out with me sleeping in the top bunk, the parents on the bottom, and my sisters on the floor in sleeping bags. I didn't think we were poor, I just thought we didn't have a pot to piss in, nor a window to throw it out of. I got very tired of this arrangement, especially when I started wheezing up from the damned heat inside that camp.

My grandfather, Harry Waterman, gave me an old Army wall tent he had bought at a surplus store. I set the tent up on a wooden platform that I'd scavenged from one of the hen pens on my father's chicken farm, and put a bed inside it. It made for a comfortable outdoor bedroom, although, some mornings, I had to kick the snow off the bed before I got up. At times, it was embarrassing to live there. I remember getting a ride home from school one day with Tommy Painter. He was a year behind me in high school, and one of these guys who always had to "have" things, like cars. Once, when he dropped me off in front of our place, he asked me if that was where I lived. I said it was. He looked at me incredulously and said, "You're shitting me?" After that,

---

† Bert later became Chief of Police of Rockland and a good friend. As a historian of the area, he wrote a book about the history of the shipyards in the Rockland area.

whenever I got a ride, I would get out up or down the road in front of a "real" house and walk the rest of the way home.

The next morning, I didn't have a hangover. We hadn't consumed that much beer. My mother had packed some of my things in a small gym bag, so I took out a pair of Levis and a shirt and put them on. I'd already bought a pair of black shoes that appeared to be military in style. They were standard black low-cuts like the dress shoes worn in all the services. My mother gave me a ride to the Greyhound bus station in Rockland. Mary, my girlfriend, was there. Both of them kissed me goodbye. I got on the bus and sat down, and it started up the street. As we drove out of Rockland, I thought to myself, "I won't be seeing this shithole for awhile."

I didn't have a clue what was in store for me. What sort of adventures lay ahead? Would I fit in with the people I would meet? Where would I be stationed? Would the Navy give me what I wanted for training, or had the recruiter been blowing smoke just to suck me in? I would soon find out.

All the way to Portland, I thought about what I had done so far in my life and how it hadn't amounted to much. I wasn't able to earn much money, most girls wouldn't give me the time of day, and my parents couldn't seem to decide where they wanted me to live. Ah, what the hell, here's my chance to punch the reset button and start from scratch.

As I reminisced about the days when I lived on Hewett's Island in the summer and went lobstering with my stepfather, all I could remember about those times was being seasick out by Two Bush Reef and puking over the side. The waves would come up and nearly touch my face as I watched my reflection in them, my glasses being full of tears from the strain of heaving my guts out.

"Nope," I thought to myself, "I am doing the right thing."

Chapter 2

Boot Camp

The bus pulled up to the terminal in Portland and I got off. The recruiter had lined up a room at the YMCA where I would stay that night. I went there and signed in. The person at the desk told me the rules and that I had to be in my room by a certain time, midnight, I think.

In my pocket was a slip of paper with the phone number of Dawn Crudell. She was a high school classmate I'd had the hots for since I'd first laid eyes on her. She was tall with dark eyes, and was the most attractive girl in Rockland High School. I had called her from a pay phone at the bus station and she told me how to get to her place. I walked to Dawn's apartment and rang the bell. She let me in. We had been talking for only a few minutes when her phone rang. It was some guy she knew from the Portland area. He said he was coming over and would bring a couple of six packs of beer. Great, I needed some jerk horning in on this. Here I was, about to take off for boot camp, alone with one of my high school friends—probably the last person I would see before boot camp whom I knew—and this turkey calls up and is going to come over with beer. She says into the phone, "Sure, come on over." I should have walked the hell out of there right then.

The minute he showed up, I knew immediately that this guy fit my definition of an asshole. He was one of those cocky, arrogant sons-of-bitches that women fall for. We drank the beer and after a couple of hours, Dawn decided it was time for us to leave. I didn't even kiss her goodbye. So, Mr. Wonderful and I walked down the street toward the YMCA. He asked me if I wanted to drink some more beer. In spite of my feelings about him, I said, "What the hell else is there to do?" I gave him a couple of dollars and he walked across the street to a small convenience store. In a few minutes, he came back with a brown paper bag. We were walking down the street sucking on our bottles when a police car pulled up and the officers got out. One of them asked us where we got the beer. Mr. Wonderful started telling the cops that we bought it "right over there in that store." He asked how old we were. I told him I was eighteen and didn't know how old "my buddy" was. He turned out to be nineteen. The cop started making noises as if he was going to take us downtown and book us. I told him that I was going into the Navy in the morning and was staying at the YMCA in Portland for the night. Then Mr. Wonderful says to him, "Yeah, we're going in the Navy."

I looked at him, then turned to the cop and spoke up.

"Bullshit! Let me tell you the truth. I don't even know this guy. I met him about two hours ago. I am going into the Navy. He isn't. He used a fake I.D.to buy the beer in that little store across the street. I don't want the old guy who owns the store to get in trouble. There was no way he could have known it was a fake I.D."

One of the cops looked at me and said, "You, I like." Then he scowled at Mr. Wonderful and uttered, "You, Smart Ass. Get in the car." The cop wished me on my way with, "Good luck in the Navy, Kid."

I thanked him and started walking to the YMCA. "Enough of that crap," I thought. I found my way to my tiny room and went to bed. The next morning, I walked down to the Portland recruiting office where I was sworn in. It was June 24, 1964.

There were about forty of us heading for boot camp from the State of Maine. I don't remember any of them at all. They were generic Maine boys. Most of them were joining to avoid the Army, or to get out of an economically depressed area. I could relate to that. Some had been in trouble with the law. I could relate to that, too, although I didn't consider myself a criminal by their standards.

After the swearing-in process, we signed more papers. Then we were loaded onto a bus and driven to the Portland Airport where we boarded a plane that took us to O'Hare International Airport. This was my first ride in a jet airliner. I had only been out of Maine twice before, once when I flew over to Nova Scotia with a local pilot out of Owl's Head Airport to deliver some engine parts for a Maine boat that had broken down in Yarmouth, and once when I went someplace in New Hampshire with my parents when I was very small.

My flying had been limited to some flying lessons with Arthur Harjula, an old bush pilot from Thomaston, Maine, and some lessons— if you want to call them that—from Bob Stenger, of Down East Airlines. All Bob did was smoke cigarettes and scream at me. Between getting airsick from the smell of the smoke and being nervous from his hollering at me, the only thing I learned from Bob was that he was a lousy instructor. I worked at the airport for one dollar an hour, which I would convert into flight time with Bob, whose rate was fourteen dollars an hour. It was an even swap, but not much of a deal. At least when I went flying with Arthur, I learned something.

Of course, we were big men now, having joined the world's largest nuclear Navy. Some of the guys tried to get the flight attendants to serve them drinks. They had already been warned by the recruiters not to. I tried to be friendly with the girls, but they'd seen too many like us, just meat to be shipped to some foreign country to the slaughter. Perhaps in their minds, we didn't count. When you're eighteen, it's difficult to fathom that someone might harbor those sorts of feelings, but when you get older it makes sense. You don't approve of it, but you know it's real. It's something that has to be experienced, such as racism and all the other politically incorrect tendencies of today.

The plane touched down at O'Hare some hours later. We walked off the plane and found our way to baggage claim. Only a few of us had any checked baggage, as some of us didn't own anything but the clothes we were wearing. At the baggage claim area, we were met by men from the Naval Recruit Training Center, Great Lakes; a couple of petty officers, and a few "service weeks" (recruits who were part way through boot camp). During service week, they had to work in the chow hall, work grounds detail, or help the drill instructors handle recruits. These guys thought of themselves as old salts, as they had been in the Navy about seven weeks longer than we had. The service weeks wasted no time in inflicting the usual boot camp harassment. I knew that was their mission so I did what I was told. Some of the boys took their insults personally and it cost them. They were down for pushups and getting screamed at up close. I did not, and had no problems. Having taken flying lessons from Bob Stenger, I was quite familiar with being screamed at by someone with a limited vocabulary. I felt right at home.

It was late at night when we arrived at Camp Barry and the Recruit Training Center where we encountered the usual intimidation. Everybody got off the bus and we had to stand around while they messed with us and made us hurry up and wait. I couldn't detect if this was intentional, or they had screwed up their scheduling. I thought it was probably the latter. Sometimes our handlers seemed as pissed off as I thought we should be. They managed to get us into a chow hall where we were fed. We couldn't go back for seconds, but I didn't need to as I ate some of the food the other guys wouldn't eat. I thought it was very good chow. At least it was free and plentiful.

The "service weeks" put us in a huge Quonset hut for the night. At about 0400, we were turned out to get haircuts, shots, and tests. There was a big building where the haircuts and shots were given. Some of us who stood in line got haircuts. When we came out, we went to the back of the line to wait for our shots. It was extremely hot out in the sun and a few of the boys passed out from heat exhaustion. The drill instructors warned us not to stand with our knees locked back. I didn't listen well. We finally started moving inside to get our blood drawn and our flu shots. When they drew our blood, the corpsmen would have us walk along in a line and hang our right arm over a sloping board. One of the corpsmen would shove a needle into a vein. We would then proceed to the next board where the next medic would drain some blood into a test tube. At the board after that, another man would drain some more blood, pull out the needle, throw it into a trash can, and put a piece of gauze on the needle hole. We were supposed to double up our arms, trapping the gauze over the needle wound, and walk along in line. Then another corpsman jabbed a syringe full of some thick marshmallow-looking goo into your biceps and left it hanging. The next guy squeezed the goo into your arm and pulled out the needle. Then we stepped up to a table and picked up a specimen cup. A left turn took us down a set of concrete steps into the coolness of the basement, where the "heads" (that's toilets to you landlubbers) were located. It was nice and cool down there, but it smelled very strongly of urine. I walked over to a urinal mounted on the wall, and the last thing I remember is looking down at my lower unit to make sure I was hitting the cup.

I woke up with three people standing over me. One guy was looking into my eyes with a little flashlight and asking me if I was okay. He said I had passed out and hit my head on something. The back of my head felt sandy, as if I had been lying on the beach. The corpsmen took me to another room, where a doctor stitched me up. I spent the next week in sickbay in and out of bed because the doctors were worried that one of my pupils was larger than the other. I told them it had always been that way. It hadn't, but I was afraid they would throw me out of the Navy if they thought I had suffered any brain damage.

Most of the people in the ward were there for broken bones from jumping out of windows as they tried to run away from boot camp. Some were there for respiratory infections or had undergone appendectomies. One individual, who was sunburned very badly, worried that the Navy was going to take disciplinary action against him for getting sunburned, as they considered it dereliction of duty and damaging government property, or some such crap.

When I reported to boot camp, I had been assigned to Company 242. When I got out of sickbay they assigned me to Company 303. It turned out to be a better deal: our company commander would not take a company that had to do a service week, so we graduated two days after Company 242. Company 303 was a diverse group made up of college graduates and barely literate hillbillies. I took the GCT (General Classification Test) and found I was right up there among the brain surgeons and rocket scientists. When I went to the classification team where we would be assigned our schools, the counselor told me that the Navy wanted me to be a sonar or missile technician on a nuclear submarine. I told them I would have none of that; I wanted to be a photographer's mate. The career counselor scoffed and referred to the rating as "titless waves" and other such derogatory terms. At the time, I didn't know what he meant. But I was insistent and, with some disgust, they relented. I was assigned to Photographer's Mate "A" School, NAS (Naval Air Station) Pensacola, Florida via nine months of "PSI (Programmed School Input) at Basic Naval Aviation Officers' School," whatever that was. Meanwhile, boot camp continued.

Each company had a drill team and a swim team. I volunteered for the swim team as I could hardly walk and chew gum at the same time. I couldn't swim the crawl or the butterfly stroke, so I tried out for the backstroke. I got on the team and we competed against other companies. I don't remember how well we did, but I do know it got me out of those damned barracks and away from the tedium of washing clothes and listening to the constant inane bullshit that was part of a recruit's daily life. We had to wash our clothes by hand and hang them out on the line behind the barracks to dry. My job as sixth squad leader was to insure that the clothes stops—those little strings we hung the clothes from—were all straight. It was not a hard job, but it was nearly impossible to teach some of the men to line the knots up and get the clothes exactly the right distance from each other. I never had to resort to violence to get the point across, but did give it some thought.

I remember one individual was just stupid. Once, an instructor asked this kid what his GCT score was. He said it was twenty-four. I couldn't believe it; the Navy had recruited a guy who had an I.Q. just a few points above bread mold. What in the hell was this kid going to do? The Navy would train him and train him and he would probably never amount to a pisshole in a snow bank. I felt it was a gross misuse of money. Another guy named Corwin, a Jewish kid from New York, got a lot of crap from the company commander, who asked the kid if he could call him "Abbe."

The kid said, "No sir." When asked why not by the company commander, Corwin replied, "Because that's not my name, Sir." I didn't know then about anti-Semitism. To me, he was just another guy in my company.

At the time, the company commanders usually used a black guy for the "guide on," the man who marched in front of the company carrying the flag. The feeling was that the black kids had better rhythm and could keep in step. Robeson, a black kid from Mississippi who was one of my buddies, said, "Those bastards better not put this nigger in front, or they're gonna find out just how bad my rhythm is." We all laughed and agreed that it would be quite interesting if he happened to be picked as guide on. He wasn't.

The company commander was a chief damage controlman. He told the company that he was also an ordained minister in some church. I never questioned as to which one because I didn't care. Any church that would have him as a minister would be one I would never attend. He wouldn't allow any of the boys to swear or use profanity, but he had to be the cruelest bastard I've ever met. If I had been stationed on a ship with him, I would have made sure he was given the "big swim." He always addressed the black kids as "boy" and one time when the dumb kid, was standing in ranks for an inspection, the company commander kicked him in the legs until he fell down. The kid had laced up his leggings wrong. In fear, he got up crying and ran for the fence. A couple of the faster guys ran after him and grabbed him before he made it over the top of the perimeter's chain link fence.

I felt sorry for the kid. To think anyone could treat somebody like that just because they had tied some knots wrong. I showed him how to tie them correctly and made sure he did it right from then on. He disappeared before we graduated. This kind of thing happened a lot. Sometimes guys wouldn't be there when we came back to the barracks. In most case, I think, the instructors may have checked the records and found something about a recruit's medical condition. In the case of the dumb kid, I think they finally figured out they were wasting everybody's time trying to train the guy. There were rumors that some of the men couldn't hack the regimentation and harassment and had jumped out of windows, hanged themselves, or slit their wrists. I heard one story about a guy throwing himself down the stairs in the indoctrination building. Rumor was that he ended up in sickbay for about a week and no one knew what became of him. I grinned because I knew that they were talking about me. They hadn't gotten the story straight, but I wasn't going to help them out.

The chow was good and we could go back for seconds once we got to Camp Porter. The place was newly constructed and quite nice. The barracks were well lit and had new sidewalks, and the lights all worked—things that most people take for granted. Once in a while, we were allowed to go to the exchange and buy things like stationery, candy, soap, and the like. My mother sent me money once in a while, usually a five-dollar bill, and I received letters from Mary and my father. Mary's father also wrote me, as he was a great one for corresponding and put a lot of heart into his letters.

As it turned out, boot camp wasn't difficult at all, mentally or physically. Some of the city slickers might have thought so, but I didn't think it was much more than an indoctrination. Rumors sometimes added spice. We heard the standard one about a whole company dying of meningitis, and that we would have to stay an extra month in quarantine because of it. Not true, of course.

Two weeks or so before we were to graduate from basic training, we were allowed to go on our first liberty. We had two choices, Chicago or Milwaukee. I chose Chicago. It was my first time on a train and I was excited. Ned Dentry[†] and I had become friends and he and I went in town together. Ned had about seven years of college and a master's degree in something. He was one of the most intelligent men in the company and was about twenty-seven years old; not the typical sailor type.

We had no desire to get drunk or chase down members of the local female population. We correctly assumed that the girls in Chicago would have had their fill of "boot camps" and not be the least bit interested in us. For some reason I didn't want to drink. The company commander told us that drinking was strictly taboo, and I believed this was a good warning, as I did not need to get in trouble. I had respect for the uniform and figured if I got drunk, I might get robbed. They had paid each of us fifty dollars, but after taking out what our uniforms cost and the rest of it, there wasn't much left. It was commonly believed by us that uniforms were free. It was my understanding. The petty officers told us if we lost or destroyed any of our clothing, we would have to pay for it because it belonged to Uncle Sam, which was bullshit, as they had taken it out of our pay.

Ned Dentry and I walked to the train station and rode to Chicago. We wandered around the streets for a while and finally went into a

† Ned Dentry now works for Nikon, and is a writer, also.

15

restaurant. I ordered fish and he, a steak. The waitress asked if we wanted a drink. I said I would have a Coke; Ned had a glass of wine. After that, we explored Chicago further. It wasn't as if the locals had never seen sailors in town. The naval training command unleashed sailors on the town frequently, and we were just another batch going through the process. I had my two little green stripes and Ned had his three. He went into the Navy as an E-3 because of his college degree. They wanted him to be an officer, but he declined.

We got tired of drifting in and out of stores and went back to the train station. The next time the company had liberty was a repeat of the same thing. I almost didn't go, but I figured it would be better than hanging around the barracks getting assigned to shit details. It felt good to be a sailor and I wanted to be the sharpest guy around. Even though I knew I was probably one of the laziest bastards ever to don the uniform, I always kept a sharp appearance. And I was not bothered by asthma any more, although one night, I awoke in the middle of a thunderstorm with a fairly bad attack. By morning, it was nearly gone and didn't have any effect on my performance that day.

The word filtered down that the North Vietnamese had attacked a couple of our destroyers using gunboats. I couldn't imagine a group of Vietnamese attacking a U.S. Navy destroyer with gunboats, and I thought that might be stretching things a little bit. But I figured if that was what was reported, then it must be true. Soon after that, rumors began flying that we would all be sent directly to Vietnam. Funny how things like that get started. I didn't think the Navy had anybody on the ground there in those days.

During the classroom phases of training, I never had any trouble keeping up. We carried these old Springfield rifles around everywhere we went. The barrels were plugged and the bolts were missing. When we went to class, we would have to stack the rifles outside, and one unlucky bastard would have to stand out there at parade rest in the stifling July and August heat to guard them. On occasion, I would be standing outside in ranks waiting to go to class and one of the service weeks who marched us around would go down the ranks asking our GCT scores.

At first, I proudly stated I had a sixty-nine (out of a possible 75). After a while, I figured out what they were doing: the training was not designed for rocket scientists, but you had to pass the tests. They would pick the guys with high GCTs to guard the rifles, as they figured they could easily catch up later on. I smartened up real quick and started quoting my test scores as being in the forties. When I graduated, I was quite near the top of my company. The numerical grade escapes me, but I knew I was one of the best. It didn't matter; I don't remember anybody flunking out who made it to the end of training.

Graduation day at boot camp had no special meaning for me other than the fact I was getting out of Great Lakes Naval Recruit Training Command. Maybe people would treat us more humanely somewhere else. I had orders for Basic NAO School at Sherman Field in Pensacola, Florida. Nobody had a clue what the school was. Ned Dentry and Dave Duchene, another guy in my boot camp class, were also going to Pensacola, and we would be in the same class in photo school. Dave, the lucky son-of-a-bitch, was getting stationed at the NAS Pensacola Photo Lab until our class started. We both would be assigned to nine months of PSI, but we didn't know what that was. They had authorized me some leave between the time I left boot camp and when I was to report in at my new duty station. Those of us leaving would fly home. My flight would take me from O'Hare to Boston. From there, I would take a cab to the bus station and then grab the Greyhound to Rockland. These events passed mostly without incident.

I remember the death-defying ride from Logan Airport in a cab driven by a foreign national. Two other sailors were also going to the bus station, so we shared a cab. When we arrived at the bus station, the taxi driver tried to hustle us out of money for putting our sea bags in the trunk. But a Boston cop walked over and gave the cabbie a little talking to, then wished us luck. There always seemed to be people very quick to rip off a military man. As life went on, I encountered more and more of this type and developed a dislike for them, unsurpassed even by my dislike for men I fought in wars or bars.

The bus ride home was a study in boredom and human nature. I could always strike up a conversation with somebody on "the many windows." In those days, riding the bus was not beneath the dignity of the common man. With the demise of passenger rail service up and down the coast of Maine, there were a number of older people and a few college students who always rode the buses. I never got along very well with the college types. Most of them had no great desire to converse with military people. Perhaps they were afraid the calling would rub off and they'd come down with a mad desire to join the service. At that time, the draft was in full swing and huge numbers of college students had deferments because of their student status. Guys I went to high school with went to college to avoid the draft, and if they flunked out, they immediately got married. Is it okay to kill off the poor and unfortunate and let the cream of the crop go on to run the country?

Who's going to pick up the garbage and sweep the streets if they wipe out all the people whose daddies can't afford to send them to college?

When I think of men like Joshua Chamberlain of Maine, I do have an attitude about the people who got draft deferments. He gambled his life for his country in the Civil War, and earned the Medal of Honor while fighting with the 20th Maine. He was a professor at Bowdoin and had to lie about wanting to go abroad and study. Chamberlain then joined the Union Army and became a hero, and later, the governor of the State of Maine. The man who trained him, Adelbert Ames, was a man from Rockland, Maine, who himself had the Medal of Honor. During one ferocious battle, Ames was wounded so badly that he had his men tie him to a caisson and wheel him around the field so he could direct artillery fire. Adelbert did so until he passed out from loss of blood. (He died in 1933 in his hometown of Rockland, not far from where I graduated from high school.) Neither one of these men had to join the military and fight, but rather they felt it was their duty to their country and to their fellow citizens. Perhaps I was following in these men's footsteps, although I didn't give it much thought. By the time I got my chance, we were fighting a different kind of war.

The idea of student deferment pissed me off. In World War II, rich guys and movie actors volunteered to go and fight. I had an attitude about draft dodgers, and still do. After being in the Navy for a while, I discovered that almost as many kids from wealthy families enlisted as from poor ones, but the antiwar people never publicized that information. Nor the fact that the number of Canadians who came to the U.S. to join our military service was twice the number of American draft dodgers who fled to Canada. That's an interesting message.

I was ready to do my duty for my country, whether the war was just and honorable or not. A war is usually looked at in hindsight with criticism once it's over, no matter how honorable it seems at the start. There will always be those who find a reason to say that war is a waste of lives and material. They are in all cases, but the results are sometimes worth it.

Chapter 3

Boot Leave

Arriving by bus in Rockland, Maine is not major event. When it pulled up early that morning, you could have fired a cannon loaded with grapeshot down Main Street and never touched a soul. The only person at the bus station was a cab driver from Rokes & Harvey Taxi Company. He was the transportation vulture who usually showed up as the "many windows" disgorged its load of sleepy passengers. For two bucks, I caught a ride home to the hunting camp I had left twelve weeks before. My mother and sisters were glad to see me. I walked over to my father's chicken farm and visited with him and my stepmother for a while. He asked me about boot camp and where I would be stationed, etc. My grandfather lived next door to him, so I walked down the lawn to his house for a visit. He had served in WWI in the Navy, but had never been in combat. Later, he had contracted the flu and nearly died. When he got his medical discharge, the doctor told his mother, my great-grandmother, Nellie, that if he was lucky, he would live six months. Well, he made it to ninety-four, as she had. That fifteen dollars a month pension he started drawing zoomed up to several hundred dollars by the time he died.

I called Mary Ware, my high school girlfriend, at her house in Rockland. There was no answer there, so I assumed she was staying down at the family's cottage on Lucia Beach in Owl's Head, a nearby town. Her mother answered the phone and I talked with her for a few minutes, then her father then took the phone and asked me how things were going and when I was coming over to see them. Mary was somewhere else. I changed out of my uniform. As proud as I was of it, I still felt a little self-conscious running around Rockland in whites. Blues always had more appeal and made you look more like a real sailor instead of the ice cream man. You can get away with more when you are wearing blues. Blues don't show the dirt as readily.

In about an hour, Mary showed up at the camp in her Volkswagen. She had heard from somebody up in Rockland that I was home. She had this old black VW bug and had obtained her driver's license before I left for boot camp. We drove to her parents' place on the water at Lucia Beach. The house was a large one that had originally been built by some people from Rockland. Her father had bought it for a small amount of money and had added on and fixed it up. From the front porch, you could spit in the ocean at high tide. What a view! It was on a dead-end road and was the envy of every summer person that set foot in the area. Mary was glad to see me and I was quite happy to be home, but something was missing about my life. I didn't know what it was.

A few nights after I got back to the area, Dwight Fifield, Nancy Wheeler, Mary, and I went for a drive. I had picked up a three-pack of condoms at the local drugstore and was quite eager to try them out. We ended up parking back in the woods off North Shore Drive in Owl's Head. Dwight had borrowed two of the condoms—I figured I would get shot down again—and was in the car slamming Nancy. Mary and I were off in the woods. During the ensuing activity, I had gained some grass stains on what should have been the knees of my pants. Unfortunately though, the knees were up near the pockets. Somehow this would have to be explained. I was wearing light colored Levis, so there was no hiding the problem.

After a while longer, we left and went up to Dwight's house. I forgot all about the too-high stains on my levis. One of Dwight's older brothers was there and chuckled a little bit. I was quite proud of them, as I knew there was only one conclusion that could be drawn, given their location. We watched the Miss America Pageant on TV and then Dwight drove us to our respective homes.

I wanted to walk the streets of Rockland at least one time dressed in my white uniform. Hell, I was a sailor now, ready to do battle with any enemy on, above, or under the water. People should be proud of me. After all, I had just gone through nearly twelve weeks of hellish basic training. I had learned how to wash clothes by hand, salute senior people wearing gold braid, and I could tie knots almost as well as when I left home. Men wearing this uniform before me had died for the red, white, and blue. Songs have been written about sailors and the sea. So here I was, expecting folks to bestow honors on me that I thought I deserved now that I was a man of the sea. But that isn't how it worked. My stepfather, Tint Drinkwater, offered me a lift into Rockland, but I didn't want to ride in his pickup truck as it might soil my pristine white uniform. I started walking along the road, and I'd gone about a half mile when he and my mother pulled up and convinced me to accept the ride. I got in. What the hell is a little dirt, anyway, compared to walking eight miles?

I made the rounds. First stop was the old poolroom where I hung out during my high school days. Next, I stopped by the drug store and had a chocolate frappé (that's what we call a shake in Maine). After that, I meandered about the streets. Very few former classmates could be found. Most of them had gone off to college by now, or joined the service as I did. Some had quit school and preceded me into the military. Vietnam was cranking up and they didn't want to miss the action. I don't think patriotism was high on the list of reasons to serve. When you are living in a coastal community in Maine your options for making a living are mostly limited to three things, all of them having something to do with lobstering, fishing, or working in a stuffy factory building. It isn't a difficult decision to jump on an opportunity to get the hell out of Dodge.

I was running out of things to do and getting anxious to see what Florida held in store—I'd never been there. I called the airline and rescheduled my flight to Pensacola.

In those days, a serviceman in uniform got to fly at half price if you didn't mind going standby. I found very little problem getting around and was almost never bumped from a flight. Military standbys also had the option of paying the full rate if they were going to get bumped. I never had to do that.

Once again, I rode the bus to Boston to catch my plane. Down East Airlines offered flights from Owl's Head Airport, but the flight was expensive. Base pay was seventy-two dollars a month, and, not having rich parents, it wasn't cost-effective to fly. The bus ride and the ensuing flight were uneventful. I arrived in Pensacola, Florida as scheduled.

Whenever I was transferred to a new unit or place, I always felt some fear and apprehension that I wouldn't like it or get along with the people there. In most all cases, this feeling abated quickly as I made new friends and learned new jobs.

Chapter 4

Pensacola

I was tired when I arrived in Pensacola and wanted to get some sleep. Hopefully, checking in wouldn't be too tedious a process. The cab driver dropped me off at NATTU (Naval Air Technical Training Unit) at Mainside. After much questioning about why I was checking in two weeks early, this turned out to be the wrong place. I grabbed my gear and the duty driver took me down the road to the administration building of NAS Pensacola. This, too, was the wrong place. Nobody seemed to know just where in hell BNAO School was, or for that matter, whether the goddamn place even existed. I had not a clue, being a boot and all, so I left it up to those I felt should know. Lesson one, assume you know more than everybody else until they prove differently, then follow the one who seems to know the most.

I finally caught a base shuttle out to Sherman Field. This, it turned out, was where they trained back-seat drivers for Phantoms fighter planes and bombardier navigators for A-6A Intruder bombers. The place where I had to sign in was in one of two buildings located on the east side of Sherman Field. I checked in with Chief Butler, the man in charge of personnel. The CO's name was Cumbie and Lcdr. Bloom was the XO. Bloom was quite effeminate. I remember that being immediately apparent. There were two Waves working in the office. One of them was Pat Busby and the other Liz Lawson. I believe Busby was from Texas. Lawson was from some southern state like North Carolina or Tennessee. They were both quite nice looking. Busby was a blonde, quite thin, and very attractive by my standards.

I was assigned to the division that cleaned blackboards, made coffee, and took care of projectors and other support activities. They called it the Training Aids Division. My assignment there may have been one of the reasons I never developed a taste for coffee until I had been out of the Navy for almost twenty years. I made about fifteen pots of it a day. It was what BNAO School ran on. While there, I made friends with many of the officer candidates. They were called OCANs. That stood for officer candidate airman. They were paid the equivalent of an E-5 or petty officer, second class. They had no rank as such, but we were told we had to treat them as though they were ensigns. They must have needed the practice.

I figured I would have it made here. The work was easy and the people, for the most part, were not screamers and thrashers. I got over calling chiefs sir in about five minutes, and soon got to know most of the men I would be working with. Among them were Saas, a knife fighter and drunk; Valentine, a skinny chain-smoker with false teeth who wasn't too bright; Facemeyer, an example of a brainless pretty boy; and Young, a fairly sharp little guy who had his own Ford Mustang. There were also a couple of twins that worked there. They spent a lot of time looking longingly into each other's eyes and often would be in the same bunk together come reveille. We didn't think much of it as long as they stayed away from us. Another kid I got to know was Robert "Frenchie" LaPointe. He was from Maine. We hadn't been in boot camp together, but we got to know one another quite soon after I arrived at Pensacola.

BNAO School was about five miles from the barracks. We lived in the old brick, two-story type that were built before World War II. The floors were concrete and they each had a long screened-in sun porch on the front of them. The showers were off to the end of each berthing area and we had open-berthing bunkbeds. I had a bottom bunk in the corner—my favorite place. Most of the time, the senior guys took the bottom bunk, but I happened to run across somebody who liked the top bunk, so I lucked out. Movies were twenty-five cents and the bus was free to anywhere on the base. I was supposed to go to photography school here and I always wondered why I didn't go right away when I left boot camp. I figured it was punishment for not going into the Nuke Program or some other brain-intensive rating. My math was weak and on top of that, I hated it, so I didn't think I would be able to hack anything that technical. I would have to wait until May of 1965 to start photo school. To pass the time, I went to the education office and checked out all the books I would need to advance to petty officer, third class. I had not made airman (E-3) yet.

Let me explain; the rate I was striking for was an aviation rating. Anyone who was striking for an aviation rating would be designated an airman recruit, airman apprentice, and airman as per their pay grade. From any of these pay grades (E-1 through E-3) one might become a designated striker, either by finishing the appropriate "A" school, or passing the test for third class but not making a high enough score to be advanced. While I was picking up the materials for the corres-pondence course for airman, I also grabbed the manual for photo-grapher's mate. The rule was that you could take the test for airman (E-3) any time you thought you could pass it. The command would keep the test scores on record and advance you automatically when you had enough time in grade. I got a 90% on it and then could concentrate on studying for E-4. When I finished the courses for petty officer, third class, I went on and fulfilled the requirements for petty officer second and first class. By the time I put on my airman's stripes, I had done all the courses right up to and including photographer's mate, first class, or E-6. I think this looked good in my record. I really didn't have much else to do during the day when I wasn't busy. The senior people liked to see kids studying.

On weekends, I would sometimes ride the bus into town. I couldn't wear civilian clothes until I made E-4, and my pay of seventy-two dollars a month didn't allow me to demonstrate a high profile. Women seemed to like guys with cars and clothes. Unfortunately, good looks didn't go very far, except with the homosexuals who seemed to prey on young sailors. When hitchhiking back to the base after dark, it was about seven-to-one odds that the person offering a ride would want something other than to help out a young, sea-going pedestrian. The standard lines were: "Gee, Sailor, you're going back to the base awfully early aren't you?" and "I can't imagine a good looking guy like you having to walk. Don't you have a girlfriend that can drive you around?" and "Hey, I know where there's a party. There are supposed to be lots of Navy nurses and Corps Waves there, and even some airline flight attendants. It ought to be fun, do you want to go?"

One time, out of sheer boredom, I accepted one of these offers. The guy drove around for a while feigning a search for the address he pretended to have forgotten. The next thing I knew, he was asking me if I had a satin lining in my dress blues. He claimed he'd had a set of them when he was in the Navy and could remember how good it felt on his crank. I told him that mine had a lining, but that I wore skivvies so my pecker never rubbed against the satin. Then I said something about having gotten in trouble for beating up some guy in the latrine at the club because he propositioned me and I wasn't supposed to be off base. That did the trick.

One of my friends told me that, if I did it again, to say that I had to get back early as I had some kind of V. D. and the doctor told me to get lots of sleep until he figured out what it was. I never popped anybody because I was diplomatic. Some of those offering rides would come right out and offer to suck my cock. As hard up as I was at that time, I am surprised I didn't take them up on it. I knew, though, that if you were caught, it didn't matter which end of the blowjob you were on, you were history. After a while, I thought I was probably a faggot and just didn't realize it. I never got propositioned by women; only men. It really got old. Probably, if I had talked to some of the other guys about it, I would have found out that I was not the Lone Ranger.

I was in a heavy discussion with some of the guys in the barracks when dumb hick Facemeyer said something and I responded by calling him a bastard. Then Young, the little guy who owned the Mustang, egged him on. He said, "Larry, did you hear what he called you? A bastard. You don't have a father, and that's what a bastard is."

Poor Facemeyer didn't have a clue. He thought that because his father was dead, it made him a bastard. He jumped me and I popped him in the face. He never struck a blow. He was a wiry little guy, but no match for a person of my level of fear. I hated pain. Still do. Somebody broke it up but Facemeyer advised me we would meet again. The next day, I was walking out of the shower wearing only a pair of Navy-issue boxer shorts and a pair of flip-flops. He came up to me and said, "Call me a bastard, you son-of-a-bitch."

I didn't really want to confront him, but I couldn't back down and look like a coward. There were a few of the others standing around. I said, "Okay, you're a bastard." He took a roundhouse swing at me. I just stepped back about four inches and started pounding him. This wasn't one of those "grab on tight so he can't hit me" fights. I stepped back and laid one punch after another right into his face. He couldn't hit me. I bloodied his nose, blackened both eyes, cut his lips and probably cracked his jaw. Finally, one of his friends hauled him off. Nobody touched me. I felt bad, as I didn't dislike the guy. He couldn't help it if he was stupid.

The next day at work, I was called into Chief Butler's office. He looked up from his desk and with a curious expression asked me, "I hear you had a little disagreement with Facemeyer. You want to tell me about it?"

I told him my side of the story and that I was sorry it had turned out that way, but I wasn't going to let people shove me around. He told me that he had to assign me some extra military instruction. In my mind, I had visions of cleaning all the pad eyes on the ramp where the planes were tied down. This was a standard shit detail for the screw-ups. I said I understood. He told me I would have to stay a couple of hours over each night and clean the blackboards in the classrooms. He added that I shouldn't let these guys get to me and get me into trouble as he thought I was better than that. I couldn't wipe the grin off my face when I left the office. I felt I had skated on that one.

Another of my duties was making the tests on the mimeograph machine. Evelyn, a civilian woman who worked there, was the GS (Government Service) worker in charge of education and training. She would make up the tests for the OCANs. Then she would give me the stencils. I would take them into the mimeograph room and run off copies of them for her, then staple them together. Any sheets that I messed up went into the burn bag. The burn bag had to be taken out about once a week and burned in an incinerator at Mainside. This was considered classified material. I gave some thought about enhancing my meager income by slipping the students copies of the tests, but figured one of them would be a snake and turn me in. That sort of thing would not look good in my record and might end my naval career prematurely.

The command had inspections quite frequently. All of us had to look sharp in uniform and have neat haircuts. I was not old enough to grow a mustache, but if I had been, that was the only facial hair acceptable at the time.

We had to keep the buildings looking sharp. The administration building got much foot traffic and the floors needed more work than the other one. The building to the North also housed the break room and the office from where the Blue Angels operated. The Team was gone most of the time putting on air shows throughout the world, but occasionally, I got to meet some of them and they gave me posters, patches, and items of that nature.

Although the buildings were old cement block and brick structures, they both had tile-type linoleum floors that can take a tremendous shine if worked properly. We had large electric floor buffers that required both hands to operate.

One day, I was busy buffing the floor. The machine I was using had a broken switch and couldn't be turned off. You had to hang onto it with one hand, bend over and plug it in, and continue buffing when it jumped to life. These things weighed about fifty pounds and were quite difficult to hang onto. On this particular morning, I was working my way down the passageway in front of the administration office when the plug fell out of the wall. I had stretched the cord to its limits and it had simply pulled out of the receptacle. Without a second thought, I walked back to the end of the cord, picked it up, and moved it to the receptacle on the other side of the buffer in the direction toward where I would be working. I remember the scream as I plugged it in. I had completely forgotten about the broken switch. When I plugged it in the handle of the buffer had swung around and nailed a lieutenant square in the nuts. He was doubled over with the dry heaves. I got the hell out of there, and fast. When I came back, the buffer was gone. That afternoon, somehow, they had found a new one for us. When that incident with the buffer in the balls happened, I had been aghast, but as I related it to my buddies the hilarity of it nearly overcame us.

Occasionally, some of us young enlisted guys had the chance to fly with the instructor pilots. They were old guys, by our standards, and we welcomed the opportunity to go up in an old Beechcraft they used for training the OCANs. I even had a chance to fly with one of the last remaining enlisted pilots, Chief Johnson.

These planes were affectionately known as "bug smashers." This was because they hated to fly very high. It took a lot of fuel to attain any altitude. One year, just about the time for Christmas leaves to begin, a couple of the pilots told us that if enough of us were going to New York, they would requisition a plane and fly us to some obscure naval air station in New York and we could catch our flights or buses out of there. I took advantage of that and flew home. Nothing stands out in my mind about that flight except the fact that I almost froze my ass off in that old plane. I rode the Greyhound from New York City to home. One of the guys was from Jersey or some other densely populated place and took care of me to make sure I didn't end up dead or lost in that thriving metropolis of New York City. We had to find a way to get back, but the money the flight saved us was considerable. I had not planned on going home that Christmas. Once home, I looked Mary up and we spent some time together. As usual, her father was quite happy to see me. He treated me as though I was a member of his family.

The rest of my time at BNAO School was quite bland. I avoided fights and got along with most of the people. I became friends with many of the instructors and students. Some nights, I stood watch in the room where they were taught the Morse code. I ran the machine that put out the coded messages at different rates. It was quite easy for me to learn code and I had nearly qualified for my amateur radio license before I went into the Navy. These future back-seat airplane drivers had to learn only five words-per-minute to qualify. I helped many a Naval or

Marine Corps officer get up to speed and probably kept them in the program. For some reason, this was a major stumbling block for a few of them. I remember one Marine captain who could do anything except learn the code. I worked with him for several nights. I even came in when I didn't have the duty. He finally learned Morse code. Although I didn't expect any official thanks or recognition for this, I felt good knowing I had helped somebody overcome an obstacle that didn't exist for me. I hoped someday I would have the favor returned. Most likely, I only sped up their induction into the ranks of those bunking at the Hanoi Hilton.

One of the men who worked at BNAO School was named Bill Smith. He was an EASCN (Engineering Aid, Surveyor, Constructionman). He hailed from Texas and was a Seabee. He was proud of both. I think he was afraid of water or something. I don't believe he ever took a shower. He had an armpit that would melt glass, and he was always rubbing his nuts. He wore tight Seafarer dungarees and the crotch of them always showed more wear than the rest from him fingering his balls. He had a strong Texas drawl that I am sure was exaggerated. Some of his teeth were rotten and he'd have a five o'clock shadow by noon. This guy was crazy. One weekend, I rode into town with him. He had a Ford convertible and drove like a wild man. He was around twenty-seven, so we stopped and bought some beer. The next thing I knew, we were heading across the Pensacola Bay Bridge at one-hundred-ten miles-per-hour. I was in the back seat and somebody else was riding shotgun. I was so goddamn scared I couldn't breathe. We made it to the other end of the bridge, slowed down, and immediately had a flat tire. As we rolled, flop-flopping into a nearby service station, we were stone cold sober. Never again! After that, whenever he asked me to go to town with him, I always had something better to do—like shining my shoes or making my rack. The Waves didn't particularly like Bill, but he considered himself a ladies man. I saw him with a couple of his "ladies" at the club on occasion. They were animals, with tattoos, front teeth missing, fat; things like that.

I would have dribbled a basketball through a minefield blindfolded to get next to Pat Busby, but she had a boyfriend who was a second class. She treated me like her little brother and I think she liked me as she would have a little brother. Some unknown person accused the other Wave, Lawson, of being a lesbian. Somebody left a note in her typewriter to that effect. She found it and broke down crying. I thought this was cruel and figured they most likely did that because she wouldn't go out with them. I never asked her to go out. Where was out?

28

Hell, all I could do was take her to the club or go for a walk. The next day, I would have gotten the third degree about whether I had screwed her or not. It is hard to believe, but I was quite shy in those days.

I used to go into town once a week, or less. Usually, I walked around looking in store windows or listening to the sales pitch of one of those "all you need is your Navy I.D. card for credit here" types. I decided if I was going to be a photographer, then I needed a Nikon camera. So I found a camera store that would give credit to a serviceman. I bought my first Nikon, a Nikon Photomic FTN, and I took pictures of everything with it. I could get free film from some of the guys at the base photo lab, but I paid for processing because I didn't know how easy it was to cumshaw things. I eventually sold the camera to somebody for less than I paid for it. I was broke and bored stiff in this place.

I asked one of the officers how hard it would be to get a ride in one of the jet trainers. He told me if I had my qualifications in the ejection seat and high-altitude chamber I could possibly get a ride, and when I got to my next duty station after school, that the qualifications might help me get on air crew status. The chief let me go one day with a group from the school to the chamber and ejection seat. These were located at Mainside right across the street from the barracks. I used to watch them fire the guys up the rail on the ejection seat simulator. It was a kick in the ass, literally. They strapped you into a real ejection seat mounted on a rail. Above you there was a pneumatic shock absorber. Under the seat was an explosive charge mounted inside a tube. This tube was inside another tube that was mounted to the seat. When you pulled the face curtain on the ejection seat, it would fire and the outer tube would slide up the rails until holes in it let the gas escape. Then the shock absorber would quickly slow you down. All this took place in about one-tenth of a second. I could never remember going up the rail, only coming down. They gave you a card that was called the OMIAS card. It stood for "Oh, My Ass". There was some truth to that. For me, it was not my ass that suffered. It was my shoulders as I was quite tall for the seat and the headrest usually hit me between the shoulder blades.

The high altitude chamber was a large, steel chamber very much like a diving recompression chamber, except it had a door to keep the pressure out, not in. There were rows along each side of the chamber where the students sat. Hanging above each station was an oxygen mask. The purpose of this exercise was to show prospective aircrew and pilots what will happen to them when they are exposed to reduced levels of oxygen at high altitude.

We all filed into the chamber and sat down. The corpsman who ran the chamber told us to just breathe normally and he would take us up. We sat there looking at each other across the small distance between the two opposing benches in the chamber and popped out ears by swallowing and yawning. The altimeter inside the chamber read the altitude as we "climbed" toward the stratosphere. We stopped at fifteen thousand feet and sat there for a few minutes. We noticed we had to breathe faster to get the same results. The corpsman, acting as the inside tender, told us of the problems of hypoxia (lack of oxygen) and how it could affect the performance and even the very lives of air crewmen. He told us to put on our masks and breathe normally, which we did. Now he put his own mask on and started reducing the pressure inside the chamber. A mist formed out of the air and coated us with a cold, clammy layer of moisture; the air was so thin that it would not hold water vapor any longer. As we reached something above twenty thousand feet, he told us to take off our masks two at a time, on opposite sides of the chamber and play a game of "patty-cake" by slapping our hands on our knees, then slapping the hands of the person opposite you, then alternating back and forth in a particular pattern as he directed us. In a short time, we were unable to perform this game, as we were on the verge of blacking out from hypoxia.

Then another couple would do it until we had experienced the light-headedness brought on by lack of oxygen. Then we went higher, and were demonstrated pressure breathing. This is when you are so high in the atmosphere that you are not getting enough oxygen, even with a one hundred percent flow. It is forced into your lungs and this makes it difficult to exhale. By the time we were back "on the ground" we had a firm appreciation for what high altitudes could do to us. The Navy demanded that oxygen be used in the daytime above fifteen thousand feet, and at night above ten thousand. The difference here is based on the extra oxygen required for the vision cells of the eye. The cones during the day need less than the rods that give you night vision.

Dave Duchene and Ned Dentry, my boot camp buddies, were also stationed in Pensacola. However, I was out at Sherman Field, where we had our own chow hall. Sometimes I would see them on weekends when I ate at the Mainside chow hall near the barracks. Occasionally, I would run across Ned at the club. I would take the base shuttle out there for something to do when I didn't have the duty. I didn't go there very much because I thought the food was better out at Sherman. Pensacola Naval Air Station was a huge base and very beautiful, and I covered every inch of it, either on foot or riding the base shuttles, which were like UPS delivery trucks with seats.

One morning, a few of us were standing in line to eat when a marine drill sergeant walked up to us and asked us to stand aside. About that time, a bus drove up and a whole group of Vietnamese troops got out and filed past us into the chow hall. I wondered, "What are those guys doing here?"

"They're being trained to fly airplanes here," somebody offered.

"I wonder how many of them are Viet Cong," I joked. Later on, I heard that they had found a couple who were just that.

I heard somewhere you could get into the OCAN (Officer Candidate Airman) program if you had two years of college or the equivalent. Not having any college, I inquired about the equivalent, which was to pass the college-level GED test. After finding out that I was eligible to take the test, I signed up. Chief Butler let me have time off for it, so I went to the base education office and sat through the test. I can't remember how well I did, but I know I passed it. I started the paperwork to become an OCAN. Around the time I completed the paperwork, the Navy came out with a directive that all NAVCADs (naval aviation cadets) and OCANs were required to have at least a bachelor's degree. That took care of my first attempt at becoming an officer.

The time was drawing near when I would be transferred to NATTU (Naval Aviation Technical Training Unit) to attend photo school. I was eager to go. Cleaning blackboards and making coffee was getting old. I was advanced to airman in March 1965 and the huge pay raise that went with it pushed my monthly pay to ninety-nine dollars. I'd made many short-term friends at BNAO School. The only one I have seen since then is Frenchie LaPointe, who lives somewhere in Maine and, last I heard, was working at a post office.

In May 1965, I checked out of BNAO School and signed in at the quarterdeck of NATTU (Naval Air Technical Training Unit) located about a half mile from the barracks where I had been living for the past nine months.

I was looking forward to finally being able to start what I considered to be my real Navy career. There was no doubt that I would enjoy being a Navy photographer, but I didn't have a clue what it would eventually involve.

Chapter 5

Photo School

I reported to NATTU and was assigned to a room on the second floor of barracks #698. This was a yellow, wooden, World War II barracks building directly across the street from a similar structure that housed NAVCADs (Naval Air Cadets). Every morning the cars would drive up one by one and a sharply dressed Marine drill sergeant would get out. Most of them would then walk around to the driver's side and kiss their wives goodbye, say a few words and then walk briskly up the steps into the NAVCAD barracks. At that point he became a screaming animal. We would hear him kicking trash cans over, upsetting lockers and generally raising hell. At the end of the day it would be the reverse. The Drill Instructors would come down the steps to the waiting cars, slide in on the passenger side, lean over, kiss the women and the car would drive off. I was amazed by the way they could make the personality shift so readily, but could never imagine doing that type of work. I had too much of a sense of humor.

I was assigned a room in the barracks with three other guys. Dave Duchene was one of them. The other two were named Willis and Noyes. Noyes slept on the bottom rack on my side of the room and Willis had the bottom rack on the other side. They had checked in first, so had gotten first choice. I was the senior person in the class except for one skinny kid named Riley. He did not outwardly exhibit signs of high, or even average intelligence. As it turned out, I was correct. He flunked out of school in a matter of a few weeks and I became class leader.

Our class lead instructor was Photographer's Mate First Class Art Giberson. His assistant was a Photographer's Mate, Second Class Berry.

32

Both of them were very professional in their demeanor and the way they handled the class.

There were twenty-one of us in the class: five marines and one coast guardsman, and the rest were male and female sailors.

I had been recommended to take the test for Photographer's Mate Third Class (PH3). On the day of the test, they were kind enough to let me out of class to take it. I blew through it in about one-third of the allotted time. Then, as I was walking back to school, I was overcome with doubt about whether I had taken enough time and care with answering the questions. My thoughts were that I had probably failed to make a high enough score to be advanced to PH3.

Photo school was not the most difficult in the aviation field. The material was comparable to college courses offered throughout the country, with the main difference being that all we studied was photography. There were no math, history or language courses as part of the curriculum.

The first piece of equipment we were issued was a 4" by 5" view camera. It was equipped with a fiberboard case that contained some cut-film holders and a lens shade. We were each issued a wooden tripod. The camera itself was not something you could use without the tripod. The first project we had was to photograph a brick wall. The shot had to be properly exposed, in focus, and a certain number bricks had to be in the frame. This required a great deal of manipulation of the camera back and forth. As you got closer, you would have to refocus and then the number of bricks would not be correct. The school issued us each one sheet of film on which to make this first historical photo. I managed to get mine done and not ruin the film, but many others got the shot, but then screwed something up in processing their film. We "souped" our film in a tray instead of the stainless tanks we would be using at photo labs after we left the school.

We were trained in portraiture, small-parts photography and damaged equipment using painted light. This technique was very interesting. The camera was placed on a tripod and the aperture closed down nearly all the way, to about f/22 or f/32. Then the photographer would take a common household light bulb in a reflector-type fixture and paint the object with light, moving it around the whole while so there would be no "hot spots." The detail in the ensuing photograph was remarkable and there were no signs of shadows. This technique was extremely useful in photographing cracks in turbine blades, and defective electric motors and items of that nature. The detail was incredible when it was properly done.

After a few weeks, we were issued small format cameras. In those days a roll film camera, the Mamiya C-3 was the standard. Thirty-five millimeter was not taking off yet. The Mamiya took size 120 film and produced twelve shots per roll. This was almost like owning a machine gun compared with shooting sheet film, which we had to load in the dark and then unload from the holders before processing. Our assignments with the 120 cameras were more of the photo-journalistic nature and we were assigned various stories to illustrate. Photo students could be seen all over the base with those bulky Mamiya cameras taking pictures of anything from men washing airplanes, to mess cooks preparing the meals at the one of the bases.

The other two phases of the school were motion picture and the aerial photography phase. During the motion picture phase, or "mopic" as we called it, we were issued the Bell and Howell 70 KRM camera. This camera was a spring-wound, turret lens, 16mm movie camera. Most of the WWII footage was shot with a B&H 70 KRM or the larger 35mm movie camera, the Bell and Howell Eyemo. The 70 KRM had a variable frame rate and took a standard one-hundred-foot roll of 16mm, double perforated film. It could also be fitted with an electric motor and a four-hundred-foot magazine, but we never used that in school. The lens had to be focused by looking through a tiny viewfinder on the side of the camera. To do this, you had to rotate the lens you wanted to focus to the position next to the viewfinder. You would turn the lens-focusing ring until things were sharp and then rotate the turret back so the lens was in the shooting position. Except when we used a wide aperture or a telephoto lens, many of us guessed at the distance and that was usually close enough. This camera also came in a heavy case and we still had the same bulky wooden tripods.

We were taught how to edit in the camera and how to tell a story using only one hundred feet of film, which lasted about three minutes when shot at sound speed, twenty-four frames per second. There are forty frames in a foot of 16mm movie film, so the math wasn't hard. Even though we did not shoot sound, we shot the film at sound speed. The first couple of feet were devoted to "slating" the film. Each of us had a slate, a piece of cardboard with our name, class number, and date on it. We would also add the name of the production.

Surprisingly, many members of our class produced excellent little projects on that short length of black and white movie film.

During aerial phase we were taught to lay out an aerial mosaic map from prints we made with negatives provided by Photographer's Mate "B" School. These students were petty officers advanced in their studies of naval photography. They learned color photography, sound motion picture photography, and got to fly to take aerials.

The trick in laying out a map is not to make any straight line cuts. You cut down the middle of winding roads and along the edges of fields, etc. When you stand back a little and look at the finished product, it is difficult to see the seams at all. The whole thing is stuck to a piece of Masonite with gum acacia. I never figured out what that was, but it was a form of glue that seemed to work well.

Things went well in school for a while. Then we started having little problems with one guy by the name of Edgett. He was always late to class and didn't quite fit in with the rest of us. It was causing disharmony to a great degree. Some of the kids in the class started griping about him. When studies didn't seem too difficult, many of us would go to the enlisted club and drink beer. We weren't old enough to drink the "real" beer, so we had this watered-down drink called three-two beer. This was 3.2 percent alcohol and it was supposedly difficult to get drunk with. Don't worry. We managed.

I had been riding Edgett quite hard to get him to straighten out, but he had been thrown out of school. One evening, I was at the enlisted club and happened to go to the head to drain off some of that good beer. As I finished "wringing my mitten" and was just completing the last in a series of shakes, I saw three men walk through the door from the corner of my eye. They were Edgett, Frank Oglesby, a black guy in X division at the barracks, and a Puerto Rican whose name I didn't know. I heard Frank ask Edgett, "Is that the dude that's giving you all the shit?" Edgett affirmed that I was.

"Why you giving my man Edgett all the shit?" he inquired.

"I am not giving anybody any shit," I answered.

At that point, he stepped a little closer and took a swing at me. I ducked it and hit him in the head with my right fist. I might as well have blown him a kiss for all it did. Next, he tried to kick me in the nuts. I just twisted a little to one side and his kick landed on the inside of my right thigh. I then punched him in the inside of his thigh on the leg he kicked me with. This hurt like hell and he dropped his guard a little. My next move was to punch him hard in the throat. Then I kicked him in the nuts and he went down. During the scuffle, my glasses got knocked off. I quickly retrieved them from behind one of the commodes. The other two were helping Frank up off the floor. He was still hanging onto his crotch and trying to get his breath.

I hauled ass out of the head and went to an area of tables by the bar. The bar was located just outside of the room housing the dance floor. I noticed Pat Busby, the Wave from BNAO School, sitting at a table with her boyfriend. She apparently caught sight of my disheveled appearance and the footprint on my thigh and called out my name, "Steve, what happened to you?"

"I just got in a fight with a guy from the barracks. There's three of them and I imagine they will try to whip the dogshit out of me," I replied, nearly out of breath.

"Get out of here and go back to the barracks. Tell the other guys in your class and they'll help you. Just don't hang around here."

There was no need for her to make it any clearer than that. I headed out the door and ran back to the barracks. I had been running the obstacle course near the Officers' Club and there was a cross-country course right behind the barracks that the NAVCADs used. A couple of us ran that every night. It was mostly soft sand, so I was in shape. I doubted if any of those guys could have caught me.

I made it back to the barracks in record time. When I went in, I woke up a few of the guys in the room next to mine. One of them, Jim Kerr, was a skinny looking guy from somewhere in Pennsylvania. He wore false teeth that were always flopping loose. His ass was wider than his shoulders and when he smoked, he tilted his head to the side and squinted one eye so the smoke wouldn't make his eye run. He told me he and the boys would handle the situation. They told me to hit the rack and they would take care of the problem. Kerr slept that night with a Coke bottle under his pillow, as did the rest of us. Anybody coming into a room would get that in the head.

Meanwhile, some of the Marines in one of the other rooms got wind of what was going on and offered their help. As it turned out, we all got a good night's sleep. Nothing happened at the barracks that night. Not so at the club.

Unbeknownst to me, after Oglesby got his balls down where they belonged, he had gone outside the club looking for me. Well, all we white boys look about the same, so he started a fight with somebody of my description. Oglesby screwed up royally. The guy he picked on was a street fighter from New York City. This kid just leaned back, snapped an antenna off a car and whipped Oglesby's face into bloody hamburger. Then he drop-kicked him to his knees and left.

I was walking through the barracks the next morning—it was Saturday—and as I passed by Oglesby's room I looked in. He was lying there in bed looking toward the door. He spotted me and said, "Hey man, sorry about last night." I said it was okay and to forget it. I don't think he ever found out who pounded him, but I wasn't going to tell. A few weeks later, he came back to the barracks when I had the duty. He came in without paying the cab driver. When the cabbie came to the Master-at-Arms shack to complain, I went and told Oglesby to pay the guy. He couldn't get his wallet out fast enough. So much for diplomacy, sometimes fear works better.

Almost every afternoon, some of us photo school students went to the swimming pool. It was an outdoor pool located about one hundred yards from the barracks. We would run the confidence course through the sand and then come back and swim and dive off the board for about two or three hours. After that, we'd go inside, change, and run to the chow hall. This was a distance of about three-quarters of a mile. I would have to say I was in very good shape.

One of the instructors at photo school, E-8 Marine Sergeant Guzman, was a real hard ass. He wanted his Marines to look "boot camp" all the time they were at school. Guzman had lived through the Bataan Death March during World War II. He was one-hundred-fifty percent Marine. I, however, thought he was a bit on the chickenshit side. If a Marine needed a haircut, he would give them a SGT Guzman Special. This involved shaving the offending Marine's head just like boot camp. I thought it was radical, so I suggested to my class that the next time he did this, we would take the bite out of it by all of us shaving our heads. I called it leadership. We did it, but the act didn't go over well with the senior instructor. I was relieved as class leader, and replaced by a Marine by the name of Kevin Dalrymple. He was a tall kid, about six-feet-five.

Near the end of the school, some recruiters came around from Underwater Demolition Team Replacement (UDT/R) training. There were posters all over the base that showed some frogmen jumping out of helicopters into the water and being picked up by rope ladders and other such things. I asked around to see if anybody else besides me wanted to try out for UDT Training. I managed to talk Frank Archuleta and Don Trimble into going with me. All the rest said we were crazy or they had something else to do on Saturday morning when the test was to be given. We took our boondockers and swimming trunks and walked to the Officer's Club near the beach, which was where we would meet the recruiters from UDT Training.

We walked in and expected to find a lot of men there. We were the only ones trying out. I couldn't believe it. There was a young rugged looking lieutenant, junior grade there by the name of Gerry Yocum, and an old wizzled up Chief Boatswain's Mate named John Parrish. They told us the requirements. It started out with a run. We had to run a mile and a half in less than twelve minutes wearing long pants and boondockers. These were low-cut combat type boot that all naval personnel wore with their work uniforms. The three of us started out. I came in second, just behind Trimble. I felt slow. Parrish, sucking on one of his two pipes, looked at his watch.

"Not bad." he remarked, looking at me through wrinkled and squinted eyes. "Have you been doing any running?"

"Mostly away from fights," I joked.

"Nothing wrong with that, son. You'll live longer that way."

I could tell he was serious. Later I learned he was one of the most decorated frogmen of World War II.

Then we had to swim. We were required to swim three hundred yards using underwater recovery strokes. Your hands were not allowed to break the surface. I knew I couldn't swim that well, but thought I could bull my way through it. I ended up swimming it in just under the maximum time allowed. The PT test nearly killed me. We had to do pushups, sit-ups, squat thrusts, and pull-ups. I just barely made the pull ups and was so uncoordinated; I had to stop and restart doing the squat thrusts. Frank and I passed the test. Trimble flunked one part and the chief told him he could come back and take it again the next weekend. His swimming was a little slow. I figured we could work on that and get him up to speed. The guy could run and do PT, no problem.

The next weekend, we went to watch Don. He cranked through the test again from start to finish. This time he made it. There was another guy there taking the test for the third time. His name was Heide. He couldn't even swim as well as Trimble. I asked him about his military background. He said he was a former Green Beret and he had joined the Navy to get into Underwater Demolition. The next time I saw him was at SEAL Team Two several years later. Of those who tried out for UDT/R, Dave Heide was the only one who attended UDT/R training. I think he tried out for training several times before he passed. Then he made it through the course, thanks to perseverance.

We still had to take a physical and our oxygen tolerance and pressure tests. The physical was no problem. The three of us went through that together and passed. Then the corpsman told us we had to take the pressure and oxygen tolerance test. Chief Parrish had told us not to sweat that, as they would give it to us when we got to Little Creek for training. I told this to the Personnel Officer, but he told me it was right in the manual and that he was not going to submit our orders until we had taken the tests. The chief at the school called Panama City and talked to the master diver there in charge of the recompression chamber. There was no mention of our medical records going with us. I didn't have a clue about procedure. We got Chief Byrd, one of the few remaining enlisted pilots, to fly us to Panama City in a Beechcraft the school used to train aerial photographers. We arrived there and learned we couldn't take the test without our medical records. This was discouraging. We flew back to NAS Pensacola very disappointed. I asked the chief if we could go again. He gave me some crap about not taking our records, but said he would see what he could do. The planes flew there several times a week and we should to be able to hitch a ride.

A few days later I was called into the office and told there was a flight at 1300 if I could get our records. I went to class and told Frank Archuleta. We were in the aerial phase and doing a performance test. In this test we were given a roll of aerial film. We had to process, dry, and print it with a continuous paper contact printer. My film had been processed and I had been waiting to dry it. Frank said he would dry my film if I would run and get the records. I took off and ran the mile or so to medical to get our records. When I got back, I was told I had cheated on a performance test and the skipper wanted to see me in his office. He told me what the charges were. I told him I was not cheating and thought somebody was out to screw me for something. This was such a stupid charge; it was not even worth his or my time. He smiled and told me if he thought I was cheating I would not have even been called to his office. He just wanted to tell me that he understood my enthusiasm, but I had to pay attention to business at hand. I asked him if we could still go to Panama City to take the test. He said, under the conditions, no, and that I should try again when I got to my next duty station. I told the skipper I wanted to drop out of school and go to the fleet if they were going to be that chickenshit. He told me it would take me more time to get a set of orders than it would to finish the course. I decided to wait it out and see how I felt the next day. I got over it and stayed.

Photo school wasn't too rough. I was quite interested in the material being presented, and Photographer's Mate is not one of the rates that require you to be a member of MENSA to be able to handle the studies. During the time I was there, I spent some nights at the enlisted club or went to the movies. For the most part I didn't go into town. I didn't like going in uniform. I always felt like a clown wearing that uniform when I was trying to have a good time. It was as if I had "screw me" stenciled on my forehead, and just labeled you as "queer bait" or an easy mark for any shop owner. We could keep civilian clothes off base, but most of us didn't bother to. I never did. The "locker clubs" were another way to rip off servicemen for money they could ill afford to spend.

A couple of weekends, Dave Duchene, one of my roommates and I went out to Pensacola Beach. There was always somebody who had a car so they would not be trapped on base. We offered to chip in for gas, so we usually found a ride and didn't have to take the bus.

Dave was a good guy. He was from El Paso, Texas and used to tell me horror stories about going into Mexico and getting in awful fights with the Mexicans. He was half Indian and rugged, I didn't need to find out how rugged.

One incident that has left a bitter taste in my mouth and wallet comes to mind. I was class leader and we were taking up a collection to have a party. I had collected a total of thirty-five dollars from people who would attend. This money was in my room, stashed in my locker. I went to retrieve it to take it to the club to pay for the beer and food we would consume at the party. It was gone. I thought I might have put it in my pants pocket or hidden it in the locker. No way. I couldn't find it. I knew Dave or Willis would not have taken it. They just weren't that type of people. However, Noyes always seemed to have more money than the rest of us. I suspected he might have done it. I went to security and told them about my suspicions. They checked him out and got him to confess to having taken it. He received brig time a fine, and a discharge. Then I went to the Yeoman who worked for the legal officer. I had read something in the UCMJ (Uniform Code of Military Justice) about reparations to people for damage and loss caused by servicemen. My interpretation of it was that I should be able to recoup my thirty-five dollars from him through the fines and loss of pay. The Yeoman gave me some song and dance bullshit about that rule was just for guys who went in town and tore up a bar or something like that. I told him I didn't see a bit of difference. I was wronged and had suffered a loss. The fact I was in the Navy should not have made a bit of difference. He got pissed off and told me that was how it was and not to bother him with it any more. I think the lazy son-of-a-bitch was afraid it would mean more work for him. I never got the money back. I also never saw Noyes.

The night I discovered the loss of my money, one of the Waves, Linda Welch, asked me to come over to the Wave Barracks (affectionately known as the Wave Cage) to help her with some of the more technical aspects of her studies. We were sitting in the lounge where men were allowed to visit. She was across from me at the table.

I was trying to help her with the homework. Every time I looked up at her, she was not looking at the books, but at me. Then she started to rub my lower leg with her stockinged foot. Jesus Christ, what a dumb ass I was. Here was the first chance to get laid in almost a year, and with the best looking Wave in the class. And I was so damned upset over losing thirty-five dollars that I couldn't even figure out what she was trying to tell me. I wore out more than one pair of shoes kicking myself in the ass for that. I think she probably told the other Waves I was a homosexual, which a lot of my class was. That took care of any future sexual activity at Photo School.

One of the other Waves, Lucy Calutti, came up to me one day while I was eating lunch and asked me where I was from. I told her, Maine. "Ain't they got any queers where you live?" she asked. "I guess so, I hadn't thought about it much."

She looked around over her shoulder and back at me to make sure nobody was listening. "Well, about a third of the guys in this class are queer."

I looked surprised. "Really, who are they?" I asked. Then she started naming them off. There was Riley, the flunking class leader, Sherman, three of the Marines, the one Coast Guardsman, and a couple of others, including Edgett who had flunked out by now.

I was quite amazed. I told her I didn't really give a shit as long as they stayed away from me and didn't try to screw me in my sleep or something. She was always a good person and never gave me any trouble about anything. We ended up being stationed in the same building some years later. She'd had a nose job and was very attractive. She was half-Italian and half-Jewish and exhibited the best character-istics of both.

One of my "friends" in the class introduced me to a black ensign named Johnson. He was in the flight program. I went to his barracks with one of the guys at school. We sat in his room and drank beer. He was a nice guy and seemed squared away. I didn't realize it then, but they were checking me out to see if I was homosexual. I wasn't, but was so goddamned naive that I never figured out what it was they were doing. I heard later that Johnson got the boot when they busted a whole bunch of them. Too bad, I thought he was very squared away.

The day came for us to graduate. The top person in the class was a graduate of Rochester Institute of Technology by the name of Stephen Nichols. I can't remember who two and three were, but I was number four. Considering how badly I had pissed some of the instructors and officers off, that wasn't bad.

I got my orders. They were to Naval Air Station Oceana, Virginia Beach, Virginia. I would be stationed in the Photo Lab. We were all buzzing around talking about were we were going. Gary Sherman, Jim Kerr, and I would be stationed there together. They were good guys and I was glad to be getting stationed with them. Lucy Calutti was going to NAS Norfolk, and some of the others were being spread out all over the place. I hoped I would see them again, but never knew if I would. We had our tickets home and then to our new duty stations. We were leaving at various times. The duty driver took us to the airport in groups. We had asked around to see if any of the instructors could tell us about Oceana. Everybody said it was a great place to be stationed. It was near Virginia Beach, Virginia. The summers there were outrageous with women everywhere. That made at least two of us quite happy.

I boarded the plane for Boston. I would go home and take a few days leave. I wanted to save most of it for some special reason. I had no particular desire to go home. Mary was in college, but maybe she would be home for a few days or something. It was September now and college was in full swing.

The plane landed in Boston. As usual, I got a cab to the Greyhound Station and took the "many windows" up to Rockland. Then I hitched a ride home. My parents and sisters were glad to see me. My grandfather was happy that I had joined the Navy. I made the rounds to all my friends and had short visits to tell them about my ventures. I hadn't really done anything, but they wanted to hear about it anyway. Mary's parents, Roland and Iva, were probably the happiest of anybody to see me. Mary was away at Colby College and would not be coming home. I didn't have a driver's license, but I could drive quite well, so I borrowed my father's station wagon and went up there. She didn't know I was coming, so I just showed up and had her paged. She was going with somebody else and acted like a real bitch to me. We ended up playing kissy-face and dry humping in the front seat of my old man's Chevy wagon. I left Colby College with the only thing I ever attained on a college campus, a stain on the front of my Levis. This was the result of many months of anticipation. On the way home, I fell asleep at the wheel and was about to run off the road when I ran over somebody's cat. The screech and thud it made snapped me wide-awake and I had no problem remaining so the rest of the drive.

A few days later I had gone to Rockland on foot and was walking home. I got a ride with some guy I didn't know. He kept saying he had been drinking and didn't feel well and needed to pull over and puke. I told him to go ahead and pull over. He said he was worried about cops.

I told him there weren't any cops around here. He insisted that he needed to pull off in some side road to puke. I was not feeling very comfortable with this character, and was prepared to defend myself. Finally, we were in South Thomaston when he made a left turn down the Grierson Road, which led through a sparsely populated, rural area. As he turned the wheel to the right to make the turn he asked me where it went. I said it just dead-ends back a little ways. He turned around and drove back almost to the beginning of the road. Then he pulled over. He got out and walked around to the back of the car. I thought he was really going out to throw up. I glanced in the rear view mirror and could see him jerking off. He got back into the car with his dick in his hand. I told him I had to get home and I would walk from here if I had to.

He reached across the seat after my crotch and said, "Ah, come on."

I grabbed his wrist, looked him in the eye, and said, "Buddy, I ought to rip your fucking head off right here."

"You wanna try it?"

"You're damn right! Right now!" I responded, and started to get out of the car.

He said, "Hey, I'm sorry. I'll give you a ride home, where do you live?"

I told him. He drove until he was in front of a house about a quarter of a mile from where I lived. I told him that was where I lived and got out. He turned around and headed back toward Rockland. I walked the rest of the way home. I got madder and madder as I walked.

Here I was, a reasonably good-looking young guy of nineteen. I had all my teeth and wasn't fat or anything. There had to be something wrong with me. I must be gay and not know it. Women won't come near me; faggots love me. What in hell is the problem? I was so damned mad that I was crying by the time I got home. My mother was awake when I walked through the door. I asked her what was wrong with me. Why did queers always come after me when I could hardly get in a conversation with a good-looking girl? She had no useful advice. I don't think she could relate to the problem. I will never know. When I left home to fly back to Virginia, I had less than a good attitude about myself or anything else.

I had no reason to hang around. There was nothing constructive to do, so I took a bus to Boston and got on the standby list for the earliest plane to Norfolk. I was hoping things would work out better there. I was about to embark on some very interesting adventures, some of which I can hardly believe, even to this day.

Chapter 6

Naval Air Station, Oceana

I arrived in Norfolk in the late evening. It was around 2200 when my cab pulled up at NAS Oceana. The Navy guard at the gate gave the cab driver directions to the quarterdeck and the cabbie drove me there. This time I got the right place the first time and didn't have to run all over hell's half acre to find the proper barracks. I signed in at the Officer of the Day's (OOD) office and the duty driver gave me and my gear a ride to the barracks. The master-at-arms assigned me a rack in one of the bays of the barracks and I went upstairs, padlocked my sea bag to the leg of my rack, crawled in, and went to sleep.

The next morning, I walked up to the photo lab and checked in with Lt. Fred Schmidt and Chief Photographer's Mate Montgomery. I can't remember his first name; I think it was "Chief." Both of them seemed quite glad to see me. Kerr and Sherman hadn't arrived yet. Apparently. they were having more fun on leave than I was. PH1 Donald Van Horn showed me around the lab. The place was immaculate. You could eat off the floors. I was assigned to the printing room for the time being. Each photographer had to get checked out in all aspects of naval photography. Some of the other guys there at the time were PH1 Hendricks, PH3 Butch Wendell, and PH3 Ed Gaulin. They welcomed me aboard and seemed to be decent fellows.

The different crews were assigned to each task for a few weeks or months, and then rotated. The print room was where our mistakes were the easiest to correct. We wouldn't ruin anything there. The worst we could do was to scratch a negative or fog a box of paper. If a job wasn't up to snuff, we had to reprint it until it was right. Usually the print crew did other things to learn the whole operation. If there were no prints to make, I went out and dried prints; stamped them with the negative number they were made from and put jobs away in big, brown, Navy-Issue envelopes. Logging negatives was a job everybody hated. We sat there with a Rapidograph pen, writing numbers on negatives, and then logged them in a green logbook by date and negative number. That must be where archives come from.

The aerial crew and the shooting crew had the best jobs. I was too new to hope to get on the aerial crew. The crash crew was assigned from the day's duty roster. The crash phone was hooked directly from Air Operations to the Photo Lab. When it rang, it rang continuously in a long, steady ring until somebody answered it. When it was answered, the person on the other end would tell you the situation. Usually it wasn't a crash. For the most, part it was a plane with some in-flight emergency, such as stuck landing gear or an indicator light that said their landing gear wasn't locked or they had no hydraulic pressure in the brake system. One runway was equipped with midfield arresting gear. If a plane needed to stop quickly, the crash crew from the airfield fire station would go out and rig it for use. The midfield arresting gear was made up of a large steel cable, some old tires cut in half, and two great lengths of anchor chain.

The plane would come in with tail hook down, catch the arresting cable that was setting up on the tire halves, and drag the chain down the runway. One man had to shoot this whole operation with a 16mm camera with the frame rate set at one-hundred-twenty-eight frames per second and the other would shoot still photos in rapid succession with a small aerial camera that used a five-inch roll of film. It was exciting having a Phantom or Crusader blast by you at over one hundred miles per hour. Sometimes a plane would blow a tire and run off the runway, or a wheel would break off and just miss the photographers. Luckily none of us ever got killed or hurt doing this.

One day right after I returned from the chow hall, I heard a horrendous noise that sounded like a plane crash. It was. I looked out toward the field just as the crash phone started its jangling. Somebody reached for the phone and the crash crew, including me, even though I wasn't on the crew, headed for the truck with duty camera bags in hand. We raced out to the field to see the ambulance already ahead of us by a hundred yards. There was debris strewn all over the runway and pieces of airplane were lying off to the sides of the concrete strip. The grass was littered with pieces of what had been an A-6A Intruder. The corpsmen had found the pilot. He had managed to eject at an angle as the plane was nearly on the ground. What had happened was one of his wings had simply folded up and the plane rolled. He ejected and was driven along the runway still in his ejection seat. He lived, but was physically and administratively bound to a desk for the remainder of his Navy days. I was glad that we didn't have to go shoot pictures of body parts. Sometimes others on the crew had had to shoot photos of heads in helmets and feet in boots. I never figured out why they were needed, but they were.

Occasionally we would be called upon to photograph an auto wreck if there were Navy personnel killed. One instance of an off base situation was when a guy tried to blow up his wife and her boyfriend with dynamite. Seems this guy's wife had been having her boyfriend over quite frequently while her old man had the duty. One day, he told her he had the duty but sneaked back to the house. He had laid a hefty charge of dynamite beneath the bed in the crawl space below the bedroom. He waited until things got going and cranked it off. Well, it blew both of them out of the bed and up against the ceiling. It drove the boyfriend's head through the ceiling and broke his neck. He was on top. The woman suffered a broken leg and some bruises. A sheet of plywood under the mattress shielded her from shrapnel as she nearly went into orbit. The boyfriend absorbed the shock of her hitting the ceiling. I heard the husband went to prison for quite a while.

We had the duty every fourth day and every fourth weekend. If you caught the duty on one Friday night, it meant the following weekend you would have the duty all weekend. Sometimes we swapped so we would have it from Friday night right through Sunday. That way you got shafted all at once. I liked working at the lab at Oceana. That was one of my favorite duty stations the entire time I was in the Navy. The base was beautiful and clean. The place was crawling with naval aviators who needed pictures of themselves and could take you flying for trade. I could get leather flight jackets and other "cumshaw" from the parachute loft. It's amazing what you can get for a color portrait of somebody.

The Red Cross was always running blood drives and the units would offer you an afternoon off if you gave a pint of blood. I had never given blood before, so I thought maybe this would be a good thing for the Red Cross and a good thing for me, so I went in and stuck out my arm. The nurse drew my blood and thanked me. As I walked through the door of the lab, one of the petty officers called my name.

"Waterman, grab a Leica and a couple of rolls of film and go out to the field. Some asshole just ran a plane off the runway into the weeds and we have to document it."

"What about my afternoon off?" I asked, knowing the answer.

"Some other time."

I got into the truck and we drove out to the runway where the incident had occurred. Before I had finished shooting, processing, and printing the film, it was late afternoon. In a few instances, I was so damned weak from giving that blood that I thought I would have to take a little nap. I could imagine what it must be like to get wounded and lose more than a pint and then have to run or try to get out of a bad situation.

While stationed at Oceana I had the chance to do some flying in various types of helicopters and propeller planes. The only time I got to go up in a jet was when the VF-11, The Red Rippers, had their fortieth reunion. They needed photographs taken from the back seat of a Phantom and I got the job. I took a Leica, two lenses and a Kodak Ciné Special 16mm camera. The pilot I got to fly with was a lieutenant by the name of, no kidding, Flack Logan.[†] That was his real name. He was Lieutenant Carl Flack Logan, USN. He drove a Model-T Ford pickup truck and flew F-4 Phantoms. He had flown in combat, was single and the women loved him. The guys in the other plane were named Charlie Iovino and Tom Brown. Tom, I think, was an ex-enlisted man, who had graduated from the NAVCAD program. He was the pilot, while Charlie rode in the back as the RIO (Radar Intercept Officer). We took off side by side and I wasn't wearing a "G" harness. Flack told me I might black out a little when we rotated as he was going to do a maximum performance takeoff. Well, we rotated and he pointed that Phantom straight at the sky. I watched the ground fall away as we headed for the stratosphere. I thought that was really something special. Then I looked out and saw Brown and Iovino go by us like we weren't moving. They had kicked in afterburners and zoomed past us like a rocket. So much for my high performance takeoff. We flew around and Tom got in formation with an old FF-1 and an F-6F Hellcat. It was a real chore for them to get lined up in formation. The FF-1 was a WWI biplane and the F-6F was a low wing, high-performance fighter from World War II. The Phantom's stall speed was just about the top end on the FF-1. He had his wheels down, his flaps down, his speed brakes out and everything except the canopy open so he could fly slowly. He was about falling out of the sky. Finally, we had to get just ahead of them and to the side. Then Tom would fly by the two older aircraft as slowly as possible and I would shot pictures. I shot some film of them with the movie camera

† Flack ended up as the skipper of an aircraft carrier and retired from the Navy as a Captain.

and some still with the Leica. Flack did a slow roll while I held the movie camera straight up. It would have been great footage except that when I took it back to the lab, Charlie Famuliner, a new guy from photo school processed it for me while I did the still film. He hadn't closed the top of the developer tank properly in the processing machine. My film was fogged. I was extremely angry, but knew there was nothing I could do about it. I didn't let him forget it for a long time. The stills came out fine and I got the cover shot on *Naval Aviation Magazine*.

That night, I went to the Officer's Club and photographed the squadron party—quite an event. Some of them put on a little skit about how the squadron insignia was conceived. Something about a gin drinking, bologna-slinging, two-balled bastard, complete with visual aids. By today's standards that would have been a sexist operation, but in those days everybody had a great time.

The pilots never seemed to treat enlisted men badly the way some of the blackshoe officers did. It might have been because all the mechanics and parachute riggers were enlisted. Even the admiral was a great guy. I got plenty to eat and just enough to drink so that I could still maintain some degree of professionalism as I shot dozens of photos. The next day I processed all of them as large format 4" by 5" film. Before the day was over, I had made hundreds of prints for the aviators at the party. I did this on an unofficial basis, but Lt. Schmidt encouraged me to do it. He knew that down the road somewhere, someone from the lab might need a favor.

I found out shortly after arriving at NAS Oceana that I would be advanced to PH3. This meant I could wear civilian clothes and live off base. By now, Charlie Famuliner and I had become good buddies. He had about four years of college, and had been training for the Flight Program. Charlie just about had his pilot certificate. He should have been a shoe-in for the NAVCAD (Naval Aviation Cadet) program. While in high school and college, Charlie used to drive Mr. Piper of Piper Aircraft around as his chauffeur. Charlie had passed the physical, the board and everything. He was a really intelligent guy and he almost had his degree. The Navy Flight Program shut him out when they stopped accepting non-college graduates.

Charlie drove an old Triumph car of some kind. It was a black and white convertible. We were tired of living in the barracks, so we moved off base into Al Schnoebelen's place. Al was a thirty-year-old surf bum who lived off his parents as far as we could tell. He was a decent guy and always had young girls hanging around his place. He'd never served any time in the military, but his father was a Navy dentist. Al owned Al's Surf Shop, which was located right on the water at 19th and Atlantic in Virginia Beach. He spent his winters in Florida. A lot of freaks and surf bums hung out there. We rented the apartment over the surf shop. It had two bedrooms, a small living room, a kitchen, and bathroom with a toilet, sink, and shower stall.

I spent most of my time next door at Bill McClellan's dive shop, "Maritime Explorations, Ltd." Bill was an ex-Army hardhat diver who had been through some Special Warfare Training. The SEALs were relatively new in 1965, having been commissioned just a few years before. Bill had been in what the Army had called the BRAT Team, Beach Reconnaissance Amphibious Team. They were hand-picked commando types, to be the Army's version of SEALs. Bill had been stationed at Fort Eustis, located near Newport News across the Hampton Bridge, on the other side of Langley Air Force Base. He was married to Joyce, a girl he'd met when he was in the Army. They had a little girl named Julie. She was a cute little kid and Bill really loved her. Bill and Joyce eventually got divorced.

A couple of years later, Bill found out he had MS. It didn't seem to affect him much, but he quit diving. He was a hell of a good guy and I enjoyed working with him. I used to hang out at his shop whenever I had time off. In fact, the first time I got off base, I discovered his shop in Virginia Beach. It was about a block from the Trailways Bus Station. I walked toward the beach on 19th Street and just ran right into it. Bill McClellan had been about the only real friend I'd had in the Virginia Beach area. I mean, Charlie and I were friends, but not like Bill. Bill was like the older brother I never had. A wiry, strong guy, he could do fifty one-arm pushups without any trouble. We had worked together on many jobs and pulled some other things that should have killed us.

Bill had a friend named Harry the Rat. Harry's real name was Harry Ross. He was one of Bill's ex Army buddies. He was the kind of guy who would pull a gun out and point it at you. Then you'd say, "Shit Harry, it ain't loaded." Then he would pull the trigger. It would go "click." He'd haul out the magazine and show you it was full. He just hadn't put one in the chamber. I didn't like things like that.

Harry showed me how to disarm somebody with a knife. He did it about five times to me. Finally, I had to have him slow down so that I could learn it. Bill told me about the time Harry and his brother had stolen a fourteen-foot boat by lifting it over a Hurricane Fence. Harry claimed he had robbed a bookie joint in Cleveland, Ohio of more than twenty thousand dollars and gotten away with it. They must not have reported it to the cops.

The summer before I arrived at the beach, Harry, Bill, and Al from the surf shop and another guy were swimming out under the Steel Pier at night with M-80s and cigars. They would grab somebody's fishing line and clip an M-80 on it with a clothespin. Then they'd light it and give a tug. The fisherman, usually drunk, would pull it up and it would explode before it got to the top of the pier. That didn't go on very long before the cops were called. Harry swam all the way up the beach for over a mile. When he got out of the water, he took off his fins and made believe he was really tired. When the "summer" cop came to him to arrest him, Harry swung his UDT duck feet around, both in one hand, and knocked the hell out of the cop. He went down on the sand and stayed there, dazed. Harry hauled ass and they never caught him. The last I heard of Harry, he was back in the Army, that he was at Fort Benning.

Another guy named Jack Wood, who used to let people punch him in the stomach as hard as they could. Sometimes he would have a guy stand on a bar stool and jump onto his stomach. He would even do it blindfolded. He could take it. He had us drive over his stomach one time with the front wheel of Al's pickup truck. I think he's probably dead by now, but one can only imagine what might have killed him?

Charlie Famuliner and I had a real snake ranch up over Al's Surf Shop except Charlie did most of the snake charming. Charlie could talk the skivvies off a nun. I couldn't make out in a Chinese whorehouse with a truckload of rice. The place had two bedrooms and a bathroom. The kitchen and living room were separated by a bar, which got its share of use. Upon arising, we might walk out into the living room to find one of our friends, or even a stranger who had come by to attend one of our social functions and found themselves unable to navigate after an evening of too much fun.

I helped my good friend, Bill, next door at Maritime Explorations, train the first class of NOAA (National Oceanic and Atmospheric Administration) divers. Signalman First Class Jack Kennedy[†] of UDT-21 worked with us that week. We both took some leave and Bill paid us to help him run the course. Jack was originally from Mile City, Montana and his father owned a major piece of Shell Oil. We asked him why he had joined the Navy and become a frogman. He didn't have a good answer, but I figured it had something to do with adventure.

We used to take the NOAA students out on the beach and run the hell out of them. Jack led the runs. Then we would do PT for a while.

† Jack Kennedy later went to Vietnam as a PRU Advisor with SEAL Team 2. He retired from the Navy and lives in Coronado, CA.

Out of eight guys who started the first class, five of them made it. The others just weren't cut out to be divers. They were either really out of shape, or claustrophobic, or clausty, as we called it. One of the members of the class was named Joe Dropp. He went on to become an Admiral in NOAA. One of the others, whose name I have forgotten, got killed in a bar. Some jealous husband came up behind him and hit him in the back of the head with a claw hammer. He didn't exactly die in the line of duty.

Bill would take on diving jobs now and then and I would always attempt to get time off from the Navy to help him. The money wasn't the driving force; it was the adventure and the chance to learn something. Until now I had no training of any kind in diving. I had dived with scuba before I had joined the Navy, but had no formal training, civilian or military. Bill had an old Mark V helmet and suit in his shop. He had hose and all the other things. I think it was something that he had "requisitioned" from the Army one dark night. I used to take the helmet and breastplate into the training tank behind his shop. I'd shove a small air hose under the helmet so I would have a little trickle of air to minimize the carbon dioxide. When we had students in the tank, I could sit on the bottom of the tank and tell them what to do next. I could holler at them and they would hear me through the water. That was the extent of my experience with the Mark V. I really wanted to go to diving school.

Bill had a friend by the name of Mike Ryan who claimed to know all sorts of people. Mike was an ex Marine and he said he had a friend over on the YFNB-17, which was the Navy's diving school where second class divers were trained in all aspects of air diving. They are also given some degree of training in salvage methods. In most cases, it is the second class divers who do the bulk of the work in the diving Navy.

Mike set up an appointment for me to go over to YFNB-17 at the Destroyer & Submarine Piers (D & S Piers) in Norfolk and take my indoctrination dive and Pressure and Oxygen Tolerance Test. I took the bus over from Virginia Beach to the D & S Piers. (The YFNB-17 was later moved to Little Creek Naval Amphibious Base.) The guard at the gate told me where the school was. I found the Hospital Corpsman, Mike's friend. He and another diver suited me up. I walked down the ladder and they lowered me to the bottom of Norfolk Harbor. There was no visibility at all. I didn't expect there to be. They told me to look around and tell me what I saw. I felt around and told them I saw some mud and an old tire and some tin cans and cable and some other garbage. Then one of them asked me how far I could see. I said that I couldn't see anything I couldn't reach with my hands. He laughed over the communications box and asked me what the hell I meant by that. I told him I had my eyes closed and was just feeling around. If I opened them I just got confused. They hauled me up and I my uniform on. One of the men told me I was the first guy to go down and not complain about the visibility. They also said I would probably make a good diver if I could get through the paperwork and get to school. Boy, did they call it right on that one! I thanked them and hitchhiked back to Oceana. The divers on the barge gave me a paper saying that I had passed the pressure and oxygen test and the indoctrination dive. I figured I had it made now, and would be able to get into diving school. Wrong.

I got back to the base and told Lt. Schmidt that I had passed the indoctrination and oxygen tolerance test and wanted to go to UDT training. He started pacing back and forth, and shouted, "Waterman I've just about had to suck a mile of cock to get some people into this lab and they'd cut my balls off if I approved your chit."

I took that to mean no.

Things went along smoothly. Charlie and I went to take the test for Photographer's Mate, Second Class (PH2) together. We blasted through it in record time. I had been advanced to PH3 on 16 November 1965. Charlie picked it up one month later. Now we wondered if we would make it at the same time. I had already done all my courses right up through chief, so all I had to do was study the manuals a little. About half of the people who took the test failed it, and less than half that passed it were advanced. It was now spring of 1966 and we wouldn't know anything about advancements until late in the summer.

Vietnam was in full swing and Oceana was full of activity twenty-four hours a day. One of the many things we had to photograph was the return of the fighter and bomber squadrons from deployment. It always sent a cold shudder through me when I heard the formations of jets coming over and looked up to see they were flying the "missing man" formation. That meant that one of the guys was not coming back. I thought about how I would never get to sit and listen to the guy I'd probably had a cold one with tell flying stories. I thought about how his girlfriend, or wife and kids would miss their family member. It was a sad experience, but one we became accustomed to. During war, one doesn't get over it, just used to it. My old division officer from BNAO School, Lt. Dale Doss, ended up as a guest of the North Vietnamese as a result of his incursion into their air space. I saw him one day in the base gedunk after he had come home, and he looked like someone who had been liberated from Auschwitz.

Late in the summer, around August, the word came down that both Charlie and I had made PH2. I would put it on October 16th and he, November 16th. This was good news. I was still only twenty years old.

We never went to the clubs on base except to buy beer. The Acey-Deucy Club was on the other side of the base. To get there, you had to drive out the main gate, take a left, drive a mile or so, take another left, go another half mile and turn left again. All that was over there was the skydiving club, the package store and the Chief's Club and the Acey-Deucy Club. The Acey-Deucy club was for first and second class petty officers and their guests. I was never carded as I always went in uniform. The clerks never could imagine that a person could be an E-5 and not be old enough to legally drink.

Pabst Blue Ribbon was eighty-five cents a six-pack for sixteen-ouncers. We could afford that. The Navy gave us sixty-five dollars a month for BAQ (Basic Allowance for Quarters) and we drew non-aircrew flight pay occasionally if we got to fly. We also drew another few bucks for eating off base. I loved to go up and shoot aerial photos. I had one bad experience. One Saturday morning when I had the duty, I asked Neil V. McDaniel (Mac) if I could go flying. He told me to go ahead, no problem. So I went flying with a commander by the name of Cumbie. While waiting for the plane to get fueled up, I ate a fruit pie and drank a carton of milk. Later, on the flight, I got sick. I may have been airsick, but I think it was the milk or something. Anyway, I was lying on the floor of the Beechcraft puking out the door. We had the door off to take aerials. When I was finished throwing up, I just kept shooting pictures. We were taking construction progress photos of the base where they were building a new hangar or some other structure. I thought no more of this. I didn't fly again for quite a while. One day, I overheard Lt. Schmidt talking to one of the other photographers. He said something about not being able to send Waterman because he got sick and puked all over everything whenever he went up. I was pissed and asked him where the hell he heard that. Schmidt said that's what Cdr.Cumbie had told him. I went over to Air Operations—Cumbie was the air operations officer—and asked him about it. He squirmed in his seat. I was quite polite about it and asked him if he would please talk to Lt. Schmidt and straighten him out, as I felt there was a misunderstanding. He said he would, and he did. I started flying again shortly after that.

On another occasion, which had nothing to do with being airsick, I caught the flu and started feeling really nauseous. This was before I had moved off base with Charlie. I told the chief I needed to go back to bed. He said go ahead and get some sleep and come back tomorrow. I started walking to the barracks. To get there I had to pass right by the chow hall. About the time I was abreast of the sign in front of the chow hall, I was overcome by extreme nausea. I was puking so hard I thought my eyeballs would come out. Tears were streaming from my eyes and I was in a world of my own. I finally stopped to take another breath and wipe my mouth and eyes. As I slowly regained use of my vision, I could see a couple of sets of shoes standing on the roadway with pants leading down to them. I looked up at two sailors, standing there watching me.

"Holy shit buddy, what in the hell did they have for chow?" one of them asked. In spite of my extreme sickness, I had to laugh. I told them I had the flu and just stopped there to puke on my way to the barracks.

One night, I had the duty and the regular phone rang. It was the duty officer at Air Operations. An F-8 had crashed in North Carolina that afternoon and they were going to need pictures of it. I asked the guy on duty with me if I could do the job. He told me to check with the chief and see if it was okay. I called Chief Montgomery at home and he said to go ahead and do it. I called the Operations Duty Officer back and got the details. The said they would be leaving for the crash site by helicopter in about an hour and they wanted just black-and-white still coverage.

I grabbed a box of cut film and went into the film loading room and filled about a couple of dozen film holders. Then I picked out a few film packs as a backup. Film packs are a low rent version of 4" by 5" film. They are composed of sixteen sheets of thin cut-film held together by tape and paper. As you shoot one, you pull the paper tab out of the cut film holder and the next one is pulled around in front. You tear the tab off and stuff it in your pocket or throw it away, depending on where you are. Processing them is a pain. You have to separate the paper from the film and be careful not to scratch the emulsion of the film. It is not as easy to do as cut-film

I made sure the strobe battery was charged and the solenoid that fired the camera's shutter had a fresh battery. It was not that far over to the Air Operations building, so I walked. We loaded aboard a helicopter and flew to North Carolina. The plane had crashed near Murfreesboro. An old farmer was standing on his porch smoking his pipe and all of a sudden a plane came straight at the ground. He said it hit so hard that he saw full-grown trees going end over end in the air.

We arrived on scene and walked to the place where it had gone into the ground. The pilot (I think his name was Lt. Wagner) had already been rescued by another helicopter. He had punched out at about twenty-five thousand feet and watched the plane go straight down through the cloud cover. He had been ferrying the plane to another base. Wagner said he was just flying along when he lost hydraulic pressure in the controls, and the stick felt like it was shoved in a bucket of concrete. The plane started a slow roll so he punched out. At twenty-five thousand feet, the pilot does not come out of the ejection seat. The seat just falls with the pilot still in it, and a small chute is deployed. This is called a drogue chute. If the main canopy opened at that speed and altitude, either the canopy might be destroyed by the speed through the air, or the pilot might die from oxygen deprivation, so the seat falls to about ten thousand feet under this small parachute and then the aneroid opening device shoots the seat away from the airman and deploys the main canopy. There are some survival items in the seat pack, including a strobe light and emergency radio. Though barely, the pilot had time to call a Mayday before he punched out. A helicopter was dispatched from Oceana, and arrived in the vicinity almost as soon as he had hit the ground. Once he touched down, the pilot called them on his survival radio, and when they were close, he popped an MK-13 smoke flare to assist the rescue. The only injury he suffered was a scratch on his face when they used the rescue sling to pull him up through the branches of a tree.

It was much too dark to do any photography, so I crawled into the back of a truck driven there by some of the ground crew and got some sleep. The next morning, the old black farmer, on whose land this thing had crashed, served us up a big breakfast.

We walked out into the woods where the plane had impacted. There was a hole in the soft earth about the size of a two-thousand-gallon fuel tank. There were pieces of aluminum stuck in the trees all around and I found the pilot's kneeboard with his note pad still attached. The plane had hit with such an impact that it had blown full size trees up out of the ground and upended them into the surrounding woods. There were pieces of the plane driven into the trees as far away as twenty yards. The investigators were probing into the hole with long metal rods. The best estimate they had was that the plane was about seventy feet in the ground. The canopy had been found in a field nearby and other items that had been blown from the cockpit were located in the woods.

I shot photos of the metal fragments stuck in the trees and the other objects that were found from the plane. The hole in the ground was so big, I couldn't get back far enough to get it in one frame, so I shot a pseudo-mosaic of it and stuck the shots all together later on.

I don't believe they discovered what caused this crash, but they never got the plane out of the ground. This was this pilot's second ejection in a few months. The other plane was recovered and it was found that it was entirely a mechanical thing, so they had no reason to believe this was pilot error. He had a good flight record other than these two incidents. I loved this work.

After I got back and processed the photos, the chief got a phone call from the CO of the squadron that owned the plane. He congratulated him on the quality of the work that I had done. This sort of thing did not hurt my reputation at all.

One day, out of boredom, I put in a chit to go to Vietnam. The chief looked at it and tore it up.

"What in hell do you want to do something like that for? That place is a shithole. Eventually, you'll get to go if you just stay around long enough. Probably once you get over there, you'll wish you'd never seen the place."

I dropped the subject.

Chapter 7

More Time at Oceana

As summer of '66 drew on, Bill, from the dive shop, started working across the river in Portsmouth at Peck Iron and Metal. This was a huge scrap yard where old ships were cut up for scrap. Bill was working with Beldon Little. Beldon was famous in his own right as there had been a book written about him. It was entitled *Raising of the Queen*. It told of how he and some others salvaged the stern section of a tanker by the name of the "African Queen" that had broken in two off the East Coast. With primitive equipment and hardly any supplies, Beldon and the others had managed to float the stern section of the vessel and tow it into Norfolk where they sold the power plant to a foreign country. It was a great book by Jerry Korn. I checked out a copy of it from the base library and still have it today. I only wish I had had Beldon autograph it for me. At the time it didn't mean anything.

Bill asked me if I wanted to help with the project. They were trying to raise a sunken dredge. It had been bought for scrap and, through neglect, had sunk alongside the dock in a slip in the scrap yard. I said I would. He said he would let me use his gear. Beldon would pay me fifteen dollars a day. I didn't have any way to get there, and no driver's license. PH3 Don Marks, at the lab, had a Honda 310 motorcycle. I asked him if I could rent it from him to make runs to Portsmouth. He told me I could. It would cost me three dollars a day, and I said that would be fine. I didn't tell him I had no license. So now I had a chance to clear twelve dollars a day as a salvage diver working under the famous Beldon Little.

The chief knew I had something going and would let me off early and I would make it up some other way. I would have other guys cover for me and I would take their duty to pay them back. It was a good arrangement and worked well for everybody. I never got stopped for driving without a license and Marks got his money when I got paid. Sometimes I took a couple of days leave, if it looked like we were going to get some work done and the weather was good.

Irving Dennis was an uneducated black guy who worked for Beldon. He was the nicest guy you'd ever want to meet. Beldon knew Dennis couldn't swim a stroke, so he trained him to be a tender. He was probably the best line tender I'd worked with then, or have worked with since. When you were diving surface supplied, you could hardly tell he was on the other end of the hose. When you needed some slack or gave him a signal to hold a strain, he was right on the ball. At lunch—Beldon always bought—we had Beanie Weenies, Pepsi, sardines, and Saltine crackers—the same thing every day. I liked it. For entertainment Bill and I would get Dennis (we thought his first name was Dennis, so we always called him Dennis) talking about his scars. He had one on his shoulder where he got knifed in a fight. He had another one on his calf where his girlfriend shot him when she caught him fooling around on her. Generally, he had some very wild stories. We enjoyed his company very much.

We were working to find where the water was coming into the sunken dredge. We worked all up and down the hull on the outside and found no leaks. Beldon got the idea that the water was probably coming in through the cutter-head on the barge's dredging equipment. We could not get to that without going way down inside the dredge barge. We had pumped with three or more big pumps but could never get ahead of the leakage.

Diving on the dredge was just short of deadly. We were working inside the thing using Beldon's old compressor and a Jack Browne mask (open circuit, surface supplied free flow mask). Sometimes we used scuba. We would work down two or three decks in total darkness with only a line to the surface. If anything had gone wrong we would still be there. One day when we were trying to move a large section of grating. We had no communications and Bill was on one end of it and I was on the other. We started to lift it and it got away from us. I jumped back and Bill did, too. We heard the thing crash and bang as it fell down into the pump room of the dredge. I was afraid Bill had gotten caught on it or something. He was diving the Jack Browne mask and I had the scuba, so he would have had a hose to worry about. I started to work over to where I knew he was when something grabbed me by the shoulder. It was Bill. We surfaced and laughed about the incident.

We spent a couple of months on and off working on that damned dredge. We pumped half of Hampton Roads through it and the most we ever lowered the water inside it was about two feet. Finally, Beldon gave up on it. Before that happened, I learned a lot about salvage work and how you can do about anything with almost nothing if you have ingenuity and common sense. Beldon was a master at jury-rigging. I would have worked for him free if I'd had to.

When I turned twenty I had an insurance policy that came due. My grandfather had bought it for me when I was a baby. I had forgotten about it. My mother wrote me and told me about it and said she needed money. She told me she wouldn't sign it off unless I gave her half of it. I figured that half of something was better than all of nothing, so I did. I had gone for my driver's license a little time before that. One of the guys had taken me out and let me take the test in his car. I had passed, somehow.

I received four hundred dollars as my half of the insurance policy, and borrowed another two hundred from my father, and headed to a local used auto dealer to look for something I could afford. I found a Simca. I had never heard of Simca, but it looked like a good car and seemed to run okay. I bought it and insured it. Well, the day I bought the insurance, I was given a piece of paper stating that the coverage wouldn't go into effect until midnight that night. By nine that night, I had rear-ended some lieutenant from New Jersey while I was driving up Atlantic Avenue. Bernie and Al from the Surf Shop were with me. I dented the chrome on his Ford Fairlane and totaled my Simca. The State of Virginia took my license for failure to have insurance. (I could have fought it) and I got fined for following too closely. I was about half in the bag at the time, but the cop never bothered to push for that. I took the wrecked car to the dealer where I had bought it and he gave me two hundred dollars for it. I went to Frank Ford Jewelers on Atlantic Avenue in Virginia Beach and bought a Rolex Submariner. That watch never got me into any trouble and I still have it.

Later that summer, Bill had a diving job on the Catawba River in North Carolina. The C.S. Lenore Pipeline Company out of Texas needed somebody to put large, concrete weights on a gas pipeline across the river. Someone had given them Bill's name. He didn't really want to do the job, as he had recently found out he had MS, so he quoted them a high price. They asked when he could be there. Bill asked me if I could get time off to help him. I told him I could, so I took some leave and we went to North Carolina and did the job. We took all the hardhat gear, and I took my scuba gear with me. I made one dive in the Mark-V and ended up doing the rest of the job in scuba. We made good money and I got paid when Bill did. Working with Bill McClellan was always fun.

Things were slack around the lab on occasion, so I would volunteer for things to do. One day somebody called and asked for one man to go to the strafing range to help pick up spent 20mm shell casings. It was clear and warm and the middle of the week, so I volunteered. We were loaded into the back of a couple of trucks full of 55 gallon barrels with one end cut out. The ride to the range was about an hour long and when we got there, all we had to do was go around and pick up the brass from the strafing runs the fighter planes made over the targets. The only problem with this was black widow spiders liked to make their homes inside the empty shell casings. On occasion, this made things kid of exciting, so we watched each other closely in case one of these little shiny critters got on us. While riding back to the base, the guy beside me had one crawl up the side of his face. It didn't take him long to get rid of that.

Back at the beach, I hung out at the Surf Rider near the eastern-most end of Virginia Beach. Most of the people hanging out there were pilots, frogmen, schoolteachers who fooled around with the pilots and frogmen, and guys like me who had a little class who thought they might get some leftovers. Jack Kennedy and some other Team guys used to hang out there. Jack was about the best-looking guy around, except he was drunk most of the time. The women used to crawl all over him. I had seen him at parties where he could barely stand up and watched one of the best looking girls at the party walk up and grab him by the hand and drag him upstairs to a bedroom. I felt I might learn from him. I never did. On Saturday evenings there would be a Dixieland Jazz band, with Vern Leach playing the banjo, at the Surf Rider. The owner, Joe Weller, was an ex Marine and treated the military patrons very well. He had to, in the winter that was all he had. The manager, Stu, was a good guy and everybody like him. He ended up killing himself a few years later. They found him dead in his garage with the car running. Too bad.

E-9 was as high as it went for enlisted. There were no illusions in my mind that it would be this easy all the way to E-9, but I didn't think it much of a challenge. I tried to help other guys study for the tests, but some of them were just not cut out for taking tests. They would freeze up whenever a test was set in front of them.

We could use Al's apartment only during the winter when Al was away in Florida. Al had gotten married to a woman by the name of "Mouse." She was very nice, by my standards. He had met her at the Surf Rider. She had just canned her husband. He was a contractor or something. She had come home and caught him in bed with another guy, of all things. He said if she kept her mouth shut, he wouldn't fight the divorce. She agreed with it. As the years went by, I lost track of what Al was doing and where he was living.

Wearing glasses was getting old so I went to an optometrist by the name of Kahn. I wanted to get contact lenses. He gave me credit even though I wasn't twenty-one. I did business with him until I left the area. Later, when I was in Vietnam, he mailed me a couple of spare pairs of lenses. I had sent him some of the travelers' checks I remaining from my reenlistment bonus. Had I waited to reenlist until I was in Vietnam, I would have received ten thousand dollars tax free. Missed again.

I decided I wanted to get into skydiving. The Navy had a club that jumped over by the Acey-Deucy Club. They were given an old building to use and it was the clubhouse where they packed parachutes. Most of the jumpers were from the Teams. Lcdr. Joe Heinlein, the skipper of UDT-21 gave me my ground school, and Davy (Diamond Dave) Sutherland and Joe Hulse of Team-21 put me out on my first and second jumps. Some of the others there that I can remember were: Tommy Sutherland (no relation to Davy), Dan Zmuda, or "Mud", Dusty Rhodes, Bobby Stamey, Stan Janecka, Hershel Davis, Bud Thrift, and Ty Zellers. Commander Norm (Stormin' Norman Olson) used to jump with us. He was quite a wild bastard and a SEAL. He was one of the nicest guys out there, always helping out the new guys and pulling strings to get us airplanes to jump from. However, he had a bad temper and use to go into fits of rage when little things didn't go right. That's probably how he got his name. Ty had reenlisted during a free-fall. It had been bogus because any oath you take while you are falling towards the earth at one-hundred-twenty miles per hour won't bear up. They wrote about him in the base and local newspapers. He reenlisted for UDT Training. Ty was an aviation electronics technician, third class. He eventually ended up retiring from the Navy as an E-8 boatswain's mate. Quite a change for a techie type.

NAS Oceana was like home to me. I knew almost everybody there and it was a friendly place. A new guy had checked in, Joe Leo, an Italian kid from New York. He was a good guy and we got along well. He and I would end up meeting again at other duty stations.

Another photographer, Neil V. "Mac" McDaniel, was from Clarksburg, West Virginia. He was a tall, thin guy. I can't remember ever meeting his wife, but I am sure I did. He always said he had a bus ticket home in a picture frame on the wall of his house. If his wife didn't like it here, she could just take it and haul ass. I think he meant it. Mac is the person who gave me the name "Lurch." Some people thought that was my real last name. One girl was asked if she knew Steve, and when she inquired, Steve who, the other person answered, "You know, Steve Lurch."

One night when Mac and I had the duty, he brought in a fifth of bourbon. I hated bourbon, but couldn't let that stop me from breaking the rules. It was Saturday night. Nothing ever happened on Saturday night. Not normally, that is. On this particular night a civilian aircraft was making an approach to Norfolk Airport when they realized their landing gear would not lock down. The tower routed them to NAS Oceana. We had the longest runways and the best crash crews. Also, they could foam the runway here. Well, the crash phone went off and we were both unconscious. When Mac finally woke up, the crash phone was ringing and there were men pounding on the lab doors, back and front, and the window of the bunk room. I knew nothing of this until the next morning. Fortunately, nobody had realized we were drunk. We didn't get into any trouble over this, but we decided not to do it again. Mac's pictures came out. He had to take a few shots of the landing gear. They had landed safely, or we might have had trouble on our hands. Mac eventually got out of the Navy and went to work for Eastman Kodak. I don't remember if I went home for Christmas in 1966, but if I did it doesn't stand out in my mind. I was still writing Mary occasionally, but she was in Colby College and on another planet.

It was 1967. I had moved into an apartment in Virginia Beach across from the Trailways Bus Station. It was over a small garage. An old lady owned it. My roommate was a Journalist from Dam Neck by the name of Adam Katala, a nerdy looking character with thick glasses and a little moustache. As I found out later, he also had a tendency to forget to repay money he borrowed from people. We had a hell of a deal on rent. The place had two bedrooms. You walked in the door and up the stairs. The bathroom was dead ahead at the top of the stairs. To your left was his room and to the right was mine. The kitchen and living room was all one. We didn't have a television, as we didn't want one, nor could we afford one. We had a cheap stereo and a refrigerator and stove. It was not exactly a high rent operation, and I think the rent there was about one hundred dollars per month. We didn't have to pay the utilities. The old woman who owned the place lived about a half block away. When I went to pay the rent, I always made it a point to stay a few minutes and tell her how things were going. I wanted her to think we were really decent young men. Huh!

In February of 1967, we got a new chief and a new photo officer. The chief was a guy from New York who had spent a tour in England. He had a phony British accent. His name was McAffrey, and he drove a Deux Chervo, one of those little French cars that look like they're made from a tin roof. I think he paid about nine hundred dollars for it brand new. The new photo officer was named Don "Bud" Sheehan. He was a warrant officer and a decent guy. He looked out for the enlisted men, as he had been one himself.

Schmidt retired. Before he did, though, he just about broke my arm. There was a custom of "tacking on your crow." This involved punching you in the arm on your newly acquired arm insignia. I was sitting down at the desk filling out the logbook. My left elbow was resting on the desk. Schmidt came up and nailed me on the left arm. I nearly flew out of the chair. If I were ever going to get a broken arm, I would have had it then. Talk about pain! I told him if it weren't for the fact that he was an officer and probably could whip my ass anyway, I would have dropped him for that. He just laughed. He retired and went to work for the San Diego Zoo as their photographer.

I was hanging around with members of Underwater Demolition Teams 21 and 22. A few of the guys were in SEAL Team 2, but they were usually deployed to Vietnam then. The only place that UDTs went was to the Mediterranean, to Puerto Rico and St. Thomas. My buddy, Jack Kennedy, spent quite a lot of time hanging around the environment of 19th and Atlantic. We consumed a lot of beer together, though I could see it was a way of life for him. He would get so drunk he would pass out while he was talking to you. In a few minutes, he would wake up and act like nothing had happened. He could hold an intelligent conversation and then just go unconscious. I never saw anything like it.

During the summers, the Virginia Beach Police augmented their forces with college kids who worked as part time cops. Some of them were law students and many of them visualized themselves as something more than they were, just part timers and not hardened veterans of the police force. Al always tried to get on their good side and many of them would hang out at the shop when they were off duty.

We knew we would be having parties and drinking out on the sidewalk and shooting off M-80 firecrackers and more, so we wanted all the friends we could get. One afternoon Al and another couple of guys were standing out front of the shop drinking beer. One of the summer cops came by and said they would have to stop drinking on the sidewalk. Al just looked at him and grinned. The cop stepped a little closer to Al and then the other two guys grabbed the cop. Al took the cop's handcuffs and they handcuffed him to a sign pole, then hauled his pants and skivvies down around his ankles and left him there. Al got his ass chewed for that, and had to do some fast-talking to keep from going to jail. The story was good for a laugh for quite a while around Virginia Beach.

The Surf Shop crowd used to go across Atlantic Avenue, the main drag there at the beach, to a coffee house. There was a black singer, Donald Leace, who performed there. Don's backup was a man by the name of John Cyr. He said he was from Old Town, Maine. Since then, I have met people from Old Town. I always ask them if they ever heard of a guitar player by that name. No luck yet. Leace was really good. Al, Charlie, Bernie (with the broken legs) and the rest of us would go over there. The place didn't stay open very long. I'll bet the fact that they didn't sell liquor had some effect on their success. There was not much room for war protesters in a town that depended greatly on the military for their economy.

One weekend, on routine training flight operations, an A-6A crashed into the ocean off the Outer Banks. The Navy was going to send a diving vessel and salvage it. They needed to know what had caused it to crash. I got the job. I took a Super Speed Graphic, a strobe and a whole case of cut film and Grafmatic film holders. I had a total of fifty sheets of 4" by 5" film with me. We went aboard an ASR (auxiliary submarine rescue). They had a barge and tug along. This was the first time I'd been involved with a real Navy diving operation. I was just an Airedale puke photographer to these guys, but I felt like I was one of them. I remember that they lowered one guy down in Mark V and he couldn't get anything accomplished. The tenders had to pull him up and send somebody else down who could do the job. They were required to rig slings on the lift points of the aircraft. It was intact except for the engines, which had fallen out as the plane impacted the ocean. Apparently the plane had run out of fuel. The crew ejected and the plane had glided into the water. It skipped along and sank.

The divers got the plane rigged so we could pick it up. Before they moved it, an underwater photographer from Combat Camera Group had to go down and photograph all the switches in the cockpit. They wanted to see what position the switches were in that controlled the fuel transfer pumps. The photographer, PH1(DV) Frank Stitt, came up with the Nikonos he was using and told me to go ahead and unload it and take the film back and process it. He trusted me. I put it in my bag where I was sure not to lose it. When they brought the plane up, I took forty-nine pictures of it with my Speed Graphic. I went home with forty-nine perfect shots and one spare sheet of film. I processed Frank's film and gave it an extra twenty percent in the developer as he recommended. The shots came out quite good. The pilot got canned as a result of those photographs Frank took. He had not transferred fuel from his wing tanks to his centerline tanks. As a result he had starved the engines. By the time the problem was discovered and the engines were dying, fuel could not be transferred quickly enough. The plane had ten total hours on it since it came brand new from Grumman Aircraft. What a waste. The pilot flew a desk for the remainder of his career.

I knew the Bombardier Navigator who had been flying in the plane that day. His name was Lt. Norm Zuchra. He was Polish, but we called him Zorba the Greek. He told us how it happened over beers. They were flying along a few hundred feet above the surf when it got real quiet. The pilot looked at the panel and couldn't figure out what had happened. The engines had died. Norm said he pointed up at the canopy with his hand and looked at the pilot. The pilot nodded his head. Norm ejected. He saw the pilot punch out a few seconds later. Norm said he was preparing for a water landing, with harness unhooked and his hand through his "G" harness, and all those those they train you to do. He hit the water and it was about up to his knees. He disentangled himself from his parachute and walked up the beach. There were a few kids standing there on the sand. One of them asked him where his plane was. He pointed out at the water. He got out of his gear, and walked over to help the pilot, who had hurt his hip when he landed on the beach. When he looked up, all the kids were gone. Norm walked up over the sand dunes and didn't see a sign of them. After a while, a helicopter from Oceana came, picked up the two downed aviators, and flew them to sickbay at Oceana for evaluation. The pilot suffered an injury to his hip, but it didn't matter, he wouldn't fly again for the Navy. They take a dim view of doing stupid things that ruin brand new airplanes. This event gave me a taste of Navy diving and renewed my interest in underwater photography.

A few weeks after this event, I received a surprise set of orders to Dam Neck, a base near Oceana. I would be assigned there as the Public Affairs Photographer for the Guided Missile School. I would have rather gone to almost anywhere else in the whole Navy. To some, this would have been choice duty, but in my mind, this was going to be shit detail. The photographer who presently held the billet, PH1 Steve Rock, was getting transferred to an aircraft carrier photo lab, and I was his replacement. He started to rub it in, as he knew how I hated PAO-type photography.

I wanted to know how I had been selected. I thought somebody had put my name in the hat. It was not the case. I just happened to be up for transfer and the bases were very close to each other. A few days later, a commander by the name of Gerry Pulley was visiting our photo lab. I knew he was the commanding officer of Combat Camera Group. Rumors had it that he'd served as Dwight Eisenhower's personal photographer during World War II. He had been an enlisted man and still acted like one. He always looked out for the troops. Everybody I ever met liked him. I asked him if they needed another underwater photographer at Combat Camera Group. He looked me up and down and asked me if I could swim. I told him I could. He looked over at Don Sheehan, the photo officer, and asked him, "Is this guy any good?" Sheehan smiled and winked at Commander Pulley and told him he had to kick me in the ass occasionally, but I was good. Commander Pulley looked me in the eye and said,

"Go ahead and put in for it, run it through me and I'll put a little note with it."

I thought that would be the end of it. I had tried to go to UDT a couple of times while I was here and they wouldn't hear of it. Now I figured this would be the same. If I could get into underwater photography, that would be a better deal. I could go anywhere with that and wouldn't have to bust my ass to go through UDT/R Training. What a deal! I wrote up my request. Don Sheehan approved it. He said it didn't matter as I was going to be leaving for Dam Neck in a few weeks anyway. I ran it through my department head and the CO of the base, and then to Commander Pulley. They all approved it. From there, it went to the Bureau of Personnel. After it went to Commander Pulley, I lost track of it. Meanwhile, I went to sick bay and traded some film for a diving physical. I wanted it in my record. I had to have a waiver for my eyesight to get into school. The requirements were "correctable to 20/30." I had 20/100 or worse, but it was correctable to 20/15, which was even better. The doctor passed me with no trouble and they filled out the paperwork to request the waiver.

My orders to Dam Neck arrived. I was allowed up to thirty days leave between duty stations, but I chose to go straight over to Dam Neck and check in, as I wanted to save the leave I had on the books. The Guided Missile School at Dam Neck is part of the submarine Navy. Submariners are a different breed. They are just too damned serious all of the time.

Most of them have I.Q.s so damn high they can't even hold a conversation with normal people.

I worked for a couple of old mustang lieutenants and a Wave ensign. She was a short, redheaded bitch who somehow felt she was superior to enlisted people.

One Saturday night, I went to the Officers' Club at Fort Story, a local Army base. I had been there as the guest of an Army major, Hugh something. He worked in Army intelligence and was one of the beach crowd. He was about thirty years old, and liked to drink beer and chase women as did the rest of us. I came back to work one Monday morning and my division officer called me to his desk. He asked me why I had been at the Officers' Club. I told him I had been the guest of an Army major who was a friend of mine. He told me to stay out of the Officers' Club. I told him I didn't understand why a civilian could go to the club as the guest of an officer, but an enlisted person couldn't. He said that was just the way it was. I agreed that I wouldn't go there again, at least not when the redheaded bitch was there. He mumbled something else and I walked away. That really pissed me off. I began to realize there was a caste system in the military. She didn't want me to know that she was either a dyke or taking on the troops. I didn't care either way, but no bitch ensign was going to mess up my social life. I went there a few more times, but was careful to make sure she wasn't around.

I was stuck at Dam Neck and hated the damned place. This was where missile technicians were trained to fire Polaris Missiles. Missile technicians and fire control technicians were crawling all over the place. The skipper, Captain Gagliano, ran the place. My job was to shoot pictures of grips and grins, reenlistments, promotions and attaboys, as we called them. There was no lab at Dam Neck, so I had to go over to Oceana to do my processing. I spent as much time over there as I could.

My second roommate at my apartment across from the bus station, Tom Hummer, was a lieutenant in UDT-21. He had been "transferred" from the West Coast for riding his motorcycle around the porch of the BOQ. He did some other things, too, but that was what triggered his transfer. Tom and the skipper of the team, Lcdr. Bob Condon, didn't get along. Condon was later killed in Vietnam. I gave Tom my bedroom when he was not deployed and I slept on the couch. He said he only needed a place to store his things when he went on Mediterranean cruises and was willing to pay rent for that. He was gone most of the time and still paid a third of the rent, which was a good deal.

It was the summer of 1967 and I was finally figuring out what girls were for. I remember one particular instance when I was at Tom's Donut

Shop. It wasn't just a donut shop. They sold donuts up front, but it was really a restaurant with booths in the back. They served the coldest beer in town. Jan, a thirty-year-old barmaid, had six kids and was married to a sergeant at Fort Story. She seemed very friendly, so I asked if she would like to go to my apartment for a beer. She said yes. I was out of beer, so I told her I would get some and meet her at my place. I ran about half a block to the convenience store, bought a six-pack of PBR, and walked the two blocks back to my apartment. She was already there. I opened a beer and offered her one. She said she really didn't want a beer and started taking her clothes off. It didn't take me too long to figure out what was going on.

At parties, when schoolteachers and nurses found out I was an enlisted man, they would usually turn their attention elsewhere. One night Tom Hummer and I pulled a trick. He told them he was as boatswain's mate third class and I told them I was a lieutenant. It worked. I seemed to get much more attention than he did, even though he looked like Ryan O'Neill and was in much better shape physically than myself. After a while, we told them the truth and neither of us made out that night. They were embarrassed to have fallen for that.

My orders finally came. They read: Combat Camera via Underwater Swimmers School, Key West, Florida. There was only one catch; I had to wait for a replacement. In a couple of weeks, my replacement's orders arrived at Guided Missile School. He would be there in mid-September, which meant I would be able to leave soon after that, according to when the class at UWSS would begin. Once I had orders for Underwater Swimmers School, I moved out of the apartment by the bus station and in with Chuck Conklin and Gene Gluhareff on 86th Street at the beach. I wanted to save the difference in rent. Chuck had been in the Teams, and now was selling cars for Checkered Flag Motors; Gene was in UDT-21. Chuck was from Maine, but had stayed in the Tidewater area when he got out of the Navy. He was one of the guys who had dived on the SS *Lusitania* with John Light. I always thought he had been bullshitting about that until I saw it on television— there was Chuck.

We lived on 86th Street almost at the front gate of Fort Story. I had to catch rides or buses to get to work each morning. I still didn't bother to get my license back. In my financial state, I had no reason to have it anyway. I couldn't afford a car. The apartment had two bedrooms, and I shared one of them with Gene as it had two beds. When his girlfriend stayed the night, I slept on the couch.

I didn't have a girlfriend. The only girlfriend I ever had that I considered to be a "girlfriend" was Mary from Maine. The rest of them were just temporary. It wasn't that I didn't want one, I just wasn't able to find anybody to hang out with me for more than a few hours.

Bill McClellan still owned the dive shop, but had moved his family out of the small apartment over the shop to a house out in one of the new housing developments. Bill gave me a key to his old apartment. He told me I could use it if I needed to for a place to sleep if I was stuck at the beach. I had made friends with another girl, Monica Kelly. Her mother owned the motel next door to the shop. She was a hippie, although we never discussed her politics. I wasn't paying any attention to Vietnam. The only thing I saw of it was the receptions they held for the pilots and crewmen returning to Oceana. Charlie and I would go over to the welcome-home parties in the hangars and shoot pictures of the aviators coming home and hugging their wives and so forth. We would trade the photos for whatever we could get, or just give them away. I spent as much time as possible at the Oceana Photo Lab. They kept very loose records of the materials I used, as they didn't really care. That's how it was in those days.

Monica told me that the song "Jennifer Juniper" by Donovan was written about her friend Jennifer Juniper. I believed her. Her mother and I got along well. Monica and I used to sneak upstairs into Bill's old apartment for evening entertainment. I never saw her again after that summer. She wrote me a couple of times, and once, when I was passing through Washington, D.C. with a buddy of mine on the way to Maine, I stopped to see her. She wasn't home, but I talked with her mother for a few minutes.

Once I found out I was going to Swim School, I began to be extremely careful with my parachute landings. I certainly did not want to get injured and not be able to attend school. Especially after I had imposed on so many people who had helped me to get to Combat Camera Group.

The rule allows thirty days leave between permanent changes of duty stations. Thirty-three days before I was due to check into Swim School at Key West, I checked out of GMS, Dam Neck. I went back to the apartment on 86th Street, packed the gear away that I wouldn't need, and got everything ready that I would need in Key West. Then I went to the beach and said goodbye to some of my friends. I took two days of leave, caught a ride to the airport, and flew to Key West. I would go home some other time. Chuck said I could store my stuff at the apartment until I came back from Underwater Swimmers School. He and Gene had been through UWSS as part of their training with UDT/R. They called it underwater track school. They told me all you did was run, swim and do PT. Before it was over, I would agree with them fully. I hoped I would be able to hack it there. I hadn't been to any physically demanding schools yet, and wondered about my endurance.

I hadn't been to Key West before. My great-grandmother showed me picture post cards of it when I was little. She had made a trip there when the railroad still ran to the Keys.

Chapter 8

Underwater Swimmers School

I caught a cab from the Key West airport and the driver took me to the old sub base, where I signed in at the quarterdeck of U.S. Naval School, Underwater Swimmers. It was in the first week of October 1967, but my class wasn't due to start until November 4. When I handed my orders to the chief in personnel he asked me why I was there so early. I told him I wanted to get in shape so I wouldn't have any trouble making it through. He looked me over and told me I would get in shape all right; I'd be a hell of a painter by the time class started. I told him where I had come from I would consider painting outhouse walls a joyful change of pace. He glanced down at my orders to see where I had come from, then grinned.

"I see what you mean," he said.

I wasn't the only one to have an attitude about Guided Missile School. He told me to grab a rack in the east wing and put my things in a locker. The uniform at UWSS was swimming trunks, fatigue shirt, Marine Corps fatigue hat with rank insignia, and white tennis shoes. I liked it.

My bunk was on the bottom of a set of two layer bunk beds in the east end of the bottom deck. Most of the guys there were UDT trainees or members of the staff of Swim School. I remember Jimmy Glasscock slept in the top bunk of the next row. Another guy, Slator Blackiston, III, had a reputation as a wild man.[†] He could do the Dance of the Flaming Asshole[‡] better than anybody.

† Slator made lieutenant after going back to college, and then was killed in France in 1984 in a questionable parachuting accident.

‡ The Dance of the Flaming Asshole is done by stuffing a wad of toilet paper between one's butt cheeks and lighting it on fire. The performer then dances around until the fire becomes too hot to bear.

One of the members of the staff was John Kirby. He was an ENFA (Engineman Fireman Apprentice) who used to work out with the UDT trainees and run on his own before and after work. He planned to go to UDT training. Well, he did and eventually became command master chief petty officer of SEAL Team 2.

The first few days at UWSS were devoted to getting to know my way around. I met many of the instructors there, Al Hale, Bill Wright, Steve Nash, and Joe Kaczmar, all West Coast frogmen. Most of the instructors were members of UDT Teams or SEAL Teams who were serving at UWSS for shore duty. In the Navy, there are several different types of duty. The Teams were considered sea duty, as the men were always being deployed somewhere and were subject to long periods away from home. Shore duty would be somewhere such as Key West, where they had a nine-to-five job much like a civilian. Some of the instructors had very interesting backgrounds. One of them, Everett Owl, was an American Indian. He was a large man and had an Indian chief tattooed on his arm. If all the Indians had been like this guy, there wouldn't be many white men living here today. Chief Owl was a great man and an outstanding instructor. We had a few talks now and then and he told me how he would do things if he were going to start over. I always liked to get the perspective from people who had been everywhere and done everything. You know, "BTDT," been there, done that. He advised me that Explosive Ordnance Disposal (EOD) would have been his choice if he were my age and had my mental makeup. I told him I was a Photographer's Mate and was being assigned as an underwater photographer to a Combat Camera Group. He told me I probably wouldn't be able to do any better than that. If I wanted to serve with any outfit like SEAL Team, UDT, or EOD, all I would have to do would be to ask and they would love to have their activities documented by a Navy photographer. They got sick of civilians coming in and making films and doing stories when they really didn't know the full story or have a grip on the "big picture." Some of these civilians wanted to play the big, bad role, and didn't have a clue what the missions were all about. They would get in the way and ask stupid questions. There really are stupid questions, no matter what anybody says.

One of the other instructors, Chief Petty Officer Bruce Lisle, a first class diver, was a seventh-degree black belt in Karate. He had won the Japanese championships in Karate a few years prior. They were very upset when an American from the Navy beat the shit out of their best guy. He was bad. He used to train students at night in the school, and had some of the UDT trainees and some other men from around the base. He beat on them harder after school than anything they had to put up with during the regular day. All of them had the utmost respect for Chief Lisle.

The commanding officer of the school was a redheaded lieutenant commander by the name of Peter Willits. He used to wander around the school holding his cat. The cat was like his wife or something. This guy was a UDT officer, but the kids in training used to think he was a faggot. Some of the trainees captured his cat one day and put it in the clothes dryer with a handful of rocks. The cat suffered a lot of pain for this and the skipper was out to can anybody from school who presented the slightest disciplinary problem to him. The members of that UDT class had to watch their asses very closely.

About a week or so after reporting for duty at UWSS, I went to a party with Ensign Rich Kuhn and Seaman Harry Hinckley. Hinckley was from Maine and I think he had dropped out of medical school to join the Navy. There was probably a draft board breathing down his neck, had I known the full story. Anyway, we three ended up at this party at somebody's house in Key West. All three of us were the clean-cut American boy type and the girls liked us. I ended up going home with one by the name of Sheila Duncan. I told her I didn't want to go back to the base as it was late and I was drunk. She said I could stay at her house and sleep on the couch. I knew that was a ruse. I got over to her house and she dragged me into the bedroom. Of course, I wasn't too reluctant to go. I got the impression she thought I was an officer. Except for Hinckley and me, all the other guys at the party were officers. Hinckley had about six years of college and used big words all the time, so they could have easily mistaken him for one. I had been hanging out with officers and people of superior intellect most of the time I had been in the Navy. My proper use of English could have led to the mistaken assumption that I might have some education.

Here I was in the rack with a Key West Debutante (we called them Key West Debi-Tramps). I wanted to make sure she remembered this enlisted puke. I gave her no rest. I was in good shape and hadn't been laid for about a month. She had trouble walking for days after that. In the morning, before I left, she asked me how I liked the BOQ (Bachelor Officers' Quarters). I told her I lived in the barracks. Now she realized I wasn't an officer, but she thought she at least had a real-live frogman on her hands. She asked me how I liked UDT training, and whether it was difficult. I informed her that I thought it was, but didn't know first-hand, as I wasn't part of it; that I was training to be an Underwater Photographer. That took care of any future dates with her. She never went out with me again. The secretary at the UWSS, Marlene, had a list of available young girls for the officers to date. Sheila Duncan was on that list. So was a girl by the name of Mary Harris. She had been the one with Harry that night. I don't think she ever went out with Harry again, either. These honeys were just like the ones in Virginia Beach and the rest of the Navy towns throughout America. They were looking to marry an officer who would help them climb in social status and live happily ever after.

One of the men in the UDT class, Rodney Wilkerson, had been kicked out for oversleeping one morning. Apparently he had been out late and had a few too many drinks. When they weren't able to wake him in the morning he missed muster. He and I were assigned to work together while the school decided whether or not to drop him from UDT training permanently. Wilkie and I did a lot of painting. One day we had to paint the buoyant escape tank in the school. There was a mermaid painted on one wall and seahorses and other underwater scenes on the other. We took turns painting, as the fumes from the paint were very strong. Before the day was out, we were both stoned out of our minds from the fumes. I don't know why we didn't die from that. We already knew we had brain damage or we wouldn't be at the school, so that was not a problem. After a while, Wilkie got back with his class and eventually made it to the Teams. He was later assigned to help train Astronauts under water in the space simulation tank in Huntsville, Alabama.

Wilkie claims he is the only man who has pissed on a man who has walked on the moon. He took a leak on one of the astronauts' legs while they were showering together after a training session. The unnamed astronaut, who has the requisite sense of humor of anybody who is in that program, thought it was quite a riot.

After my month or so of painting and shit details were up, I started my course. The UDT class was about to graduate. One day there was a commotion in the recreation room on the first floor of the school. Somebody had been stealing chocolate milk out of the vending machine and the XO of the school. An old mustang lieutenant we called Shaky Jake was determined to find the culprit and have him thrown out of school. He got some fluorescent powder that shows up under ultraviolet light and dusted parts of the machine with it. Sure enough, somebody stole some milk and he brought out the black light to catch the thief. The first two guys he shined the light on were a couple of young frogman candidates, Bill Barth and Wellington (Duke) Leonard. They had to be the culprits. Their careers in Naval Special Warfare were going to be abruptly halted by a vending machine theft. The black light clearly showed they had been handling a fluorescent material. Their platoon officer, ENS Rich Kuhn, talked to the two men and they swore they were innocent. Rich believed them. He went in the back room and got a handful of Baralyme dust. This was the barium hydroxide compound used to scrub carbon dioxide from the breathing gas in a mixed-gas, or closed-circuit diving rig. He walked out into the recreation room and asked Shaky Jake to shine the ultraviolet light on the dust. It glowed brightly. Rich told Jake that all the men had been handling the compound and that's why their hands glowed under the light. Jake didn't like it, and threatened to throw them out anyway. Rich informed him that if he did, the whole goddamn class would quit in protest. That would not look good if seventy-three of the Navy's finest young frogman candidates quit a few days before graduating. Jake backed off and never did find out who had been stealing. That was my first taste of how frogmen and SEALs will stick together in a bad situation.

My class finally started. It was made up of Marines who were going to Force Recon and men who were starting EOD School. There were only five enlisted in the class of over twenty some students. We were paired up according to our swimming ability. I had been practicing with fins and had bought a pair of Scubapro Jet Fins from a corpsman, Hospital Corpsman First Class Martin, who ran a small dive shop out of sickbay. It turned out I was the fastest swimmer in the class. I could also hold my breath of over two and a half minutes underwater if I wasn't swimming. That impressed the instructors. My swim buddy became a Force Recon officer, First Lieutenant Jones of the Marine Corps. He was a pretty nice guy—for a Marine. Jones was an ex-enlisted man, so he was very sharp, all in all and understood how things were supposed to "work."

Of all the things we did in training, I liked the underwater relay races and the "Town Runs" the best. The underwater relay races were conducted between two halves of the class. They would break us into two teams. Each team took a Jack Browne weight belt,[†] then a man would jump into the water and run underwater to the other end of the pool. Then he handed the belt to the next guy in line, who jumped into the water and ran underwater to the other end. This continued until all the men had swapped ends. The winning team got to sit down and rest; the losing team was split in two and had to compete with each other. Once

† The Jack Browne weight belt is about forty pounds and made of leather with lead ingots bolted to the belt. It has shoulder straps, also of leather.

again, the winning team could sit down and rest. Pretty soon, it was down to two guys competing with each other. When they finished, all the rest of us had to get up and continue with whatever training evolution came next. This practice was called "IT PAYS TO BE A WINNER." Nobody argued with that. Sometimes we swam with a fin in each hand and none on our feet. Other times, we had a towel in each hand and it had to be slapped on the water with each stroke when we swam the crawl. One day, the instructors had us swimming with a bucket in our hands. Also a lot of fun was lying on our backs on the edge of the pool with a face mask full of water, singing, and doing flutter kicks. It's hard to sing with water in your face mask; it runs up your nose and down your throat, and you start coughing.

We had a Marine major in the class. Old, by our standards, and hard-core, he wore a skinhead haircut and was always chewing tobacco or smoking a cigar. If he wasn't smoking it, he chewed it, even on the runs. I liked the guy, even though we all thought he was a bullshitter. He was thirty-three but looked fifty. His swim buddy was a little Marine private. They got along great.

On our final compass swim, the longest one and at night, the major, who had never had any trouble with his compass before, ended up swimming slightly off course and landed on the beach right in front of the Officer's Club. Another strange coincidence was that he just happened to have a twenty-dollar bill stashed in his trunks. All the rest of us landed on the beach, guided by the headlights of a truck, but the major was nowhere to be found. After a few minutes, he and his enlisted Marine swim buddy came walking down the road with their tanks on their backs. Each of them had a beer in their hand and a shit-eating grin on their faces. The instructors didn't get too upset over it, as I am sure most of them, being frogmen, had done the same or worse.

We practiced doing hull inspections, and made some free ascents from thirty feet in the harbor by the old submarine piers. This was a safety precaution in case one of us ran out of air. For our final qualifying deep dive, we were taken offshore to a depth of one-hundred-thirty feet where we would dive to the bottom, staying on a descending line, and swim around for about ten minutes and then surface. The instructors had us stop at ten feet for a safety decompression stop. Ray Gladding, an EOD man who was an instructor, was in charge of that evolution. He told us the story of a Master Diver, Chief Garlick, at the school who had saved the people inside a chamber when a fire had started. Somehow he had vented the chamber quickly enough to keep the occupants from being incinerated. I believe he got an award for this. In all the other chamber fires I have ever heard of, everybody was burned to a crisp in the high oxygen content atmosphere.

Less than half of our class was enlisted. Most of the officers were okay. They didn't pull any rank. All the instructors were enlisted, so if they saw any of the student officers treating the enlisted trainees badly, they would cram it to them hard. One instructor, Pappy Hewitt, was about fifty years old. I was lying on my back doing flutter kicks one day. I was not particularly enthusiastic about my performance and Pappy Hewitt happened to run by me. He stopped and looked down.

"How old are you kid?" he asked.

"Twenty-one," I answered.

"How old is your father?" he asked.

"Forty-two."

"Shit, I'm over twice your age and older than your old man, and I can still run your ass off. Now put some ass behind it."

That made me a little humble. I was wearing tennis shoes, a T-shirt, and a pair of trunks. I was in good shape and this old chief could run me into the ground wearing combat boots. Pappy Hewitt was a legend in Key West.

One day, a huge, fat hospital corpsman checked in. They asked him why he was there. He told them he was there to attend school, as he wanted to become an SOT (Special Operations Technician). They were the corpsmen who operated with Special Warfare types. They had to be well trained in diving medicine, field surgery, and other things conducive to emergency medicine in the field under combat conditions. The instructors took one look at this guy, Dick Wolf, and told him he didn't have a snowball's chance in hell of getting through the school in that condition. He would have to lose over fifty pounds and get in shape. Wolf told them he would do it if they would give him a chance. They wouldn't let him start the class he had been assigned to, but told him he could start the next one and work out with the one he was supposed to be in. He agreed. They had never seen anything like it. He melted that weight off and got into excellent physical shape. When he had arrived at Swim School he had had a bad attitude and was a prick. As he got thinner his attitude improved until he was a nice guy. He no longer started fights in town and bad-mouthed people. He finally graduated from the school and went to one of the Teams. He was killed in Vietnam a few years later when he got hit in the head by a helicopter blade. At the time, he was working with SEAL Team 1.

We only lost two guys in our class. One of them was an enlisted guy who couldn't handle the academic part and the other was a chief who just couldn't keep up physically. All of us graduated in the first week of December 1967. I was the only Photographer's Mate. All the rest of them went to their respective duty stations. The only ones I ever saw again were Lt. Dichiachio and Lt. Lashutka. They eventually got stationed at Fort Story, Virginia, after the navy started stationing EOD Teams out there.

The instructors gave us our class rankings and our diplomas. I was number four in the class. We left right after we received our diplomas. Some of us buddied up on cabs and headed out to the airport through the driving rain, typical for a fall day in Key West.

I boarded a plane to Norfolk and reported in at Combat Camera Group. I was really proud of that little black scuba diver patch on the right sleeve of my uniform. Anybody qualified as a diver was designated by a "(DV)" after his rank, so I was now PH2(DV) Steve Waterman, a really special guy; one of the elite, even more so than a frogman. I was a Navy Underwater Photographer, even though I had never taken a single underwater photograph in my life.

Chapter 9

Combat Camera Group

I signed in at Atlantic Fleet Combat Camera Group (AFCCG). When I went to see the skipper, Commander Gerry Pulley, he gave me the usual greeting. He stood up and quickly walked out from behind his desk. Then he reached out and grasped my hand and shook it warmly while slapping me on the right shoulder. He kept shaking my hand for a few seconds and told me how glad he was to have me aboard. He was about as enthusiastic about meeting me as anybody I have ever met. Gerry Pulley was someone I would never let down if I could avoid it. He made you feel he was genuinely glad to see you, because he really was.

After I met the XO, Lt. Dick Wade, I went to the diving locker and met the guys. PHC Dick Johnson, a rugged thirty-year-old man was six-foot-one with brown hair. He had a slight stoop to his shoulders, which, I later found out, was the result of milking cows at a very young age. Dick was a native of California, and had recently been promoted to chief.

PH1 Ron Hamilton was a thin blonde with a crew cut and glasses. He was not the typical robust, swashbuckling sailor-type, although he was one hell of a cinematographer, and I liked working with him. He had attended the Naval Cinematographer course at USC, as had Dick Johnson. On one of the training films, they worked with George Lucas who was a student at USC at the time. The production was called *THX-1138*, and it featured Dick as a person called "Perfectbody." There were a number of other Navy photographers, students in the USC Motion Picture Director's Course. One of them, Dan Nachtsheim,[†] worked in the editing section of Combat Camera Group. He had been the "star"

† Dan has since passed away.

of the film, though all he did was run through the airport with a fearful look on his face as though trying to escape from something. This first film got Lucas a contract, and he made a release version of the film. It bombed, but George Lucas has made some spectacular films since, and is very well-known in the movie industry.

PH1 Dave Graver was more of a typical sailor-type who was seriously under the impression that every woman wanted him, and badly. Dave was a good underwater cameraman, and an all around good hand with boats. We always got along well and went on many jobs together.

PH1 Art Cutter was getting ready to be transferred somewhere. He was a good man with a movie camera, and had served on the DOD (Department of Defense) Photo Team in Vietnam. This made him popular with the old Korea and WWII Veterans.

PH2 Howard Trotter was a fanatic for neatness and doing the job right. He would spend more than his fair share of time drinking, which was not unusual for some of us in those days. He was married to a younger woman and we used to kid him about that all the time.

PH2 Gus Kennedy[†] was from someplace out west and wore a belt buckle with a bucking horse on it. He claimed he used to ride broncos. Gus gave me a hardly-worn belt buckle with a miniature Mark-V diver's helmet soldered on it. He was a good shipmate and would do anything for his friends. We got along well.

PH3 Bill Curtsinger[‡] was waiting to go to Underwater Swimmers School. Bill was a skinny, blonde serious type. He was one of Gerry Pulley's favorites. The skipper saw much potential in him. Bill could handle a Nikon. He could also hustle his rejects to magazines and photo agencies. In the Navy when a photographer shoots pictures and sends Kodachrome off to the Naval Photographic Center for processing, NPC sends back the rejects. If he shoots enough film, which we all did, he gets a lot of good images that he can unload wherever. It wasn't exactly ethical, but we all did it when we could. Curtsinger was the king.

PH1 Frank Stitt, the underwater photographer I'd met on the A-6A job, was still in the diving locker, but was due to transfer to some better deal on the West Coast he had hustled. He was very uncoordinated. Frank was about six feet four and as gaumy[§] as they come. The rest of the crew started telling Stitt stories shortly after I arrived. There was the one about him trying to change lenses on a Nikonos camera while

† Last I heard, Gus Kennedy had moved to Hawaii.
‡ Bill Curtsinger made a name for himself as a contract photographer for *National Geographic Magazine*. Both of us lost our wives to breast cancer a few years apart.
§ Gaumy is a Maine term meaning extremely uncoordinated.

underwater. I couldn't believe anybody would do that, but they convinced me it was true. He was sitting on a stool in the diving locker one day and had his feet stuck through the rungs. When he went to get up, his feet were trapped and he fell flat on his face on the tile floor. He was a damn good cinematographer and director. I think he went on to some civilian job in Hollywood and made good.

PH2 Harry Kulu, a native Hawaiian, was an excellent diver and photographer in and out of the water. Harry and I had the same measurements except for height. He was one rugged bastard, broad of beam and not an ounce of fat. He had dropped out of school at a young age and this was a disadvantage to him when it came to getting promoted. His wife, Debbie, had a PhD and taught college at Old Dominion University in Norfolk. When Harry got drunk, you didn't want to piss him off.

One night, we were at the Stag Lounge at the Acey-Deucy Club at Norfolk Naval Air Station. Harry and I were indulging in some social beverages. After a while, we rode out to his house on his Harley Hog. Later on Harry went out for some more beer and got a ticket for drunken driving. Harry would come up to a stoplight and forget to put his feet down. After two repetitions of this, a Virginia Beach cop following Harry pulled him over. The cop, who was a motorcycle owner, told Harry he perfectly understood having a "hog" fall over at a stoplight, but after the third time, he just had to check the driver out.

Combat Camera Group was heaven for a photographer. We could sign out an Arriflex 16S motion picture camera (A German-made, high-end 16mm motion picture camera) and shoot "training film" on weekends. If you wanted to go diving for fun, you could take your gear and fill your tanks with the Navy compressor. All you had to do to get film was go up to the supply office and sign it out. There was a certain budget for training and, unless guys were selling the film on the black market, (which happened only once, that I know of) there was plenty of film for training. We had a big responsibility to the archives, and the Navy wanted to insure we were as good at our trade as possible.

After I had been at AFCCG for a couple of days, Chief Johnson drove me to the local dive shop and I was measured for my first custom-made quarter-inch wetsuit. I also picked up my fins, mask, regulator, weight belt, life jacket, etc. The owner of the dive shop was Hyrum Mulliken, a retired Navy master diver. He had all the open purchase Navy business in the area. The men from the Teams got most of their open-purchase items there, too. Open-purchase items were things that were not in the Navy supply system—usually things such as wetsuits, specialized clothing, and other items that were not bought in large quantities. Our wetsuits were all custom-made, so could not be stock items. The Navy had an "approved" list of regulators, so we had to choose one that was on the list. I chose the same equipment as the rest of the team so there would be fewer spare parts to stock.

Back at the unit, I was assigned a locker to keep all my gear in. The chief issued me my PT gear. He was a big one on physical fitness. We had PT three days a week. Most of the time, we would go over to the gym, change, go for a two-mile run and then do PT for about a half hour. Sometimes, we would swim in the pool if it wasn't being used for training. There was a Dilbert Dunker there. That is the device used to train pilots to escape from a downed aircraft that has landed in the water. The instructors strap a man into this thing that simulates the cockpit of a plane. Then a brake is released, and the Dunker runs down a track, crashes into the water, flips over, and sinks. When the safety diver taps the victim on the top of his helmet, he unstraps and pushes out of the cockpit to swim away and surface. We were surprised how many flyers had trouble with this simple procedure. Marine pilots were the absolute worst. They tended to panic almost every time. We worked as safety divers a few times on the Dilbert Dunker and, when the Marines were training, you could count on getting your regulator kicked out of your mouth a couple of times.

The first job I went on with AFCCG (Atlantic Fleet Combat Camera Group) was in Key West. The chief had finagled a job to go down and train with the Naval Ordnance Unit at the Naval Station in Key West. We had an old mustang (former enlisted) photo officer by the name of Matson who was going down with us. He hadn't been a diver for years and was no longer a qualified diver, but he was going to go along anyway. It was a vacation for him, and a chance to get back into the water, albeit illegally.

The crew going to Key West was Ron Hamilton, Dick Johnson, Dave Graver, Harry Kulu, Bill Curtsinger, and myself. Bill would be staying on at Key West, as his class at Underwater Swimmers School started before the job was over. Part of the assignment was to shoot film of some aquanauts from Canada, England, and Australia who were part of the SEALAB program. There was an exchange program going on and Combat Camera Group had to document it. Although ninety percent of the filming would be done topside, we carried along all of our underwater gear so we would be able to get some training in while there. Ron Hamilton and Dick Johnson[†] were the guys with the formal

† Dick Johnson retired from the Navy and moved to Montana. We stay in touch.

training in filmmaking. The rest of us just knew how to operate cameras and ended up being "grips."

The Navy graciously supplied a plane for our trip down and we loaded all the gear on board. We had just taken delivery on some new 16mm Milliken DBM-5 and DBM-123 underwater motion picture cameras and we were anxious to try them out. They had a "water-corrected" lens. That meant the front element of the lens was not in contact with the water, but the front port had a slight minus correction that made up for the magnification factor of the water. All it did was correct a little for the fact that water has a greater optical density than air. Topside, these cameras didn't shoot clear and sharp footage, but underwater, they were good. Rechargeable batteries powered the cameras and these had to be treated with care so as not to ruin them by overcharging. The DBM-5s would take a four-hundred-foot spool load and the DBM-123s took a two-hundred-foot spool load. The DBM-5s had a Milliken movement in them. This was a movie camera mechanism that was an all ball-bearing or roller-bearing movement. The DBM-5s could be driven up to four hundred frames per second by changing the drive motor and the cam on the drive sprocket. We thought the 123s were mostly garbage as they were nothing more than Bell & Howell Filmo mechanisms in a Rebikoff housing. However, these cameras were still better than what we had been using as they had internal rechargeable batteries and would shoot a whole load of film without having to be rewound or messed with in any way.

We were given a couple of Pegasus vehicles to test. Dmitri Rebikoff also made these. The Pegasus looked like a stainless steel torpedo with aircraft controls. The theory behind it was to mount a camera on one and use it for underwater mapping or some other purpose. I think we only ever used them as toys. The one benefit of the Pegasus was when we sold the old Yardney Silver-cells back to Yardney for scrap silver and put the money into our "slush fund." We used the extra bucks to buy some new swimming trunks and have a party or two now and then. They were fun to fly, but I felt they had no practical use. Some of the UDT teams had them and I believe they arrived at the same conclusion. It was quite a job to hang onto it as it flew through the water, and wore you out. Its speed was about three knots, but if the water was cold, you got cooled off too much with the movement through it. If you turned your head and your facemask was not on tight, it would be ripped off.

While we were in Key West, we thought it would be good if we could get some photos of hardhat divers at work. The divers at the Naval Ordnance Unit had some Mark V gear, old standard Navy Hard Hat equipment, and agreed that it would be good to give them an excuse to dive it. They took us out and anchored their dive boat in about thirty feet of water. We took turns going down and shooting photos and film of them picking up rocks and putting them in a tool bag. This was just for effect, but the people at the Naval Photo Center in D.C. didn't care.[†] Some of the divers at the Naval Ordnance Unit were very avid spearfishermen. I wasn't much of a sportsman when it came to shooting fish except for food, but I liked to tag along and shoot movies. One of the men, First Class Petty Officer Nielsen, was a very good spear-fisherman. Several of us took out one of the larger boats to where the good fishing was and we were going to spend the day shooting fish for the freezer. I was following Nielsen around as he dived down to more than one hundred feet to shoot grouper and snapper. I used up two sets of double scuba air bottles. After I used the last set and we were heading back to shore, I figured out how much bottom time I had against me and how little time I had spent on the surface between dives. Then it hit me that I had stayed way over the tables and most probably would get hit with decompression sickness. I started getting nervous and was expecting to have numbness, or paralysis occur in some part of my body. The other divers were also concerned about me. I sat up on the foredeck and tried not to think about it. Before long, my right hip started aching as if I had pulled a muscle. "This is it," I thought, "my first case of the bends."

By the time we returned to the dock, it had gotten a little worse. It felt like a pulled muscle, or a sprain, but with no sign of relief no matter what position I moved. It was a dull, throbbing ache.

The divers drove me over to a submarine tender, the USS *Bushnell*, at the wharf near Underwater Swimmer's School, and we went aboard. Of course, it was Friday and payday, to boot. However, the dive gang stayed around to treat this dumb bastard on a Recompression Table One A.[‡] Their oxygen system was out of commission so the whole treatment was done on air alone. As a result, it was several hours before I was allowed out of the chamber. I had to sleep aboard the ship in sickbay for the night. I swore if I did something stupid like that again, at least I would have the decency

† Twenty years later, I was working as a commercial diver and one of the divers in the company showed me a picture of his uncle, who had been a Navy warrant officer and diver in EOD. It was a photograph I had taken in 1968 at the Naval Ordnance Unit in Key West. Small world.

‡ The Table One A was the shortest treatment schedule for simple decompression sickness without supplemental oxygen. It lasted much longer than the oxygen tables, due to the effective partial pressure of oxygen n the breathing gas used during treatment.

to do it on a Monday morning and not on a Friday evening on payday. The crew had a good sense of humor about it.

When we returned to Norfolk, I got the word that I would be going over to Little Creek to attend SERE School. SERE stands for Survival, Evasion, Resistance, and Escape. The school was designed to provide some basic survival skills to those who might find themselves out in the boonies as a result of an aircraft accident or being shot down. It also included a mock prisoner of war camp.

First up was firearms training. We were loaded onto stake trucks and driven over to Dam Neck, right past Guided Missile School. I shuddered at the thought of being stationed there again. At the firing range, Marine firearms instructors, with the help of our Navy instructors, broke us in on the use of the M-16, M-60 machine gun, and the .50 caliber machine gun. We all got to fire the weapons and, for me, it was the first time I had fired any of them. Although I had been around guns all my life, I had never fired a machine gun. It was quite an experience.

After this phase, we had one day of booby trap orientation. As we filed into the classroom from lunch on this particular day, one of the instructors, who was standing outside the classroom door sucking on a cigarette said, "Be careful in there, fellas." He had a grin that accompanied his warning. I knew what was next.

The class moved into the room, carefully looking around to see if they could detect any booby traps. Then one of them threw an empty soda can into the trash can, which resulted in an explosion. The trash can had been booby-trapped, resulting in a loud "bang." The booby traps were very small noisemakers, but they were effective in getting the point across.

For the survival and the "camp" phase of the training, we were bussed to Camp A. P. Hill some distance from Little Creek. After the survival phase came the "camp." One of the staff, who called himself the "friendly partisan," was supposed to help us keep from being captured by the "bad guys," but it turned out that he was one of the bad guys. During the "green," or survival phase, we had to build shelters. The "friendly partisan" came into our area where my group was camped and looked over the shelter we had built.

"I think you boys have built yourselves an 'Aw, shit'," he said, spitting some tobacco juice at his feet. One of the guys asked him what that meant.

"You'll know, when the time comes."

That night, the shelter was so crowded that I slept on the ground in my sleeping bag some short distance away. Around midnight, I heard a crash as the sleeping platform collapsed.

"Aw, shit!" was the first thing I heard after that. Now we all fully understood what the "friendly partisan" meant.

When we made our next move in the morning, we had to cover some territory to go to some "safe" place. Of course, the "bad guys" were waiting for us along the way.

We were all captured and interrogated. There was no food, only water, and you just about had to beg for that. The instructors (bad guys) had a mattress glued to the wall and they would bounce us off that until our teeth rattled while they were screaming at us and telling us we would be shot if we did not cooperate. The object was to get us to tell them certain things that we were not supposed to divulge. Hardly any of us talked. One of the men that was just wandering around the camp acting neutral was a lieutenant by the name of José Taylor. He wore Navy jump wings on his uniform. At that time, the SEAL insignia had not been developed, so we all thought he was a SEAL. He just as well could have been a parachute rigger that had become jump qualified.

None of us died or got seriously injured in SERE school, and we were all happy to be returning to Little Creek to graduate. I thought I had learned a lot in this school. I learned that I would not eat rabbits and could go a long time, by my standards, without food. The instructors gave us one rabbit to kill and share, but I didn't eat any of it. I could eat a snake, any type of bird, frog, or rat, but for some reason, not a rabbit.

The next goody that was waiting for me was a set of orders to Little Creek for a two-week course in small craft operation. Harry Kulu and I were selected to attend this course. I was looking forward to this and thought it would be fun. We were trying to get some boats for the Underwater Photo Team, and often we had to run boats on some jobs, so it just followed that we should be checked out in their operation. I had already had some boat handling experience before I joined the Navy, and Harry was from Hawaii and spent a lot of time in and on the water before he enlisted, so we were the right ones to pick.

I moved to the barracks at Little Creek and walked back and forth to the school for that course. We were in the class with a lot of Bosun's Mates, Enginemen, and other black-shoe ratings. We were trained in the operation of small landing craft. These were the wooden type with the bow ramp that dropped to let people and small machinery roll-off. They were Landing Craft, Vehicle and Personnel (LCVPs) left over from WWII. Harry and I finished the class with a standing of number one and number two. Not bad for aviation types, one of us not even having started high school, let alone finish it. We got our diplomas and Harry gave me a ride (his wife rode his motorcycle to work) over to my barracks at NAS Norfolk.

The barracks were only about a hundred yards from Combat Camera Group, so it was convenient. I knew I would be gone a lot and wouldn't have to pay any rent while I was gone, as I would have if I lived off base. There are advantages to living on base, but damn few. One evening Gus Kennedy and I were over at the Petty Officer's Club on the base. We made friends with a couple of married women who were there without their husbands. The one I was after was black, but she was much better looking than the white one Kennedy escorted. Neither Gus nor I had a car, so we caught a ride with them to one of their apartments. We went to the black woman's place. Their children were all there, asleep. Any respect I had for them disappeared when I realized the women had left their kids alone while they went looking for some action. Gus and I realized we were two horny sailors looking for some strange with the wife of an E-8 chief at his house with the kids there. I looked over at Gus and he was looking at me with that "you've got to be shitting me" look. It was the middle of the night with the weather outside colder than a witch's tit, and we were sobering up. We made an excuse about needing to get back and thanked them for a great evening. After stumbled out of there, we began walking toward the base, two white boys in the heart of the black section of Norfolk. We'd heard stories about white guys being beaten up there just because of their color. It was so damned cold out that night, though, we were the only ones crazy enough to be outside. Finally, we caught a cab and returned to the base.

Gus went straight to bed, but I was hungry after all that exertion. I walked to the hall where they kept the gedunk machines. There were two white guys and a black guy beating on one of the machines. I walked up and asked them what the hell they were doing. One of them looked at me and said the goddamn machine had taken his money and he was going to fix it. I informed him in my quiet, subtle way that he was not going about it in an approved manner. He should write his name on a piece of paper and take it to the Master-at-Arms' office. When the vendor came to fill the machine his money would be refunded. In so many words, he told me to mind my own business. I reiterated my position on the machines and informed them that I ate most of my meals out of these machines and considered them almost like my mother, and that I would not take kindly to them beating on my mother. I then advised them I would kick the living shit out of all three of them if they didn't leave the machines alone. At that, one of them pulled out a knife. It was not a large knife, but it was a knife. I looked at it and told him he would soon have it shoved up his ass unless he was either very good with it or threw it away. He threw it away and jumped me. I grabbed him and sunk my teeth into his throat in an attempt to rip out his jugular vein. Mind you, I was still pretty drunk and did not have the force in my jaws necessary to complete the task. He screamed and jerked away from me. About this time the black guy jumped on my back and tried to choke me from behind. I reached back, grabbed him by the hair, shoved a thumb in his eye, twisted him and got him in a headlock so that his body was behind me. I then ran his head into the brick wall of the barracks. This served its purpose and he was out of the fight. The other white guy chose to be a bystander and merely stepped on my glasses that had fallen to the floor. He actually won the fight. Up until then, I had suffered no injury. Now I was nearly blind. The fighting was over and we all left. The gedunk machines were intact. I got something to eat, and went to bed.

The next morning PH1 Dave Graver took me aside and asked me what had happened in the barracks. He had heard that I tried to kill somebody. I told him that had been the general idea. There had been three of them and only one of me. What else was I supposed to do? He told me that if I put in a chit, they would approve it and I could live off base and draw sixty-five dollars month in BAQ (Basic Allowance for Quarters). I thought it over for almost as long as it took me to find a pad of special request chits. I put the request in and it was approved. Chief Dick Johnson said I could move into his place and we'd split the rent. I could sleep in the living room. There was a couch, but it wasn't long enough for a person of my height, so I found a cot and a mattress somewhere. I took an old parachute and used that for a blanket.

The place was certainly not a palace. The rent was only forty dollars a month total, but in the winter the heat cost more than that. The wind blew right through it. The apartment was a small house over on Chesapeake Street in Ocean View. It was not very far outside the gate near the Petty Officers' Club, and it was about a half mile from the beach in Ocean View. At that time, Ocean View was a low rent area. Dick had an old blue Buick he drove back and forth to work. At this time I didn't have a car or a driver's license, so I had to depend on the good will and friendship of those who possessed these handy items.

Just before daylight one morning, I was awakened by a loud crash. Some drunk had come around the corner and slammed into Dick's car, which was shoved up onto the sidewalk and nearly onto our front porch. Dick's car was a total loss. We had to walk to work or to the base and catch the base shuttle, a pretty unreliable method of transportation. A week or so later, Dick bought a big orange Harley motorcycle. It didn't have "buddy pegs" on it and he only had one helmet, so would ride it to the other gate that was closer to Combat Camera, I would then get off and walk the rest of the way. That worked for a while until the Navy made a rule that anybody in uniform had to wear a helmet. Then I'd catch rides with other guys who lived nearby, or start early and walk.

When I was in the Navy—before it became politically correct—there used to be a tendency for military personnel to drink maybe a little more than they do now. The men of Combat Camera Group were no exception. PH3 Jim Kerr, who I had been stationed with at Oceana, was now stationed at the NAS Norfolk, Photo Lab, so we saw each other about every day when I was in town.

The NAS Photo Lab shared the same building as Combat Camera and we had use of their facilities for Black and White, and Ektachrome processing. Jim had a car, which endeared him to me.

One afternoon we went to the club out by the back gate near where I lived and started to drink. I was trying to impress somebody as to how much I could drink, so began slamming down double shots of vodka and chasing them with pitchers of beer. I soon realized this behavior was destined for a bad ending. I leaned over to Kerr and asked him if he would give me a ride home. He told me he would in a few minutes. I asked him if he could carry two hundred pounds. He got the message. We left and I staggered to his car. By the time Kerr had driven the half-mile out the gate to my place, I was nearly comatose. I couldn't walk so Kerr to drag me into the apartment in front of the neighbors sitting on their porches enjoying the warm, afternoon sunshine. The skinny bastard pulled up in his old blue Chevy, got out, and dragged my big, blonde, drunk body across the sidewalk and onto the porch. Once we were inside, I told him I was okay and thanked him for the ride. Somehow, I turned on Dick's stereo, then sat down on the couch and leaned over to untie my boots. That was the last thing I remember until I woke up several hours later. I could hear music, but I couldn't see anything. I thought I was dead and that I was hearing funeral music. I had fallen off the couch, passed out on my back, puked straight up in the air, and was unable to move before it came down. My glasses were covered with puke and I was lying in a puddle of the yellow liquid. I came to my senses, cleaned up the place, took a shower, changed my clothes, and got back to normal. I don't think I even had a hangover.

Dick used to keep a loaded Colt 45 in his room. It was one of those revolvers that took .45-caliber ammunition, but if you used automatic ammunition you had to put the rounds in the little circlips. He used to keep three blanks and three live rounds in the gun. One night, he came home drunk, which was not unusual back then, and broke out the gun. I was in the other room. He hollered out, "Hey, Waterman!"

As I looked toward him, he pointed the gun off to the side and pulled the trigger. Plaster went everywhere. He looked at the wall, dazed, and mumbled that the bullet was supposed to be a blank. Apparently, somebody had rotated the cylinder so that a live round had been fired. He put the gun away and went to bed. The next day, he was at it with spackle and a putty knife. That was the last time he played with guns after he'd been drinking.

Dick and I decided this was no place for civilized people to live. We had two plates, two forks, one big spoon, a frying pan, and a saucepan. Dick had a stereo and a reel-to-reel tape deck. All I had was my clothes and my parachute. Neither of us owned a camera. We started to look for another place to live. We looked at some ads in the local paper and finally found an apartment. It was brand new, an upstairs apartment with two bedrooms, a kitchen, a bathroom with a shower, and it was furnished. The rent was only one-hundred-forty dollars a month. They didn't mind renting to sailors, even single ones, as long as we were white. It was an easy walking distance to the supermarket, and not too far from the main gate to the Naval Air Station. With the assistance of somebody with a pickup truck, we moved our gear into it.

While parachute jumping in Suffolk, I made friends with Electronics Technician Wesley Boles, a tall, skinny, squirrel-faced guy who was very smart. He hailed from Texas and had the drawl to match. We had a common interest in skydiving and women. He had a car. We used to go out to Suffolk Airport on weekends and jump. I had started jumping again when I got back from Underwater Swimmers School. I'd bought a new parachute rig with a loan from the Navy Federal Credit Union. It was a Para-Commander made of all the colors they had available except olive drab. The pattern was called the Clown. There were only two of us around with this particular pattern. The other guy was from West Point, Virginia. His name was Acey Bryan and he used to come to Suffolk on weekends once in a while to jump with us.

I also had a new type of reserve chute, a twenty-three-foot tri-conical, in a Crossbow piggyback pack so that the entire affair could be worn on my back. With the piggyback arrangement, you have the main ripcord on your right (if you are right handed) and the reserve ripcord was a little "panic handle" that was more like a triangular shaped knob on the left. If you had a malfunction, you had to release your main chute using the Capewell quick release buckles on the risers. The piggyback was rigged so that, as you fell away from your cut-away main parachute, one of the riser straps would pull the ripcord housing off the reserve chute, thus opening your reserve.

Before I went to UWSS, I made one last jump. Denny Morse, a chief machinery repairman and a navy master diver, had jump-mastered on my third jump. Just before we reached jump altitude, I leaned over to Denny and told him I was scared shitless. He just gave me a shit-eating grin and said, "Fuck it." I made the jump with no mishaps. Denny was a short, rugged guy about thirty-two years of age. He and I became friends. He was stationed on board an ASR at the D & S Piers in Norfolk and, at the time, was one of the youngest master divers in the Navy. In 1964, he and three other divers had successfully salvaged the statue of Admiral Andréa Doria from the bottom of the ocean inside the sunken vessel *Andréa Doria*. This was quite an accomplishment, given the fact that the water was more than two hundred feet deep and the entire operation, including blasting through the hull and hacksawing the statue out, was done on scuba gear with air as the breathing medium.

Wes Boles and I spent a lot of time drinking beer and chasing women. We also jumped out of airplanes a lot, nearly every weekend. Most of the time we went out to Suffolk DZ at the airport in Suffolk, Virginia. Once in a while, we drove to somewhere like West Point, Virginia or Roanoke Rapids, North Carolina where a jump meet was taking place. I met Frank Genovese as a result of my parachute jumping. He was supposedly the nephew of Vito Genovese of the New York Mafia. Frank was a great guy. He was a nut for military weapons and parachuting and had a hell of a sense of humor. He never served in the military, but had an I.D. card that said he was a lieutenant on active duty. I didn't ask him where he got it.

When Wes had the duty or was at sea, I rode out to the drop zone with Frank, who kept a pet boa constrictor in his house. He would go to the pet shop and order "two white mice to go" to feed the thing. Frank had his pilot's license and would fly us when the other pilots didn't show up. The club owned a Cessna 180 tail dragger, and members flew it a lot of hours on weekends. Sometimes we would go out during the week to make some jumps if we could get enough people together with time off.

Dick Johnson had his pilot's license and would fly us now and then. He made a couple of parachute jumps, but preferred to fly, rather than jump. Later on, he acquired his flight instructor's license and I took a few flying lessons from him.

Off and on, we had underwater photo jobs at Andros in the Bahamas. The Navy had a contract facility there that was operated by RCA. It was at AUTEC where all the torpedoes were tested by firing them from submarines. The water was a thousand fathoms deep and the club on the base was called "The Thousand Fathom Club."

This particular job required us to do some underwater motion picture photography of a naval vessel as it passed by overhead. Dick Johnson threw a crew together consisting of Harry Kulu, Bill Curtsinger, and myself. We flew to Andros for three days. The weather was nice and we had no mechanical problems with our gear.

Later on that summer, Dick Johnson, a few topside photographers, and I went aboard a small ship and headed up the Chesapeake Bay to cover the testing of a fiberglass-hulled minesweeper. The idea was to fire a one-thousand-pound charge of HBX that would be located sixty feet from the hull and sixty feet underwater. Dick and I were just on site to shoot photos and motion pictures of the exterior of the hull in the event a lot of damage was incurred. As the helicopter carrying the motion picture crew hovered over the scene, the shot was fired. The ensuing geyser of water came very close to knocking the chopper out of the sky. We thought it was pretty funny afterward, but the helo crew didn't appreciate our humor.

Chapter 10

Panama City, Sunken Barge "Salvage," In the Azores

Panama City

When we got back from the Bahamas, Graver, Trotter, and I were sent to Panama City, Florida to work with the SEALAB Program. We were supposed to do some underwater photography with the habitat and the Aquanauts. The weather was very windy, so the work we were supposed to do was canceled. The whole trip ended up being a drinking binge. We stayed at a small motel near Panama City and drove out to a large hotel on Panama Beach.

One night, we were sitting at the bar, Trotter and Graver paid the bartender to slip 151-proof rum into my rum and Cokes, instead of the standard booze. Before long, I was pretty out of it. In my stupor, I noticed a painting on the wall. It was of an extremely beautiful woman clad in nothing but a grass skirt. To anyone who would listen, I said aloud that I would really like to meet her. An older woman three stools over asked me if I would like to have dinner with her and the woman in the painting. I asked the fifty-something woman how she knew the model. After telling me her name was Ann, the woman told me she was the artist who painted the picture, and that the girl was upstairs in her room getting ready to join Ann for supper. A few minutes later, the subject of the portrait sat down at the bar. I don't remember her name, but I remember she was better looking in person than in the painting. Here I was, hammered almost beyond coherence, being introduced to a girl who looked like she'd just stepped out of Playboy Magazine. I apologized for my obvious state of intoxication, and explained that if I'd known I was going meet someone like her, I would not have touched a drop of alcohol. Ann and the beauty invited me to join them for supper in the restaurant on the second floor, Ann's treat. Ann had to stop in her room for something so I had a chance to talk to the beauty queen alone. I asked if she would be up for a little action later in the evening. She told me that Ann usually went to bed about ten o'clock at night and we could get together then. I had the impression Ann watched out for her. The beauty queen may have been leading me on, but under the guise of going to the bathroom, I rented a room for the night. When I returned to the table, our steaks had just arrived and I had taken one bite when Trotter appeared and motioned for me to come over. I went to him and he told me that they had just received a call to go to another job as this one was shut down due to weather. I asked him when we had to leave. He said, "Right now." I said I would be with him when I finished eating.

"No. Right now," he repeated.

I went over to the table and apologized for having to leave. Then I got a doggie bag for my steak and walked downstairs to the bar. Graver and Trotter were sitting at the bar. I went up to them and said, "Let's get going."

Trotter turned around with his shit-eating grin. "Go where?" he smirked.

I'd been had!

"You bastards! You sons of bitches!" I shouted at them. I told them that maybe Jesus forgives people for stuff, but I sure as hell don't. They both just sat there grinning. The band had stopped playing and people were beginning to pay attention to me. I decided I'd better leave before I started stomping the shit out of them and got myself arrested. I turned and stormed out of the place, threw my steak in the back seat of the rental car and ran down the beach for ten miles or so to where the beach became so narrow, I had to use the street. I hitchhiked a ride with an Army helicopter pilot who was home on leave and made it back to the motel. I wanted to kill those bastards. The best looking woman I had even been close to and they screwed it up! Maybe I should have gone back to the table and explained that I was working with jerks, but I was too embarrassed about falling for their trick.

I felt like killing them both. I thought about getting my KA-BAR knife and climbing on the roof of the motel above the door. When they came back, I would jump down and cut their throats before they knew what happened. While I was planning this, I fell asleep. They came back in the morning and woke me up. I was still pissed. I told them, once again, that I would never forget this or forgive them. I haven't yet. We got along and had fun together after that, but I always reminded them that I hadn't forgiven them.

After eating breakfast, we drove back to the hotel, one of the largest hotels on Panama Beach, and went to the bar for some Bloody Marys. I called up to the beauty queen's room and Ann answered the phone. She said she thought I had left. I told her my "friends" had played a trick on me and I owed them big time.

"Sounds like you've got some great friends there." Ann put the beauty queen on the phone, who said she'd be down in a few minutes. About twenty minutes later, I watched her walk into the bar. She looked even better than the night before, perhaps because of my improved vision. I was angrier than ever at the two losers I was with. The beauty sat down next to me at the bar.

"Let's go to the beach where we can talk," she said. She grabbed a blanket from her room, and we walked out on the beach. Neither of us was wearing beach-appropriate clothing, but we laid on the blanket anyway. It was cold out and nobody was around. The beauty told me she owned a chain of health clubs in the Atlanta area and that her boyfriend was in what I would call the Mafia. Her artist friend, Ann, was her "babysitter," but Ann thought I was a pretty nice guy and would look the other way in this case. After about an hour of talking, I got her name, address, and phone number, and we left the beach. The guys and I had to catch the plane—for real this time—and I never saw her again. I think I may have tried to call her once but not gotten through. C'est la vie.

Trotter and Graver had made arrangements for us to fly through Atlanta on the way home. On the plane, we had a few drinks. It so happened that the day we went to Atlanta was the day of Martin Luther King's funeral. Rioting was great concern among some of the white people, but I didn't think anybody would because most people, including a large number whites, were upset over the death of Reverend King. The solemnity of the occasion, however, did not detract from my energies in the humor department. As we approached Atlanta, I stood up and announced, "Ladies and Gentlemen, we are now approaching Atlanta International Airport, where the weather is mild, with a light rain and the small arms fire is light to moderate." Then I sat down. Graver and Trotter damn near crawled under the seats.

We were stuck staying the night in Atlanta. My two friends had met three women in Key West and had fixed me up with the youngest one, Pat, who was shy yet quite nice looking. The women said we could stay with them whenever we came to Atlanta so we called them when we landed. We left about a day and a half later.

Sunken Barge "Salvage"

A week or so after we returned from Panama City, Dick told me he had arranged for us to go to Roosevelt Roads, Puerto Rico for a few days and do some diving there. We could train and get some time in the water where it was clear. We loaded our gear in a pile, checked out some film and made arrangements with one of the squadrons, VRC-40, to fly us down. Usually there were a lot of cargo flights going back and forth to Puerto Rico, so it was not difficult to get a ride to and from the island.

When we got there we were settled into the barracks and had arranged to have a vehicle and some boat support. The chief got the word that a Navy fuel barge had sunk while it was being towed to San Juan. He asked me if I wanted to go up to where they were trying to salvage it and get some pictures of the operation. I told him that I would love to, so I got my gear ready, grabbed a topside and an underwater still camera and caught a boat up to the salvage scene.

When I got there, two Navy ships were rafted up together. They had an ASR and an ARS. The ASR (auxiliary submarine rescue) had the most qualified divers, mostly first class divers, and the ARS (auxiliary rescue & salvage ship) had a few, but they were mostly second class divers. Between the two ships they had over two-dozen divers capable of diving to the depth necessary to work on this barge. The water was warm and this was not the worst place to dive. The barge had been partially loaded with diesel oil and a tug was towing it up the coast to dock in San Juan. There had been a piece of plate missing in the hull above the waterline. The workers had replaced it with canvas and just painted it gray, so when they got underway, the canvas fell out and the water came in and sank the barge. Now it was on the bottom in about seventy-five feet of water halfway between Roosevelt Roads and San Juan.

There was a Navy master diver on the scene. He was one of those cigarette-smoking, hard-looking Navy divers that I was familiar with. He didn't say much, but you better damn well listen when he did talk. Because of the "environmental considerations" of this salvage job with the oil leaking out and everything, there must have been a dozen commanders and above running around the ships who acted like they knew something about salvage diving. The master diver simply ignored them.

I asked the master diver if I could make a dive on the barge and get some photos. He told me to go to the diving locker and talk to the chief. I did, and soon I was all rigged up in my brown UDT swimming trunks, life vest, and a set of scuba gear. I had a Nikonos underwater camera and a dozen number five flashbulbs stuck in a strip of rubber we used for carrying them. The chief told me to follow the hose of one of Jack Browne divers down to where they were working on the barge. I did that and arrived at the barge a few minutes later. The water was clear and I could see the men rigging salvage balloons on the barge. They were chaining them to the bollards and then rigging the air hoses to them. The barge was lying on its side at an angle. The plan also included putting air into the barge internally to float it onto the surface. This would, theoretically, allow the crew to quickly find and patch the holes before it sank again.

I shot what film I could and used up all my flashbulbs. Then I returned to the surface and climbed up the ladder. After I washed the salt water off in the shower and got dressed, I went out on deck. The master diver was standing there with one foot up on a chock along the side of the ship, and staring off into space with a cigarette in one hand and the other in his pocket.

"Hey, Chief. What's the plan?" I asked.

He looked me up and down a little before he spoke.

"Well, they are hooking lift balloons onto the thing and then they are going to pump air into the hull and lift it to the surface. Why?"

"I don't want to piss you off or hurt your feelings, Chief, but I sure hope you aren't the one that came up with that scheme."

He looked around at me with one eye a little squinted.

"Why's that?"

"Well, it isn't going to work. That's why."

"How come it isn't?" he asked. I was beginning to think I had strayed into forbidden territory.

"Well, they ought to be putting enough balloons on to almost lift the whole thing when they are full, and then winch it to the surface and let them blow off the excess air. That way it won't get away from them. They can put extra ones on to blow on the surface to keep it up here. The way they're doing it, it'll just come up to the surface all right, but the air they blow inside the barge will rupture the internal bulkheads and the damn thing is just going to sink again and be harder to raise on the next try."

I thought I had pissed him off. He just looked at me for a few seconds. Then he took hold of my right arm and moved me a little so he could see the scuba patch sewn onto the right sleeve of my tropical white uniform.

"Okay, now let me get this straight. You're a scuba diver, I am a master diver and we are the only two sons-of-bitches on this whole damned operation that knows what the hell is going one. Why do you think that is?

"Well, Chief, for one thing," I joked, "I don't own a slide rule and don't know how to use one. I just know what air does when it expands three times and it hasn't got any place to go."

He smiled. "You're right, kid, but you aren't a commander and neither am I. I don't think either one of us has to worry about either making admiral or pissing one off."

We stood there watching the operation for a while. I didn't say anything more. It was a good feeling to be around somebody who had proved they had their act together. The master diver knew that no matter what he said or did, one of those hotshot diving salvage officers would come up with a better idea. He had committed himself to the fact they were going to shit and then fall back in it. Nevertheless, it wouldn't make the difference of a piss hole in the snow to him or his diving career.

By late afternoon, the divers had all the air hoses rigged and were ready blow the barge to the surface. Somebody made the decision not to blow it until the next morning so they would have plenty of daylight to work in if they had any problems. We ate chow, watched a movie on the mess decks, and went to sleep. I slept in the diving locker on some duffel bags with a blanket over me. There was a shortage of racks due to the large number of people on board.

During the night, I was awakened a couple of times by salvage balloons blasting to the surface. Apparently, the divers had not secured some of them well and they had worked their way loose. They would rocket upward as the air in them expanded and filled them to overflowing. Once the balloons arrived at the surface, the pressurized air from the ascent hissed out like an angry, black, round sea monster and a some seamen would have to man a boat and recover them.

We arose around 0600 the next morning and everybody was anxious to see how the barge would float. First, the divers would have to dive again and reattach the balloons that had come loose. There had been no wind that night and it was easy for a couple of the ship's crew to go out in a boat and tie off the salvage balloons as they floated on the surface near the ship.

The first set of divers was able to get the balloons back in place. Apparently, working back and forth on the bitts where they had been attached had loosened the lashing that held the chains, allowing the chains to unwrap. This time, they used wire to secure the chains to themselves.

Now it was show time. All the men topside had cameras. I was standing beside the master diver at the rail. As they began the compressors to blow air into the balloons and the barge, he turned and winked at me. I just grinned.

Before long, some roiling of the water and air bubbles appeared on the surface. This was a sign that the balloons were full and blowing off. Then, a large mass of air bubbles and oil appeared. The barge was coming up. I hoped the corner of it did not hit the bottom of the ship, but I imagined we were far enough away. One corner of the barge appeared on the surface and then another. Then the flat surface of the bottom came up—it was upside down. One balloon came off, and then another, then the barge lost upward momentum, hung there a few moments and started to fill up again with water. One by one, the tops of the salvage balloons disappeared as the barge dropped back to the bottom. The master just turned around and rolled his eyes.

A diver went down to confirm that the barge had, in fact, landed on the bottom. Now it was flat on the bottom, and that made the water deeper for the divers to work in, thus reducing their available bottom time. Additionally, all the internal bulkheads had been ruptured as a result of the trapped air expanding rapidly upon ascent.

I left that afternoon, and learned later that they finally sent some men down with explosives to blow the thing up and make it into a "fish sanctuary." The reason they gave for blowing it up was to ensure that no fuel was trapped that would come leaking to the surface over time.

In the Azores

In late 1968, I had an underwater photo job in the Azores with PH1 Howard Trotter, PH1 Dave Graver, of Combat Camera Group, and Joe Gordon and Denny McLenny, both civilians, from the Underwater Sound Lab out of Groton, Connecticut. Denny was the former PHC in charge of the diving locker at Atlantic Fleet Combat Camera Group. Denny was a gruff type of guy who really had a soft heart. He acted hard-core but was a pretty decent guy all in all. Joe was a civil servant who was a GS-13. He was all-professional and originally from New York. We were going to be working with a black Navy master diver by the name of BMC "Bubba "Davis."[†]

† Master Diver Davis died a couple years ago.

The three of us caught a commercial flight out of Norfolk. After an uneventful, nearly empty flight to Lisbon, Portugal, we flew on an old DC-3 to Ponta del Gada in the Azores. This was, no shit, one of those flights you hear about with chickens and goats on the plane. We touched down on a grass strip and caught a cab into town. We were supposed to catch the USS *Spiegel Grove*, an LSD out of the Atlantic Gator Navy. It would not be in for a few days, so we had some time to kill. I spent some money on a couple of sweaters, and some local guy took me to one of the local riding academies where I was introduced to an Azorian honey about eighteen years old who was quite interested in my escudos (Portuguese money).

One morning, the three of us were walking along the dock on the other side of the harbor when we saw a large sailing yacht flying an American flag. We walked closer to check it out. When we moved nearer we could see a man sitting in the cockpit reading a magazine. One of us called out that that was quite a boat and asked him if he was the owner. He replied he was the skipper and the owner was ashore on business. We walked closer and struck up a conversation. His name was Walt Pikula and he was from Newport Beach, California. The boat, *Blackfin*, was brand new and had just been built in Bremerhaven, Germany. She was a 65-foot aluminum ocean racing yacht. The crew was taking it across the Atlantic and through the Panama Canal to California. Walt invited us aboard. Turns out he was an ex-Navy diver and we had something in common. The owner, Ken DuMeuse[†] was an ex Marine who had fought in Korea. Walt offered us a beer and we started slamming down Beck's Beer. Before long, Ken, the owner, came back and we met him. He turned out to be a genuinely nice guy and was not all caught up in the fact that he was a multi-millionaire. We drank some more beer and he offered to take us to supper.

In the Azores, dining out is not a big social event. If you can find a place to buy a roasted chicken and a gallon of cheap wine, you're in. That is exactly what happened to us. Ken, Dave, Howard, Walt, myself and the other two crew members, Germans from the shipyard where the boat was built, made our way to some small outdoor restaurant and started eating chicken. Before long, the drinking caught up with us. Dave Graver asked Ken if he had learned to eat glass while in the Marine Corps. Ken replied that he hadn't, but would be a most willing pupil if we would teach him. Dave grabbed a wine glass and bit a chunk out of it and chewed it up. Ken asked to see it again, so Howard did it, then I showed him. Before long Ken tried it. He acted as though he was

† Ken and a daughter and son were killed in the crash of his private plane in 1969.

the caveman who invented fire. I've never seen anyone so impressed by something he learned. Especially something that cannot possibly have any redeeming social value whatsoever. If lucky, one won't cut the hell out of one's mouth or gums. Ken told us he was going to demonstrate this procedure at one of his wife's "stuffy social functions." We thought that to be about the most appropriate use for this skill and advised him to practice so as not to appear the least bit nervous, acting as though he did it every day.

We said goodbye at the restaurant and thanked him for the evening, and the day of beer-drinking. The next day, the *Blackfin* was gone. Ken had offered to take us on as extra crew if we wanted to go. Before our job was over, I wished I had gone with them.

In a few days, the *Spiegel Grove* showed up at the pier. We got out our uniforms and went aboard. Chief "Bubba" Davis was there and we met him. We got the impression he probably knew what he was doing. This was before affirmative action had taken hold in the military, so blacks and other minorities still had to be able to compete legitimately to be advanced in pay grade or become a specialty, like a diver or pilot. There were very few black divers and only two Master divers that we knew of. The other one, Carl Brashear, had lost one leg and was allowed to stay on active duty because of his good physical condition and determination. I personally knew Carl, and though he was as sharp and knowledgeable as they come, I thought he was a cocky son-of-a-bitch, as did many of us. Davis was not like that, not in the least.

I made a distinct impression on Bubba the first day I met him. Bubba and I were standing at the rail of the USS *Spiegel Grove*, and I hawked a lunger downwind toward the water. There was a vortex that grabbed it and lifted it up. I watched as it flew back and landed on the front of Chief Davis' khaki shirt. As he wiped it off with his handkerchief, he just looked at me and asked, "Been at sea long, Waterman?"

"About an hour, Chief," was my only reply.

Our job in the Azores was to map out a section of the bottom of the ocean off the island of Santa Maria in a depth of water shallower than one hundred feet. Below that depth, the submersible, Alvin, would be making the charts. The Navy was installing a hydrophone system (SOSUS) for listening to Russian subs as they moved south in the Atlantic ocean. The job was "unclassified," but I got my ass chewed out for talking about it in a bar one night. McLenny said I shouldn't tell people what we were doing. I replied that I had been told that it was unclassified. McLenny explained that there was no classification because most of the people couldn't be cleared that high, so they just called it "unclassified" and "don't talk about it." I never figured that one out.

Boatswain's Mate Seaman (BMSN) Bill Hooten was the coxswain who ran our dive boat. He was a high school dropout, but was very intelligent. His brother was a doctor. Bill and I became buddies, and one night, we decided to go into town and drink some wine. We really wanted to get laid, but our second choice, due to the high percentage of Catholics and black-clad widows on Santa Maria, was to get drunk. We ended up in a bar drinking with some EOD (explosive ordnance disposal) divers from the Portuguese minesweeper, the *St. Gorge*. They spoke minimal English and we spoke even less Portuguese, but as the night wore on, we became unilingual. We were speaking Igboo, the universal language of drunks. It is a type of mental telepathy accentuated by guttural sounds and much drooling. One who is not intoxicated cannot hope to enter into the conversation.

After consuming several bottles of Mateuse Rosé wine, we thought it appropriate to go to the airport bar, which had a band, where we could probably pick up some women. In our drunken state, we imagined ourselves to be the epitome of what any young Azorian woman would want to take home.

We caught a cab and headed for the airport. Once there, we sauntered into the lounge expecting to be welcomed with open arms by all sorts of Portuguese sweeties. Well, that's not at all what happened. The skipper of the boat was there with his all-purpose "follow him around from port to port" girlfriend from the States. He was a naval aviator who was serving as skipper of a Gator freighter to get his ticket punched for bigger and better things. I have forgotten his name, as he mine, but he was a decent guy.

I asked his woman to dance with me, which she did quite readily, as I was very cute and had a nice ass in those days. We danced a few times and I felt I might be getting out of line a little. The executive officer was there, also. He took himself a mite on the serious side and tried to be too military, by my standards.

Bill and I made up our fogged minds that it was time to leave. We had to get back to the ship. While at the airport lounge, we didn't let the fact we were already almost ossified deter us from consuming more wine. Before we left, I was determined to have a souvenir of our trip to the airport lounge. The tables had beautifully embroidered tablecloths on them, no doubt the work of the many old, bent widows who occupied the island. The black-clad widows probably sat around all day missing their dead husbands and embroidering tablecloths. I casually, and without anybody observing me (yeah, right!), wadded up one of tablecloths and shoved it down the front of my pants.

When we went out the door, we didn't have a clue how we were going to get back to the pier. It was midnight and we knew the last boat left at 0100. We thought it would be appropriate if we stole the XO's VW bus. We looked in it, but the keys were gone.

"What the hell," we thought, "we can just push it and coast down to the dock. It's only four or five miles."

Wrong. Bill jumped into the driver's seat and I opened the passenger door, pushing against the door frame. This way, I would be able to jump into the seat as soon as the bus started rolling at a good pace. We made it down the first hill and had enough momentum to get over the one that followed. But when we arrived in the bottom of the valley between the second and the third hills, we lost inertia and found ourselves trapped between the two hills. We got out, pushed the van to the side of the road, and started walking toward the pier. We were so damned drunk that Bill walked on one side of the road and I walked on the other. We had trouble tracking straight down the sides of the road.

It took us until nearly 0200 to get back to the dock. We had missed the last liberty boat and were now officially AWOL, or "over the hill" as it was called. I had never had this happen to me in my life and expected to be shot or worse as a result.

"Aw, the hell with it," I said. "Let's swim back to the ship. It's only about a mile or so."

Bill wasn't very excited about this prospect and advised me he was not a great swimmer. I told him I would make sure he made it, that I'd swim right along beside him in case he got into trouble. We took off our hats and shoes, tied our shoes to the backs of our belts and stuck our white-hats inside the waistbands of our trousers. Then we walked down the stone steps of the dock and into the warm water of the mid-Atlantic Ocean.

We had gone about two hundred feet when Bill told me he didn't think he could swim that far. I didn't encourage him to try as I felt he would probably not make it if I pushed him. Even in my drunken state I had a little sense left. I escorted him back to the stone wharf and he climbed out and sat down on a bollard. I turned back toward the small well-lighted shape of the *Spiegel Grove* in the distance. She was the farthest ship out in the harbor. Later I would estimate it to be nearly two miles from the dock.

Things were going well. The water was pretty warm and the seas were calm. I breast stroked for a while, then side stroked. Every so often I would lie on my back and float for a little breather. Finally I started getting tired. Not dead, dog tired, but just a little tired. I thought it would be nice to have a place to lie down and take a nap for a few minutes before continuing the swim. The only thing nearby was a large yellow buoy used for off-loading tankers in the harbor. I attempted to scale the side of it to no avail. It was not designed to be climbed onto from the water. I gave up this idea in short fashion and continued toward the ship. About a half mile farther I discerned the outline of the *St. Jorge*, the Portuguese minesweeper the EOD divers had come from.

"Aha!" I thought to myself. "I'll sneak aboard and steal one of their life rings with the name of the ship on it and keep it as a souvenir."

Brilliant idea. I quietly swam around the ship looking for a method to climb aboard. My only chance would be to climb the anchor chain and slip up over the foredeck. I started climbing the chain and had reached the hawse pipe where the chain goes through the forward bulwarks. I was about to reach over the bulwarks for a handhold to climb into the deck when I heard voices.

"What in hell is going on?" I thought. "Shit, these guys are getting under way." Then I realized the chain was slowly being drawn up into the hawse pipe. I did a back flip off the chain and dived headfirst into the water. I breast stroked underwater as far as I could to get out of pistol range of these guys. I imagined they were armed with .45s at the very least and were not especially good shots. They never fired and all I heard was a bunch of Portuguese shouting and some commotion on deck. I repeated my evasive swimming maneuvers until I was well away from the vessel. I lay on my back with just my face above water to catch my breath. In a couple of minutes, I started swimming for the *Spiegel Grove* again.

Suddenly, I heard somebody called out, "Waterman!" I didn't recognize the voice, but I figured it had to be the good guys. I looked back toward the shore and it was the liberty boat coming toward me. I could just see the starboard running light reflecting its green glow in the water. By now the wind had started to pick up and there was a slight chop forming in the harbor. I raised an arm and they easily spotted my white sleeve against the blackness of the water.

The boat approached me and two of the sailors grabbed me by the arms and bodily dragged me unceremoniously out of the water and onto the deck of the boat. Bill Hooten was standing there grinning. The boat had gone in to look for us and found only Bill standing there soaking wet. The crew asked him where I was and he told them I had started swimming for the ship. It had been a fairly simple matter to track me down. They had seen me hanging from the chain of the *St. Jorge* and were heading in that direction when I dived off.

We got back to the *Spiegel Grove* and I walked up the brow. The warrant boatswain, who was Officer of the Deck asked me, in a most serious voice, how I got wet. I told him I had dropped my hat overboard and reached to retrieve it and somehow lost my footing. He just gave me one of those "You've got to be shitting me!" looks and told me, "You've got until tomorrow morning to come up with a better one than that. Now hit the rack and get some sleep."

I awoke with a bit of a hangover. I had the top bunk. What a strange dream that had been—at least it seemed that way until I looked over the edge of the bunk. There on the floor of the compartment were my whites, except they really weren't that white any more. The entire front of them was covered with rust.

"Oh, shit," I thought, "now I am screwed. They'll probably court martial me and ship me home for violating some international law or something."

About this time, Denny McLenny, one of the civilians we were working for, came into the compartment.

"You little shit! What in hell did you think you were doing last night?"

He was trying to act pissed off, but I could tell he was quite amused by my actions. I got up, threw on a set of fatigues and went to the mess decks. We had to go to work and regardless of my condition, I would have to dive today and shoot more underwater film. When I got up to the mess decks, some of the sailors were pointing at me and whispering things. Nobody got in my way and there were undercurrents of some newly gained respect from the crew. Guys would walk by, nod to me and say, "Good morning," or "How's it going?"

I wondered what in hell was going on.

"The senior civilian on the Alvin crew walked up to me and slapped me on the shoulder. "Helluva swim, kid," he said with a broad grin.

That was it! Everybody thought I was really cool for getting drunk, missing the liberty boat, nearly drowning a shipmate, attempting to board a foreign warship in the middle of the night, and leading a boat crew on a wild goose chase. Not to mention stealing the XO's van and running it off the road, and stealing an embroidered tablecloth from the airport lounge.

The other guys showed up and joined me at the table for breakfast. I ate the usual amount of eggs, bacon, sausage, biscuits, grits, milk, fried potatoes, and orange juice. I knew I'd probably puke it all up later, but at least I might get some use out of it before that happened.

We all climbed aboard the LCM-8 (Landing Craft, Mechanized), our dive boat and, with a hung over BMSN Bill Hooten at the helm, steamed for the work area around the other side of the island. It took about an hour to run to the area where we were doing the survey. The job was to lay out a piece of rope from one hundred feet of depth to the shore and then swim along it with our 16mm underwater movie cameras and document the type of bottom and the amounts and types of obstacles that would have to be blown up or circumvented by a cable. I believe we had to do this in something like five locations so they could pick the best route. Today was overcast and the wind was breezing up a little. It wasn't long before I was down on my knees puking my guts out. That Mateuse wine has a tendency to do that even to the hard-core drinkers like myself. Joe Gordon and Denny McLenny were just laughing at me, as were Dave Graver and Howard Trotter. Bill was trying to hang onto his breakfast too and Bubba Davis, the Master Diver, just kept looking at me and shaking his head.

We got to the site and put the first two guys in the water. They shot their film and came back to reload. By now the wind had come up some more, so Joe said we might as well pack it in. That was good news to me. Now I could go back to the ship and crawl into the rack and recover.

When we got back to the ship, we drove the boat into the well deck inside the ship and they pumped the water level down so the boats inside were high and dry. That way they wouldn't bang around as they would if tied off to the boat booms beside the vessel. LSDs are designed with an open well-deck. They can carry many small craft inside and when they arrive at the area or operation can flood the well deck, lower the stern ramp, and the boats simply drive out.

I dragged myself off the boat. After going to the galley for a little chow to replace what I had sprayed overboard, I went down to the compartment and started to get out of my wet gear. A messenger came and told me the XO wanted to see me in uniform in his office in a half hour.

"Shit! This is it," I thought. "They're going to send me off to Leavenworth or something terrible like that."

I dug out another set of whites, took a quick shower, shaved and put on my still-wet black shoes. Fortunately I had brought two white-hats with me, being the squared away sailor that I was.

Dave Graver went to the XO's office with me, probably more for amusement than anything. I walked up to the XO's office and knocked on the door. A gruff voice told me to come in. I walked inside, uncovered, and stood at some version of attention. I was still not feeling up to speed. The XO just sat there looking at some papers on his desk. Then he looked up.

"PH2 Waterman, are you in the habit of boarding foreign warships in the middle of the night?"

"No, Sir, not usually."

"Well, then, why did you decide to do it last night?"

"I don't know, Sir. I guess it just seemed like the thing to do at the time," I answered back.

"Ever been shot at?" he asked.

"Yes sir," I lied. "But they missed."

He looked down at the same mystery papers on his desk and things got really quiet for a minute, then he looked up again.

"Well sailor, fortunately for you I am in a good mood and Petty Officer Graver here speaks highly of you. The captain of the *St. Jorge* was quite impressed with your dedication to return to the ship in spite of having missed the last boat, and he said for me to congratulate you on the long swim. Now get out of here and don't ever do anything like that again while you're aboard my ship."

I was a free man. Jesus, that was lucky. I thought, I'll never do anything like that again, period!

The ship left Santa Maria when we finished the project, then steamed over to another Azorian Island, Lajes, where our team left the ship. From there, we were to catch a flight back to the States.

We managed to spend a couple of days on the Lajes Air Force Base where I went to the exchange and ordered my first three-piece suit. It was made by Alexander's of London and cost me almost one hundred dollars. In the States, it would have been three hundred dollars or more. It was dark green, and of worsted wool. I figured I wouldn't see the damned thing but, in a few weeks a package came from England and there it was. It fit perfectly, and I got some good mileage out of it.

Graver, Trotter, and I went to the airport and got a room while we waited for our flight. That night, a British Overseas Airline plane came in and the crew stayed at the hotel. I met one of the flight attendants and we seemed to hit it off. Her name was Eileen Thornton. She was extremely attractive and lived in Sussex, England. We wrote back and forth few times and, at one point, I even planned to go and visit her, but nothing ever materialized.

Our flight back to Norfolk via New York City left in a few days, and was quite uneventful with the exception that one of the flight attendants sewed up the crotch seam of my double-knit pants after they had split. Fortunately, I was wearing skivvies that day.

Chapter 11

Back Home
from the Azores

When my crew returned to Norfolk, I got together with Wes Boles and we decided to take some leave together. We went to Maine via Orange, Massachusetts, one of the primo skydiving places on the East Coast. We loaded up his Ford Mustang with our jump gear and my cameras, and headed up the coast. When we arrived at Orange, we got a "room" at the "Inn at Orange." This was a bunk room over the bar in an old house located at the drop zone (DZ). We made some jumps, tried some relative work, and I did a relative work jump with Lew Sanborn. He was a legend among skydivers. Nate Pond also jumped with us. Lew had United States Parachute Association license number D-1. Nate had D-69, which he received by special request. There is some sense of pride in having a low license number. Lew had been injured seriously in a plane crash some time back and had plastic surgery done to his face. They did okay, but he still looked a little screwed up. He was extremely lucky to have lived through the crash. Wes and I hung around Orange a few days and then drove for Maine. Wes met my mother, father, stepfather, and everybody else around. Mary was gone somewhere, so we didn't see her. I had planned on making a jump while home, but it didn't work out. I showed Wes around the local area and a few days later we drove back to Norfolk and continued our boring lives as sailors in the world's largest nuclear navy.

Sometimes Wes and I would frequent the 56 Club (E-5 and E-6 only) at Little Creek. On one occasion, we happened to become "introduced" to a couple of fairly decent looking women who seemed interested in our minds and, more than likely, our bodies. We left with them and went down to the Duck Inn, a restaurant that was famous for cold beer and good seafood. After a few cold ones, we took them back to their car. They invited us over to their places a couple of days later. The one I was with, it so happened, was the wife of a fairly well-known SEAL officer. I did not feel that there was a strong future in this relationship, and didn't pursue it.

A number of days later, I was out in the little lawn area between the apartment buildings where we lived. I had my parachute stretched out on the ground and was packing it to get ready to jump that weekend. This extremely attractive girl came out with a bucket of hot water and some car washing gear. She stopped and introduced herself to me as Joan, my new neighbor. She lived with her husband, Bob, across the hall from Dick's and my apartment. Her husband was an aircraft mechanic in the Navy on board a carrier at sea, and she worked at High's Ice Cream in Norfolk. Joan told me she was new in the area and had only met one person. I mentioned that I loved black raspberry ice cream.

A few days later, there was a knock at the door and Joan had some black raspberry ice cream for me. I thanked her and put it in the freezer.

"Wow, this is great," I thought. "Free ice cream. This sort of thing just doesn't happen."

I never thought for a minute that Joan might be interested in something else. A few nights later, when Dick was out, there was a knock at the door. It was Joan. She asked if I knew anything about televisions. I said I didn't own one, but I would see what I could do. She said hers wasn't coming in clearly. I walked the six feet to her apartment and went over to the TV. Joan offered me a drink.

Another freebie! "Sure. Rum and Coke, if you have it."

While she mixed the drink, I frigged with the knobs on the TV set. Joan had turned all the adjustments around so the TV wouldn't work properly. All I did was readjust them so that the picture came in perfectly. Then it hit me. She was on the make! What a dumb bastard I was, twenty-one years old and still couldn't tell when a woman was interested in me.

I walked up to the counter where Joan was standing with her back to me, still mixing the drinks. I just brushed up against her back and started to put my arms around her to lean on the counter. Joan spun around, threw her arms around me, and kissed me.

Christ, another freebie, I thought.

We managed to get to the couch, and turn off the TV and some of the lights. It became a regular thing until her husband came home. Apparently, Joan had never had sex with anybody other than her husband, and from what she had heard and read about sex, he seemed to be a dud. One of Joan's friends told her to try out somebody else and see if it was she or her husband. That's where I came in. Well, it must have been her husband because she told me she loved me and wanted to leave him. That scared the living shit out of me. Had I to do it over, I might have said, "Go for it!"

When her husband, Bob, came back from the cruise, I invited him over to the house to have a drink and meet him. He was a pretty decent guy, not too bad looking and fairly intelligent. The conversation came around to sex and I asked him if he had managed to gather any strange while he was down in Puerto Rico. He went into detail about a couple of schoolteachers he and a buddy had supposedly turned every way but loose.

"Hell," I thought, "the best woman you'll ever have is right across the hall." I don't know what was wrong with that guy. He must have thought his wife didn't have any sex drive or something. The first night he had the duty, she came over and molested me heavily in my room. She was crying and didn't know what to do, as she just wasn't enjoying his technique. I told her to try to change his habits. She should pick up some books on sex and leave a couple lying around the house. He would be sure to ask about them, and maybe she could drop the hint that he could use a little work on his technique.

"If that doesn't work, dump him before you ruin your life and start having kids," I told her. I decided to hang it up as a marriage counselor.

A few days later, the phone rang again. This time it was Beldon Little, my salvage diving friend. He wanted me to see if I could get some "powder" and blow a propeller off an old Menhaden fishing boat down in Elizabeth City, North Carolina. I told him I'd see what I could come up with. He only had blasting caps and no primacord, which I much preferred to use rather than putting caps into the water. I called some friends and finally located a guy who had about three pounds of C-4. Of course, it was illegally obtained from somebody in the Teams. After procuring the explosive from the guy, I called one of my other buddies and asked them if they wanted to go to "Carolina" and help me do this job. I didn't really need any help, but I thought they would have an interesting time.

We drove to where the boat was. Beldon was there with Skinny Travis, a professional scavenger. He was into salvaging anything that could be sold for scrap. I asked Beldon once again if he had located any detcord (primacord). He had not. Somehow, I was going to have to get the C-4 to do the job that four feet of primacord would have done.

Beldon had a length of radiator hose in the back of his pickup truck. I asked him if he had any motor oil. He reached into the back of the truck seat and came out with a quart. I took the C-4, put it in an empty can and worked it with the motor oil until it was thick goo that I could stuff down the radiator hose. Before I put the mixture into the hose, I ran a piece of thin line through the hose. Then, with a small piece of a tree branch I jammed the C-4 oil-mix into the hose until it was full. I taped up one end of the hose, stuck an electric cap in the other end, and taped it up, too. Now I had a charge I could tie around the shaft and force the propeller off.

I climbed into my scuba gear and went down with a large pipe wrench in my hand. The wrench was four feet long. I put it on the nut on the end of the shaft that keeps the propeller on. It took one hundred percent of my strength just to loosen the nut. I removed it the rest of the way by hand. One of the topside people handed down my special charge and I tied it around the shaft forward of and against the hub of the propeller. Then I got out of the water and climbed onto the old boat. The boat was just aground in the mud; it was not submerged all the way. I made sure all was clear around us and gave Beldon the signal to fire the shot. He raised the hood of his old truck and snapped the firing circuit wires, which ran to those coming from the cap onto the terminals of his battery. There was a WHUMP! from under the boat and the stern rose up an inch and dropped back. Fish started trying to walk on water, flipping around on the surface and then disappearing. I went down again, and the propeller was about six feet from the end of the shaft. Retrieving it was simply matter of putting a piece of chain through the hole in the prop and dragging it ashore. It weighed about three-hundred-fifty pounds and was solid bronze.

It was late in 1968 and, again, I didn't go home for the winter holidays that year. Fred Yelinek was a skydiving friend from Richmond, A few days after Christmas, he, his girlfriend, and I headed for Florida to go skydiving at Paul Poppenhager's place. It was near Indiantown and was a famous drop zone in Florida. All the heavies would be there, including Steve Snyder, co-inventor of the square canopy, and several others that I had known when traveling around the jumping circuit. We traveled in Fred's van and I drove some, even though I didn't have a driver's license. I still hadn't reapplied since I'd lost it in 1966.

We made it to Pop's place and jumped and drank for several days. I was starting to lose interest in jumping, but I managed to get one in on a new, square-type canopy. Steve Snyder[†] let me jump it. When

† Steve Snyder was killed in a plane crash a few years after I met him.

jumping this rig, due to the fact it was an experimental chute, one was required to wear two reserves. I hopped out of the plane and popped the chute at about thirty-five hundred feet and flew the thing into a cow pasture by the Okeechobee canal. What a thrill! The damned thing had a twenty-miles-per-hour forward speed. I really had to brake hard to keep it from slamming me into the ground. I braked it down to the minimum speed just off the ground but still went head first into the grass of the cow pasture. I managed to miss any piles of cow shit.

The next day it was hot and nearly windless. I'd made my last jump of the day and was nursing a Pabst Blue Ribbon. We were watching some of the jumpers guiding their parachutes over to the canal and landing either on the bank or in the water. Some of them would drop out of their rigs just above the water. Then somebody shouted that one of them dropped out of his rig about a hundred feet above the canal. I heard somebody loudly moan "Aw, Shit!" I looked over quickly, and all I saw was a canopy with nobody under it fall slowly to the ground. I took off running for the canal. It was about three hundred yards from where I was standing. By the time I got there I was out of breath. The people by the canal were standing around in shock. I asked where the guy landed and it took a couple of seconds for me to get a straight answer. One of them pointed to the water and said he had landed in the water in a hands and knees position and immediately gone down. I jumped on a raft that was there in the canal and they quickly guided me over to the spot. I was still about out of wind from the run. The hot weather and cold beer was taking its toll and I was pissed that I was not stone cold sober. I jumped into the water and dived to the bottom repeatedly. The water was around twenty feet deep and cold near the bottom. There was no visibility and I didn't have a facemask. I kept making surface dives and sweeping along the bottom with my hands until I was so exhausted, I could barely only climb onto the raft with help. I couldn't find the guy. The sheriff's people came after a while and dragged him up with one of those rigs with all the fish hooks on it. Gruesome. I felt he could have been saved if we had found him quickly enough. Too bad.

That night, there was a dance in the hangar at the drop zone. I danced once with a girl who was really quiet. One of the jumpers told me that she was the guy's girlfriend. Maybe she had gotten over his death, but most likely she was still in shock. It was tragic and there was no excuse for the accident.

After a couple more days of parachuting, Fred, his girlfriend, and I headed up the coast and back to Norfolk. The neighbor couple was not home when I got there; apparently they were on leave, as I never saw them again.

When I arrived at Norfolk, I decided that I should probably stay in the Navy forever, so I talked it over with some of the senior people and they told me to go for six more years, that way I wouldn't have to make any decisions for a long time. I thought it over for a little while and put in my papers to ship over, as it's called. A few days later, I raised my right hand and swore, once again, to uphold the Constitution and to defend the country from all enemies, foreign and domestic—at least for another six years. I got about eleven hundred dollars for reenlisting for six years. I went to the bank and purchased Traveler's Checks with it and stashed them in my locker.

A few more days passed before the word came down from Chief Dick Johnson that Graver, Trotter, and I were going on another operation. This time it was to Project Tektite and would take place in Lameshur Bay, St. John in the Virgin Islands. We would be working with civilians and be there for at least a few months.

Most people would jump at the chance to dive in the Virgin Islands doing underwater cinematography—and get paid, too. Dave and Howard weren't bad to work with, so long as they stayed away from booze and women. The trip would be a joy ride. We wouldn't have to stand duty on board the ship, as we were passengers.

This was an ideal opportunity for anybody who liked to dive and take pictures in warm, clear water. We could drink cheap beer and rum, and might even run across a girl or two to make friends with. I was really looking forward to the trip.

Chapter 12

Heading for
the West Coast

Once again, I would be working with Graver and Trotter, the same two guys who had messed me up with the beautiful woman in Panama City. They were not bad guys to hang out with, but they were messed up socially. Howard Trotter exhibited signs of being an alcoholic and Dave was always worrying about his wife when he was out of town. I was junior man in the crew and thought that might result in me getting the shit end of the stick while we were working there.

The three of us and our gear took a commercial flight to Philadelphia, and there at the Philadelphia Naval Shipyard, boarded the USS *Hermitage*, an LSD (Landing Ship Dock). On this job, we would be involved with a civilian/military experiment in air saturation diving at a shallow depth. Some civilian scientists would spend about sixty days in a two-part habitat in the beautiful waters of the U.S. Virgin Islands in Lameshur Bay, St. John. Most people would kill for an assignment like this. I had to kill to get out of it.

My unplanned adventure started while I was on the USS *Hermitage* headed for St. John. We were heading there to install the Tektite Habitat for this underwater saturation experiment. We had been out of Philadelphia for a few days when a message came in requesting a volunteer of my particular skill (PH-8136 Underwater Photographer) to go to Underwater Demolition Team-13 on a WESPAC cruise (I knew what that meant) to serve in the intelligence department of that Team. Most people thought I was crazy to give up a soft assignment in the Virgin Islands to go off to a war nobody wanted to fight. But I was the adventurous type and thought it might be interesting to do some of the things that others would not do.

I decided I would take my chances with the Viet Cong instead of a couple of guys who would probably make sure I got all the shit details.

As it turned out, I was the only one in the entire Navy to volunteer for this. The ship pulled into Puerto Rico and I got off with my gear. One of the men from the Combat Camera Detachment at Roosevelt Roads came and picked me up at the ship and took me to the unit where I was cut a set of orders. I spent the night in the barracks and the next day they issued me a TR (Transportation Request) to get a ticket back to Norfolk. One of the photographers gave me a ride to San Juan to the airport and I got out and checked my baggage. Then, in true navy tradition, I headed for the bar. I began shooting the shit with a German who most likely thought I had a cute ass, because he started buying me Heineken. I happened to glance down the bar and noticed a righteous looking honey looking me over. Pretty soon, her interest in me was obvious and I motioned for her to come and join me. The German had to catch his plane.

The girl introduced herself as Barbara Malyska, and told me she lived in New Jersey. She had been injured in a car wreck. She showed me the scar on her back from her surgery. She was a nurse and had rich parents. Her father had paid for her to come to Puerto Rico for a vacation to recover and have a little fun since finishing physical therapy. She wanted me to become part of that physical therapy. I was all for it, but my gear was checked including my shaving gear. She wanted me to stay and so did I, but finally, they called my plane. I kissed her goodbye. She gave me her phone number in New Jersey. I called her a few times, but the last time, her father answered, and he told me she didn't want to talk to me any more. Another "relationship" down the tubes.

I had a few days to get moved out of my apartment and pack up my things. After giving some of my belongings away, I filled up a suitcase and two duffel bags with my clothes.

I went back to the unit on the last day and shook hands with all my friends. They wished me luck, told me to keep my head down, etc. I went to the skipper's office and told him I was sorry to bail out on him, but I was ripe for adventure, which, for me, didn't include being stuck in a tropical paradise with a drunk and an unhappily married guy. He smiled and wished me luck as he shook my hand. He knew the story.

Dick Johnson gave me a ride to the airport in his newly-acquired, beat-up station wagon. I had planned it so that I would have time to catch a standby flight for San Diego. That way, I could cash in my ticket and just pay half price. If the plane had been full, I would have had to wait for the next flight. In this case, the plane was full, but not the first class section. The flight attendant put me up front with two Marines and "the rich people." I think she took great pleasure in bringing us free drinks and all the chow we wanted. It was a slap in the face to the sometimes-smug types who ride in first class who don't want to get dirty sitting next to low-life scummy servicemen. In this case, had I taken my regular ticket I would have been in the back of the cattle car. By going half price, I rode first class! You gotta love it.

The two Marines and I had a very pleasant conversation during the flight. They worked in technical fields, so we talked about electronics, radio gear, and fire control systems. I surprised myself with what I knew about a these subjects.

Chapter 13

Reporting for Duty with UDT-13

The plane landed in San Diego, and I caught a cab for Coronado. The ferry was still running across the bay, as they hadn't finished the San Diego Bay Bridge at that time.

Tom Hummer, my former roommate now lived in South Mission Beach. He had left the Navy and had become a stockbroker with Merrill-Lynch. It was too late to call him and I was tired, so I stayed at a cheap motel in Coronado. The next day I caught a cab the Silver Strand and checked in at the Quarterdeck of UDT-13. As soon as I checked in, the guys I knew from Little Creek that were there as part of a "fleshing out" of UDT-13, came around to greet me. There were not enough bodies on the "left" Coast to make up the full compliment for Team 13, so they "borrowed" some guys from UDT-21. I had parachuted with some of these guys at Suffolk back on the East Coast. By virtue of the fact I was greeted warmly by "real frogmen", the stigma of being an "admin puke" was less. The frogmen of UDT-13 were, for the most part, veterans of Vietnam having been drawn from all areas of the Special Warfare Community. Some of them had several tours and a few had even been over there before we officially were over there.

Things after that were hectic. Everybody was getting ready to go to WESPAC and all the gear that had not already been shipped with the advance party had to be packed up and put on pallets for the flight over.

HMC "Doc" Worthington of UDT-13 and Doc Meyers, from UDT-21, finished the job of giving us our shots. The chief in the supply room issued me my combat uniforms and other gear. "Chicken" McNair in UDT-11 sold me a Browning 9mm pistol for fifty dollars, as I thought I needed a handgun for the upcoming trip. I stuffed it in my gear and never used it except for target practice off the ship and when I went on liberty in Vietnam. I carried it in a shoulder holster under my cammie shirt. You see, in a war zone you are not supposed to carry personal weapons, as you might get in a firefight and hurt somebody.

Out of sheer boredom we went over to the rifle range at North Island Naval Air Station and burned through a few cases of ammunition. I got to fire the M-16 for the first time since I had attended SERE school. It was an easy weapon to learn and it had almost no recoil, so your aim was not messed up by any fear of the upcoming recoil. In later life, I would fire Expert with the M-16 rifle on several occasions. We were now ready for shipment to Vietnam.

We did not go directly to Vietnam, as the UDT headquarters were in Subic Bay, Philippines. From there we would go to whatever detachment we were assigned to and then to Vietnam. Some of the platoons were in Vietnam, and others were stationed aboard a submarine. Some other platoons were assigned aboard surface ships as part of the Amphibious Ready Group, or ARG. We would relieve these platoons as we made our move overseas.

My friend from the East Coast, Tom Hummer, let me use his spare bedroom until I headed to Vietnam. I had a couple of weeks to hang out in some of the bars where the Teams went drinking and met some of the people I would be working with. For the most part, they were pretty sharp. Some of them had some good stories about their former trips with SEAL Team 1 or one of the other UDT Teams.

I remember drinking a few beers with Frank Bomar at the Tradewinds in Coronado. He was a guy about my height, but with a sizable beer gut on him. I asked him about that. He said they told him he could keep it as long as he could carry it around. He carried it right through training and up until he, and another guy in his unit by the name of Riter, died two years later in Vietnam.

A few nights after I arrived in California, I was at a party and met a girl by the name of Chris. She was standing in a doorway as I squeezed past to get another beer out of the kitchen. She gave me "the look" and introduced herself. She said her name was Chris. I told her I was Steve and she said I ought to look her up sometime, and I said I would. I didn't get her last name. A few nights later I was again in the Beachcomber and asked the bartender (and owner), Parker Jackson, who she was and where she lived. He knew her. She was a schoolteacher and lived almost across the street from the bar.

I walked over and knocked on her door. A woman came to the door and opened it. I asked her if Chris was there. She said, "I'm Chris."

She was wearing glasses and I didn't recognize her.

"I'm Steve. We met the other night. I thought you might like to have a beer."

"Sure. Let me get a sweater."

We walked the three blocks to my place and went upstairs to the apartment. Needless to say, beer wasn't really what Chris was after. It was a good night. We hung around together a while. She was very nice, quite intelligent, and had a good disposition, not one of the standard bar flies that some of us were used to meeting.

One night, I was at Chris' apartment and we were both naked, about to perform some unspeakable acts, when there was a knock at the door. It was Charlie, a medically retired Marine Captain. I told her not to go to the door, but she was half drunk and opened it. I grabbed my clothes and ran to the bathroom to get dressed. Charlie came in, grabbed her, threw her naked over his shoulder, and lugged her down the street to his place. By the time I got my clothes on and came out of the bathroom, they were gone. I ran down to his place and he was gone, but Chris was inside lying on the rug naked. All the doors and windows were locked so I couldn't "rescue" her. Perhaps he was just saving her from me. Later, I asked around and learned he was not really too stable. He had taken some shrapnel in the brain housing and had not been the same old Charlie after he got back. I backed off a little bit and faded out of her life. I didn't need to die for something stupid such as that. He wasn't in love with her or anything, he just had some fixation that he was her guardian. I talked to him once and he told me he didn't want to see her get hurt. I told him that I had no intention of doing anything to hurt her, as I liked her a lot and he might have the wrong idea about us. I figured it was time to put a shine on that relationship if some whack job was looking out for her. I would be leaving in a week or so, and thought I would save myself for the Viet Cong. Charlie wasn't too bad a guy when he wasn't drinking, but that wasn't very often.

I never saw Chris again after that night. She had given me one of her college graduation pictures. I kept it in my wallet with the only other picture I had, one of Mary, my girlfriend back home.

We hung around the Team area, doing PT and keeping the place clean. Some of us tied up some loose ends and bought things we though we would need. I went across the road to the Navy Exchange and purchased a large Buck, folding knife that had a leather case, so I could carry it on my belt.

One of the frogmen in Team 13, James Boyce, "borrowed" forty dollars from me and "promised" to pay it back before we deployed. Well, I didn't know it, but he was about to get canned out of the Teams for not being up to snuff. He was basically a thief and a lazy bastard. What a waste of good training, I thought. I never saw him or my forty dollars again, and thought it just as well.

In a few days, we would be heading for Subic Bay and then to Vietnam. We had several false starts, which was typical in those days. The airplane would have a mechanical problem, or the pilot would get sick, or something. I think we lugged several trucks full of gear over to the North Island Naval Air Station about three times before we finally broke ground. Even the last time, we wondered if it was just a drill, and whether we would have to turn around and go back.

Chapter 14

Overseas with Team 13

It was very cold at cruising altitude and, as I remember, very few good things happened on the way—except our first stop at NAS Barber's Point, Hawaii. Lt. Chris Lomas, one of the officers, had a friend there who loaned him a car, so a few of us had a good tour around the island. In true Navy fashion, we managed to get drunk a few times sitting under the trees or in a club while waiting for our plane to be repaired—they ALWAYS broke down in Hawaii. All of the people who flew back and forth to Vietnam via Naval Air were way-laid in Hawaii, as the crews' families lived there. It was the only way for them to get a break from the schedule.

We stopped several other times for fuel at places such as Guam, Wake, Midway, or some of the other islands we took away from the Japanese in World War II. We also fueled up our personal tanks. There are regulations against drinking on military aircraft, so we had to guzzle our drinks before we got back on board the plane. This caused a very heightened level of intoxication. It was so damned cold in the plane that I thought we would freeze to death before we got to the Philippines.

When the plane landed at Cubi Point Naval Air Station, Philippines, we all thought we were stepping into a steam bath. Jesus, it was hot! Our clothes stuck to us like wet, gooey washcloths. The starch in our utilities turned to glue. Being from the East Coast and having grown up in Maine, I was used to cooler temperatures. However, I could get used to most anything. I stepped off the plane and walked into the terminal. There was a set of scales used for weighing baggage, so I assumed they were accurate. I stepped on them. With my boots, hat, and wallet, I weighed exactly 225 pounds. Oh, for those days again. There was a bus and some other vehicles waiting for us. Some men from UDT-12 were waiting to haul us over to the Team area and help us get settled into the barracks. Some of the UDT-13 men were already at Subic as they had come over with the advance party to sign for weapons and things of that nature. The trucks dropped us off at the barracks and one of the officers told us to go to the Team area after we grabbed a rack and locker and stashed our gear.

YN1 DeLorme took me in to introduce me to the XO. His name was Lt. Bob Peterson. He had served with SEAL Team 2 and had been awarded the Silver Star on some hairy-assed operation with Bob Gallagher where Gallagher had received the Navy Cross. This gave Peterson respect among the boys in the Team. Sometimes the award is more awesome than the deed, but in his particular case, those who knew felt he had earned it. I walked into his office. He stood up and shook hands with me.

"Well, Waterman, are you already to take pictures on enemy beaches?" he asked.

"Sure am, Sir. Whatever it takes to keep me off the streets."

He didn't quite know how to respond to that answer and gave me an odd look. Perhaps he thought I was a macho asshole, and, thinking it over afterward, it was a dumb thing to say, however, he got over it.

One of the first things that I did there, of course, was go to Olongapo on liberty. Sonar Technician, Second Class (STG2) Arles "Steve" Nash was going to show me the town. He was one of the guys in UDT-13 who had been an instructor at Underwater Swimmers School in Key West when I was a student there. The first place we stopped was the U & I Bar, where Nash introduced me to Crazy Amy, one of those Filipinas who would have been a millionaire had she been in the States. She owned the bar and still did a little hooking on the side. She liked frogmen and she was my introduction to sex in the Philippines. Not very impressive, but it was better than nothing—barely. She charged six dollars, which was a lot of money in those days.

My first assignment was to the USS *Cook*, LPR-130. There were fourteen of us from the Team. The *Cook* was a small ship about one-hundred-twenty-five feet long upon which Detachment Bravo of UDT-13 would live for a month until we rotated to another detachment. The skipper, Lcdr. Bruce Tager, was a former enlisted man. He had been a gunner's mate before he was commissioned. All of us liked him, as he was extremely intelligent and had an excellent sense of humor. The job of the UDTs on the *Cook* was to make hydrographic maps of the coastline of Vietnam. I was issued a Nikonos amphibious camera, and PH1 Chip Maury, from UDT-12, had signed over his Leica M-2 for me to use. It was a standard military issue Leica with 50mm, 35mm, and 90mm lenses, all contained in an olive-drab leather gadget bag. By the time my tour was over, that Leica was destroyed from the humidity and dirt. I had a lot of Kodak Tri-X film and some Kodachrome and Ektachrome I'd scrounged from my old unit in Norfolk, Combat Camera Group. I bought a number of Kodak mailers at the Navy exchange, as I planned to shoot the color film and mail it to Kodak. I used my father's address as a return address. That way I wouldn't have to worry about losing the film for security or any other reasons. As it turned out, it was a good thing I did it that way.

We went aboard the USS *Cook*, LPR-130, at Subic Bay. Our rack (bunk) assignment consisted of us throwing our gear onto the one we wanted. STG2 Steve Nash had his own personal CAR-16 carbine so he let me use his issue M-16 rifle. This was not a high budget operation. I slept with my rifle under the mattress to keep it from getting exposed too much to the salt air, although during the day sometimes, we would wade through salt water to get to the beach. To keep in practice, I fired it from the deck of the ship as much as I wanted. The famous Marine Corps general, Lewis B. "Chesty" Puller always said, "If you don't hit 'em, you don't hurt 'em." I subscribed to that doctrine and wanted to be as good a shot as I could be. I never carried more than a couple hundred rounds of ammo, so I felt I had to make them count. We were never expected to get into any prolonged firefights, just keep the bad guys' heads down while the beach party and swimmers extracted.

On board the *Cook*, our routine was to awake in the morning around 0500, get our gear together, and load it onto the boats. Then we would recon a beach. This involved putting a number of the frogmen in the water on what is called the swimmer line. More of us would be on the beach party, the only ones armed. Two men were on forward security, two on rear. When I was in the beach party, I was always on rear security with Machinery Repairman, First Class (MR1) Charlie "Tobacco" Lewis. There was also an officer in charge and the cartographer, who would note on his clipboard the terrain features. Two men with the cartographer would man the range poles. These were two poles with different colored flags on the tops of them, one flagpole longer than the other. The cartographers would lay out a base line on the beach, then line up the range poles at ninety degrees to the line. When the swimmers could see they were lined up, the cartographers would take a sounding with a lead weight on a length of nylon string. Then the range pole guys would yell, "MARK!" and move to the next line, usually twenty-five yards farther down the beach. The swimmers had always just arrived on line when the beach crew hollered, "MARK!" so nobody got to take a breather when we swam the beaches.

These numbers were recorded on a Plexiglas slate with a lead pencil. I swam about six miles of beach one day, and by day's end, had no trouble sleeping. I hadn't gone through UDT training and this was my first experience swimming a beach. It kept me in shape. I think they had me swim those beaches just to see if I could hack it. I did, but every time the guys on the beach yelled "Mark!", I had only just gotten on line and I had a hell of a job recording the depths while swimming to the next sounding. I asked if I was the only one who had this problem. The guys just grinned and said that was standard procedure.

On several occasions, we were met with unfriendly persons who were intent on killing us. The first time this happened, I was with Lewis. We had two men named Lewis. The other one was a member of UDT-21 from the East Coast. The one I'm referring to here was nicknamed "Tobacco" a ruddy-complexioned guy who had a tour in Vietnam with SEAL Team 1. Lew always had a chew of tobacco stuffed in his cheek. He would take out his chew, set it on his tray, eat chow, and then stuff it back into his mouth after he finished his dessert.

The Team would go to the beach in a small wooden boat, called an LCPR (Landing Craft, Personnel Reconnaissance). It was made of plywood and had a small ramp on the front. On the way in, we would know the direction the swimmers would be working, so when we felt the boat hit the beach, we always knew which way to run as soon as the ramp dropped. Lew and I were always the first out of the boat. We would go to the rear, which would mean either right or left of the rest. This was the worst part. I would be crouched down behind that little wooden ramp, damned near out of breath. I asked Lew how come I was all out of breath and hadn't even run or anything yet. He just grinned and told me I'd get over it after a few trips onto the beach.

We got out of the LCPR and onto the beach. Lew and I went over a large sandy berm toward some vegetation. We crawled into the bushes, and Lewis eased himself up and looked toward the inland area. The next thing I knew, he was standing up and shooting. He shouted for me to run and tell the rest of the men to get the fuck out of there. I made it down the berm in about five steps, as it was almost a forty-five-degree angle downward and back onto the beach. All of us ran into the water, put our fins on, and swam out to where the boats could pick us up. Steve Nash had left his fins on the ship that day and had to ditch his ammunition to keep afloat and swim. We were all wearing the gray UDT life jackets, but it is quite a job to swim with sneakers or coral booties on and no fins. Later, we harassed him about it. To the best of my knowledge, nobody shot at us that morning, although there were some near misses from our boats' .50 caliber machine guns shooting over our heads at the shoreline.

That same day, we were to recon another beach some distance from the first. When we went ashore, a little guy came up to talk to us. He was wearing beads and had long hair for a military man. He was a Marine who was stationed near the village. His equipment didn't look too squared away to me. We told him we would be working down the beach and past a point of land that stuck out into the ocean. He told us we were crazy to go down there. Then a chief hospital corpsman came out of the village. He said he would walk down the beach with us for a ways. I talked to him for some time. "Doc" had fought in the tail end of WWII and had been awarded the Purple Heart. Then he had fought in the Korean War and had been wounded twice. So far he had been hit twice in Vietnam. I think he had a couple of Silver Stars. Doc told us we were crazy to go down past the point, too. I thought maybe there was something to this advice.

By then, I was walking in the water up to my ankles and scanning the tree line quite intensely. The Doc left us and wished us luck. I was walking rear security with Tobacco Lew. Lewis was walking about six yards ahead of me and slightly up the beach from the water's edge. All of a sudden, the bullets started flying. I could hear them zinging off the sand and splashing in the water around me. The VC had opened up on us with a machine gun. I laid in semi-automatic fire along the berm and tried to see if the other guys were getting off the beach and into the water. We felt pretty safe in the water. All of us had shot at small targets the size of a human head in the water and knew how hard it was to hit them. We imagined it was even more difficult if the "heads" are shooting back at you.

Nash, the guy who had forgotten to brings his fins that morning, spotted some Viet Cong in the bushes setting up a machine gun. He'd caused the VC to start shooting before they were ready for us. He probably saved a few of the guys from being hit. He shot two of them and the rest of us ran to the water, firing into the berm as we did to give the swimmers a chance to get offshore a little further. Then the rest of them swam out to sea as the gunners on the boats poured fire into the bushes on the beach. This time, I could hear the rounds zinging by and see the little puffs of sand as the bullets hit near me. Nash burned up all of his ammo retreating to the water as the rest of the beach party extracted.

I waded out into the water and kept firing at the berm. A large wave upended me and I was rolled over in the surf. As soon as I regained my footing, I stood up, hauled back the charging handle on my M-16 and blew out the water in the breech. I then chambered a round, took aim at the berm again and pulled the trigger. The rifle blew up in my face. I must not have cleared the buffer spring housing completely of water.

That was the end of Steve Nash's M-16. I took some harassment for that. Fortunately, I had been wearing contact lenses and I didn't get any powder flecks in my eyes. I borrowed another rifle for the remainder of my time in Vietnam.

The boats offshore started firing their machine guns at the shore and some of the rounds were hitting the water around us. It was bad enough to have the VC shooting at us, but we were not impressed by our own guys walking their guns through the swimmers.

The LCPR boat picked us up and, as we were counting heads, a woman ran out of the bushes with a stick across her shoulders and a parcel hanging from each end. Nash wanted to fire on her and asked for a magazine. Lt. John Hollow, the assistant platoon officer wouldn't give him one. Nash called him a cocksucker, or something like that and Hollow said he couldn't talk to him like that. Nash replied that after the shit he had pulled having the .50s walk fire through the water while we were swimming out, he could talk to him any fucking way he wanted to. The woman escaped down the beach and the Marines took care of her later that day. She was a reloader for the Viet Cong. I don't think the rest of her day was very pleasant.

When we returned to the ship, I remarked to Tobacco Lew that rounds did zing and snap when they went by, just like in the movies. He looked at me with one eye squinted and a slight hint of tobacco juice running from one corner of his mouth and said, "No shit!"

The rest of our trip with Detachment Bravo on the USS *Cook* was quite uneventful except for getting thrown overboard fully-clothed on my birthday and having to swim around the ship twice before they let me back aboard. It was all in great fun. Near the end of our trip on the USS *Cook*, the ship pulled into Hong Kong for ten days of R & R. Three of us, ETN3 Kent Larsen, BM3 Dan Sager, and I got a room at the President Hotel in Kowloon and went to see the sights. I bought some hand-made, monogrammed shirts, a three-piece suit, and some other things. I never spent my money like a drunken sailor, even though, on occasion, I was one.

One pleasant thing about Hong Kong that stands out in my mind was a night the three of us were eating in a restaurant. An older couple was at the next table, obviously American. The man asked if we were in the military. We said yes and that we were taking a few days off from the war in Vietnam. He offered to call our parents when he got back to the States and let them know we were in good health and so forth. We figured we didn't have anything to lose by trusting them, so we gave him our parents' phone numbers. Later on, my father told me the man had called with the message that we looked good and seemed to be in good health. I have always remembered that kindness and hoped someday to be in a position to do that for some young kid away from home who is in a dangerous situation.

Larsen elected to go back to the ship early for some reason, and Sager and I decided to have a couple of the local talent come and spend some quality time with us in our rooms. After that, I decided I would stick to "round eyes," what we called American women. There's something nice about being able to hold a conversation with your partner, even if you don't have a hell of a lot to say.

The USS *Cook* returned to Subic, and I learned I would be advanced to photographer's mate, first class, having taken the test in the fall before I left Combat Camera Group. This, in the Navy, is pay grade E-6, one grade below chief petty officer. I would be advanced on 16 April 1969. I had been eighteen when I joined the Navy and had over four years in when I headed for Vietnam. I was a little bit older than most of the guys in the Team, except for the chiefs and officers.

I spent a few days in Subic, got laid a few times, caught a "gentleman's cold," got it cured, and prepared to go back to Vietnam to see some action with the other detachments. I hated sitting around when there might be some action going on. It's hard to shoot combat photos if you aren't in combat.

This time, I caught a bus to Clark Air Force Base and would be flying out on a C-141. When we went aboard, I realized there were no seats. All of the passengers had to sit on aluminum pallets with a strap across our laps. I thought this really sucked. I looked around and to my right was a warrant officer, and on my left, an Army major. Apparently, rank has no privileges when it comes to being cannon fodder or baggage.

We landed in Da Nang at night, and somebody from Frogsville—the name of our compound—came out to the field to pick us up. We went back to the Quonset huts and found our racks. The berthing area was well air-conditioned and I damned near froze to death the first night. After that, I found a blanket. The Da Nang Detachment didn't do much.

Mostly, they went up rivers and blew things up and sometimes got shot at a little bit. The guys water-skied, laid about, and went over to Camp Tien Sha to try to meet the nurses. I didn't partake of any of this, with the exception of going to the EOD compound in Tien Sha with my buddy, Steve Nash, and to drink a little beer. Tien Sha was chickenshit. You were supposed to have your boots bloused and all that REMF crap. There were even white picket fences around some of the officer's buildings. The frog types, of course, did not subscribe to peacetime standards.

One night, an Army sentry at the gate between Tien Sha and our area stopped our OIC, Ltjg. Robbie Robertson, who had been drinking. The sentry asked the drunken officer where his pass was. Robbie leaned over and grabbed his left lapel and shook his lieutenant, junior grade bars at him. "There's my fucking pass," he said, and drove on.

Mouse, a Vietnamese woman married to a Vietnamese Army officer, worked at the compound doing laundry and cooking. Her cooking sucked, and I heard later from one of the guys that she did, too. One day, Larry Whitehead, on loan from UDT-21, got pissed off at Mouse for some of her poor cooking. He was about to shoot her until one of the men talked him out of it. Perhaps I was just naive or something, but I missed out on a lot of probably not so hot fun. Some of the men used to go out and smoke dope in one of the bunkers. I could hear them out there laughing and listening to *In-A-Gadda-Da-Vida* by the Iron Butterfly all night long. They were West Coast types and that was part of their makeup. It was in their blood.

I was pretty bored there and needed to do something interesting, if not dangerous. One day, I made some crack to Tom Winter of UDT-21 about needing to go down to Ca Mau and to kill somebody. He looked at me with a strange look. "You're nuts, Waterman." I felt stupid for making that remark.

Somebody higher up decided that some VC bunkers up a river (the Song Bo De, I think) needed to be destroyed. We had some old, outdated demolitions in the bunker, so we loaded them onto a Swift Boat, steamed up the river, and blew them up. We took a few stray rounds that day, but didn't shoot back. It seemed as if they were from a firefight off in the distance because we could barely hear the weapons as they discharged. The best part of going out with the Swift Boats was they always had great chow on board. When we went with them, we raided their freezers, which were loaded with frozen steaks, ice cream, and things we didn't have access to. The crew didn't mind as we usually had something to trade and chow wasn't hard for them to get.

We went up and down rivers looking for bunkers, some that had been spotted from the air, others that fired upon boats in the rivers. I went on three operations, all without incident. On one particular day, we had to blow up a small section of a river that separated two different parts of it. The Swift Boats couldn't cross to the other part of the river and chase the VC until we did. The little bar between the two sections became nothing but a column of water, mud, and sand shooting straight up into the air.[†]

The frogmen in Da Nang had built themselves a great compound, Frogsville. When I was there, they were in the process of building a chain link fence around it. Perhaps so nobody could get in and steal the cold beer. The field caught on fire after a Marine in a vehicle ran over a flare locker near the Freedom Hill Exchange. It was blamed on the Viet Cong. The fire had burned down the Exchange and ruined most of the beer. Some enterprising frogmen had gone to the Exchange with a truck and gathered up the cans that hadn't burst. They washed them off and chilled them down. Then the beer was sold to sailors on boats at the deep-water piers. A couple of the boys also stole a brand new outboard motor that was still in its crate. It was setting on the dock just inviting somebody to take it. They beat it up a little with some chain, painted it flat black and mounted it on our Boston Whaler. It towed many a UDT water skier around the harbor, including me.

We used a photo of Stanley Neal being towed behind the boat in the *UDT-13 Westpac 1969* cruise book. We were going to entitle it "Trolling for Alligators," but Ltjg. Pete Upton, my partner in the creation of the cruise book, thought it might offend him. I don't think it would have, as Neal had a hell of a sense of humor. He loved to give the PT and swim test to guys who wanted to try out for the Teams. He liked to squash the stereotype of the black guy that couldn't swim. Neal looked like a real seal when he got in the water and could have probably out-swam one.

While in Da Nang, one of the scariest things I did was go out diving with MR3 Gary Cronin. He was a rugged little guy who was always getting into trouble for either catching VD or beating up fleet officers.

---

† In 1993 in a restaurant in Rockland, Maine, I was eating a meal with my son when a man noticed the SEAL TEAM shirt I had on. He asked me if I used to be a SEAL. When I told him I had served with UDT-13 in 1969, he said I resembled one of the guys who blew up the sandbar for him in the river near Da Nang. Small world, again.

We didn't have anything to do one day, so Robbie, the OIC, asked us if we wanted to look for a fifteen-thousand-pound anchor the Seabees had lost. We figured it would be a chance to do a little diving and cool off, and maybe the Seabees had something to trade. At the very least, they'd owe us one. Gary and I checked out a hand-held sonar unit, took the truck over to the area where we met up with the Seabees, and put our gear on their boat. We burned a set of double tanks each, and during the whole dive, all I could think about was some gung-ho boat crewman dropping a grenade on our bubbles thinking we were VC frogmen. It didn't happen. We found the anchor. That was good for some more building materials for the compound. We could always trade something when we needed gear, paint, fencing, weapons—most anything.

Another time, Gary Cronin and I were on a search-and-destroy operation and Gary was carrying an M-79 grenade launcher. There were some bunkers made of blocks of stone in an area we were crossing. Gary said, "Hey, watch this," and fired an HE (high explosive) round at the entrance of one of them. The bunker was only a few yards away. The round hit the stone entrance to the bunker and bounced back without exploding. Before I could react, Gary picked up the dented M-79 round from the ground and threw it into the river.

"Jesus Christ, Gary, that could have gone off when you picked it up, don't ever do that shit again!"

He just grinned. Some of these guys were dangerous to themselves and to others in the unit.

Detachment "Charlie" was aboard the USS *Tunny*, which had pulled into the harbor on Friday for liberty for its crew. I planned on going aboard to document some of the SEAL Delivery Vehicle (SDV) operations there. I already knew all the guys on the detachment, so it would not be a big change of pace for me.

On Monday morning, I went aboard the USS *Tunny*, LPSS-282, an old diesel submarine of World War II vintage. I'd read a lot about submarines and seen them in WWII movies, but until I served with UDT-13 in Vietnam I'd never been aboard one. My first experience on board the *Tunny* was to be led to the "UDT bunk room." The guys in the Team were quartered up in the hangar. The *Tunny* was an old fleet submarine that had been converted to fire the Regulus Missile, and then turned back into an "SS" boat. In January 1969, she'd been converted from an "SS" boat back into an LPSS. Her sole purpose was to support UDT operations and insert commandos on special operations.

To get to the "bunk room," we had to go down a hatch on the deck of the *Tunny*, through the control room and up through a hatch in the crew's mess. The hangar was a big steel cylindrical tank with a huge, hydraulically-operated door on the aft end. Two large hydraulic rams opened this door and, in the old days of the Regulus missile, the crew rolled a missile out onto the aft deck along tracks and set it up, cleared the decks, and fire control cranked it off. Once the weapon had been launched, the deck crew rolled the launcher back into the hangar, the sub would dive and everybody would live happily ever after—except maybe the guys downrange. The Regulus missile was never used in combat and was designed after the WWII German V-1 buzz bomb so fondly remembered by the civilian population of London.

The Regulus missile was relegated to the dust heap of outmoded military equipment, and the *Tunny*, not the latest and greatest example of our undersea technology, was assigned to support UDTs so they would have shelter for swimmer delivery vehicles (SDV) operations. Ltjg. Robbie Robertson, of UDT-21, was OIC of this UDT detachment, and the only UDT officer with us.

Frogmen used the SDV for clandestine beach recons. With two swimmers and a driver, the SDV motored in toward the beach submerged. The driver would set it on the bottom in thirty feet of water and the two frogs in the back seat would swim in toward the beach on a compass heading. They would be attached to the SDV by a heavy fishing line wound on a huge fishing reel. The SDV driver would let it reel out as they swam toward the beach, then reel them in as they started back. That was about the only part of the operation that was nearly free from Murphy.

One of the swimmers carried a little Plexiglas tube containing a clock mechanism with an end closed off with a fairly heavy latex material. As the depth changed, the rubber end would respond to the pressure change by being pushed in or out. A stylus connected to the rubber marked a roll of paper. The paper moved at a known rate, so it acted as a clock. The stylus made a black line on the paper that was representative of the gradient of the bottom. All the cartographers had to know was how deep the device was when the swimmer turned it on, and they could extrapolate the depths from there. In spite of it being a primitive piece of gear, it worked very well.

The *Tunny* pointed her bow to sea, and we headed out of Da Nang Harbor. That night we steamed toward our area of operation. The sub, being conventional, was just a submersible surface ship, so it was more at home on the surface. We made our way offshore and, after dark, started creeping shoreward toward our objective.

At about three in the morning, the sub dived. It was just like in the movies. I was sleeping in my bunk up in the hangar and the klaxon horn blew, "Ahoogah! Ahoogah!" followed by the command, "Dive! Dive!" I could hear the rumble of the diesel engines' RPMs drop quickly, then silence. The sub's main induction valve closed and my ears popped a little. In a few short moments, the water was sloshing under the hangar, and then beside and over it. The gurgling passed by the steel outside of the hangar past my head and then all became quiet as the sub completely submerged. It was an eerie feeling to hear that sound and feel the slight downward angle of the boat as she slipped quietly beneath the South China Sea. Now I knew what Captain Nemo felt like on board the Nautilus, safe and out of sight of the bad guys.

We needed to conduct SDV operations during daylight hours, but had to be in place to launch the mini-sub before the sun had come up. The skipper of the *Tunny* ran his boat toward shore until we were at a depth of ninety feet. As the sub touched down on the seabed, I felt the slight jarring as we bounced along the bottom and finally came to rest. The submarine crew secured the electric propulsion motors and went to other tasks. By now, the UDTs and I had crawled out of our racks and we had our scuba gear ready for the day's work.

On this particular day, ace SDV driver QM2 Bill "Jake" Jakubowski would be at the controls. SN Bill Shearer and SN Steve Abney would be the swimmers riding in the back seat.

In the SDV, on top of the battery containers, was an array of aluminum ninety-cubic-foot scuba bottles. These were for "boat air." On the way in to the beach and back out, the crew of the SDV breathed the air from these bottles. In spite of the telltale bubble trail left by these rigs, open circuit scuba was being used on these operations. Although classified at the time, our SDV operations were not conducted north of the DMZ (demilitarized zone), and the topside Vietnamese were thought to be "friendly." Each man wore a set of double 90cc bottles on his back and the usual belt, KA-BAR, flare, and UDT life vest. They kept their "duck feet" stashed in the sub when not using them. On these operations, the men wore a wetsuit top at the very least. Although the water was warm, they would be in it for a long period of time.

All the support divers and SDV crew moved to the forward torpedo room. I would be locking out as well and and working with the SDV deck crew. Radarman, Third Class (RD3) Walter "Mole" Roberts and I climbed up into the escape trunk and stood back-to-back in that very confined space. Neither of us was a small guy, and it is no place for someone who can even spell claustrophobia. We almost had to take turns inhaling. It was tight. Mole and I had to do a little dance so the submariners in the torpedo room below could get the lower hatch shut. That left us in total darkness. At this point, the flood valve was opened to flood the trunk. The water started to rush in around our feet and quickly rose up to our chests. Just before it reached my mouth, I yelled out, "Trunk's flooded. Secure the flood," and we shoved our scuba regulators into our mouths, hoping we'd remembered to turn on the air before we donned our rigs. The operator acknowledged by securing the flood valve leading to the trunk. Then he opened the air valve to pressurize the trunk to ambient sea pressure. I put my foot against the door of the trunk and held it with a slight pressure, so that when the pressure outside and inside the trunk was equal, the door would easily swing open on its hinges. The door opened and I sounded off, "Door's open. Secure the blow," and then I ducked down and swam out and onto the deck of the submarine. I turned back to make sure Mole was right behind me. We stopped at the edge of the opening in the sub's deck long enough to pull our fins on and then continued aft toward the conning tower looming up in the clear water.

I'd been diving since I was thirteen years old, but had never locked out of a submarine before. All the "real" UDT guys had done lockouts in training. It is an eerie feeling to swim along the deck of a submerged submarine and realize the only safe place is inside that gray, steel hulk lying on the bottom under you. Above you is the unknown and maybe death, but under you in that gray cylinder of U.S. Government-issue steel is hot chow, a rack, a place to take showers, your teammates, and the crew who is there to support your mission.

We had no shortage of fresh water due to the fact that this boat still had the Kleinschmidt vapor compression system installed as original equipment.

Mole and I swam aft along the deck toward the SDV where it was secured on deck behind the hangar. He was on my left and I was near the edge of the sub's deck. As we passed by the conning tower, I looked off to my right. There was a yellow sea snake swimming in formation with us about five feet away. I'd read about sea snakes and how they could kill you if they bit you and all that, but I'd never seen a live one. All of a sudden, the damn thing pulled a ninety-degree turn, and swam right for me. It came right at my face and bounced off my facemask. I was too scared to panic, so I just kept swimming. The snake turned and swam away. Maybe he thought his reflection was mating material, or even the enemy. I didn't care. He went away.

Mole and I moved to the SDV and started loosening the chains holding it to the deck. The scuba tanks and the batteries in the SDV had been charged the night before. In a few minutes, two more guys locked out and swam up on deck beside us. We were only about fifty feet below the surface, so we had plenty of air in our tanks to do whatever we needed to do. When the crew had insured the SDV was ready to go, they gave a series of taps on the hull and Jake, Bill Shearer, and Steve Abney locked out. They wasted no time in getting to the craft and climbing in. Jake gave it a quick preflight check and nodded with thumbs up. We released the chains and he flew the small submarine off the deck and into the hazy green gloom of early morning.

None of us had been outside the sub long enough to worry about decompression, so I locked back in with Machinist's Mate, First Class Harry Lapping, another guy on the deck crew. Mole locked in with the second member of the deck crew.

Chow on board a submarine is the best in the entire U.S. military. They have four meals a day, plus "soup down" in the afternoon when the galley offers a bowl of soup and a sandwich. To those of us in UDT-13, it was hog heaven. We ate all we could hold. The fare included steaks, ham, French fries, even ice cream.

Ltjg. Robbie Robertson, MM1 Harry Lapping (both borrowed from UDT-21), and a couple more of us stationed ourselves in the conning tower. The UQC (underwater communications unit) transceiver was there. The SDV trailed a thin, disposable wire behind it that was connected to the UQC on the *Tunny*. The *Tunny* had two-way communication with Jake in the SDV for a while, and then it went dead. Robbie kept messing with it and trying to raise Jake, but no luck. The wire must have broken. We all started grabbing quick glances at our watches as the time passed slowly by. Pretty soon, we realized the boys would be out of boat air and have to go on scuba. This meant pretty soon the SDV would have to surface.

By now the sub was rolling gently back and forth, side to side in a ground swell. It got deathly quiet in the darkness of the dimly lit conning tower, and the serious expressions on everyone's faces added to the solemnity of the situation. There was no question that things were getting tense. The skipper ran up the periscope and we all took turns watching the surface toward the beach for signs of our little sub and its three-man crew. Daylight was rapidly fading and the sky was overcast. The seas were getting rougher and nobody was talking who didn't have something to say.

Finally, Robbie shouted, "There they are. I see a flare!" He had just taken over the periscope when he spotted the SDV on the surface. Jake had an MK-13 Day/Night Distress Flare burning hotly in his hand. The skipper surfaced the *Tunny* to decks awash and we rushed out on deck, pulled the small sub on board and chained it down. The SDV crew had run out of air and they were nearly exhausted and were getting cold. We helped them get below to warmth and hot chow. They were happy to be home.

The mission was compromised, even though we got some good hydrographic data, and the after-action report showed some points that needed improvement on future missions.[†]

Thanks to these Vietnam missions, SDV operations nowadays have a whole new set of procedures, equipment, and missions. The attitudes of the men of UDT/SEAL Teams are the same now as then, and their spirit is universal within the U.S. Naval Special Warfare Community. They just don't make sailors any better.

After a week on the *Tunny*, I went ashore and back to Frogsville in Da Nang. The boredom of hanging around the Quonset hut in Da Nang, became overwhelming, so I caught a flight to Saigon and from there, another to Phu Quo Island. At the Swift Boat base there, I got a boat ride to the USS *Terrell County*, LST-1157, an old Landing Ship Tank (LST) at a two-point moor off the mouth of the Song Ong Doc River. This was where Detachment Golf was based.

Just prior to my arrival at Detachment Golf, the *Terrell County* replaced the *Westchester County* as the base of operations for UDT-13, Detachment Golf, and a SEAL Team 1 detachment. On the evening of 12 April 1969, around 1700, Detachment Golf of Team 13 suffered several casualties on the Duong Keo River. They were on board PCF-43, which was the trail boat in a group of four PCFs, PCF-5, PCF-31, and PCF-38. Before the day was out, PCF-43 was totally destroyed. It carried the full complement of UDT-13's men. The VC were set up in thick vegetation on the west bank of the river and waited until the other three boats heading up river had passed their position. It is assumed that once they opened fire on the boats that the ones upriver would turn to run and have to pass through the kill zone to escape.

† RD3 Walter "Mole" Roberts of Burley, Idaho, was the last person to ever lock in aboard the USS *Tunny*. He was number 3,680. In June 1969, the LPSS *Tunny* was decommissioned. On 19 June 1970, she was used as a target and sunk by a torpedo from the USS *Valodor* (SS-490).

The first two rockets struck PCF-43. HMC Robert Leroy "Doc" Worthington was killed when he was hit with a B-40 rocket during the first minutes of the ambush. The shrapnel from that rocket wounded Seaman William "Randy" Piper. His helmet was blown off by a piece of shrapnel from the blast that killed Doc. The steel pot flew straight up in the air and fell back on the deck. He didn't know he'd been hit until blood started to run down his forehead. GMG3 Ricky Hinson took some shrapnel from the same blast. Seaman Mike Sandlin from Roosevelt, Utah, one of the youngest members of UDT-13, was struck by an AK-47 round through the thigh. The corpsman gave Sandlin a shot of morphine, an M-16, and two of the frogmen carried him forward where he could fire back without moving around too much.

Lt. Lomas ran to the pilothouse to give first aid to the wounded there. A second rocket that entered the wheelhouse killed the skipper of the PCF-43, Ltjg. Don Droz. The blast from the rocket knocked out the coxswain for a few precious seconds. He died a short time later. With nobody at the controls, the PCF-43 ran itself up onto the bank at full throttle and ended up careened onto its starboard side almost on top of the VC positions. From this angle, its .50 caliber machine guns were useless as they could not be depressed enough to fire at the enemy. The thick foliage prevented the VC from using more rockets, and the proximity to their position precluded the use of mortar on board the PCF-43.

Signalman Third Class Bob Lowry, of Spokane, Washington, and Art Ruiz from Tulare, California were trying to set up the crew's M-60. Ruiz was hit in the abdomen and seriously wounded by grenade fragments during this attempt. Lowry dragged him back to the boat and went after the M-60 that he had dropped into the shallow water by the bow of the grounded Swift Boat. The VC kept throwing grenades at him. Lowry was determined to get the M-60 and take out the VC that were throwing the grenades. He got into a snowball fight (with concussion grenades) with two VC who were in a spider-hole shooting at the men on the disabled Swift Boat (PCF-43). Lowry lobbed a concussion grenade into their hole and blew them physically out of it.

After some time, another Swift Boats came and took off the survivors. PCF-43 caught fire and exploded into nothing but aluminum shrapnel. What remained burned and there was nothing left but a hulk with the two Detroit Diesels sticking out of it. The name "PCF-43" was still visible on the stern, but that was about all. The men of Detachment Golf stayed the night on the river, not risking a nighttime transit back to the *Westchester County*, LST-1167.

For his actions, Lowry earned the Silver Star. To look at this kid, one would think he should have been out delivering newspapers or bagging groceries instead of throwing hand grenades at the bad guys, but he came through, and most likely saved the lives of many of his fellow frogmen. Later in his tour, he picked up the Purple Heart on another operation. SM3 Art Ruiz[†] was the only one of Team 13 who had to be discharged for his wounds. Art later returned to active duty and served again with Naval Special Warfare. Shrapnel also wounded Ltjg. Pete Upton during this firefight. The men not wounded on this operation were SM1 John Campbell, QM3 Patrick Broderick and SM3 Bob Lowry.

When I went aboard the USS *Terrell County*, LST-1157, there were no available bunks in the UDT compartment. I had to share mine with somebody from SEAL Team 1, something called "hot bunking." The SEALs would sleep during the day. As we returned from daytime operations, the SEALs would be preparing to go out at night. When they returned in the morning, the frogmen would be getting ready to go.

The Team 1 officer in charge, Lt. Tim Wettack, was a decent guy. None of us wore any rank insignia, and sometimes it was a joke to see whom the other guys thought was in charge. Some of the guys in that detachment were Richard Solano, Jim Gore, Lance Farmer, "Moki" Martin, and a skinny guy by the name of Dwight Daigle. Later on, a helicopter's transmission seized and the entire crew went down, killing some of these men. (Dwight has passed away from cancer.)

During our time in Vietnam, we heard that a few guys in a SEAL Team platoon were blown up in an accident involving the removal of the demolition charge from a Chicom 82mm mortar. It was a foolish accident and never should have happened.

Two Navy Seawolf helicopters from HAL-3 (Helicopter Attack [Light]) were on board the USS *Terrell County*. These airmen gave us close air support and medevac if we needed it. The crew used to let me fly with them whenever I wanted to. On days when the OIC didn't think there would be any action, I would go up in a helicopter to shoot pictures and try to shoot seagulls from above with the M-60 door gun. Some fun. Sometimes when we were up high, we would throw out white phosphorous grenades to watch them explode in midair—expensive fireworks, but impressive.

Our officer in charge was a fellow by the name of Lt. Bruce Dyer, a graduate of the Naval Academy. He was as fair a person as I'd ever

† Ruiz has since passed away from cancer.

seen, and gave everybody the chance to work at his full potential. The second in command, Ltjg. "Rudy" Wiggin, was a nice enough guy, but somewhat of a wimp when it came to standing up to brass. I had a roll of film confiscated and destroyed by the CO of the USS *Terrell County*. I felt this situation could have been avoided if Rudy had stood up for me. Had I to do that over, I would have had a dummy roll ready to relinquish. Hindsight is 20/20.

Lt. Tim Wettack and the Army lieutenant advisor to the Regional Forces and Popular Forces[†] (Ruff Puffs) had flown upriver in the Loach. They landed when they saw some footprints going into a bunker. After several attempts to get whoever was inside to come out, one of them threw a concussion grenade into the bunker. It turned out to be a woman in her early thirties. She was not badly injured, but when the Loach flew her back to the ship for medical help, the skipper told everybody to get the cameras off the flight deck. I felt that, because I was an official Navy Photographer and had the credentials to prove it, I was exempt from this order. I shot about six or eight shots of them unloading her from the helo. The captain called me up to the bridge and reamed my ass, royally. He asked me what in the fuck I thought I was doing out there with a camera after he had ordered everyone to stop taking pictures. I told him I was an official photographer and it was my job to document everything that happened.

He said, "Well, official Navy Photographer, give me that fucking official Navy film out of your fucking official Navy camera!" Then he threw the film roll overboard out the window of the wheelhouse and told me to get off his bridge. Fortunately, I had control of my temper. Besides, we were in a war zone and I was not sure just what my rights were. I just shut up and left, confident that Rudy was a chicken and that this would never happen again. It probably would have been fruitless for Rudy to say anything to the guy.

I went on my first operation with the men of Detachment Golf after a couple of days there. The Song Ong Doc River runs through the Ca Mau Peninsula on the Southern tip of Vietnam. It drains into the Gulf of Thailand adjacent to the South China Sea. On this day, in May 1969, we were to travel up the river with a small flotilla of six Swift Boats, take aboard some RFPFs, then proceed further up river in an attempt to locate and destroy bunkers and other structures that could give the Viet Cong cover during attempts at ambushing and destroying American and South Vietnamese Riverine craft.

† RFPFs (Ruff Puffs) were Regional and Popular Forces, Vietnamese troops like our National Guard, not regular army.

At approximately 0400, the members of Underwater Demolition Team Thirteen, Detachment GOLF, and six Swift Boat crews ate chow, checked gear, and went on deck to prepare for getting under way. Our standard operating procedure (SOP) was: reveille, eat chow, load magazines, and then assist the boat crews in loading demolitions aboard the Swift Boat (PCF). We would carry several cases of C-4, 5.56 ammunition, 81mm mortar rounds, high explosive rounds for the M-79s, concussion, fragmentation, CS, and a few smoke grenades. Usually, at this time in the early morning, the squad of men from SEAL Team 1, who were also operating from the *Terrell County*, would be returning from night operations, often with a prisoner or two for interrogation.

On some other operations, we would bring the Ruff Puffs to the ship and feed them and show them movies at night, etc. None of the Team members had a warm, safe, fuzzy feeling about living offshore on a ship carrying both Vietnamese troops and tons of high explosives. One evening, I took a detour through the tank deck on my way to the galley. Our supplies of explosives and ammunition were stored on pallets on the tank deck. I walked along the deck admiring the numerous stacks of ammo and explosives. As I approached the door that led off the tank deck toward the galley, I heard a sound. There was a sailor, supposedly on watch, sleeping on top of one of the pallets of ammo, snoring away. A real confidence builder! At this particular time, we had Vietnamese troops on board. Any one of them could have been Nguyen Van Hardcore. All he would have needed was a length of time-fuse, a cap, and a match. In a heartbeat, he would have been a hero and we would have been history.

My mind raced back to the year before. The USS *Westchester County* had been moored in a similar fashion off the Coast of Vietnam and was also being used as a base for the Riverine Forces. Viet Cong sappers had sneaked up and planted limpet mines on the hull. The ensuing explosions killed twenty-five Americans, making this the "US Navy's greatest loss of life in a single incident as the result of enemy action during the entire Vietnam War." It was the heroic action on the part of the crew and others on board the *Westchester County* that kept the ammunition stored on its tank deck from going off. I felt my concern over this guy sleeping on watch was well-justified.

The sun was creeping toward the horizon and we were anxious to get the operation under way. The boats were loaded and the crews properly briefed. Diesel engines were fired up and the formation of Swift Boats struck out for the mouth of the Song Ong Doc, a few miles inshore from our anchorage. The plan was to take those VN troops that were on the ship with us and pick up a few more from a village up the river a few clicks. The two Seawolf helicopters on the *Terrell County* would be coming in later. The crews would be monitoring our radio frequencies and wouldn't take off until after we had left the pickup point with the Vietnamese troops. No sense orbiting around burning fuel. With Murphy's Law as the order of the day, they would most likely run low on fuel about the time the action started.

The Song Ong Doc was a typical Vietnamese river, brown, shallow in depth, and meandering slowly toward the ocean. The vegetation was heavy on both banks. We stopped at our prearranged rendezvous point near a small village and picked up the Ruff Puffs who would be operating with us.

Our boat's skipper pushed the bow onto the mud of the riverbank, and some of us jumped off. The officer in charge of the Ruff Puffs was standing a few yards from our landing point. He motioned for us to get off the boat and follow him. An Army captain on board our boat, the adviser and interpreter for the Vietnamese troops, turned and told us to come into the village and have a Coke or something. Our OIC, Lt. Bruce Dyer, didn't relish the idea. We agreed. The less time we spent screwing around, the less time the Viet Cong would have to set up any surprises for us. The RFPFs, a slack looking bunch, climbed on board several of the boats and we headed up river. They were equipped with World War II vintage M-1 and M-2 carbines. Some of them wore sandals and had brightly colored scarves around their necks, a method of unit designation. I got the distinct impression they were not crack troops.

The stern of the Swift Boat was crowded with its crew members and the members of our Golf-Detachment. A .50 caliber machine gun was mounted on the stern deck and a twin-fifty was mounted in the gun tub topside behind the wheelhouse. I was sitting under the stern .50 caliber with my back against its mount. We were all trying to make believe nobody could see us; that the Viet Cong didn't know we were coming. It is the most naked feeling in the world to be sitting on the deck of a fifty-foot, aluminum-hulled boat with two Detroit GM V8-53 diesels screaming underneath, assuming nobody knows you are there. There's no place to hide. You try to get very small. We called it the "fishbowl effect." You couldn't sneak up on anybody. With the noise of the engines, you can't even tell you're being shot at. Maybe we'd see rounds hitting the water, or catch a glimpse of muzzle flashes. That's what I thought, anyway.

141

Without warning, a huge geyser of water erupted fifty feet astern. It was equidistant between the boat to our rear and us. Nearly every weapon on the boats opened up. I didn't have a clue what the hell was going on, but figured I better get involved. From where I was sitting, a few feet back from the rail, I didn't have a clear field of fire, so couldn't bring my weapon to bear on the riverbank. Suddenly I had a searing pain in my back. I thought I had been hit. The fifty-caliber shell casings were falling down between my flack vest and my shirt. I rolled over and got the vest off in a hurry! No harm was done, but I learned quickly why that place where I had been sitting was so readily available. The skipper of the boat pushed the throttles wide open and the sound of the twin diesels increased from a roar to a scream and the boat forged ahead. The muddy brown water from under the stern churned into froth as we sped up river to get clear of the kill zone. We traveled nearly a hundred yards around a slight bend when the skipper throttled back and pushed the bow ashore on the bank of the river.

There were six boats in this formation. Ours was the second boat from the front. When the ambush began, the three lead boats sped upriver, and the three in the rear did one-eighties turning down river. The boats, with Ruff Puffs and UDTs aboard hit the bank in order to insert and encircle the bad guys.

The boat slid to a halt in the soft mud of the riverbank. Equipment Operator First Class Oliver Dean "O.D." Nelson,[†] on loan from UDT-21, moved to the bow and told the Ruff Puffs' advisor to get his troops off the boat. They wouldn't move, and milled around indecisively, as if they had no direction and were afraid to get off the boat. O.D. then told the advisor he would open fire on them if they didn't. They got the message.

I made a graceful non-Hollywood exit from the bow by jumping down and driving both legs into the soft mud up to my knees. Then I fell forward onto my rifle. Normally this fiasco would have elicited laughter, but most of the others landed the same way. We pulled each other out of the mud and tried to move inland as quickly as possible, having no idea what size force we might be fighting if the enemy had not run off.

The Seawolves were airborne and heading our way. Even before they were within sight, we could hear the Hueys and knew some Viet Cong were spotted running away from the riverbank. The staccato sound of their M-60 flex guns came from the sky as our soldiers took VC under fire. We watched the smoky trails from rockets shooting

† Dean Nelson is now deceased.

earthward, fired at a position hidden from us by the foliage. Over the radio, one of the commanders on the ground ordered our side to hold their fire unless they were well away from our ground forces, as the flex guns' brass casings were landing around our troops on the ground. Getting hit by brass dropping from a thousand feet could ruin your whole day.

Paths crisscrossed in this swampy area. The one I chose to follow intersected a small stream where tree branches hung low to the ground. I passed under one and it brushed the top of my head and shoulders. Suddenly the back of my neck felt as if I had been hit with a bucket of hot coals. I grabbed for my neck and went down on my knees. When I looked at my hand, it was full of big red ants. Jesus, that hurt! Those damn things were three quarters of an inch long and at least a third of that length was teeth. I cleared them off, buttoned my collar and sleeves, and packed handfuls of mud around my neck and wrists. Then I smeared the gray mud over all the exposed skin of my face and hands. In the heat, this mud poultice dried to a concrete-like consistency. I didn't much care what it looked like, as long as I didn't hurt. That was my last problem with ants.

Boatswain's Mate Third Class Bob Lewis[†] from UDT-21, nicknamed "Machine Gun" Lewis,[‡] and Hospital Corpsman, Third Class Larry Williams, and myself moved out ahead and to the right of the Ruff Puffs. They didn't have our aggressive attitude, or else they knew something we didn't. We were moving across a small open area when I heard a loud explosion. I learned afterward that a Viet Cong in the bushes to our front had fired a B-40 rocket that passed harmlessly between the three of us and hit the trees a number of yards behind us. Nobody was hurt. Lewis opened fire with his M-60. "Rambo" was making R-rated movies back in the States, but if he could have seen Lewis with that '60 on his shoulder and the bandoleers of ammunition crisscrossing his body in Pancho Via-style, he would have been inspired. Doc Williams and I were moving forward on either side of Lewis. We spotted movement in the bushes, but hesitated for a moment before opening fire. Bruce Dyer was somewhere on our left flank with the Ruff Puff advisor, and Larry Whitehead, Dean, and some others were on the right. We also knew we had three boatloads of good guys coming in from somewhere in front of us. We didn't want to take a chance on shooting our own men. All this decision-making took place in the course of a few seconds. It didn't take Doc and me long to realize those movements in the bushes were not friendlies. The Ruff Puffs were firing

† Bobby Lewis is now deceased.

randomly past us. Lewis got off about thirty rounds when he stopped firing and went down on one knee. Doc Williams[†] and I were firing our M-16s to cover him, and I moved over, kneeling down beside Lew to see what was wrong. I realized he was trying to clear his weapon. The extractor had broken off the end of a shell casing and the brass was stuck in the chamber. He couldn't clear it and had no spare barrel.

About then, the Ruff Puffs moved past our position, firing their weapons sporadically. Lewis gave up on the M-60; the firefight was over. The Ruff Puffs ran by us and into the bushes. As I moved closer, I could see the body of a dead Viet Cong lying nearly hidden in the bushes. One of the little Ruff Puffs ran up to where he was lying and emptied a full magazine into the guy's chest. They dragged his body and two others out of the bushes. It appeared these Viet Cong were in their late teens or early twenties. There was an AK-47 plus a few magazines lying beside one of them. Beside another were a B-40 launcher and two more rockets. The third Viet Cong had been running toward a small canal when he had been killed. We found more weapons in the canal. Apparently some of the Viet Cong had ditched their weapons and made a run for safety. Some of them were killed on the other side of the canal. One of the Ruff Puffs came up and pointed to the Buck knife on my belt. He was asking to borrow it. I let him use it not knowing what he was going to do. He returned shortly with a big betel-nut-stained, shit-eating grin on his face and showed me the set of testicles he had cut off one of the dead Viet Cong. I was not impressed.

As we worked our way down to the riverbank, we found two more B-40 rounds and a bamboo frame full of G.I. batteries in a small depression. There were twelve D-cell batteries in series fitted into a long tube of bamboo strips held together by rubber bands. This was the power source used to fire the command–detonated water mine that had exploded astern of our Swift Boat. A pair of wires led into the water and revealed the direction where the mine had been placed. Apparently the man who fired it had his timing off. Luck was with us on that one.

Following SOP, we got a body count. It is difficult to comprehend how those numbers meant anything. There were thirteen dead Viet Cong, but each unit made separate claims, and by the time the numbers were added up, the total in the message traffic far exceeded the actual number of dead. This was typical, and I believe it was done to make our efforts look more productive than they actually were.

† Williams was killed the next deployment when he tripped a booby trap. Another frogman, Luca Palma, was killed with him, and Seaman Tim Nichols lost an eye.

Somehow, the politicians equated military victory with how many of our enemies were killed versus how many of us were lost. It was as if we were nothing but points on the scoreboard of some permanent basketball game.

The captured weapons were gathered up before we slogged back through the mud to the Swift Boats. We stopped at the village to drop off the Ruff Puffs. This time we went ashore and drank some Coke. The Ruff Puffs kept the captured weapons. Thinking it over, we joked that we would probably be shot at again with them the next time we went out. Most likely, that would be the case.

The villagers were very impressed with the little anatomical packages these macho heroes brought back. I felt only revulsion for anyone who could cut up the dead; no impression of bravery, only of cowardice. Men are killed in combat. Having achieved all he could ever do for his cause, once a soldier is dead, he should be afforded the privacy of death. Those false heroes should have saved their energy for running the country after the war was over. Then bravery, character, and fortitude can truly shine, even if it is all a facade.

As an afterthought, some of us totaled the cost in ammunition for that day's operation. As nearly as we could estimate, it came to about twenty thousand dollars per dead Viet Cong. If there had been some way to offer those guys a reward just to go the hell home and forget it, we all might have been better off. But soldiers don't fight for financial gain. Only the politicians reap the rewards from the efforts of warriors.

We were back aboard the *Terrell County* in time for steak, French fries, and ice cream. What a way to fight a war! From death, mud, mosquitoes, huge ants, and defoliated swamps, to movies, a shower, hot food, and bunks. Talk about culture shock.

On another foray into the jungle with Detachment Golf, the team came upon a small hooch where some Viet Cong had been living. We found empty ammunition and crates that had contained our C-4 explosive. I made note of the lot number and date on the crate. When I got back to the ship, I checked the numbers with the supplies on board. They were the same. The VC had been getting the excess we threw off the ship and carrying it back to their hooches. Pretty industrious, I thought.

It was so hot that day, HMC "Doc" Algeo passed out from the heat. He came around soon after collapsing so we didn't have to carry him out. That would have been a bitch. It seemed as though the bigger guys always had more trouble with the heat.

We were supposed to make all the bunkers we came across unusable. On a foray up the river, we planted bags of CS (an irritant) powder in bunkers and stuck a sock of C-4 under them with a length-of-time fuse. Then we ran back to the Swift Boat that had inserted us. The goddamn boat was aground and downwind of the bunker. When the C-4 went off and blew the CS all around the bunker, we got a taste of it and we were crying a little before we got the boat off the bank. After that, we always grounded the boat upwind if possible when we blew CS.

On one of our trips down the Song Ong Doc, we had to walk point for a Navy captain (O-6). He was there with some other men to survey the area in preparation for putting in a floating naval base, to be called Sea Float. They installed it later that year and SEALs were stationed on board.

When I was ready to leave Detachment Golf and head back to Subic Bay, a number of the crew were ready to rotate out. I wasn't due to rotate. I was making a tour of the detachments to shoot pictures. We rode a Swift Boat back to Phu Quo Island. This boat had been in many firefights and had a number of unpatched holes above the waterline that were not a problem. At least they weren't until we started into some rougher seas. We had a twenty-three hour boat ride ahead of us. The whole SEAL detachment was seasick. I was wishing I were dead. Dean "O. D." Nelson (of UDT-21) and the commodore, a captain in charge of the squadron of Swift Boats, were the only two of us not sick. I was lying on top of the port engine cover on the stern deck. On the other one, was a man from the CIA we had picked up from some obscure island. I was puking straight up, as was he. We would throw up, and then the next wave would wash it away. I looked over at him and said, "I sure hope dying doesn't hurt this bad." He agreed. We got to the base on Phu Quo Island and ate some half decent chow. I couldn't believe there were Vietnamese women making the beds and cleaning the hooches. Talk about lax security.

I caught a C-123 to Da Nang. From there I took a flight to Clark Air Force Base in the Philippines. That was the easiest place to get in and out of. We could always hitch a ride back to Subic with somebody, or take the bus that ran every day from Clark AFB to Subic.

I had been able to make some illegal parachute jumps while in Subic Bay. The skipper, Lcdr. Jim Wilson, didn't stand on formality when it came to operating. I had one-hundred-thirty-five parachute jumps when I went to UDT-13, but they were all sport jumps. Here, we jumped out of any aircraft we could, including amphibious planes, transports, and helicopters. A couple of us even made a demonstration jump at the San Miguel Naval Station on July 4th trailing smoke. I landed in a large puddle of water that was up to my knees. I didn't care much for that. The chow was very good. We made the jump, ate a hamburger, and got back on the helicopter to return to Subic.

We had the usual PT (physical training) every day during our time in Subic. It got incredibly hot soon after dawn and, during the runs, usually with a hangover, guys would sweat incredibly. Some of us would take off ahead of the pack and hide behind a bus stop, and when the more dedicated members of the team ran down the hill, we would sneak out and join them from the rear. It didn't take them long to figure out what we were doing. Some days, we would play "jungle rules" water polo in the swimming pool near the Quonset huts where we were head-quartered. The goal was to try to drown the skipper, or get the ball into the makeshift net at the end of the pool. I never had much luck doing either one, but I could keep up with the best of them in the water. This was a serious workout and served as a more realistic training evolution than just doing PT in the oppressive heat.

We had our share of beer parties in Olongapo. I really missed American women. It wasn't the physical relationships with them I missed—at least that's what I told myself—but being able to hold a good conversation with somebody who spoke the same language and had a similar background. Mary, my girlfriend from high school, was in college somewhere. Chris, whom I'd been dating in San Diego, wrote to me that she married her new boyfriend. I burned her picture in a big glass ashtray.

During my stay in Subic Bay, I went to Camp Magsaysay in the Philippines with Parachute Rigger First Class Al Flud,† a rather large Indian from Okmulgee, Oklahoma, to train some members of the Philippine Navy Underwater Operations Unit (UOU) in static line parachute jumping. That was an experience. We rode to Camp Magsaysay in the back of a truck with the UOU men. The ride must have been a hundred miles. I remember looking out from the back of that truck only to see straight down the side of a mountain. These guys had live ammo in their weapons. I asked them about that. One of them told me they got ambushed by the Huks all the time and had to be ready to defend themselves. Great, I thought. I should have brought something besides a pocket full of pesos and a camera. During the long ride to Camp Magsaysay we sat in the back of the truck listening to dirty jokes I had heard in high school. There's something quite humorous about listening to old dirty jokes told by a guy who barely speaks English—even if the jokes aren't that funny.

† Al Flud is now deceased.

147

We arrived at the barracks where we would be staying for a couple of nights. There was no running water. The toilets were overflowing with shit and the showers, of course, were inoperable. There were no mattresses on the beds. I took a blanket and stretched it over the springs and slept on that. The insects nearly ate us alive. We ate lots of rice and whatever meat that was in it. They were a really good bunch of guys, though, and we had fun doing this. Most of them would end up being much safer when they jumped. These UOU men were good guys. They looked out for us when we were in town. Dave Hostetter was breaking up a fight between a Filipino and his girlfriend when somebody stabbed him with a butterfly knife. While on the ground, injured, the boyfriend stole Dave's Rolex watch. At the hospital, as Hostetter was recovering from his near-fatal wound, one of the UOU men came to visit. He grinned at Dave and tossed the Rolex onto the bed. Hostetter asked where he'd found it. The UOU man grinned and told Dave that someone shot the guy and left him in a ditch. All he'd done was recover the watch.

Some Special Forces troops from Okinawa came over to Subic so UDT could teach them how to do cast and recovery, and scuba diving. While they were in Subic, of course we took them into town to knock back a few cold ones. We were at the U & I club or Ding's, I can't remember which, when a fleet sailor threw something at one of the SF sergeants. The sergeant walked over and asked, "Did you really throw that or did I imagine it?"

The sailor said, "Yeah, what the fuck you gonna do about it?" The sailor didn't have to wait long to find out. The place instantly erupted into a typical TV-type free-for-all. Chairs and bottles were thrown, people knocked out, and others just running from the club. The Filipino singer on the bandstand threw down the microphone and pulled a piece of the mike stand out and started swinging it at anybody in the crowd.

I am not prone to violence, so I just stood up, turned and walked over to the bar, and ordered another San Miguel. A young "hostess" walked over to me and asked me to sit down. Just then a Filipino came running at me with a chair to hit me. I grabbed the chair out of his hands and made believe I was going to hit him with it. Then I put it on the floor, sat down, and started drinking my beer. That's when the "hard hats," full-time Shore Patrol, came into the bar. They had guns and some of them carried M-3 Grease Guns. They looked around the bar and walked directly over to me.

"Let me see some I.D., Sailor," a lieutenant commander said.

"I'm not in the military."

"Word is you started this fight."

"That's a crock of shit. But if you insist, I'll go with you."

"We insist," one of them said.

I walked down the stairs with two first class petty officers. As we walked down the street toward their paddy wagon, each one held one of my arms. I was talking to them in a friendly manner, and all of a sudden I jumped forward as if I was trying to get away. They tried to hold me back but I just pushed my arms against their grips. They weren't expecting the reversal and lost their grip on me. I jumped back and hauled ass up the street. I could run quite fast in those days and had no fear they would catch me. However, there were other SPs on the street that night who were far thinner and in better shape than the two clods who had captured me. One of them, a real track star, came after me from the sidewalk across the street. I knew he would catch me, so I slowed down to save a little energy and feigned being tired. I waited until he ran up behind me. As soon as I felt his hands on me, I elbowed him in the face and he went down. I started running again and ran into the hood of a stopped Jeepney. By the time I got my shit together, the other two had caught up with me. This time, they held me a little tighter. I told them I didn't mean to hurt the guy who caught me and that I hoped he was all right. They relaxed their grip a little and I pulled the same reversal thing again. I only ran about twenty feet, then stopped and turned around.

"See, I could have gotten away."

That pissed them off. Now I knew I was in deep trouble. They took me to the paddy wagon and put me in it along with a kid who had been picked up for drinking as a minor. The driver took every back road in Olongapo and bounced us around for about an hour. We finally ended up at the Shore Patrol Headquarters inside the gate. When they opened the back door and I got out, there were two rows of SPs with their clubs out just waiting for me to try something.

"Nice night, ain't it fellas?" was my only remark as I quietly walked the gauntlet and into the Shore Patrol building, where I quickly produced the I.D. card I claimed not to have.

The next day, YN1 DeLorme came up to me with a sheet of paper. He handed it to me and asked me if I did all those things. I read it and handed it back to him. He asked if I wanted it in my record.

I said, "No, I don't think so."

"Well, you better get rid of it then," he said. I did.

Around June, some new guys checked in at UDT-13. They were Gilles, Gillen, Baresciano,[†] Czerwiec, Dudley, and Kozlowski. All of them were fresh out of Coronado's BUD/S Class 50 and had not been to jump school as of yet. On the second or third operation off the USS *Cook* with Detachment Bravo, Second Group, the rookies got into a fire fight on the beach. Kozlowski jumped up to run from a bad place with no cover to try to get to the water (there is not much cover on a white sand beach, anyway) and was shot in the arm. As a result, he was medevaced out, and had about an inch taken out of his arm, so that one was shorter than the other. He soon received a medical discharge with disability.[‡]

Some time later, I was in the barracks and Parachute Rigger Al Flud had the duty as the Officer of the Day. He went to the club and got drunk. When he returned to the barracks we were all asleep. He came into the barracks and started making noise about somebody had taken the extension cord to his fan or something to that effect. I woke up and told him to go to sleep and worry about it in the morning. He mentioned something about "your generation," and then started talking about how he had fought in the Korean War. I had the jump on him there. I had heard these stories before and thought it was bullshit, so I had asked DeLorme, the yeoman, to look it up in Al's record. He told me Al had joined the Army after the war was over and had crossed over to the Navy after his hitch was up. Al kept on ranting. He was pissed off because I was twenty-three and had made E-6 only six months after him, and, at the time, he was thirty-three.

Finally I said, "Al, you're full of shit. I've been shot at more than you've been fucked."

It was nearly pitch dark in the barracks. Al walked over to where I was lying in the top bunk. I had started to go back to sleep. It was dark and I had my eyes closed. All of a sudden he punched me in the face and broke my nose. I jumped out of the rack, blood streaming down my face.

"Good job, asshole! You broke my nose."

Al was standing there ready to hit me again. I told him to go to bed before he screwed himself further. I think he might have sobered up a little. I opened my locker, got some clothes on and went to sickbay. The corpsman there told me my nose wasn't broken. Christ, it was right over sideways. I could feel the bone crunch when I tried to straighten it. The next morning I went to the medical clinic up at Cubi Point Naval Air Station. The corpsman there had a different diagnosis. The next thing I

---

† Baresciano was seriously injured in a motorcycle wreck some time later and was discharged from the Navy.

‡ Kozlowski was wounded when shot in the forearm. The Army doctor treating him wanted to amputate, but a Navy doctor convinced him to save the arm. Kozlowski is working today as a commercial diver.

knew, I was sitting in a dentist's chair with a drumstick or something in my nostril. The dentist had sprayed some cocaine solution up there to numb it, but might as well not have bothered for all the good it did. I think he lifted me out of the chair by my nose during the procedure. I heard it snap back in place and then the pain came became a dull roar. It has never been the same.

Six weeks before we were due to return to the States, Pete Upton and I gathered all the material we would need for the creation of the cruise book.[†] Ltjg. Pete Upton was one hell of a writer. He could put things into words better than anybody I have ever known. I had shot a good number of pictures for it and we hoped to produce a good book. We lined up Dai Nippon Printing Company to do the work. Before our trip, we had asked all the men in the Team to write stories and draw pictures and anything else for us to put in the book, so Pete and I went there with a briefcase full of memorabilia of our tour.

I stayed at the Akahane Hotel in Tokyo for a few nights. One evening I was in the bar on the first floor when I struck up a conversation with two Japanese guys. Well, it wasn't much of a conversation, because we didn't speak each other's language. One of the hostesses there did the translating. These men were with the Teijin Tire Cord Company, manufacturers of Bridgestone Tires. They invited me to go with them to a Japanese Country and Western bar. How could I turn down an invitation like that? We left and walked to the train station. After a short train ride, we walked some more to a place that had Hank Williams music blasting out of the door. People were singing in English even though they couldn't speak a word of it. They just mimicked the words. We went inside. The two men wouldn't let me take out my wallet, insisting the night was on them. They bought tokens from the girl at the door, and we paid for everything with them. Money only changed hands at the front counter where the cash register was located.

We had a few drinks and ate some sashimi, my first and last. Then we left and started back to the hotel. By now, the subway was deserted. We stopped at a little stand to get some fried tofu or something. I heard violin music. I looked around and saw an old man playing a violin and begging money. This was too good to be true. I play the fiddle! I walked over to him to persuade him to let me play his violin. He was very reluctant to part with it, but the two guys with me told him I was okay. There I was, a six-foot-three American, drunk, in a Tokyo subway

† FindTech, Ltd has recreated *The Underwater Demolition Team 13: Westpac 1969* cruise book and it is available for purchase at *http://find-tech.biz/udt13*.

after midnight, playing country music on a Japanese violin. Since then, I tell people I am an internationally acclaimed violinist.

We made it back to the hotel where they had met me earlier and they asked if I would like to go out again tomorrow night. I told them I would so we agreed on a time. The next night, they had a girl with them. She was one of their sisters. I had the feeling she wanted to marry an American. I didn't feel comfortable with that situation, but went with them to the Tiger Beer Garden for some Japanese entertainment. Once again, my money was no good. They were great people, but I never saw them again, nor did I get their addresses. There are so many things I would do differently if I could do them over again.

Pete Upton arranged for us to stay at the BOQ (Bachelor Officer's Quarters) at Camp Oji. This was an Army Hospital where men with orthopedic wounds were operated on and left to recover. There were men all over the place, some in wheelchairs with limbs missing, and others with horrible chunks missing from their bodies. Pete, myself, and several other men who were going to study Karate at the Shodokan in Tokyo stayed at the BOQ at Camp Oji. It cost us fifty cents a day for the room, which included maid service and a refrigerator. I thought that was great. The food in the chow hall was wonderful, and all the officers and enlisted ate together.

Pete and I took a cab or train to Dai Nippon to work on the book. We made friends with the Japanese fellows who helped us, Naoyoshi Saato and Hiroyoshi Mizogui. Mr. Saato took us up to one of the top floors and introduced us to the president of Dai Nippon. They were the second largest printing company in the world. I was impressed by their work ethic. They printed the Far East version of Time Magazine and other publications for American publishers.

On the way back from Tokyo one night after watching the Karate class at the Shodokan, we stopped at a bar outside the Camp Oji gate. Before long, we made the acquaintance of the kick-boxing champion of Japan. We started drinking this liquid called Absinthe. An American had told us not to drink it as it contains a narcotic that we weren't supposed to have. By the time I left the bar that night, I was wide awake and drunk, and the kick-boxing champion was passed out in the corner on his hands and knees with his face on the floor in a puddle of his own puke. So much for Japanese being able to drink.

During some of my time off, I went into downtown Tokyo and bought some Nikon camera equipment. I had owned a Nikon when I first joined the Navy, but sold it when I had access to equipment as a Photographer's Mate. Now I wanted my own again. The price was right, so I spent most of the money I had been saving since I reenlisted in December 1968 on camera gear.

Pete and I, along with the cases of cruise books, needed to get a hop back to Clark Air Force Base. When we tried to get a flight out of Tachikawa Air Force Base, the Air Force sergeant at the desk told us the "no-cost" orders we had were worse than no orders at all, so he threw away our orders and told us to say we had lost them. He got us on the next plane out. When we got back to Subic, UDT-11 had started moving their gear into our spaces. I looked for the negatives that I had stored in a filing cabinet in the office, and couldn't find them. Nobody seemed to know what happened to them. All the black-and-white photographs I'd shot during my tour were gone. I had only a couple dozen 8" by 10" prints to show for all that work. I was upset and to this day wonder who took them. I expect to see them in print some day. Then I will know who the culprit is. Also my sport parachute rig had been stolen. It was a Para-Commander in a crossbow piggyback rig. The reserve chute was tri-conical, of a special design. I didn't have the serial numbers, but knew I could get them from Hugh Bergeron, who owned the West Point, Virginia dealership where I bought the rig. I think the parachute theft pissed me off as much as the theft of my negatives. But, right now I would give about ten of those parachutes to get my negatives back.

We drank our way back to the States, by way of Naval Aviation. When we got off the plane in San Francisco at the Air Force Base, some of us didn't want to screw around waiting for a military flight, so we hired a cab and headed for the PSA (Pacific Southwest Airlines) terminal at San Francisco Airport. We'd changed into civilian clothes by now and had bought tickets for San Diego. Most of us had rings in our ears and didn't look too military, so we didn't catch any garbage from the anti-war types. When we arrived landed in San Diego, I called my friend, Tom Hummer. He came out to pick me up in his Jaguar and drove me back to South Mission Beach. I took a shower, changed clothes and walked down to the Beachcomber, my favorite hangout in those days. I walked in and sat down at the bar. One of the guys there, whom I knew, looked over at me and said, "Hi Steve, ain't seen you around for a while, where you been?"

"Vietnam," I answered.

"Well, Jesus Christ! Welcome home! Let me buy you a beer."

The first publication of **Just a Sailor** contained fifty-five photographs. This publication has eighty photos, twenty-eight of which were in the first publication. Some of the photos in this publication of **Just a Sailor** are being published for the first time ever, such as the one of the **Apollo 12** recovery.

Many of the photos in the original publication were from the **Underwater Demolition Team 13: Westpac 1969** cruise book. This cruise book has been recreated and put into circulation by FindTech, Ltd. It is available for purchase at booksellers and at **http://find-tech.biz/udt13**.

Photo credits for photo section head pages:
Civilian Adventures:
Steve Waterman carrying Larry Theorine's MK-V helmet after he and Larry made the first dive on the China Wreck.
Photo by Ray Curraco

Combat Camera:
Steve Waterman photographing a coral head with a Nikon F inside an Ocean Eye housing.
Photo by PHC Richard Johnson

Vietnam:
Steve Waterman getting ready to leave the USS *Cook* for a beach recon mission. It takes a lot of self-discipline to look this hard core.
Photo by Pete "the Pirate" Carolan, UDT-13

Miscellaneous:
Steve Waterman with his two younger sisters, Cheryl and Heather. They were all on active duty at the same time. Cheryl retired from the Naval Reserves as a commander and Steve retired from the Reserves as an E-7. Heather left the service as a lieutenant.
Photo by NAS Norfolk Photo Lab

Unless otherwise noted, all photographs in this book were taken by, and are the copyright of, Steven L. Waterman.

Civilian Adventures

Bay King Salvage 1967

The *Bay King* on the surface ready to be pumped.

Part of the crew that salvaged the tug, *Bay King*, from the ocean floor off Solomons, Maryland. Waterman is front right, "Jitterbug," the skipper of the *Bay King*, is top right.
Photo courtesy Steve Waterman.

The *Bay King*, shown from an in-water vantage point.
It's resting in slings while the crew prepared to
pump it dry and tow it back to Norfolk.

Steve Waterman tending Larry Theorine
on the salvage of the *Bay King*.
Photo by Beldon Little

Right: Beldon goes over some details with Larry Theorine before he makes his first dive on the *Bay King* to rig slings under the vessel in preparation for lifting it to the surface.

Below: Larry is being lowered into the water.

"China Wreck" Salvage 1968

Salvagemaster Beldon Little goes over some of the details of our upcoming salvage of the dishes from the "china wreck" off Lewes, Delaware.

Below: Tending Larry Theorine on the china wreck adventure. Left to right: Unknown, Jerry Smith, Lem Brigman in the background, author. *Photo by Beldon Little*

Author's good friend Bill McLellan at the helm of the schooner *Lister* sailing up the Eastern Seaboard to Lewes, Delaware in hopes of getting rich salvaging china from a sunken wreck

Lem Brigman, co-owner of the Schooner *Lister*, plots our course up the coast to Lewes, Delaware on the ill-fated "china wreck" adventure. Below and below right.

Lister

The schooner *Lister* was built in Lunenburg, Nova Scotia as a swordfish longliner. She was owned by partners Riley Davis (left), now deceased, and Lem Brigman, a retired Navy chief bosn's mate.

Opposite page.
Top: *Lister* at the dock.
Bottom left: the bow of the *Lister* as she heads up the Eastern Seaboard.
Bottom right: Bill McLellan working on the rigging of the *Lister*.

Miscellaneous 1974

Rear Admiral Jim Cobb, USN, Ret., a good friend, and a mentor when it came to sailing seamanship. Through him, Steve acquired enough sea time to get his USCG captain's license. "Cobb was one of the nicest people I have ever met."

Steve's friend, PH2(DV) Ike Johnson of the USN Underwater Photo Team serves up hot chocolate in the galley of a WestSail 32, as Steve skippered it up the Intracoastal Waterway from the boatyard in North Carolina to Hampton, Virginia. Ike was the only one of the crew who didn't lie to Waterman about his qualifications. They only ran aground a couple times, with no damage.

Steve and crew took a new WestSail 32 sailboat up to Virginia from the factory in North Carolina. This is a photo of them running before the wind in the Albemarle Sound.

Ltjg. Timothy L. Jones, UDT-21, was a friend of mine, and had cut an album of songs he wrote. Tim was one hell of a guitar player, but had trouble with his singing. Steveshot this portrait for him (original in color) at the photo lab at NAS Oceana. He paid Waterman with a bottle of expensive Scotch.

The author after landing at the drop zone at West Point, Virginia.
Photo by Mary Waterman

Combat Camera

Dr. Jerry Stachiw (left, getting into the NEMO) was in charge of the NEMO project. Until his retirement from the U.S. Navy in 1994, Dr. Stachiw was the staff scientist for Marine Materials in the Ocean Engineering Division of the Engineering Department at the Naval Ocean Systems Center in San Diego, California He received his undergraduate engineering degree from Oklahoma State University in 1955 and his graduate degree from Pennsylvania State University in 1961. He passed away in 2007.

Most of the Atlantic Fleet Underwater Photo Team posing on the stern of a sunken Navy landing craft off Andros Island, Bahamas.

Right: Waterman in front of NEMO.

Photo by PHC Richard Johnson

Below: This underwater photo of the NEMO was taken at about 500 feet from the Perry Oceanographics submersible, *SHELF DIVER.*

On a project in Andros Island, Bahamas, clockwise from outboard motor: Paul Whitmore, Mitch Wilson, Earl Bullock (now deceased), Gene McCraw (now deceased), Jack Sharpsteen, Dick Johnson, Bob Hasha.

Steve Waterman after making PH3 at NAS Oceana, November 1965.
Official U.S. Navy Photo

Steve Waterman after making PH2, October 1966.
Official U.S. Navy Photo

Left to right: Gary Seibert and Ray Fine (human guinea pigs) have a conversation with Cmdr. Claude Harvey, MC,USN in the chamber during the SHAD (Shallow Habitat Air Dive) at the Naval Submarine Medical Research Lab in Groton, Connecticut in 1974.

Waterman steering the Pegasus 2.
Photo by PH1 (DV) Dave Graver.

Waterman outside of the
Underwater Swimmers' School.
Photo by PHC (DV) Richard Johnson

Going home to NAS Oceana. Pilot Tom Brown turns left over the
coast of Virginia with Charlie Iovino in the back seat as they
head back to base after Steve photographed three of VF-11's
aircraft in flight formation.

Three aircraft of VF-11, The Red Rippers.
These represented different eras of Naval Aviation. Steve shot this
photograph from an F4 Phantom flown by Lt. Flack Logan. An F-6F
low-wing, high-performance fighter is on the left; an F-4 Phantom is
center; and on the upper right is an FF-1 WWI biplane.

RECORD OF COMPLETED FLIGHT TIME
OPNAV FORM 3760-37 (REV. 2-59)

TO: *(Pilot's activity)*					FROM *(A/C Custodian)*							
NAS, OCEANA					FITRON ELEVEN							

Ref: OPNAV INSTRUCTION 3760-8 (Navy Flight Records and Reports Manual)

PILOT *(Name - Last, first, middle)*				RANK		FILE NR.			DESIGNATOR			
WATERMAN, STEVE, L.				PH2		904 28 07						

SIGNATURE *Eleven J. Watermam*   I certify that I was in a duty status during the flight recorded below.

DATE	MODEL A/C	A/C BUNO	CODE	TOTAL PILOT TIME	FLIGHT TIME AS				INSTRUMENT		NVFR	LDG	INSTRUMENT APPROACHES
					FP	CP	DP	SC	DAY	NIGHT			
2/21/67	F4B	153068	1A1					0.7					

REMARKS

I certify that while under competent orders to duty in a flying status involving operational or training flights and while
in a duty status the above named individual performed the flights as indicated and that a record of these flights has been
or will be made in the permanent records of this activity.

NAME, RANK, TITLE *(Type or print)*   SIGNATURE
   G.F. LOGAN, LT, USN

Opposite bottom: The only record of Steve having flown in the F4 Phantom with Lt. Carl Flack Logan, USN (pictured with the Steve above). Fighter pilots usually choose a call sign, so people were surprised that Flack was his given middle name.
He become the skipper of an aircraft carrier later in his career. Flack was on board the USS *Forrestal* when it caught fire.

Vietnam

A typical day doing beach recons on the coast of Vietnam.

Some of the boys fooling around at the UDT compound.
Left to right: Marvin Dukes, Bob Barton, Bill Pozzi, (the car is Pozzi's),
Steve Waterman, Al Starr, Phil Czerwiec, and Pete "the Pirate" Carolan.
Photo by Lt. George Green

HMC "Doc" Algeo of UDT-13 makes his way across a small stream in South Vietnam as the men move forward on a Search and Destroy mission.

"This is a booby trap made of U.S. 81mm mortar round. If this area hadn't been defoliated, we may have tripped it, which would have turned some of us into hamburger. That's my half-sock of C-3 set to detonate this booby-trapped round."

Lt. Bruce Dyer was our platoon leader at detachment Golf on the Ca Mau Peninsula. He let the men who knew the area best call the shots. That's leadership. The Teams lost fewer men that way. War is no place for ego trips.

The USS *Tunny* "hangar," which had been used to house the Regulus Missile, a forerunner of the Polaris.

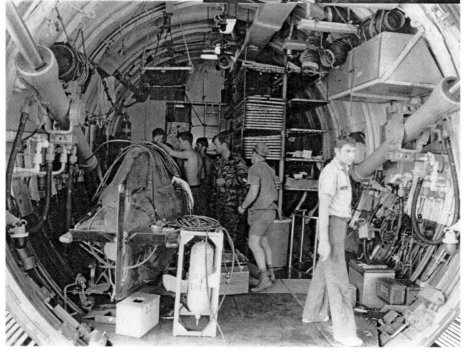

Some of the team after getting shot off a beach. Steve's rifle blew up because of seawater in the buffer spring housing. Left to right: Lt. Paul Plumb, Tobacco Lewis, and Daniel "Micky" Holland.

After Steve was upended by the surf and lost his hat, Lew grabbed it and put it on. The next wave knocked them down again. Lew was hanging onto his rifle with his left hand and Steve's hat with his right. It was funny afterward.

Waterman crossing a small canal somewhere on the Ca Mau Peninsula of Vietnam.
Photo by Bob Lewis, UDT-21 (With Steve's camera. Bob carried an M-60 machine gun.)

Waterman, "My ass was dragging this day. We were out in the swamp tracking down some VC who probably heard us coming a mile away. We found nothing but water jugs, ammo crates, a calendar on the wall of one of the hootches, and footprints in the mud. "
Photo by Doc Algeo

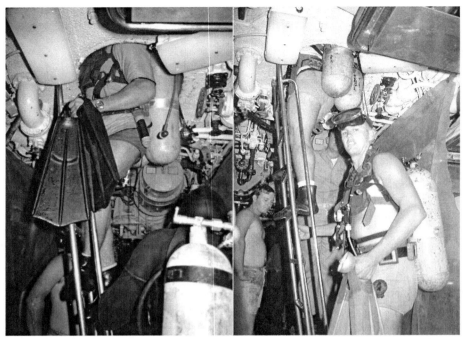

Locking out of the forward escape trunk of the USS *Tunny*.

Waterman getting ready to enter the lockout. "This was no place for a person who could even spell claustrophobia. Two of us had to squeeze into that small, steel chamber with our double scuba tanks and fins. You almost had to take turns inhaling." *Photo by Larry Whitehead, UDT-21.*

HMC Algeo with water casks after UDT-13 destroyed them.

"On our way to the drop zone at Castillejos, Philippines for a routine admin parachute jump to maintain qualifications. We were riding in a Navy amphibious aircraft in this photo. We jumped out of whatever aircraft we could. Clockwise, starting on left: Pete Upton, Mole, ETC Burger, SN Nichols, ET3 Larsen, Lcdr. Jim Wilson (our skipper), and PR1 Al Flud (now deceased)."

RDC Mel Hardman of UDT-13 indicating insertion point for landing beach recon team. Left to right: Airman Mark Buland, UDT-13; RDC Mel Hardman, UDT-13; USS Cook Crewmember; Lt. Paul Plumb, UDT-13; MR1 Charlie (Tobacco) Lewis, UDT-13; Ltjg. Ernie Jahncke, UDT-13; USS Cook Crewmember.

Mouse was the wife of a Vietnamese officer. She cooked (poorly) and did the laundry for the boys at the Danang detachment.

LDNN (Vietnamese frogman) Von. He was working with Moki Martin, Tim Wettack, Dwight Daigle, and some other SEALs from SEAL Team One down in the Ca Mau Peninsula. This was taken on board the USS *Terrell County* about a week before Von was killed in action.

Photo from collection of Steve Waterman.

Fate plays tricks on all of us. Here, Doc Worthington gives Mike Sandlin an inoculation. Within a couple months Doc would be dead and Mike would be recovering from a serious gunshot wound to the thigh. Both were hit on the same operation.

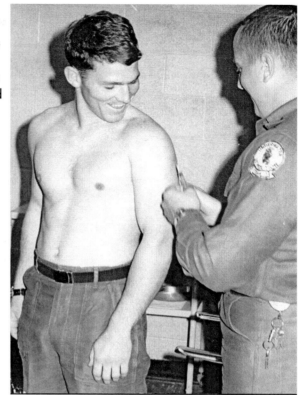

A typical day of non-operation on board the USS *Cook* off the coast of Vietnam.

Award ceremony for UDT-13, January 1970. Left to right: John Lowry, John Campbell, Robbie Robertson, Steve Nash, Mike Sandlin, Pat Broderick, Randy Piper, Bill Morterud, and Steve Waterman.
Photo by SMC Lou Boyles, NSWG

Here, the admiral presented Waterman with the only personal medal he received in Vietnam: the Navy Achievement Medal with Combat Distinguishing Device for Outstanding Combat Photography.
Photo by SMC Lou Boyles

The author on liberty
in Hong Kong.
Photo by BM3 Dan Sager.

Below, one of the many
cartoons drawn by frogman
Pete "the Pirate" Carolan
(*PatriotSEAL.com*).
Pete helped illustrate the
**Underwater Demolition
Team 13 Cruise Book:
Wespac 1969.**
(*reproduction available from
http://find-tech.biz/udt13).

Deep Sea Diver

by *Steven L. Waterman*

I could have been happy above
If I'd never donned
The cumbersome copper carapace
And dipped my head beneath the waves
To hear the muddled
Man-made sounds

Distorted
And dreamlike droning
The whir and thrash
Of a distant propeller,
The tumultuous thundering thud
Of fogbound freighters.

Mud underfoot,
No sights,
Except the grasp of a diver's trained hand,

Dreaming of distant lands and sunny places
Knowing all the while this is what I love
Not the blue skies and wondering faces
above.

Canvas, rubber, brass, copper and glass,
Leather and lead,
Mud and sweat,
Heaving around in dark damp depths
Seldom seen by most
Yet talked about by all.

As if a sunny, happy place
Where mermaids and seahorses play
And chests of gold are lain bare
Untarnished by salt and time
For all to grasp who are bold enough
To go below...

Copyright Steve Waterman © 1973

187

A slug of compressed air is shot out of a torpedo tube on Gould Island off Newport, Rhode Island as part of torpedo exploder testing.

This may be the only photo ever taken of Steve in a Mark V Diving Rig.
He wasn't a Navy diver when this photo was taken by Bill McLellan at his dive shop in Virginia Beach using Steve's camera after Bill rigged him up.
Photo by Bill McLellan

Commander Gerry Pulley, USN. Gerry believed in Steve, which gave him the courage to become a Navy diver, and subsequently a member of the Combat Camera Group's Underwater Photo Team.
Official U.S. Navy Photo

Al Schnoebelen and Helen (Mouse) behind the counter at Al's Surf Shop, 19th and Atlantic, Virginia Beach, Virginia. (1966)

Maritime Explorations, Ltd., Bill McLellan's dive shop.   Al's Surf Shop.

The crew at the NAS Ocean Photo Lab in 1966. Left to right: Charlie Famuliner, Steve Waterman, Jim Kerr, Joe Leo, Don Marks, Steve Rock (kneeling), Ray Mauldin, Valentine, Ray Robeson.
Photographer unknown.

The class at Naval School, Deep Sea Divers, Washington Navy Yard, summer 1975. Left to right, front to back: Lt. Duignan, Training Officer, Lcdr. Tony Esau, Commanding Officer, HT2 Turok, Klobertanz, Alley, Powell, unknown, Mills, Barefoot, Gauthier, Hill (Steve's swim buddy), unknown, unknown, PH1 Steve Waterman. *Official U.S. Navy Photo*

Barracks #602 NAS Pensacola, Florida.
Steve's first home-away-from-home after boot camp in 1964.

Waterman's graduation class from Naval Technical Training Unit (NATTU),
Pensacola, Florida 1965. The class included Marines, Coast Guard, and
Navy. (Steve is third from the left in the front row.)
Official U.S. Navy Photo

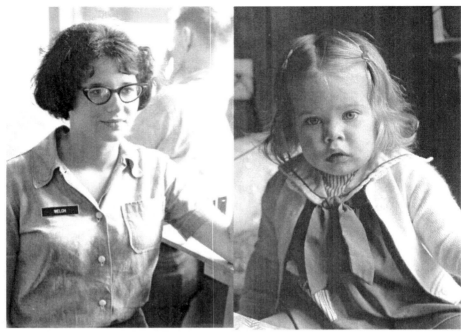

Photographer's Mate Airman Apprentice Linda Welch was one of the cutest Waves in the class at photo school.

Steve's daughter, Emily Olga Waterman, at eighteen months. Today, she is married to a Navy man and has three children of her own.

Steve's younger sister, Heather Waterman (center) is taking the oath of enlistment into the Navy as an officer candidate as elder sister, Ensign Cheryl Waterman—still in her internship at Peter Bent Brigham Hospital—administers the oath, and Steve documents the occasion.

Photo by Mary Waterman

"Mary Jewett Waterman, née Ware, my wife of thirty-three years, was the main inspiration for my writing this book. She fought three battles with cancer. The third one was almost a tie. Mary passed away at home at 0600 on January 17, 2006, with her family by her side. I scattered her ashes over our property on Criehaven Island from an airplane. Criehaven is about twenty miles offshore from our home in South Thomaston, Maine."

Lcdr. Joe Heinlein, skipper of UDT-21 was a great guy. No one ever figured out how he became a frogman. He's the man who trained Steve for freefall parachuting at the Tidewater Navy Skydivers at NAS Oceana. Joe's twin brother was a Catholic priest.

Ltjg. Robbie Robertson, ST2 Steve Nash, Bill Pozzi, and Pete "the Pirate" Carolan were on this mission when UDT-13 was tasked to be the recovery team for Apollo 12.
Photo by PH3 Bill Pozzi

Chapter 15

Back in the States, San Diego

When we arrived back in the States, some of the new guys who had gone to Vietnam with us and some of the men who were just reporting to the Teams out of training had to get jump-qualified. There were men from UDT-13, UDT-12, and SEAL Team 1. Lcdr. Wilson, our skipper, told me I could go to Fort Benning with them and attend Basic Airborne Training, often referred to as "Navy Appreciation School."

We were given commercial airline tickets and flew to Georgia in our civilian clothes. An ex-enlisted lieutenant, junior grade by the name of Jim Dentice of UDT-11 was in charge of our detachment.

We checked in and received the same lecture the skipper had given us before we left: we were guests of the Army and they would not put up with any crap from the Navy, Marines, Air Force, or even the Coast Guard if any of them were present. The chow was awful and the instructors, although quite professional, were pretty much on the numb side. The officers didn't have to do anything except show up for class. They stood no duty that I knew of. Before long, all the Army E-6s had quit or dropped out for some medical reason and I became the company first sergeant. I didn't have a clue what a first sergeant was. All they told me was that I was in charge of my company—half the class. There were 640 men (no women in those days) in the class. The first day I was in charge, the instructor, SFC Nunez, told us there would be a police call. We had to pick up all the cigarette butts between the parade grounds and the PX. Being the fair-minded individual I am, I decided that anybody who didn't smoke shouldn't have to pick up cigarette butts. I told the men who wanted a cigarette before we began to fall out. When they did so, I told the remaining guys to go back and shine their boots and work on getting their uniforms squared away. I was chastised for this as it was not the Army way of doing things. I was advised that everybody goes to police call!

During the runs sometimes, the guys from the Teams would fall out and run around the Army formation as they ran along the road. On hot days, this could be a real bitch, but we tried not to show it.

Al Starr[†] and I had a private room together. Fresh out of training and a former fleet sailor, Al was a second class storekeeper from Team 13. Starr woke me one night and told me that a lieutenant was giving someone in our barracks some shit. I jumped out of my rack, put on a pair of pants and walked out into the squad bay to confront Army Second Lieutenant Fox, who was chewing out one of the men. Most of the soldiers in this barracks were Army reservist parachute riggers who were required to go through jump school to fully appreciate the importance of what they were doing. Most of them had college degrees, and they were about as squared away as any Army types I have met. The man who was the brunt of the lieutenant's harassment had a master's degree and owned a chain of barbershops with his father. He flew his own personal plane to attend jump school, and he was a sharp troop. To make a long story short, on inspecting the barracks after taps, the lieutenant had found a man in the latrine, polishing his boots, and was chewing him out for not being in his bunk after lights-out.

I lost it. I told Lt. Fox that the Army had put me in charge of this barracks. The men in it were my responsibility and I expected to be notified before anybody talked to them. Any future infractions of this rule would result in me or my men physically throwing the son-of-a-bitch out of the building. Fox looked at me in disbelief and left. The men who had been awakened by the sound of loud voices slowly made their way back to their bunks, shaking their heads in that "Oh, shit!" manner.

"Damn," I thought, "I'll get it in the morning."

I figured they would probably throw me out of jump school. The skipper of Team 13, Jim Wilson, had told us that anybody who got dropped from jump school, for any reason other than physical injury, would be back in the fleet as soon as he could cut the orders.

The next morning at formation, Lieutenant Fox came up to me, took me aside, and quietly apologized for coming into the barracks without checking with me first. He said he had been out of line and shook my

† Al Starr retired from SEAL Team as a Master Chief

hand. I told him no problem and that I shouldn't have jumped in his shit so hard. I humbly accepted his apology, we saluted, and parted amiably.

One of the soldiers who was on light duty and worked in the office at Spec Four had been injured playing touch football. He ran messages and drove the instructors around. He seemed like a decent fellow. We became buddies after a while. One night, he asked me if I had any civilian clothes. I told him I did. He invited me to go into town to some joint that had a band. I knew it was against the regulations for students to go off base, or even be seen in civilian clothes. For about ten seconds, I hesitated.

"How will we get there?" I asked.

"I've got a car," he replied.

"Well, as long as we don't get into any trouble, I can handle it," was my response. I went back to the barracks and slipped into Levi's, a shirt, and a pair of shoes. When we walked to the parking lot, I saw that the kid drove a brand new Corvette.

"Where in hell did you get this?" I asked.

"Bought it," he replied.

"Jesus. Are you a rich guy?"

"Well, my dad gave me the American Music Corporation for my twenty-first birthday and told me not to piss it away."

"What in hell are you doing in the Army?" I asked.

"I thought I should serve, like everybody else," he said. "I got fed up with those chickenshit assholes running away to Canada and the like. Besides, I always wanted to be a paratrooper."

We ended up in some redneck, shit-kicking place in Alabama. I was dancing with a reasonably good-looking woman and my ride was with another one. I noticed a man watching us. I asked my dance partner who the guy was. She said it was her husband, that he was the jealous type. The Spec Four and I left shortly after that and drove back to the base. The way he drove scared the shit out of me because we were doing one hundred miles per hour at times. After that, I decided to stick to jumping out of airplanes. It was safer.

While attending jump school, I only went on liberty one other time. Lieutenant Dentice and all the guys from the Teams went to a bar in Alabama. We were drinking beer and trying not to draw fire from the indigenous population. Before long, the cops came in and dragged a woman out in handcuffs. I asked the waitress what it was all about. She said the woman shot her husband. We left shortly thereafter and took cabs back to the base.

The class graduated from jump school en masse. We had to sit in a very hot auditorium—the air conditioning must have been broken—and one of the instructors handed us a cigar box full of jump wings. We passed it up and down the rows and each took one, some of us took two. Then they drove the Navy guys to the airport and we flew back to San Diego.

Almost as soon as we arrived, we received orders to go to Hawaii for surf training and to train in the submarine escape tank. I really didn't want to go as I figured it would be a classic clusterfuck. After three false starts, we were on a four-engine prop job for Hawaii. We landed at Barber's Point Naval Air Station and soon were ensconced in the barracks at Pearl Harbor Naval Base. It was hot. We had to go to Sunset Beach and "train" in the surf. That meant body surfing and learning how to handle the big waves. I wasn't interested in this. All I wanted to do was chase women, but most of the women were already being chased and, for the most part, they didn't like sailors.

The best part of the trip was working in the submarine escape tank. It is one hundred feet deep with locks at the bottom and at various depths along the sides. Submarine sailors are trained to make free and buoyant ascents from it. Sailors are put into the locks, which are then pressurized. One at a time, the men are released to go to the surface. Instructors stationed at various depths up the inside of the tank insure that the students didn't hold their breath, which could result in an air embolism.

We had to prove how hard-assed we were, of course, by making a free dive to the bottom of the tank. We tied our sneakers together and threw them into the tank. When they hit the bottom, we would grab the cable pull ourselves all the way down to the bottom. The goal was to grab your sneakers and have them on by the time you reached the surface. I made it to the bottom and succeeded in getting my sneakers, but the knot stuck where I had them tied to together. I damn near blew out my sinuses trying to untie the knot, and didn't get them on. My mask was half-full of blood when I got out of the water. So much for that trick. Only about twenty of us made it to the bottom. Most of the men thought it was a dumb idea to do it and didn't bother to try.

When I got back from Hawaii, I started hanging out more and more in the photo lab. Officially, it was known as the Naval Special Warfare Photographic Laboratory. Those of us who hung out there, SMC Lou Boyles, a SEAL, and PH2 Charlie Renaud, an admin type, and myself used it almost strictly for cumshaw. Now to the uninitiated, cumshaw is just another word for grand theft, but in the Navy cumshaw is frequently the only way to get things you need to do your job. But not always. It's an informal system of barter, exchange, and deception. The word "cumshaw" is what sailors called beach time in Hong Kong. They thought it was a Chinese word, and few knew it was a slurred contraction that native hawkers once yelled to entice sailors into their dice, girl, and opium action, "Come ashore."

As I was not "ship's company" in the lab, Lou asked me if I'd shoot the photo for the annual SPECWAR Photo Lab Christmas card. He said we needed a couple of weapons and sent me to the SEAL Team armory to check some out. At the armory, the chief in charge gave me an AK-47, a grease gun, and a Swedish K with a silencer attached. I got back and showed them to Lou. I asked him about the Swedish K; I thought silencers were against the Geneva Convention or some shit like that. His eyebrows jumped a little and I took the "K" back to the armory.

There was a small, oriental-looking guy working at the lab who would pose as the captured Viet Cong for the Christmas card. I shot the picture and we printed up a bunch of them. They were mailed throughout the Navy to all the photo labs, to our friends, and to other members of the SPECWAR community.

Underwater Demolition Team-13 was selected to be on the recovery team for Apollo-12. PH3 Bill Pozzi, one of the guys I had trained to become a photographer, was going along. He came and asked me if he could borrow a Nikonos to take along as he would be jumping into the water and helping the astronauts out of the capsule and then assisting them into the sling for the lift to the helicopter. I told him I would let him have a Nikonos and all the film he wanted, but I wanted first choice of his best shot. I would get to keep the original and I would give him the rest. He kept his word. When he came back he told me they had confiscated all his film except the first roll he shot and he gave that to me. I processed it and have, to this day, the slide. It was a shot that had all the astronauts, the capsule, the recovery helicopter and the ship they would be flown to all in the same shot. Great photo, never been published.†

In southern California, the teams made all their land parachute jumps at Roll's Farm Drop Zone south of San Diego near the Mexican Border. I made a couple of night jumps there. During one of the Boy Scout demonstrations, I made two water jumps into San Diego Bay.

† This photograph is on the last page of the photo section in this book, being published for the first time.

That was about the most fun you could have parachuting. I heard that the Boy Scouts loved it. After we hit the water and were recovered by the boats, we went back and washed the salt water out of our chutes and hung them up to dry. Then we all hit the beach for some cold beer.

When I arrived back in the States, I had bought a Honda 350 motorcycle from Lt. Jahncke, who needed the money for a car. The bike had only a couple thousand miles on it. I think I paid five hundred dollars for it. I made a trip on this bike through Big Sur and almost up to San Francisco. I shot several rolls of color film and made some good photographs. While traveling through Santa Barbara, someone took a shot at me. I wouldn't have recognized what it was had I not previously experienced it. I was zipping down the road and heard the shot snap by and then heard the snap of the rifle. It only happened once, but it was enough. I don't have a clue why or who it was. I just kept going.

When I returned to my apartment, two new kids from Team 13 were walking down the stairs from my door. I asked them what they wanted.

"Master Chief Walsh, the command master chief, sent us to tell you that you have Shore Patrol Duty in San Diego." I went back to Coronado and checked in early off leave. I went and talked to BMCM George Walsh about it. He told me that they needed a first class petty officer to stand Shore Patrol. It was a rotating thing and we had to take our turn. No problem, I told him, happy to do it. This would be for thirty days and I wouldn't have to pay tolls to cross the Coronado Bay Bridge any more. I knew Master Chief Walsh was a real operator. He had been one of the frogmen in the old days and was a friend of Roy Boehm, who started the SEALs, and Hoot Andrews, an original SEAL. Some of these "old" guys had gone into Cuba with closed circuit rigs from a submarine. It was not one of your average swims. I figured if George Walsh wanted me to do this, then I would gladly do it, no questions asked.

I went into the office, picked up my orders and jumped on my bike— I had traded my Honda to QM2 Bill Jakubowski of UDT-13 for a Triumph 650 Bonneville—and headed to the Shore Patrol Station in downtown San Diego. I checked in with a chief by the name of Sims.

"Jesus, they sent us a first class," he stated.

"They told me that's what you guys requested," I answered.

"Hell, all we ever ask for is a petty officer over twenty-one. They must have felt they didn't need you around that badly."

I began to see the handwriting on the wall and knew my time with peacetime Special Warfare was going to be short-lived.

200

Chief Sims was on light duty, recovering from surgery after he shot himself in the shoulder with a shotgun while drunk. Sims took me in to introduce me to the shore patrol officer. He turned out to be a Marine captain named Dave Hamilton, with whom I had spent many a night drinking beer at the Beachcomber. I hadn't known what he did for a living. He recognized me and stood up, shook my hand, and told me to have a seat. He advised me that this was really a tit job and there was not much to it. I should consider it almost like a vacation. I would be assigned to booking. My job would be to lock up military personnel who were brought in and insure they were not in need of medical attention. Also I was responsible for making sure they didn't have weapons on them and the like. Not too hard.

A week after I checked in at San Diego Shore Patrol Headquarters, I came through the front door and spotted a young Marine first lieutenant sitting on the bench where people wait to see someone at SP headquarters. I took a quick squint at the ribbons he was wearing. He had three rows, but the one that stood out was the light blue one on top with five white stars—the Medal of Honor. I had never seen one of those on anybody before. I walked into Dave Hamilton's office and told him about it. He came out and walked over to the lieutenant.

"Hello, I'm Captain Hamilton, the Shore Patrol Officer," he stated as he offered his hand.

The lieutenant stood up and shook his hand and introduced himself.

"What can I do for you, Lieutenant?" asked Dave.

"I just got out of Balboa Naval Hospital—I was wounded—and I'm on light duty for thirty days, so they sent me here to work with you on Shore Patrol until I go back to my unit."

"That's the Medal of Honor, isn't it?" queried Dave, knowing that it was.

"Yes, sir."

"Where is your home?"

"I live up the coast a little, this side of L. A.," the lieutenant answered.

"Tell you what, Lieutenant. No Medal of Honor recipient is going to be working Shore Patrol while I'm in charge here. You go home and give me a call once a week and let me know how you're enjoying your vacation. I'll see you in thirty days."

I was really impressed that Dave would do something like that, being a gung ho Marine. He definitely garnered my respect.

My job there wasn't too rough. Sometimes staying awake was the hardest part. The biggest crime most of these kids committed was drinking underage. The San Diego Police Department Vice Squad brought in several of them every night. Usually there was no problem. We explained to the sailors that the police were doing a courtesy to turn them over to us; that the they didn't have to do it. One night, the cops brought us a real asshole, handcuffed. He had been in a fight and was quite belligerent. The cop who arrested him was a decent guy, about forty years old. When he took off the cuffs, the sailor took a swing at him. One of our guys grabbed him. I looked at the cop and shrugged. The SP chief said, "You can have him. He just fucked up. Now you can get him for assault in addition to being drunk underage."

Another time, a guy came in with a cut on his lip from being in a fight. When the corpsman asked him if he would like to have the cut looked at, the guy spit a mouthful of blood all over the corpsman's white uniform. This irritated me. I went into the cellblock and open the cell door. I asked the guy if he'd spat on the corpsman.

"Yeah, what the fuck's it to ya?" he snarled.

"Well, I'll tell you what, pal. Nobody spits on a corpsman on my watch. He's just trying to help you. You can either come out here, or I'm coming in there after you, asshole!"

The guy gave me that "fuck you" look. I walked in and dropped him with one punch. I made sure he was still breathing and left the cell. The next day, when I showed up for watch, Captain Hamilton wanted to see me.

"Some guy we had locked up last night claims you hit him."

I'm sure Dave was expecting a story about how the guy must have slipped and fallen and hit his face against the bars. Not this time.

"Goddamn right I hit him, sir," I related. "The cocksucker spit on the corpsman when he went to look at a cut on the man's mouth. I knocked the prick on his ass."

"Well, his division officer is coming here with him to lodge a complaint against us for that. Are you sure that's how you want to leave it?'

"Yes, sir. That's what happened and I'd do it again."

A couple of hours later, a mamby-pamby lieutenant in khakis and thick glasses drove up in a gray Navy-issue pickup truck, parked out front, and he and the sailor whom I had punched walked in. Captain Hamilton sent for me. I walked to the door of his office, knocked, and was invited in.

"Petty Officer Waterman, this lieutenant is from the USS Whatever. He is Seaman Dipshit's division officer. Seaman Dipshit claims somebody who fits your description punched him in the face. Do you know anything about this incident?"

I started, "Yes, sir. I knocked the son of a bitch on his ass last night."

I could see the lieutenant's eyes light up a little. He was thinking. "Ah, I'm gonna get these fucking Shore Patrol assholes now."

"Petty Officer Waterman, please tell the lieutenant why you hit Seaman Dipshit?" asked Hamilton.

"Well, sir, I just got back from Vietnam. I served with Underwater Demolition Team 13. One of the things we did when I was with the Teams is treat medical personnel with respect. After all, sir, they were sometimes the only thing between us and one of those sleeveless gowns made of waterproof fabric we all know as body bags. Anyway, sir, this guy spit on the duty corpsman when he went to him to offer medical aid. Something just snapped, Sir. I had to hit the bastard."

By now the sailor tried to crawl into the top of his jumper.

The lieutenant glared at him. "Did you spit on the corpsman?" he yelled.

"Well, er, ah, yes, sir," he answered sheepishly.

"Get your sorry ass out to the truck. You're goddamn lucky it wasn't me here last night when you pulled that shit. Captain Hamilton, Petty Officer Waterman, I'm sorry to have wasted your time. You men keep up the good work. I don't think you'll see Seaman Dipshit in here any more."

That was the end of that.

Another time, a young kid about eighteen years old was brought in by the vice squad. The kid was very drunk. He was about six-foot three and probably weighed two-hundred-fifty pounds. From looking at him, it appeared he was most likely one hundred percent American Indian. The vice cops were really treating him like shit. When we took the kid's things from him—wallet, cigarettes, etc.—he went apeshit. One of the vice cops jumped on his back and choked him until he passed out. While he was unconscious, they put handcuffs on him. When he came to, I explained to him that we were going to put all his things in an envelope and seal it. He would sign across the back of the seal and when he got out, he would get all his property back. He couldn't seem to grasp this concept. There was a picture of his little kid in there and he was upset that we weren't going to let him have that. He must have thought he would not get it back. This kid was really drunk! I couldn't understand why that would be a problem and planned to give it to him when these vice cop assholes left. In the meantime, we put him in a cell and took off the handcuffs. He settled down on the bunk and went to sleep. The vice cops filled out the release forms and left. Once outside, one of them stood up on a plastic milk crate and sprayed Mace on this kid through the bars of the cell window. I was put off by that, and it gave me a bit of an attitude about San Diego vice squad cops.

A day or so after I returned to UDT-13, another challenge came along. After PT one morning, BMCM George Walsh informed Seaman Dudley and me that we had a mission. He told us that an organization such as the Black Panthers, or a bunch of radical bikers, might try to steal explosives from military magazines. The Teams needed a couple of us to "volunteer" to go to Miramar Naval Air Station where we kept all our explosives and make sure they were well-guarded.

"No problem, Chief. What do we draw for weapons?"

I thought they would give us M-16s.

"Go see the chief in the armory and draw a .38 and a box of ammo."

"You gotta be shitting me, Master Chief. I'm supposed to guard a fucking magazine full of TNT and C-4 against some radical group of crazed biker assholes, and you're sending me up there armed with a little pissant .38?"

"We can't be sending you down the road in a civilian vehicle carrying a fully automatic weapon. Besides, Dudley hasn't been in combat, so I am just having one weapon issued."

That made sense. Seaman Dudley and I jumped on my Harley with our sleeping bags tied on the back and the .38 stuck in my belt, and went to Miramar to guard the magazine. I hid my Harley, which I'd traded my Triumph for, in a building in the same area as the magazine. Dudley and I crawled under another building that overlooked the magazine. We thought we would just lie there and "gather intelligence" if they broke through. There was no fucking way I was going to launch an offensive with the two of us and one beat up Smith & Wesson thirty-eight. Fortunately, nothing happened. This assignment only lasted two days. The base security rigged up an alarm on the magazine to replace us.

I was barely back at the Teams a week when Master Chief Walsh† told me I would be the new barracks master-at-arms. My job was to maintain law and order in the UDT barracks on the base. This was the straw that was putting a hell of a strain on the camel's back. I asked him if I had "Fuck me" stenciled on my forehead or what. He told me that I wasn't a UDT operator and therefore was expendable as far as they were concerned. These jobs really weren't considered shit details as they were almost work-free and had no adverse effects on my record. I could still jump and dive with the Teams and was still drawing my diving pay.

† Master Chief Walsh died of cancer a few years ago.

Nevertheless, I didn't like it. I think MC Walsh was under orders to coerce me into requesting UDT training. I went out and ran the obstacle course one day. I didn't see how the hell those guys did it so fast. I talked to one or two of the guys and asked them if they had that much trouble running it. They just laughed and said some of them could barely do it when they started training. I didn't feel like such a pussy.

During the latter part of February 1970, a woman moved into the apartment two doors down from me in South Mission Beach. Her name was Rosalyn Clausen.[†] I helped her carry some of the heavy items up the stairs to her apartment. She lived there by herself and worked someplace in San Diego. She invited me in for a cup of coffee—the only time I drank it was for an excuse to talk to a woman—and said she wanted to introduce me to her daughter. A few days later, I met her daughter, Judy. We started hanging out together and jumping one another's bones with increasing frequency. It got serious when she started taking birth controls pills. I asked her to marry me. I had jumped out of airplanes, locked out of submarines, been shot at, and I felt that now it was time to do something really dangerous. She, of course, accepted. A few nights later, I got shit-faced and called Mary, my old girlfriend from back home. I asked her to come out to San Diego. She said she couldn't right then. I took that to mean she had other plans. Judy and I went to Fairhaven, California to one of those instant marriage operations and got married on March 21, 1970. A civilian friend of mine lent me his Corvette for the occasion. On the way back, I got a ticket for speeding and the vehicle turned out to be unregistered. I should have taken that as a portent of things to come.

I had requested a transfer back to Combat Camera Group and it went through. I would be going back to the East Coast in April 1970.

In March, UDT-11 returned from their six-month WESPAC Tour. One of the men in the team, PH2 Terry Muehlenback, told me he knew who stole my parachute. I didn't even think about asking about my negatives. He told me a parachute rigger by the name of PR2 Craig had done it. I went to SMC Lou Boyles, who ran the photo lab at Special Warfare Group, and asked him for advice on how to handle it. He told me to see Lieutenant Commander Bell, the CO of UDT-11, and tell him the situation. I went to PHCM Gene Gagliardi who ran the parachute loft and told him about it. He said he would impound Craig's gear when it came back in the Conex box with his other things. Meanwhile,

† Rodie killed herself a few years later. She had terminal cancer.

Lieutenant Commander Ron Bell talked to Craig and tried to get him to admit he stole my things. He said he didn't do it.

When the gear came back from overseas, Master Chief Gagliardi impounded it and I got the serial number off the canopy of the Paracommander. Then I called Pioneer Parachute Company in New Jersey and asked them to run the number. The person I talked to said that it was a bogus number as they had never issued that one. When confronted by this information, Craig broke down and admitted that he had stolen my gear. I asked him where the piggyback rig and the reserve chute were. He said he had the reserve at home and that the piggyback rig had been burned. I tried to get Bell to put it to this guy hard, but he gave me a song and dance about how courts martial take a long time and we might not even get a conviction. Bell asked what my second choice would be. I told him that I'd like it if I got all my gear back, got all Craig's gear, and Craig was transferred so that he never serve with Naval Special Warfare again. Bell said he could do that. I recovered my canopy, my reserve chute, and some other things that Craig had. I sold all but his reserve chute and my gear. I had a feeling that Bell might be lacking in some areas of leadership, but he was still a lieutenant commander. He didn't show the amount of aggressiveness that many other SEAL officers would have under these conditions. Thievery was not looked upon lightly among Team members. However, he may have had more important things weighing on his mind.

I was ready to head back to the East Coast. I tried to sell my Harley. I even left it outside my apartment hoping somebody would steal it, but no such luck. I arranged to have somebody ship it to me in a crate. That turned out to be a stupid move. A couple of weeks later, I moved out of my apartment and stayed with Judy in hers for a few days before flying to the East Coast. She would follow once I found a place for us to live.

I checked out of the Team and said goodbye to all my friends there. I knew I'd miss operating with these guys. The skipper, Lieutenant Commander Jim Wilson, had offered to send me T.A.D. (temporary additional duty) across the street to training, but being an underwater photographer was looking to be a much better deal than being a peacetime frogman. Most of us realized the war in Vietnam would soon be over, and with us in second place. I told Lieutenant Commander Wilson I appreciated his confidence, but that I had a good deal as an underwater photographer. There were only about fifteen of us in the whole Navy. Besides, my bad eyesight was a well-kept secret. I couldn't pass the physical without my contact lenses. Knowing the amount of time spent in the sand, mud, and water, there would be no chance I could see well enough to function on some of the training evolutions, especially at night. In retrospect, I should have stayed there and made another tour with Team 13, but that is history now.

I went and said goodbye to Judy's mother, Rosalyn, then Judy gave me a ride to the airport and we kissed goodbye. The flight was non-stop to New York. From there, I had to take Allegheny or some other tree-top airline to Norfolk.

Chapter 16

Combat Camera Group Again

Combat Camera Group Again

When I arrived at Norfolk airport, Dick Johnson came out and picked me up. Christ, I was glad to get back to the East Coast. Things seemed more realistic back here.

After I checked in at Combat Camera Group and settled in at Dick's place, I found an apartment on Waco Street in Norfolk. Two brothers named Wright, the Wright Brothers, were developers and had several apartment buildings they had recently completed. I talked to one of them and he said he had a place. He asked me if I had one of those "mixed marriages." I told him that I didn't. Nowadays, he could get into trouble for asking that question. The apartment I rented was on the first floor and close to a large supermarket, the Giant Open Air Market, and only about two miles to work.

Judy flew to Norfolk and we bought a used Coronet 440. As a wedding present, her grandmother had given us the money to buy it. We didn't own it very long before we traded it in for a bright yellow VW Super Beetle. It cost just less than two thousand dollars brand new.

My Harley Sportster hadn't arrived from San Diego. There was a truckers' strike on and no clue when it would end. When the bike finally arrived, it had rust on it and had obviously been sitting on some back lot in storage. I couldn't get the headlight to work without it killing the engine. I took it to a Harley shop in Norfolk and they screwed around and bypassed the light switch so I could at least run the headlight. I tried to get rid of it and finally got some guy to buy it. That Harley was the worst piece of machinery I've ever owned. I know they make them better now, but I still can't get the nasty taste out of my mouth from that experience.

During May1970, Dick Johnson, Bill Curtsinger, Charlie Curtis, and I went to Freeport on Grand Bahama Island. We would be working with the inventor of the Plexiglas dome, Dr. Jerry Stachiw, a Russian engineer. Jerry had developed a method of taking thick sheets of Rohm & Haas Plexiglas cut into pentagons and, with a heating and vacuum process, bending them into a spherical shape that was capable of withstanding much pressure. The Navy had built a sphere out of these plastic pentagons at Southwest Research Institute. A couple of their physicists came up and would be diving this thing to five hundred feet. The Perry Oceanographics submersible and the support vessel, *Shelf Diver*, were on site for support. I talked my way into a dive in the *Shelf Diver*.

The pilot and I sat on the bottom in about five hundred feet of water and waited for the NEMO (Naval Experimental Manned Observatory) to come down beside us. I shot some movie footage and some stills photos of it. I was shooting High Speed Ektachrome out of the forward port in the *Shelf Diver*. The light was very dim and I had to rate the film at four hundred speed and push-process it when I got back. This was my first experience in a small, dry, one-atmosphere submersible, but it would not be my last.

My assigned job was underwater cinematography. Bill Curtsinger would shoot stills underwater and each of the other men on the crew would shoot whatever was required topside. Charlie Curtis[†] was the motion picture guy, and Dick Johnson filmed cut shots with the hand-held 16mm camera.

Whenever possible, topside, I would shoot stills. One of my color photos was used on the cover of *Navy Magazine*. Some of my movie footage was used in the Navy's production of *Eyes Under the Sea*. This was a movie about the Navy's underwater photographers. The script started out as corny as it gets, but by the time we gave it a reality check, it was believable. The writer had beautiful women coming out of the surf with cameras and that sort of thing. We read it with a jaundiced eye and made so much fun of it that Volker "Hasi" Seifert, an optical engineer we were working with from the Naval Photographic Center, told us to go ahead and shoot wild footage with no script and then have one of our editors see what he could do with it. We did, and the editors pulled off a hat trick and made a good documentary of it. I think the scriptwriter was sent to Adak, Alaska.

† Lcdr. Charlie Curtis died of cancer a few years ago.

Much of the footage for the film was shot topside in Norfolk. PH2 Rick Mason and I used my motorcycle with a sidecar to shoot motion picture film of the guys while they ran PT. Some of the other footage was filmed in the diving locker. All together, it was not a bad production and we received some good reviews on it within the military film-making community.

There wasn't much to do in the Bahamas. The food was not gourmet quality, to my palate, except for the Chinese fare at the International Marketplace. The British beer was warm and I couldn't get used to that. Other than the diving, I had no use for the place. Flip Schulke, a civilian, showed up to work with us. He was making a film about the NEMO testing. This sort of thing used to really piss us off. We had the best equipment in the world, but the military heads would assign a civilian with a trust fund or government grant to do a story; or someone who was into "film" would decide they wanted to tell the "true" story of an operation we were on. They, or their crew, would show up with an old Bolex wind-up camera and bum film of us and, without possessing the necessary technical expertise, write about and document what was "really" going on.

My motorcycle at the time was a BMW R-60 with a Steib sidecar, a thing of beauty. I used to ride it to Suffolk when I went parachute jumping. It was silver and the sidecar had red upholstery. Early on, I broke the windshield of the sidecar by trying to bend it too quickly to snap it into place. I went to a plastics shop in Norfolk that specialized in making custom objects out of Plexiglas. Emanuelson was the fellow who owned the shop. I vaguely remembered his name from somewhere, then I recognized his son, Bo. He was one of the kids who had hung out at Al's Surf Shop when I lived in Virginia Beach.

Mr. Emanuelson made the windshield from smoked Plexiglas and it fit perfectly. On one of the first long rides on the bike after that, PH2 Rick Mason and I decided to go out to the backwater area of Virginia Beach and just ride the roads a little. Rick was small and easily fit into the sidecar. We drove for a while and ended up in Pungo, Virginia. Jay Bender lived there in a big house. He was a friend from Virginia Beach who used to own the Steamer, a small restaurant that served steamed corn and hot dogs. We found Jay's driveway. It was a long one that looked like something out of a swamp setting for a Stephen King movie. The house looked as if it was about to fall down. The outside was faded and weatherworn. It was hard to tell if somebody actually lived there.

We rode up the driveway to the front door. As we got closer, I could see that the windows and all the doors were fairly new, they just didn't look it. Jay came to the door and invited us in. I made introductions and we sat and talked for a while. Jay asked if we would like some home-made bourbon.

I looked at Rick. He had a shit-eating grin on his face. I looked back at Jay, who already knew the answer. Jay broke out a mason jar full of clear liquid. First, he gave us a small shot. It was pure moonshine, and of good quality. Then, he put some sugar in a frying pan and caramelized it on the stove. He poured the moonshine into the pan after the sugar had cooled off a bit. He poured this mixture over ice for us. Jesus, that was a smooth drink. Pretty soon, we had quite a buzz going.

Jay asked us if we wanted to go for a boat ride. We said sure. He led us outside to a small, decrepit, unpainted boathouse. We went inside and there was an airboat with a one-hundred-eighty horsepower Lycoming airplane engine. Jay pushed it out of the shed. We hopped aboard as he cranked her up. We spent about an hour zooming through the swamps of backwater Virginia Beach. By the time we returned to Jay's house, the effects of the moonshine were starting to wear off, so Jay gave us a few more shots and some to take with us. Rick and I made it back to Norfolk, but I don't know how.

The anti-war movement was going full blast, and almost every weekend there would be a rally in Washington, D.C. A photo mate friend from Combat Camera Group, PH2 Jim Call, and I decided we would go to D.C. and see if we could get some good photos of the situation. I wore a pair of combat boots and Levis, and Jim dressed similarly. We each carried a couple of Nikon Fs and shot color slides. We found almost every denomination of radical church, and anything else you could imagine. Many of the kids were smoking dope. The religious right was there with Reverend Carl McIntyre, the supposed guru of patriotism. We wandered around hoping for some good photograph opportunities. Someone tried to recruit me into a white supremacist organization called ROWP, Rights of White People, headed by a Marine sergeant in North Carolina. I don't think they had much success with their recruitment.

Jim and I went to D.C. twice. We slept in the car and ate at available hot dog stands. After those two trips, we decided it wasn't a productive way to spend our time and didn't go again.

Later in the summer, Jim and I went to Little Creek and photographed Class 49's UDT/R Hell Week. We made an audiovisual presentation using two projectors with the song, *Raindrops Keep Falling on My Head* as background music. At the graduation party for that class, Jim showed the production to the new frogmen. They loved it.

I was still parachute jumping out at Suffolk occasionally. The first time my new wife, Judy, came out to watch me, I had a bad partial malfunction. I had jumped with a guy named Fred Farrington, who we called Fred Farkel after a character on *Laugh In*, the TV show. We left the aircraft at twelve thousand feet and were going to hook up to do some relative work. I blew the exit and he got away from me, so I decided to just pull high and screw around. I dumped my main at about thirty-five hundred feet, which is a thousand feet higher than the normal parachute opening in sport jumping. As soon as I got the shock, I looked up and saw a ball of colored rags where my Paracommander parachute should have been. My chute was badly tangled. I pulled the steering toggles down and alternated them. Then I pulled on the back risers and tried to shake the thing loose. I looked at where Fred was and noticed I had fallen past him, even though I had opened way above him.

"Oh shit," I thought, "the reserve I have is the one I got from that dickhead, Craig, who stole my parachute in the Philippines.

I wondered if there was even a parachute in the damned pack as I hadn't repacked it since I got it from him. I figured I was going to die either way, so I cut away from my main and opened the reserve. It was a twenty-six-foot conical parachute. However, Craig had cut a modification in it to make it steerable and in doing so, he'd cut to within thirty inches of the apex of the chute. This made me come down like a rock. I knew I was going to hit hard. I could see people running to where I was going to land. All their faces were turned skyward. My legs started to shake as I approached the sun-dried, plowed ground between the runways of Suffolk Airport. I was making maximum effort to make the perfect parachute-landing fall (PLF). I hit in a front left PLF and rolled over so quickly that I actually bounced off the ground. My left shoulder was sore near my shoulder blade, but otherwise I wasn't hurt. As I rose to my feet, I heard somebody exclaim, "Jesus, he got up!" I knew then that I had hit very hard.

Fred landed not far from me a couple of minutes later. He came over and congratulated me on living through a real bastard of a landing. He had seen how fast I was coming down and figured I would at least break a leg.

The fellow that sold me the BMW motorcycle and sidecar told me that he wouldn't sell it to me unless I promised him I would sell it back to him if I wanted to get rid of it. I did so, and he turned around and sold it to get a different bike. I bought Judy an MG Midget. She had always wanted one, and a chief who was getting transferred was selling his. I paid him seven hundred dollars for it and Judy had her sports car. We used the VW whenever both of us needed to go somewhere, as I could get into the MG, but could barely move around in it.

A new guy, PH1 Eugene McCraw,† transferred into the Underwater Photo Team. He was a short, stocky guy who had finagled his way into being a saturation diver while he was stationed at Experimental Diving Unit in D.C. Mac smoked at least one-and-a-half packs a day and was usually last on the runs at PT. Mac could fix anything mechanical and was one hell of a nice guy. He had a way of getting "things" out of people when we deployed together. His wife, Jeannie, was from somewhere in Texas, and she could cook as well as anybody I have ever met. They made one fine pair, both of them real characters.

We were needed in Puerto Rico for another underwater photo job. I don't remember the assignment, but we managed to sneaked Mac's 90cc Honda motorcycle into one of the packing crates. Mac was drunk and he passed out on the plane before we took off. On the way down, he woke up just long enough to drink some more of the vodka and cranberry juice we had in a thermos cooler jug. We all partook of the spirits during the flight.

When we arrived at Puerto Rico, we were put up in some barracks away from the rest of civilization. There was a bowling alley nearby and I went there to make phone calls home and drink beer. I remember the cook made one hell of a good grilled ham and cheese sandwich.

One night, after going to Fajardo and consuming vast quantities of malt beverage, I walked along the road heading for the barracks back gate. The road running to this desolate gate goes through a large cane field. Behind me in the darkness, I saw a single point of light coming my way. Then I realized it was a motorcycle. As he drew closer, I saw it was Mac. He stopped and I got on behind him. I weighed two-hundred-thirty-five pounds and Mac was pushing one-hundred-ninety pounds. Somehow both of us got on the bike. Mac was sitting on the gas tank and I had the back two inches of the seat. There aren't any buddy pegs on a Honda 90, so my heels were on the nuts that held the back wheel on. We were cruising about twenty miles per hour down the paved road and managed to get through the gate and past

† Eugene is now deceased.

the Marine sentry when I noticed a car following us. We had to stop at a stop sign where the road branched off. I waved the car by. The guy didn't move. I waved again. He still didn't move. I jumped off the bike and walked back to the car. There was a lone person in the vehicle.

"What the hell are you doing, goddamn it? Why don't you come around us and get the hell out of here. If I fall off this bike, I don't want some dickhead running over me"

"Watch your language, sailor," he said. "I'm Lieutenant So-and-So and I'm president of the base motorcycle club. I don't want to see anybody get hurt."

"Well, I don't give a flying fuck who you are. You're the only one who's going to get hurt if you don't get the hell out of here right now." He left and I never heard another word about it. Mac and I made it back to the barracks in one piece.

I decided that if I was going to stay in the Navy, I should probably go to Second Class Diver's School, as I eventually wanted to become a diver, first class. One of the prerequisites for first class school is to be a second class diver when you apply for school. The course was at YFNB-17 at Little Creek Amphibious Base. It was ten weeks long and covered every aspect of air diving, salvage theory, and a small amount of demolitions training. I put in a chit and it was approved. There were sixteen of us in the class. A couple of the guys were from SEAL Team 2: Rex Davis and Fred Keener. Rex was a big guy, but was out of shape. Fred was a quiet blonde, and a hell of a good guy. He had been a heavy-duty operator in Vietnam and there are stories about him told to this day. Our class instructor was a Mexican-American by the name of Hernandez. He was a bosun's mate, first class. Others there were Bill Manning and a man by the name of Royce who looked like Howdy Doody. The chief at the school was Ross, a short little prick nobody liked. One day we were going out for PT and I said, "Hey guys, Chief Ross will lead the run and PT today." He looked at me with fire in his eyes. This guy couldn't run if his ass was on fire. After that, because I had poked fun at him in front of the class, he was out to get me. One day, we were swimming underwater in the pool over at Norfolk with scuba gear. We had taken our masks off to practice swimming without them but the pool had recently been chlorinated and our eyes started to really burn and hurt. I felt that there was no need to screw up our eyes for the sake of a stupid drill. I stood up in the pool and told him if he wanted to screw with us, why didn't he just get us out of the pool and make us do flutter kicks or something. He said, "You really like it here don't you Waterman?" I said, "Yeah, Chief, I really fucking love this place."

The next day, they called me into the office and told me I had to quit school or they would shitcan me. I told them they would have to throw me out, as I wouldn't quit under any circumstances. You guessed it. I was gone the next day. Boatswain's Mate Hernandez had been on leave for a family emergency at the time. When he came back, he asked somebody where Waterman was. "He got dropped for having a bad attitude," one of my former classmates said.

"Shit, he was the only one in this whole goddamn class that had the right attitude," Hernandez retorted. I returned to Combat Camera Group and explained what had happened. I told them I would like to go back sometime later and take the course again. Nobody gave me any shit and they said I could when things were right.

In late summer 1970, I went home to Maine and ended up seeing Mary a lot. Her father warned her not to become correspondent in a divorce, and she, of course, took his advice seriously. I had brought my two Nikons and a quantity of Uncle Sam's film, so I spent a week on Graffam Island shooting pictures of an old lobster fisherman I had known as a kid. He and I had some long conversations about life, women, war, and things of that nature. After some time out there, I returned to the mainland and headed back to Norfolk.

A few weeks later, I got a phone call from my old friend, Bill McClellan. It seems Beldon Little, of salvage fame, had another idea how we could make some serious money. Somebody had located an old shipwreck up off the coast of Delaware that was loaded with ironstone china. Beldon did some checking around and thought we could make a few thousand dollars apiece if we went up and cleaned out the wreck and sold the dishes on the antiques market. The crew would consist of Beldon, Bill, Jerry Smith, Larry Theorine, Ray Curraco, and me. Beldon was the brains behind the operation, Ray would be the cook, and the rest of us would dive. Beldon had lined up an old Nova Scotia-built schooner, the *Lister*, which would be our diving operation platform. The owners, Lem Brigman and Riley Davis, had bought the one-hundred-ten-foot vessel and were living on it at the old ferry dock near Little Creek. After we removed the sails from the schooner and put them in storage, we loaded aboard all the supplies, compressors, diving gear, and so forth that we would need for this adventure.

In addition to being a crew member and a diver, I was also going to be the photographer. I put in for a week's leave and it was approved. Then I "borrowed" a couple of Navy underwater cameras and "requisitioned" some film for "training," assembled my diving gear and went aboard the *Lister*.

The *Lister* was an old schooner built in Lunenburg, Nova Scotia for sword fishing on the Grand Banks. She was wood and had a Rolls Royce diesel engine. The *Lister* got her name from the Lister Diesel Company, which offered to give the builders a Lister generator for free if they'd name her after the company. That was easy. She had been lying at the wharf in calm conditions for several months. Water had not touched her above the waterline for quite a spell. The seams above the waterline had dried out and started to open up a bit. Beldon had allowed for this, so he had rented a large air compressor and a couple of submersible, air-driven pumps. We knew she would leak badly once we were under way, but expected the seams to swell and close quite quickly.

We left the ferry dock the next morning and headed up the Bay. After passing over the Chesapeake Bay Bridge Tunnel, we hung a left and steamed up the eastern shore of Virginia and Maryland. I started to get a little queasy as we passed the first point of land off the eastern shore. Before long, I was throwing up. The swells kept increasing in size until we were taking green water over the bow. We stood two-man watches every two hours. Beldon had gone on ahead of us in his truck, as he didn't want the people in Delaware to know what we were up to. He had loaded a case of dynamite or two on board in the event we had to blow the wreck to get at the cargo. The China Wreck, as we called it, was a favorite fishing spot for the charter fishermen to take their fishing parties. It was out of sight of land, but still pretty shallow, about fifty feet. As we progressed up the coast, it got dark and the wind picked up. Before long, all of us were puking except Riley and Lem. Bill was so sick, he was lying under a piece of canvas on the lazarette. Soon, we were getting soaked by the water that ran over the deck with every other wave as the bow plunged into the swells. The wind was howling at forty knots, and I was wondering if this might be my last voyage. Lem's cabin was just forward of the steering station. He came up and looked around for any landmarks or red lights on radio towers. His electronics consisted of an old HF radio and a Loran A receiver.

Lem calculated our position and started down the steps. Just then, a large wave broke over the bow and the green water washed down both sides of the trunk cabin along the deck. He felt the thud as the bow dug into the swell and jumped back to where I was steering. We both grabbed for Bill just as he started to float back over the stern rail. Lem rolled him down the steps to the trunk cabin and that's where he stayed until we got to the wreck. That was close. Had Bill slipped overboard, I doubt very much that we could have recovered him under those conditions. Larry and Jerry, both ex-Navy frogmen, were throwing up. We were all cold and miserable, but had no choice but to stand our watches every two hours. It was fifty-seven degrees and I was as cold as I'd ever been, before or since.

By the next morning, we had recovered, and the seas and wind had abated to reveal a very nice day. We got the word from Beldon over the radio to not show up at the site of the wreck, but to just lay over the horizon until he had pinpointed its location. After a while, he gave us the "secret code" and we steamed for it. Beldon had marked the spot with a buoy thrown from a fishing boat that he had conned into taking him to the site. He paid the skipper of the boat fifty bucks and loaded his gear onto the *Lister* from the party boat. The charter fisherman left and went back into Lewes. The get-rich-quick part of the trip commenced. When I signed on, my cut was to be twelve-and-a-half percent of the take, plus whatever I would make for doing the photography. Ray, the cook, had chosen to get paid a salary of one-hundred-twenty-five dollars for the trip.

Larry and I set up the gear. He was going to dive in a Mark V hardhat and I would dive scuba. Larry had no hardhat training, but he was a good diver and could use any kind of gear quite handily. We got rigged up and loaded Larry into a big steel box that we were going to use to bring up the "treasure." Lem lowered him down into the water using the *Lister*'s main boom, and he rolled out of the bucket. As soon I heard him say he was on the bottom, I jumped over the side and followed his air hose down. We prowled around the wreck and started to load dishes into the bucket by the armload. We finished getting what we thought was a full load and Larry told Beldon over the diver's radio to take up the bucket. It disappeared from view and in a few minutes came back near where we were. Larry and I dragged it across the bottom to another location and filled it again. We had been hoping that we would find some silverware or something valuable, but didn't. We loaded the bucket a few more times and then Larry climbed in with the dishes and they hauled him up. After he got out of the bucket, they dropped it down for me to I climb in, and they recovered me from the water. We had around two-hundred-seventy-five plates and various dishes from the wreck. We called it a day as we felt we had cleaned out whatever was there. The dishes had been packed in hay inside wooden barrels, which, of course, had rotted away over the years. Many were broken, but a large number were intact.

We hauled anchor and steamed for Lewes, Delaware. My Vietnam record of twenty-three hours being seasick had been broken, and I received one plate from this recovery. As I had to be back at work in a day or so, I rode back to Norfolk with Beldon in his pickup truck. We found out later that the type of dishes on this ship were the cheapest that could be made as they were heading for a prison. In those days, of course, paper plates had not been invented. Our dishes were the ironstone equivalent of paper plates.

I arrived back at Norfolk and made it to work on time, checked in "off leave" and things were back to normal again.

Judy and I decided to go home to Maine for a few days so she could meet my family. We drove up in the VW and made the rounds. My mother treated her quite badly and it upset her a lot. We didn't stay in Maine long, and soon drove back to Norfolk.

Lane Briggs, a "good old boy" from Virginia who owned Rebel Marina on Willoughby Spit, called me. Lane also had a small diving company called Rebel Marine Service and did work as was called for. He didn't have any full-time divers; Lane just hired people when he needed them. This time, he had a job in North Carolina shoring up a small dam on a river. The bottom of the river had washed out underneath the dam. We had to put fiber-form bags under the downstream side and pump them full of a cement mix. This would take three or four days. I had lots of leave on the books, so I had no trouble taking some time off.

Judy and I did not have any major problems with our marriage and seemed to get along well for a while. However, we weren't communicating with each other. One week, Judy took off and drove to Akron the visit her grandmother. She called me and asked me to come up and be with her. I did, and things seemed to go well, but I think we both knew her trip was the beginning of the end.

The Salvage of the *Bay King*

In the summer of 1971, I was asked to go on another salvage diving job with my friend, Beldon Little. A tug, the *Bay King*, had sunk in the bay off Solomons, Maryland. The *Bay King* had been towing a barge loaded with sand when it had simply rolled over and sunk right out from under the crew. The skipper, a North Carolina native by the nickname of Jitterbug, had barely gotten off the boat alive. He couldn't swim a stroke. Later, he told me what had happened.

They'd been steaming for Solomons, towing a sand barge. Jitterbug made a slight turn to port and the *Bay King* just kept on rolling over to starboard as they made the turn.

"I knew she was full of water," he said. "The cook and the engineer were standing in the wheelhouse, and their eyes starting getting real big. They headed for the open wheelhouse window and began to squeeze through it. I knew there was no time to wait for them, so I dove for the open wheelhouse doorway and pulled myself through, even though water was pouring in. As I pulled myself up the rigging towards the surface, I felt the stern of the boat hit bottom. When I got to the surface, the cook was hanging onto the bow of the tug. Air was bubbling up all around him and I knew the bow was going down any second. Pieces of wood and other debris were floating in the water from the deck of the *Bay King*. I grabbed a sheet of plywood and shoved it toward the cook. He grabbed onto it just as the boat went down. The engineer was hanging onto another piece of blocking that had washed up from the tug."

Some local fishermen had seen the mishap and rescued the three men. Later, the Coast Guard went out, cut the hawser that had been hooked to the tug, towed the barge to Solomons, and placed a lighted wreck buoy where the oil slick was forming. The *Bay King* was diesel-powered and a continuous upwelling of fuel oil leaked to the surface, marking the spot on the water with a wide sheen.

Before we could do this salvage job, we had to outfit a barge at Lockwood Brothers in Hampton, Virginia. Beldon and I went there and figured out what we would need. His plan was to find the tug, rig slings under it using divers, pull it to the surface using two cranes (one on the stern and the other on the bow), pump it out, and tow it back to Norfolk.

It took a couple of days to rig up the barge with the two cranes and the diving gear. We then went aboard the tug for the ride to the *Bay King*. I slept most of the way, and the other divers, Skip Barber, and Larry Theorine, did, too. Once in a while, we went into the wheelhouse to inquire about our position. The next morning, we anchored the barge near the site and I suited up in a wetsuit and scuba gear. Beldon rigged a circling line on a cinder block, threw the block overboard, and passed me the end of the line. I jumped over the side of the tug into the water and started searching for the wreck. Despite having its buoy nearby, it took me nearly a full tank of air to find the *Bay King*. I found it in the limited visibility of the Chesapeake Bay, tied the circling line to it and surfaced. The tug came over to me and I handed the line to Beldon. He tied a Clorox bottle to the line as a float, and I climbed aboard. We had a small discussion as to which direction the *Bay King* was lying on the bottom. I told him where on the sunken boat I had tied the line and Beldon had the tugboat go over and hook up to the crane barge. They pulled the barge over the *Bay King* and, using a bow and stern anchor, placed it almost exactly over the top of the sunken vessel. The water depth was fifty-five feet deep at high tide.

I got out of my scuba gear and we rigged the dive station for surface-supplied diving. Larry got into long underwear and a canvas diving suit. We bolted him into the breastplate and Beldon gave Larry instructions as to what needed be done. Larry was a good man in the water and had no trouble figuring out exactly what was needed. We lowered him into the water with one of the cranes and he went to work. After he had done a survey on the *Bay King* and checked around to see how much of what Beldon wanted could actually be accomplished, he passed word up that he was ready to have me come down and help him. I climbed back into my wetsuit, strapped another bottle of air on my back, and jumped overboard. I followed Larry's air hose to the bottom and tapped on his helmet to let him know I was there. Using a rope, the deck crew lowered a steel cable sling to us. Larry took one end and walked around the side of the stern. I grabbed the other end and fed it between the shaft and the bottom of the tug. Then I swam back over and gave him a thumbs-up. The topside crew lowered the hook the rest of the way and we pulled it over to us using the same rope that the sling had been tied to. I helped Larry hook his end of the sling onto the hook and went over to retrieve mine.

By now, it was getting late and Beldon decided to call it a day as Larry and I were pushing our bottom times. We left the barge and tug there. The crew of the tug stayed aboard. Beldon, Skip, Larry, Jitterbug, me, and a couple of other guys from Lockwood Brothers went ashore and stayed on the third floor of some firetrap hotel. Beldon smoked all the time and would fall asleep in bed holding a lit cigarette. This scared me more than any part of the job. When I woke Beldon in the morning, he'd be lying on his back, and between his fingers was a cigarette stub with two inches of ash on it burned clear back to his flesh before extinguishing itself. If that wooden building had caught on fire, I might not be around today.

After a large breakfast at a nearby diner—Beldon had only coffee and a donut—we headed back to the barge. The weather was flat calm and the water was glassy smooth. When we got to the tug, we made sure that the crane was still hooked to it. Before surfacing, I had mouthed the hook with a piece of manila rope to make sure the hook did not slip off the slings.

We fueled up the compressor and started up the Moretrench pumps to make sure they would run when we needed them later in the day. For this dive, I suited up in the hardhat rig. The crane took a strain on the sling under the stern and lifted it off the bottom. The dive crew lowered me into the water with the other crane and I started down to the wreck. A second sling was lowered to me and it was my job to pull it as far forward as I could under the bow, working forward from the stern of the *Bay King*. The tug was seventy feet long and had been built in the 1800s out of iron plate. Riveted not welded, it was an extremely heavy vessel. I worked my way along the hull and put the loop of one end of the sling over one of the bitts near the bow. I then went back as far as I could and shoved the other end under the keel of the sunken tug. Next, I walked around the bow and found the end and pulled it out and forward as far as possible. All this took a while to accomplish and the compressor kept quitting. I could feel my air decrease in volume and asked them topside what was going on. When Beldon replied, I noticed the lack of compressor noise in the background.

"Now, Steve," Beldon would say over the dive radio in his North Carolina drawl, "we have a little problem with the compressor—nothing to worry about. We'll have her running in a minute. Just take a little breather and we'll have her cranked up in just a second."

In a few minutes, the airflow volume increased slightly. The air control valve on the suit was all the way open, but there was never any danger of me blowing up to the surface. I was getting just barely enough air to survive. I was sweating and had a headache from carbon dioxide buildup, but managed to get the sling under the bow. It was then a simple matter to rig a third sling under the keel near where the original sling had been rigged. We wanted the full weight of the boat to be on the keel, so the crew lowered the *Bay King* back onto another sling I had put under the keel and tied off to the bitts. Then I took the hook off the uppermost one and re-hooked it to the one that went under the boat. Now we were ready to lift her up. I made one final check to make sure nothing would screw up, and told Beldon I was ready to leave the bottom. Before I did, I made sure that the shackles in the rigging were secure so there was no chance we would drop the sunken boat once we started to lift it.

"Steve, where are those decompression tables?" Beldon inquired over the diver's radio.

"I think they are in the tool box with the spare fittings," I replied.

I heard nothing for a few minutes and he came back. "They ain't in there. You got any idea what the decompression schedule is for three hours at sixty feet?"

"No, but I better take a long stop at ten feet," I suggested.

They ended up hanging me off at ten feet for about a half hour and I surfaced. I didn't seem to suffer any bends and felt none the worse for wear. After I surfaced, I kept imagining I was getting pains in my legs or arms, or was about to pass out from a central nervous system hit, but it never happened.

It was about 1030 on Friday morning and we were ready to lift the *Bay King* and pump her out. I got out of my diving rig with the help of the tenders, and headed for the galley of the tug to get some chow. I was hungry as hell from that long dive, heaving around cables and fighting to get enough air to breathe. After eating, I went out with my cameras and shot pictures as the two cranes took a strain and began lifting the *Bay King* from its temporary watery grave. The antennas started showing above the water and pretty soon the top of the wheelhouse broke the surface. We had all the pumps rigged with hose and were ready to drop the suction ends into the tug when she came up. I put my wetsuit back on and prepared to go aboard to help get the suction strainers where they needed to be.

As soon as the main deck was awash, Larry and I went aboard the *Bay King* and opened up the engine room hatch. We shoved the hose down through, and Beldon lit off the eight-inch Moretrench pump. Water started flying out of the discharge hose and we could see the level in the engine room dropping. Before long, the boat was lively in the slings and we knew she would stay afloat. Now it was time to explore. Larry went into the galley area. Next thing I knew, he was out on deck, puking over the side. I asked him what was wrong. He said he didn't know, but when he opened the refrigerator door, something made him puke. I went in and opened the door. My stomach knotted up and I did the same as he had done. Later in my diving career, I understood what had happened. There had been a package of steaks and some hamburger meat that had rotted in there in an anaerobic environment. Hydrogen sulfide formed and when we smelled it, the natural thing for our bodies to do was reject it.

Four years later, I was taught in First Class Divers School that it could be fatal to breathe hydrogen sulfide. What you don't know *can* hurt you. We finished stripping the water out of all the compartments except the engine room. The crew and the insurance adjuster, who had come aboard that morning, tried to find the reason the *Bay King* sank. We located it. What happened was pretty simple and pretty stupid. There was a through-hull fitting that did not have a shutoff valve directly connected to it. Instead, there was a piece of rubber hose between the valve and the hull. The hose had rotted off, and a small stream of water about the size of a garden hose had filled up the engine room to just below the breather. When Jitterbug made that last left turn in the calm sea, the free surface of the water in the engine room caused the *Bay King* to roll to starboard. The engine room hatch had been opened and propped up so that the engine would get plenty of air. Seawater cascaded into this large opening, and the *Bay King* went to the bottom in a hurry.

We rigged the tug so it could be towed alongside the barge. Then Beldon and I went ashore and drove back to Norfolk in his truck. Another adventure in the life of an amateur salvor. I was paid three hundred dollars for my part in the operation. Beldon was paid ten thousand dollars, which was pretty cheap for what we had done. I went down to Bay Towing some time later and went aboard the *Bay King*.† She was all outfitted just like new—they even had fresh meat in the reefer.

Late in the fall of 1971, word came down that a crew was to go to the Naval Underwater Sound Lab, Newport Naval Station, Newport, Rhode Island, and do missed-distance studies for the Naval Ordnance Lab on the Mark 48 torpedo. This was a photo-instrumentation job and boring as hell, but Newport was a good place compared to Norfolk, and we'd be living in a motel and drawing per diem, sixteen dollars a day. Big money. I was there a week when I got a call from Judy. She told me she was leaving and going back to California. I felt bad about her leaving, but knew we were not hitting it off that well. We had no children and it was probably better that she went on to finish her life elsewhere.

A few weeks before she had decided to leave, I was driving down to the Outer Banks to photograph a hurricane and I hit a deep puddle, hydroplaned, and rolled the VW. It landed back on its wheels, but the wreck caved the roof in and broke out all the windows. Neither the guy with me, PH2 Don Middleton, or I got hurt. I put some rags over my face to protect it from the driving rain and drove back to Norfolk through the storm. The damage estimate was fourteen hundred dollars, and we had only paid nineteen hundred dollars for the car. I wanted the

† The *Bay King* sank again a few years later and they didn't salvage her.

223

insurance company to declare it a total loss, but they wouldn't do it. The car never was right after that, and the repair shop that did the work wouldn't make it right.

I asked Judy what she was taking when she left. She told me the stereo and the VW. I tried to get her to take the MG as I couldn't fit into it, but no. Her mother convinced her to take the VW. I wanted to stick it to the guys that repaired the car and make them eat the goddamned thing if they couldn't fix it properly.

Judy took the Volkswagen back to the West Coast, and I got stuck with the MG. I didn't know what to do with it, so I put an ad in the Trading Post, a local sell-it paper. Soon, I got a call from Jerry George, the guy I'd bought the BMW sidecar rig from some time back. He told me he was looking for an MG Midget, so I traded the MG for his BMW R69US bike. Now I had one vehicle—with only two wheels. So I got some other junk together and traded a rifle and some money for a Datsun pickup truck.

I didn't need the big apartment any more so I took over PH2 Larry Cregger's lease on a third-floor place in Ocean View. The rent was cheaper, the utilities were free, and it was not far from the back gate to NAS Norfolk. I spent about a year there in that snake ranch. I was single again and trying to make up for lost time.

I had a queen-size waterbed on the third floor—probably not too smart as it weighed a ton and the building was very old and none too sturdy. My landlord, a Navy chief, used to "borrow" my apartment to use as a place to screw his girlfriend. When I came home sometimes, I would find money under the pillow, usually nearly a month's rent, so it was a good deal.

While stationed at Combat Camera Group, we always had time for Friday afternoon beer parties. Funding for them was collected either from passing the hat among the attendees, or from the "recreation fund." By default, I became the manager of the recreation fund. My "job" was to raise money for this noble cause. The usual method was running a raffle, with the prize generally a shotgun, or "six-pack" of half-gallons of liquor. I wanted to make a lasting impression, so I decided to try something different—I would raffle off a hooker. The holder of the winning ticket would go to my apartment when I had duty, and the woman would show up at the assigned time and take care of business. There were no women assigned to Combat Camera Group at this time, as it was considered sea duty. That was the way things were.

I called my buddy Medford Taylor, a reporter/photographer at The Virginian-Pilot/Ledger/Star, the largest newspaper in the Tidewater area, and asked if, in his travels, he had found a woman of this particular occupation who might like to be the prize in our raffle. Medford told me he didn't know anyone, but he knew somebody who would know. He hooked me up with Bill Abourjille, a reporter who worked the crime scene with the local cops. Bill gave me the name of a woman whom he thought would like to be the raffle prize.

I drove down to her place and explained what I had in mind. Donna was a tall, attractive blonde, and built well. I could tell that she had some education from our conversation. Donna told me she owned the apartment she lived in and a motel, and was planning to retire with her boyfriend before she was thirty. We talked for a while and I told her that I'd call her with the address to my place and the time come.

Everything went like clockwork. Most of the guys bought tickets, married or not. Due to the nature of the mission at hand, I decided to rig the lottery so a married guy would not win. I figured I would be in enough trouble if the word got out about this without contributing to some marital strife on the part of a shipmate.

I drew the lottery on the date as specified—on a day when I had the duty, and would be staying at Combat Camera Group for the night. I didn't have to rig the lottery after all, as the name I drew was of a single guy who claimed he had not been laid in months. It was a simple matter to give him the keys to my place, call Donna, and wait for a report back. I gave him half the money from the lottery, as agreed upon with Donna, and he was on his way. I think the take was around one-hundred-fifty dollars, so Donna ended up with a bit more than her usual fee, and my buddy got taken care of in style. It was not long before I was replaced as the manager of the recreation fund.

In the early part of 1972, I had to go to St. Croix in the Virgin Islands to do some underwater motion picture work of a fast-attack submarine. There was a problem with the wire that fed the guiding signal to the Mark 48 torpedo. It would vibrate and send a harmonic signal down its length and mess up the guidance. The Navy engineers had designed some material that looked like plastic seaweed to cover the wire so it would not set up these vibrations and they needed motion picture photography of this while the sub was steaming along at ten knots.

We gathered our gear and took a civilian flight. While on the plane, I met JoAnne, a girl who worked for the Peace Corps on an island called St. Kitts. She was returning to the Caribbean after visiting her parents in Tempe, Arizona. She invited me I to visit her, and offered to put me up in a large farmhouse they rented near Basseterre on St. Kitts. Some months later, I went to visit for ten days. We explored the Brimstone Hill fort and climbed Mount Misery, a recently active volcano. Inside the crater, there were still sulfur pits and hot sulfur boiling up out of the ground. This was my first experience in the crater of a volcano. We took the ferry over to Nevis, the birthplace of Alexander Hamilton, and spent a few days there.

On the way home, I flew from St. Kitts to San Juan. In San Juan, I climbed aboard the plane in my dress blues to get the standby rate, and changed into civilian clothes as soon as the seat belt sign went out. Some kids on the plane had just come from a big rock concert in Puerto Rico. They were smoking pot and carrying on. The flight attendants said they had better get rid of the marijuana before New York, as the narcotics people would be waiting. I hadn't seen anybody smoking dope on a commercial airliner before.

During the trip to St. Kitts, I shot fifty rolls of Kodachrome. When my slides came back from the lab, my friend Rita and I went through them and picked out the best ones. I sent these to my agency, Photo Researchers, a stock photo agency in New York. Later on that year, I went to NYC and visited Clifford Dolfinger, the man who handled my photos, and Jane Kinne, one of the owners of the agency. I figured a face-to-face meeting couldn't hurt. While in New York, I met Linda Blazer, a food writer for a magazine. She wrote a story on a recipe that I had for fish chowder and did an article about me being a Navy underwater photographer.

In Norfolk, I was calling Mary Ware on the phone and talking with her on a regular basis. I knew her background and her parents and figured if I was going to have kids, they might as well be from genetic material that was a known factor. I called her one night and asked her to come down and live with me. She agreed and flew down a couple of weeks later after quitting her job, putting her old horse to sleep, and selling her VW. We married a few days after she arrived.

The day before we were married, I went to a bike shop and bought a brand new BMW motorcycle for seventeen hundred dollars. The following day was payday, so after getting my check, I took off early and we drove to Elizabeth City, North Carolina. There was another couple at the Justice of the Peace office. The woman's name was Miriam Ware and she was from Canada. The couple were sailing south and had stopped at Elizabeth City to get married. What an odd coincidence: another person named Ware, and with almost the same first name as my girlfriend. Mary and I said the words, paid the money, and then went for some fried fish and a couple of beers before driving back to Virginia Beach.

Rita, the optometrist's assistant I had been dating since shortly after Judy left, was very upset that I had married Mary without at least a warning, but she and Mary later on became good friends.

When I returned to work at Combat Camera Group, I received orders to go to Naval Special Warfare Group, Atlantic. That command was at Little Creek and was the parent command of SEALs, UDT, Beach Jumpers, Boat Support Unit, and a couple of others.

Shortly before Mary had arrived, I had moved my things to an apartment off of Shore Drive, on the other side of Little Creek Amphibious Base. The roads are lined up so that, in the summer, the sun sets and rises almost directly in front of you, depending on which way you're heading. I thought I would probably die in a car wreck if I had to drive facing the sun in both directions. Mary and I rented a house near Fort Story off of Shore Drive, our first place together. Shore Drive ran along the coast from Virginia Beach to Norfolk. The road was one hundred yards from the beach, and we could hear the surf pounding at night almost as loudly as the cars roaring by on Shore Drive.

A month before my orders went into effect, I was hanging out in the Combat Camera office. I told them I wanted to check my record and make sure everything was in there. As I was going through it, I noticed a sheet of paper that said I had been involuntarily disenrolled from Second Class Diving School. I jokingly said, "I guess I don't need this shit in here," pulled the paper out and, without crumpling it up, threw it into the nearby trash can. The administration officer, a Lieutenant Williams, wrote me up for that. He called it, "intentionally destroying official military records." I got a captain's mast out of it, and a suspended bust from first class to second class petty officer.

I meant it as a joke; I had no intention of destroying that piece of paper. If I had, I could have easily done it with nobody watching and no one would have known. However, I had made a nasty remark about a friend of the administration officer's on a previous occasion. The friend had made warrant officer. He was a good enough guy, but a consummate ass-kisser of extreme skill. He had been to all the right schools and punched his ticket quite effectively. I made the loud comment one day, "If that guy can make warrant, any asshole can." I was wrong about that. I never made warrant or limited duty officer.

A few weeks later, before going to Little Creek, I was late to work. The power had gone out and my electric alarm clock didn't wake me. I was thirty minutes late. This was not uncommon for most people, but I hadn't been late before except for two cases of auto trouble en route. This time, though, the officers had a hard-on for me and were going to stick it to me. When I got to Combat Camera, I went straight to the administration office.

"Am I on report for being late?" I asked.

"I guess so," was the answer I got.

Immediately, if not sooner, I was across the hall and in the operations officer's office. I did not ask to see him and he did not ask me to close the door. I just walked in, closed the door and sat down in a chair opposite his desk. Lieutenant Commander Dixon, an ex-enlisted man, was the operations officer. I leaned over his desk and looked him in the eye. "I understand that I am on report for being late this morning."

"Well, er, I, er, guess that's the story," he offered.

"Tell you what, Sir. I ain't standing by to get busted a pay grade for this chickenshit rap. If you want a stripe, don't stop there. Keep ripping until you have the crow, the uniform, the sea bag, the I.D. card, and even the fucking dog tags. And furthermore, this ship ain't going to go down without taking some of the rats with it. Perhaps you would like the NIS (Naval Investigative Service) looking into all of the travel claims from this command." He started to mellow out and turned a little pale. I continued, "I know some stuff on people here that would really embarrass the hell out of this command all the way up to AIRLANT (Naval Forces, Atlantic Fleet). I would hate to do it, as I have a lot of friends here. If Commander Pulley were still CO, this shit would never have happened."

He sat back and looked at his fingernails.

"Tell you what, Waterman. I think perhaps I can see a way out of this for both of us. The skipper wants your ass, and so does the administration officer for that remark you made about his warrant officer asshole buddy. I'll recommend that they drop all of this if you'll go see a shrink. I'll tell them you were still upset over your first wife taking off."

I went along with it as I was checking out in a couple of weeks, heading for my new command at Naval Special Warfare Group. I thought they would forget all about sending me to a shrink.

Wrong again.

Chapter 17

NavSpecWarGruLant

NavSpecWarGruLant

I checked in at NavSpecWarGruLant (NSWG) and met the guy who was running the Photo Lab. Ryder, a radarman third class, had a knack for photography, so they had assigned him there. He was transferred out a short time after my arrival, and I replaced him. At the lab, there was also a real dufus-type, Photographer's Mate Airman Powell. He shuffled when he walked, wore thick glasses (thicker than mine), and couldn't pour piss out of a boot with the instructions written on the bottom of the heel. Nevertheless, Powell was a good kid and everybody liked him. There wasn't an evil bone in his body.

The Photo Lab was located behind SEAL Team 2 in a windowless gray trailer. Wooden steps led up to the door, but there was no sign to say what it was. Fortunately, the air conditioning worked most of the time. Hot weather was common in Little Creek, Virginia. There was a phone in the Photo Lab so I could make calls to anywhere on the base and off. We had a setup for color slide processing and any black-and-white film. The budget was not too restrictive and I didn't usually have any problem getting materials.

My actual boss was Chief Photographic Intelligenceman (PTC) Scotty McLean.[†] He was a SEAL and had changed his rating from cook to photographic intelligenceman. This guy thought he was Ansel Adams when it came to photography. He had a cute little beard and was always sucking on his pipe as though deep in thought. I believe he was deep

† Scotty McLean and his daughter were killed in an auto accident a few years after I left the Navy.

in thought all right, but most likely he was thinking, "How can I fuck Waterman this time?"

His boss was a slightly more mature version of Powell, with many of the same physical characteristics. His name was Williams, a lieutenant who was supposed to be an intelligence officer. Well, he sure as hell never exhibited any intelligence that I could detect. Between Williams and Scotty McLean, I made the determination that I wouldn't go to the administration building unless I absolutely had to. A couple of days after I checked in, PH1 Joe Leo, my old buddy from Oceana days showed up at the door of the lab. Turns out he was the duty PAO (Public Affairs Office) photographer for the admiral. This was a great job and he loved it. All he had to do was shoot reenlistments, and grips and grins—what we called award ceremonies.

One day, I got a call from the Commodore of NSWG, Captain Bill Thede. He wanted to see me in his office. He received a call from Combat Camera Group. They wanted to know if Waterman had contacted a psychiatrist yet about his "problem." I told him that I intended to go down to the clinic when I got my things in order. He looked at me over the top of his reading glasses and advised that I do it soon. I said I would. Next thing I know, Leo is in the lab asking me if I am nuts or something. I laughed and told him the story. He said that Scotty McLean asked him to keep an eye on me to see if I exhibited any irrational behavior.

"What the hell happened to doctor-patient confidentiality?" I asked him. He just shrugged.

I called the neurology department at Boone Clinic ("Boone's Farm," we called it), and made an appointment with a shrink. A couple of days later, I went to see the doctor. Ryder went with me for something to do. I walked in the door and told the Gray Lady volunteer that I had an appointment. There were two doctors sharing one receptionist, so she didn't know whether I had an appointment with the shrink or with the neurologist. After a few minutes, she asked if I was there to see Doctor Green or Doctor White. I told her I was there to see Doctor White, the shrink. I detected an immediate change in her demeanor. She started talking down to me as though I was a little kid or a deranged maniac about to go apeshit with a chainsaw.

"Well, just have a seat over there. There are some nice magazines to read until it's time for you to see the doctor."I expected her to hand me a coloring book and a handful of crayons.

"Jesus Christ, lady, I don't need a straight jacket… yet. I just need to have an evaluation."

She looked at me in fear the entire time I sat there. Some real winners must have gone through there.

Finally, it was my turn. I walked into the office, sat down in the chair facing the doctor's desk, leaned forward, and started asking this young-looking shrink some questions.

"How old are you?"

"Twenty-eight."

"Ever been shot at?"

"No."

"How much time have you spent in the real world? I mean, not in school?"

"Not much, but probably enough."

I leaned farther over the desk and asked him how in hell anybody who was only twenty-eight years old and had eight years of college, had never left the warm comfort of academia and worked in a room without any windows could possibly relate to anything in the real world.

Apparently, he felt I was hostile because he put me down as being dangerous to others and myself and pulled my jump and diving status. This pissed me off, not only because of the loss of money, but also the loss of status, and the fact that people would start to look at me as if I had tits on my forehead. I was very pissed off when I left.

The doctor gave me a chit to take back to the CO indicating I was to be removed from jump and diving status. I had only been able to draw jump pay at this command, as it was not a diving billet. Jump pay was fifty-five dollars a month then, and diving pay for scuba divers was sixty-five dollars. The guys in the Teams got one-hundred-ten dollars for double hazardous duty pay, jump, and demo. The officers got two-hundred-twenty dollars, which was not fair to the enlisted SEALs as they did more jumping than most of the officers, and most of them intended to make the Teams a career. Most of the officers were there for the thrills and chills of being a frogman, after which they went on to the Fleet. In those days, being an officer in the Teams was akin to being a leper. There were no career paths in Special Warfare for officers.

Now I was a marked man: mentally unstable, dangerous to others, and myself etc. Joe Leo joked about it and told me I wasn't nearly as crazy as he was as well as most of the people he knew. I agreed that I was not nuts, but once you had the label, there was no getting rid of it.

My wife, Mary, didn't like the fact that I'd been railroaded into going to a shrink and felt it would screw up my naval career.

"Now, that's a crock of shit. It won't have any effect," I responded. I found out later that she was right.

Scotty McLean had Leo watching me, and I began to catch curious looks from some of the other people on the staff. The asshole I worked for, Lt. Williams, was one of those types you just want to grab and pound into a mess of unidentifiable, gruesome goo. Later on, I found out that I was one of a large number who felt that way, including a few senior officers.

Occasionally, my photographic duties would take me down to the building where the SPECWAR sick bay was located. A young doctor named Kent MeWha worked there. He was a physical guy and worked out with the Teams when he could. He drank, chased women, and all those things that would ingratiate him with SEALs and UDTs. One day, I was telling him about my medical record and the things in it that had me painted as a liability to myself and to others. He looked up my record, said something derogatory about shrinks, and proceeded to write a high recommendation, which ended up placing me back on full status. Kent added that, of all the people he had come in contact with in NavSpecWar, I was probably one of the sanest and most reliable. That took care of that bullshit, and I started to draw jump pay again. I thought he was doing this as a friend, until one day I walked by sick bay and overheard a SEAL chief in there crying, I mean "boo hoo crying" about "not being able to hack it any more." I never found out who he was, and didn't care to.

One of my first assignments after Mary and I married, was to Roosevelt Roads, Puerto Rico with UDT-21. After that, I was to work with RDT&E. The USS Barnstable County would take me to Puerto Rico with a detachment of frogs from UDT-21, and I would stay at the UDT barracks in Roosevelt Roads. "Whew!" I thought, "I'll be getting out of here and away from this bunch of staff jerks."

Lt. Williams told me that I was to report back to him on a weekly basis and keep a logbook of my daily activities. This guy wanted me to shit and fall back in it. Just to get him off my back, I told him I would do that. I asked him if he had one of those green logbooks that I could take. He took that as a sign I was "coming around."

I drew some film, packed my gear, and loaded it aboard the USS Barnstable County. The officer in charge of the UDT detachment was Lt. Brian Barbata. He was a decent guy and liked to do all the frogman things, although I could tell he was not the career type. On the ride down, we played cards, ate, slept, did PT—all the boring things that passengers on Navy ships do when their mission is ashore. The chow was good. We watched movies at night, and didn't stand watches. We all hated standing watches.

We stopped in Guantanamo Bay, Cuba to drop off some Marines and vehicles, stayed there for about two pitchers of beer, and got underway again.

When we arrived in Puerto Rico, we were met at the dock by some of the support guys who stayed there all the time and maintained the area. We loaded our gear onto the trucks and they drove us to the barracks which had a swimming pool behind it. There were two buildings away from the rest of the base used to house UDTs when they were in Puerto Rico. They were originally built for UDT training, but the training was now called BUD/S and was conducted in Coronado, California.

Each day we would have PT in the morning or play jungle rules volleyball, or run. The rest of the day we would do something that "needed to be done." This could range all the way from taking a swim to lining up some beer for a party.

Atlantic Fleet Combat Camera Group had a detachment on the other side of Roosevelt Roads Naval Station and I there to meet the crew. They didn't have a photo lab, so the chief at Combat Camera told me to go to the base Photo Lab and talk with Senior Chief Photographer's Mate (PHCS) Don Husman, he would take care of me. Husman was a great guy and let me use the lab for processing black-and-white and color.

There was a problem with rats in the other UDT barracks; not the one we lived in, but the one we used for storage, etc. Electrician's Mate, Chief (EMC) Scotty Slaughter,[†] a crazy bastard, like me, had a penchant for playing with explosives. He rigged a rattrap that consisted of a couple of pieces of wire, an electric blasting cap, a battery, and a piece of cheese. We set it up so that the cheese was on a piece of wire hanging down through another loop of wire. Then a blasting cap was placed on the floor near the cheese. When the rat moved the cheese, the wire would swing and make contact with the loop, closing the circuit. The rat would be demolished at that close range. We would set it up, then go over to the other building and drink beer while we waited for the explosion. Rat guts were everywhere. It worked twice before the other rats figured it out and stayed away from it.

I had brought my ten-speed bicycle with me on the ship to Puerto Rico, so I had a means of getting around the base. I eventually sold the bike after I moved down to the SEAL area, as I could use the SEAL vehicles whenever I needed to, and they were much easier to pedal.

† Scotty Slaughter died of cancer a few years after this book's first publication in 2000. He was a friend of us all.

One day at noon, the chief gathered us all together and asked if any of us would volunteer to go to Loquillo Beach and look for a young boy that had drowned. All of us offered to do it. The chief chose men who were older and had done body searches before. I was one of them. We ran a pattern parallel to the beach looking for the kid, but never found him. I was sad that we didn't find him, but happy that I was not the one to stumble across his body had he been found. The senior person in the Civil Defense unit at Loquillo Beach wrote each of us a personal "thank you" letter.

A few weeks after the search, I moved from the UDT barracks to the SEAL area by the new Chiefs' Club on the beach. The SEALs lived in what used to be the old Chiefs' Club. It had a bar and a number of small rooms. One area was like a bunk room with many bunks, the two-tiered type.

The officer in charge of the SEAL area was Lt. Terry Grumley, whose class I had photographed during Hell Week. Grumley was only putting in his time there. Nobody was fooled into thinking he was a career officer. He did his job low profile and didn't get in our way. Things ran a lot smoother that way.

My friend Dick Stauffacher, a petty officer in UDT-21 at Little Creek, had asked Mary if we wanted to take over his house when he left the Navy. It was on Lauderdale Avenue off the end of Pleasure House Road, which is the first road going toward the beach east of Little Creek. Lauderdale Avenue dead-ends against the chain link fence of the Amphibious Base. We accepted the offer, and Mary and Dick moved all our things out of the place on Hatton Street into the small two-bedroom house practically on the beach. The rent was ninety dollars a month and included all the sand you could track into the house.

Mary decided to fly down and visit me. I agreed as she hadn't been to Puerto Rico before. I wrangled a truck and driver out of someone at the SEAL area and he drove me up to pick up Mary when she arrived at the airport in San Juan. I was glad to see her and she looked good. We drove back to Roosevelt Roads and took her gear over to PH1 Hudson's house. He was a black guy who worked in Combat Camera, a hell of a nice man who had offered to put us up if Mary came to visit. We stayed there a few days and then I was able to pull some shit and get a private room over at RDT&E in sick bay. Hospital Corpsman, First Class (HM1) "Doc" Pacuirk arranged for us to use the space, which had a shower and a bunk. He gave me the key and things worked out quite well.

Mary rode the chase boat on a few operations, one with SDVs while testing some new closed-circuit scuba gear, and another time when we were testing a new hand-held sonar devise. At first they weren't going to let her go, then BMCM Corney Leyden, the master chief in charge of RDT&E said if Lt. Tommy Hawkins' wife (who was down there visiting him) could go, then he guessed maybe Mary could go, too. That took care of it. She hit it off with the frogs and we had a good time. I still have my wife,[†] but I hear Tommy replaced his later on.

Master Chief Gunner's Mate (GMCM) Everett Barrett, Lt. Joe DiMartino, Lcdr. Pat Badger, and Lt. Jim Harper[‡] were some of the older frogs in RDT&E. They had all been in WWII except Harper, who was somewhat younger and an ex-enlisted man. Barrett and DiMartino were the salt of the earth. It was a pleasure to operate with them. One of the missions we had while there was testing some new explosive hose. This was not like Mark 8 hose, which is nothing more than fire hose filled with granulated TNT. This new hose was made of a type of plastic explosive that looked like olive drab modeling clay except it was more rugged and came in hose form. On each end of the hose were valves to let water in. This way, a swimmer could flood it and tow it along. The concept didn't work very well from the swimming standpoint, but it sure as hell was powerful as an explosive. We shot the hell out of it and thought is was good product—if you didn't have to tow it underwater very far. On the surface, it was okay. You could drag quite a few lengths of it behind you.

We took a Mark IV boat over to Pinéros Island, a small island that UDT had been using for demolition operations for years, and set off some large charges. There was a restriction on the size of the charge we could shoot, but somehow we never paid much attention to it. One day we shot about a thousand pounds in one go. We had Mark 8 hose, C-4, the new hose, and a couple of ammonium nitrate cratering charges all linked together with primacord. When it went off, the shockwave went skyward, reflected off the low cloud cover, and came right back to the UDT barracks a few miles away, where one of the guys was in the shower. The shock wave focused right onto the building and knocked the light fixture off the ceiling. It came crashing down around him and glass went everywhere. Nobody was injured, but It scared the shit out of him.

A representative from General Electric was at RDT&E to run tests on the new GE Mark 1500 closed-circuit scuba. There were a number of companies vying for the contract to produce this equipment and Joe was there to oversee it. The GE guy was an ex-Navy diver, so he fit right

† My wife, Mary, died January 17, 2006
‡ Jim Harper has since died of cancer, as has Joe DiMartino.

in with the frogs. Lcdr. Chuck LeMoyne arrived with some men with funny accents. We found out that they were Israelis in the U.S. to learn about our SDVs and to try out the closed circuit rigs. They were on tourist visas, so they were not really supposed to be at RDT&E. One of the Israeli Frogmen, Shaoul Ziv, was the CO of the Israeli Navy Commandos. He was a commander and a very nice guy. He had seen many days of combat and lost a few men, from both accidents or combat casualties. The Israelis had a good time and our men liked them. Later, I met a whole platoon of these frogmen in Little Creek when they were training with SEAL Team 2.

The Mark 1500 was a mixed-gas, closed-circuit rig. It had two small flasks of gas and a Baralyme canister in a fiberglass shroud, which the diver wore on his back. The diver wore an instrument console on the left wrist. This gave the status of the gas mix and the supply, battery life, etc. By today's standards this thing was primitive, but it worked. I don't know who got the contract, but I know it worked well and nobody drowned swimming with it.

RDT&E made a run to Vieques using this rig in one of the SDVs and I rode along in the back seat. During the lengthy ride, I read a paperback crotch novel, and tore out the pages as I went and let them float away. The chase boat on the surface could tell what chapter I was in by the debris left behind.

Many nights at the SEAL bar, I drank until I was almost in a coma. We had a rule. The bartender drank for free, but had to relinquish the job when he was too drunk to make change. Some of the SEALs and divers would drink until closing and then get up and run PT the next morning. This, I could not do. Many mornings, I paid the price for staying in the bar too long, having too much fun. Sometimes the nurses from the base came and danced to the music playing on jukebox. I don't know where the jukebox came from and never asked.

Joe DiMartino could hold his own with the boys, slamming down rum and Coke or beer until the sun came up. His personality never seemed to change. Occasionally, he had a little problem with certain words, usually quite late in the night. Joe was an icon in the Teams and everybody loved him. However, the promotion board didn't for some reason. Joe was an ex-enlisted guy but never made it past lieutenant. He must have screwed up, or pissed off someone. Joe told me that his "hell week" was on Omaha Beach during the Normandy Invasion.

I had been working with RDT&E for about a week and a half when either Barrett or DiMartino called Lt. Williams at SPECWAR and told him that I wouldn't be sending any situation reports or keeping a logbook. They told him what I was doing was classified and that I had enough work without keeping any stupid records.

One of the men working out of the SEAL area was named EMC Phillips. He was a fat chief electrician's mate from Indian Head, home of the EOD (Explosive Ordnance Disposal). Phil was a sharp cookie and never missed a trick. When his civilian flight landed at San Juan Airport, he called and asked for a driver to be sent to pick him up. The kid on the phone asked him his name and rank. He told them he was a chief. The kid said, "I'm sorry, Chief, we are only allowed to provide transportation for commanders and above." Phillips, (we called him Filthy Phil) called back in a few minutes and disguised his voice. He told the dispatcher that his name was "Commander Clump." (A clump is the weight on the end of a descending line to keep it taut when a diver descends. It is usually a lump of lead or steel with an eyebolt cast in it to connect the line. All divers recognized the term. Not so the "admin pukes.") They sent a truck and Phil bought the driver a meal on the way back, so he never said anything about it. From that day on, Phil was known as Filthy or Commander Clump.

Phil had a lot of money. His father had died years earlier and left him fifty grand. Phil knew he'd piss it away, so he gave it to a broker and told him to make him rich. The guy did. He invested in soybean futures back when it was a hot investment. He sold at the right time and Phil had a pot full of money. One of the guys asked him if he was going to get out of the Navy now that he was rich. His response, was, "What, and let them screw me out of my retirement?" The only visible toy he bought was a new pickup truck.

I spent many hours at the base photo lab near the airfield. PHCM Don Husman, the master chief in charge of the Roosevelt Roads Photo Lab, took great care of me there and made sure that I had all the things I needed. When I had to order more photographic supplies, he had his supply guy fill out the paperwork for me and make sure it was right. Then I would take it back to the SEAL complex, requisition a vehicle ("Hey Chief, I need the truck."), and head up to Bayamon where Kodak was located. It was a good ride and I stopped along the way to take pictures or eat at a restaurant.

Time flew while I was in Puerto Rico. Even the work was fun down there. Mary was still with me and we were trying to figure out how to get her home without spending money to do it. Finally, Corney Leyden said we'd just put her on the frigging airplane. We didn't have much gear and there were only seven of us going home. So we just went over to air operations, loaded our gear on the C-141, climbed aboard, and

took off. We managed to slip a little cocktail material on board to help
the time go faster. Mary ended up sitting in the flight engineer's seat in
the cockpit shooting the shit with the pilot, who had to fly the plane
manually as the autopilot had died. When we landed at Norfolk Naval
Air Station, we threw all the gear on a stake truck headed to Little
Creek, where one of the guys had left his car. He gave us a ride the rest
of the way home. Things continued on as usual at NavSpecWar.

At Little Creek, there were usually a few foreign military personnel
training with the SEALs. At a beer party one afternoon, I happened to
meet a couple of men from the Pakistani Navy. Both Ali Khan and Sham
Din were officers; Sham was a chief petty officer.

Sham Din had been aboard a Pakistani ship being attacked by the
Indians. Knowing he would have to swim to safety, Sham ran to a deck
locker for his swim fins, but was wounded in the foot. I felt sorry for him
and asked him if he'd like to come out to the house for supper and
meet my wife. He accepted and we headed home. A few days later, I
he came over for another visit. He started showing up at the house after
I left for work. He told Mary he was in love with her and wanted her to
go back to Pakistan with him. She didn't much like the idea of that. I
thought the whole idea was humorous.[†]

One day, I wandered into Lt. William's office. A new guy working for
him, a senior chief yeoman, was an intelligence specialist handling all
the top secret material. I spotted a *top secret* item lying on the desk.
As I got closer to it, I started laughing. I didn't have a *top secret*
clearance then. Williams spoke up, "Waterman you aren't supposed to
be in here when we have top secret papers out."

I answered back, "Well, you're gonna look like an asshole if you send
in this report."

"Oh, yeah? Why's that?" he questioned, cocking his pointed little
head to one side.

"Well, you've got the wrong pictures with the bios."

"How do you know that?"

"Well, I drank with these guys for a week. I oughta know their names
by now." His face turned red and he went over and switched the
photographs of the two Israelis to where they should be. He had Ziv's
picture switched with the engineer's. I turned and walked out of the
office. I couldn't get the grin off my face.

† In 1991, I was in Pakistan on a diving job. We were "backed up" by some
  Pakistani divers. I asked them if they knew a former Pakistani frogman by the
  name of Sham Din. They all looked at each other incredulously and exclaimed,
  "Sham Din was our instructor." Small world.

My parachute jumping continued and I made some friends at the parachute loft. Pierre Ponson, Stan Janecka, Norm Olson, Danny Zmuda,[†] Hershel Davis and some of the others still jumped a lot. A short version of HALO school was going to be taught at Little Creek. The real HALO school in Fort Bragg was too much money for their strained budget, so they talked SpecWar into funding the school there. We would take a short ground course, and then go out to Suffolk and jump, either out of C-1As or helicopters. Lt. Norm Carley, Lt. Al Horner, Lt. Tom Steffens,[‡] and some enlisted guys were all going to take the course. I conned my way in with my camera, as usual. All of them liked to have pictures of themselves doing different activities. We made four or five jumps with oxygen equipment and a parachute bag full of sawdust strapped to our asses. We jumped T-10 parachutes (T-10 parachutes were standard issue for paratroopers and not very steerable) or olive drab Para-Commanders (PCs), for those of us who had experience with that canopy. I don't remember if I had a PC or a T-10, but I remember that I didn't pull my ripcord too late and managed to find my way to the ground. The part I didn't like was the way the goggles and oxygen mask completely blocked the view of the altimeter, which was strapped on top of our chest-mounted reserve. If I cocked my head to one side and pulled my chin way over, I could just barely see it. I decided I would trust the team leader and just pull when he did, as we were supposed to. If I got so low that I could read the labels on beer cans on the ground, I would pull. Nobody was hurt, except the taxpayers.

My shore duty stint was almost up, so I decided I would like to return to Combat Camera Group, which was considered sea duty. The Navy had decommissioned Naval Special Warfare Group while I was in Puerto Rico, and all of us were transferred to NAVINSWARLANT. That stands for Naval Inshore Warfare, Atlantic. I never figured out why they renamed it, but they have since re-commissioned Naval Special Warfare Group.

I put in a chit and asked to transfer to Atlantic Fleet Combat Camera Group via second class diving school. I had spent a little over two years at NSWG. I received my orders and checked in at YFNB-17, the school. YNC Ross, my old nemesis, had since retired or been transferred. One of the first stories I heard was about him getting the shit kicked out of him in some bar by a guy to whom he had mouthed off while in the

† Danny "Mud" Zmuda has since passed on.
‡ Tom Steffens retired as a rear admiral.

Navy. I liked it and wished I could have been there to see, or even take part in it.

In this class, we had several Puerto Rican State Police officers. Most of them were not high speed, but they were good people and tried to do what they were supposed to. They didn't act like they were just along for the ride. We weren't assigned permanent swim buddies as at some schools, so we rotated. I never had any problem out-swimming and out-diving the other men in the class, but that was not the challenge. The challenge was keeping my mouth shut when I saw somebody screwing off that shouldn't be there.

One of my duties at the school was standing junior officer of the deck (JOOD) watches. This was a four-hour exercise in staying awake, drinking coffee, and fielding phone calls for guys who were supposed to be on watch—at least according to their wives who called to talk with them. One night, I had the eight-to-twelve watch and a seaman from Maine came up to the quarterdeck. We were just talking when another sailor came up and started harassing him verbally. Before long, the other guy hauled off and slugged the kid from Maine. I grabbed the asshole and nailed him a couple of times. I hit him hard, but it didn't take him down. He ran down the brow and onto the pier with me in hot pursuit.

"Nobody starts a fight on my quarterdeck," I shouted after him. I caught up to him and grabbed him around the neck in a headlock and tried to push him down between the camel and the pier where he would be crushed when the surge of the swells moved them together. Two of the Seabees in my class had been walking up the pier and saw what was going on. They didn't want me to kill the guy, so they both jumped me and tried to break it up. Finally, I let go of him. Both of them looked incredulously at each other and then at me. "Jesus, Waterman. Didn't you know we were on your back?"

"No, I didn't. Were you?"

They cast each other the same glance. "Hell, yes. You were a crazy man! I'm glad it wasn't us who pissed you off." After that, I tried to control my temper a little more.

The remainder of the time at second class diving school passed without major incident. We graduated and said goodbye to each other, and I continued on to my "new" command, Combat Camera Group. But by then, they had changed the name of it to Naval Audio Visual Command, Atlantic. No more Combat Camera Group. The Navy was becoming politically correct and somehow combat and cameras were seen not to mix. Even so, we still called it Combat Camera.

One night in early fall 1973, I received a call from Lane Briggs, the owner of the Rebel Marina and Rebel Marine Service. The clam-dredge, *Christy*, had hung its dredge down and then managed to get the towing line in one of its two screws. She was anchored in seventy-five feet of water in the Chesapeake Bay somewhere. Lane wanted me to meet one of their other dredges, the *Ocean View*, at the dock and go out and cut the dredge loose. They would buoy it off and go back later and recover it. I told him I needed another man to go with me, so I called PHC Dick Johnson, the chief I had worked for at Combat Camera Group. He said he'd go and brought tanks for both of us, as I didn't have access to them at NavSpecWar, so we got our gear together and headed down to the dock where Miles Brothers Clam Company kept their boats.

We arrived at the *Ocean View* and met the skipper, Richard Miles, one of the company's owners. He and one of the crewmen helped us get our diving gear aboard and we headed out. It was starting to get snotty out on the bay, and I wondered if it would be safe to dive, being dark out and with the wind blowing at twenty-five knots. By the time we got on station, I was puking my guts out in true seafarer style. I crawled into my wetsuit and scuba gear. I had a hacksaw, which I would use to cut through the huge polypropylene hawser. I told them I would go down to where it was connected to the dredge and saw it off. When they felt it part, I would count thirty seconds before surfacing so that the *Christy* would be well out of the way. I did that and it worked quite well, although, as I sawed, the swells kept tightening up the hawser like a large black violin string until the last stroke of the hacksaw, when it just parted.

When I surfaced, I popped an MK-13 signal (a Navy-issue day/night distress signal flare: one end is orange smoke for daytime, the other is a red flare) and the *Ocean View* came right over to me. I had one hell of a job getting back aboard, as the swells were level with the side of the boat. Finally, they threw the boat out of gear upwind of me and I just let them drift to me until I could slide over the coaming onto the stern deck. Dick was there to help me out of my gear. It was time to go home. We slept all the way back. I was worn out, more from the puking than from the diving.

The next day, I went down to the dock and cut the hawser out of the *Christy's* propeller. It was quite a job in itself. Later that evening, Lane called me and said we needed to go back out and recover the dredge; that it would cost about fifteen thousand dollars to build a new one, and take a long time to have one made. I called PH2 Larry Cregger and PH2 Ike Johnson, two members of the Combat Camera Group's Underwater Photo Team and asked them to do the job with me. We had worked together a lot on other diving projects and I had confidence in their abilities. I told them I would pay them fifty dollars apiece to come along and one hundred dollars if they had to dive. That was big money in those days. They agreed.

We loaded our gear aboard another boat owned by the Miles Clam Company. I think this one was called the *Hampton Creek*. It was not a clam dredge and the only piece of electronics on it was a VHF or CB radio. The compass worked, and I think the skipper had a chart. We put to sea in the *Ocean View* and headed for the *Christy*. The *Hampton Creek* went ahead of us to locate the buoy the skipper had put on the end of his haulback wire.

In a couple of hours, we were on site. Cregger and I dived, so Ike stayed in the boat. Our mission was to go down to the dredge and attach the haulback wire to it using a metal shackle made up for the job. There were several holes in the bracket where this could be attached, and Captain Ben of the *Christy* told us that it didn't matter which one we used. This cable was about an inch and a half in diameter and I knew it was going to be a hell of a chore to drag it over the bottom, so I told them I wanted a block (sheave) to tie onto the dredge. Then, I had the crew lower that down to me with some line woven through it. I took this to the dredge and tied it off. Then I had them pull on the line, which was attached to the cable's end, and pull until it stopped. After that, I went down and cut the rope and easily put the shackle on the dredge. That was all there was to it. I imagined what would have happened if we had tried to pull that big cable by hand over to the dredge. I'd probably still be out there screwing with it!

We steamed for Little Creek. By now, it was starting to snow and it was very cold in the boat. I climbed into the top rack in the wheelhouse bunk and Larry Cregger got into the lower one. It was rough. Before long, we were taking seas over the bow. Ike had gone forward into the forecastle to try to sleep. The skipper of the *Ocean View* and Richard Miles, son of the owner of the Miles Clam Company, were at the helm. It was so rough that they fell down a couple of times and I thought we might not make it back to shore. A fuel drum rigged up on deck broke loose and went overboard and the stack for the galley stove was carried away. We hoped Ike was okay in the forecastle. When we got back, he said that he figured he wouldn't be any worse off there than anyplace else on the boat. At least he was dry, if not warm.

242

I went out clam dredging a few trips on board the *Christy* and quickly found out why guys who work on clam dredges had such huge arms and the sixty-fathom stare. I think I had about two hours of sleep out of thirty-six, and that was in fifteen- to twenty-minute naps on deck between tows. We shoveled clams into the large baskets with aluminum scoops each time the dredge came up. It was hard work.

Richard Miles and I became friends. He was a millionaire, but worked harder than most fishermen I've met. Eventually, Richard became skipper of the *Christy* after Captain Ben died. Ben weighed in at around four-hundred-fifty pounds, and had to have a special table built for him down below just so he could sit and eat. Brother could he eat!

Shooting the USS *California*

I had been back at Atlantic Fleet Audio Visual Command—we still called it Combat Camera—for a few weeks when we got a call that a team was needed at Atlantic Undersea Test and Evaluation Center (AUTEC) on the Bahamian Island of Andros. This was good news. We used any excuse we could to go to the Bahamas on a job. It was no problem getting volunteers. The water was warm and clear, and the beer was cold and cheap. There aren't any women available, but what the hell. Two out of three ain't bad.

Chief Dick Johnson picked the team. It consisted of Mac McCraw, yours truly, and another guy whom I can't remember. In addition, there would be some frogmen from UDT-21 as our swim buddies. The CO of Team 21 sent a new lieutenant, junior grade as OIC of the frogs, and told him he'd be working for us. The entire job was under Lcdr. Chuck LeMoyne, of Naval Ships Systems Engineering Command. I had met Chuck in Puerto Rico, but hadn't actually worked with him. Chuck was a UDT/SEAL officer and was doing his time on shore duty to get his ticket punched on his way to admiral.

We arrived at Fresh Creek International Airport, a dirt strip with remnants of aircraft lying about the perimeter. A van ferried our gear to AUTEC compound. A platoon of civilian engineers had already arrived from another one of the naval engineering commands. Chuck was with them. During an impromptu meeting that we photographers weren't invited to attend, the frog officer told Lcdr. LeMoyne that we, Underwater Photo Team, were just photographers, and that they, the frogmen, were the ones trained to do scary shit. The frogmen felt they should be shooting the film, and we should just be there to support them. Chuck quickly put an end to that line of thinking, and things went on as planned.

When the ship exceeded eighteen knots, the sonar had such a loud ambient noise level that they couldn't hear anything over the passive sonar. The engineers believed the problem was being caused by cavitation along the sonar dome. Cavitation occurs when uneven pressures in the water, caused by irregular surfaces, pull air bubbles out of the water. When the bubbles collapse, noise is created that can screw up sonar. We had a boom-buoy system set up that would give the helmsman of the USS *California* (a six-hundred-foot nuclear powered frigate), a target to aim for. This system was nothing more than a couple of floats on ropes leading down to weights at the end. A boom made of neutrally buoyant aluminum tubing kept the sides separated a specific distance. The ship would go between the buoys in the same direction each time.

We would have photographers stationed in various places along the boom system. I would be halfway from the waterline to the keel on the starboard side shooting with a DBM-9 movie camera set at two hundred frames per second. We would wait on the surface hanging off of large inner tubes until the ship started its run. At a certain point, the ship would blow its whistle and the team would submerge and take up stations. When we arrived at them, on Chuck's hand signal, I would start shooting film of him firing a .357 magnum bangstick[†] into a five-gallon can we had tied off on the buoy line. This gave the ship an acoustic marker for reference. From that point on, I had to keep the trigger down on the camera to keep continuity. The ship came by at about twenty-two knots on the first run. I shot my film and noted my distance seemed to be a little father from the ship than I had wanted.

Between each run, we divers would surface and hand our cameras to photomates in the Zodiac inflatable who would reload them for us. Chuck would put another round in his bangstick, and we'd hang off of the inner tubes in the three-foot seas, conserving air and getting more and more seasick.

The two crews had become acquainted the night before in the dimly lit interior of the Thousand Fathom Club. Being short of women to impress, we simply got drunk and were not early to bed. This was taking a toll on the crew and me. I started to get seasick. Before long, I was puking and so were Chuck and a couple of the other guys. We were eager for the ship to return so we could be where it was calm. By now,

† A bangstick is a device that resembles a pistol barrel on the end of a pole. A cartridge is inserted into it so that when the end strikes anything solid, the cartridge moves back against the firing pin, causing it to fire. They are used against sharks for protection and for bagging large food fish.

the ship was supposed to be steaming by at thirty-two knots. I figured if they were going to have an observable cavitation problem, it would be on this last run. I'd be goddamned if I was going to miss it. This time, when I went down, I worked my way out to the middle of the boom after I filmed the bangstick. I looked back to check my distance from the line on my side of the boom system and realized, "Oh, shit. I'm too far out," and began swimming to where Chuck and another frogman were hanging off of the line.

Out of the gloom, in the three-hundred-foot visibility, came the bulbous sonar dome of the USS *California*. I was just to the starboard side of the dome and was going to get run over by it. I kicked my young, dumb ass into overdrive and just about broke the blades off my duck feet, keeping the camera switch jammed down hard. If I made it, this would be some wicked footage. I swam at warp speed until the hull stopped getting wider. I realized I was safe now, so I turned around and faced the hull. The ship was about ten feet from me and she was coming by at thirty-two knots.

I exhaled to get negatively buoyant and started to drop below the bilge keel. I could see the screws churning through the water, and dropped below the hull to shoot them from about thirty feet away, as the ship blasted by overhead with the sound of one hundred locomotives thundering in my ears. I swam into the prop wash, ready to be slammed all over the tongue of the ocean. I wasn't disappointed. With the camera shoved against my facemask, I rolled up into a ball and waited for the blast of water. It was as if I was an ant getting hit with a fire hose. The water was nothing but froth, throwing me all over the place, as if I was in a blender full of whipped cream. When the froth finally cleared, I looked around for my swim buddy, one of the frogmen who'd wanted this job. He was about thirty feet below me. I think his eyeballs were bugged out right against the faceplate of his mask.

Later that afternoon, as we relaxed in the air-conditioned comfort of the Thousand Fathom Club, Chuck stood up with glass in hand. "I just want you guys from Combat Camera to know that we'll swim with you anywhere, anytime." The frogmen echoed his sentiments in the background. That felt good to us "titless WAVES"—what photographers were often called.

Chuck LeMoyne made admiral some years later. He died of throat cancer in 1996. I was sorry to hear it. I thought he was a good man.

I never saw my footage from that job.

Chapter 18

The SHAD Project

The crew at Combat Camera now consisted of PH2 Bob Hasha, PH2 Paul Whitmore, PHC Dick Johnson, PH2 Harry Kulu, and PHC Dave Graver. Graver had made chief. PH1 Trotter, who had been there when I left for NSWG, had gotten himself into trouble for screwing the Navy on a per diem job. It was 1974 and there wasn't much work for the Underwater Photo Team, so I went to work drumming up some business. I called around and found out about a project called SHAD: Shallow Habitat Air Dive. The plan was to put a couple of divers in a chamber for thirty days at the equivalent depth of sixty feet on air. This would give them the effect of breathing a hyperoxic mix of gas and they would have more than the normal partial pressure of oxygen. There were plans to use air instead of the more expensive gases and equipment for saturation diving.

I volunteered. At first, they were not going to take me as I was not a first class diver, but they decided that I would be okay because I had a lot of experience. I am not sure that was the reason, but I didn't care.

I packed my gear and headed up the coast for Connecticut. I was driving a 1963 VW bug with a sunroof and a 6-volt system. It ran great, but was a piece of junk, and at night, the lights weren't much better than kerosene lamps. I had no trouble with it during the trip to Groton, though. When I got there, I signed in at the Naval Submarine Medical Research Laboratory (NSMRL). There, I met Dr. Claude Harvey, MC, USN, and a number of other doctors, both medical and Ph.D. types. I would be working with a crew of first class divers, and they didn't let me forget it, jokingly. The place was slack militarily, and everybody was on a first name basis. Ph.D.s and M.D.s and physiologists and shrinks surrounded us. I felt right at home. I was there under the guise of documenting the project for the Naval Photographic Center—where the Naval Photographic Archives are located—using my own personal cameras and Navy film. I was getting paid per diem, which was still about fourteen dollars a day. After check-in, I was put with Ray "Superfine" Fine, a hard-core diver who was very biased against other races, ethnic minorities, and just about anybody else. He carried a .44 magnum stuck in the crack of his ass whenever he went on liberty. Ray told me he had to pull it out once when he was accosted coming out of a bar. Two non-Caucasians grabbed him and pulled him into an alley. By the time they pulled him around the corner, he had shoved his pistol into the stomach of one of them, and they suddenly realized they'd grabbed the wrong guy. They apologized and Ray didn't shoot anybody.

Ray was intolerant of just about anything and anybody. The other three guys, Jack Welch, Burton, and Gary Seibert, were decent to work with. Gary and Ray were chosen to be in the chamber, and the rest of us would be topside as control subjects. As usual, the Navy did one hell of a fine job picking candidates for an experiment. I was the only one who didn't smoke at all or drink heavily.

The experiment depended on having people live about the same on the outside of the chamber as those on the inside. This meant we weren't supposed to smoke or drink and we topsiders had to carry a bottle with us all the time. Every time we urinated, it was to be collected in the Clorox bottle. Ellie, "the pee lady," as we called her, was an organic chemist or biologist who analyzed all the urine. Each morning, we'd come in and trade our full bottles for new ones. There was a slight amount of hydrochloric acid in the bottles to work as a preservative, and man, did it stink! It would almost make your eyes water whenever you had to uncap that jug. We were not welcome in restaurants for some reason, carrying these bottles. When we got up in the morning, we had to chew a piece of paraffin and spit it into a bottle so the doctors could get a bacteria count to determine if we had tendencies toward tooth decay. The dentist said I was very close to being immune to tooth decay, something true for only one out of 5,000 people. We also had samples of parotid fluid taken from the parotid glands in our cheeks. I didn't know there was such a thing as a parotid gland. They are part of the salivary gland system in our mouths.

We all were administered EKGs under stress, and had our carbon dioxide levels measured, both resting and under stress. Color vision, night vision, stereo vision and tonometric readings were taken of our eyes. An x-ray regimen began including images of our knees, shoulders, hips, and chests. We were told not to eat ice cream, gelatin, or chewy candy bars, as they contain alginate, or hydroxi-proleen. This would give the same readings as if you were losing bone mass. There was a room at the lab with a bed in it and copper screen all over the walls, floor, and ceiling. This was where we went for EEG tests. The screen was to filter to ground any extraneous electromagnetic energy. It turned out that none of us was a flat liner.

At exactly 1400 on March 15, 1974, the chamber was pressed down to sixty feet with Ray Fine and Gary Seibert inside. That night, I went in to the NSMRL to get checked out on the emergency back-up generator that would be put on line to keep the compressors running if there was a power failure.

We were briefed on chamber emergencies. For a failure of a fitting on the inside lock where Ray and Gary were, this was the scenario: The operator would jam on the air supply to override the loss and attempt to maintain depth. One of the other topside people would grab a toolbox with special plugs and a wrench, get into the outer lock, and run it down to depth (sixty feet). Now the inner door could be opened. The two "divers" would come into the outer lock, and the topside man would get into the inner lock and close the door. The outer lock would be maintained at sixty feet of equivalent depth. Then the inner lock could be drained, and the fitting that failed would be replaced with a blank plug. The inner lock would then be repressurized to sixty feet, and the fittings tested with a soap solution as well as an ultrasonic listening device that could hear air leaks, no matter how small. When it was determined to be safe, the inner door would be opened and the two "divers" would swap places with the topside man, who would go into the outer lock, close the door, and be brought back to the "surface."

While looking over the chamber, I wondered about something else. When they designed the hookup that would enable the men to take showers in the chamber, something had not been considered. There were two water heaters hooked up in parallel. The system pressurized them to about thirty-five PSI over bottom pressure. In most cases, though, water heaters receive cold water through the bottom and feed the hot water out the top. In this hookup, they had rigged it so that air pressure could be added to the tanks. However, when air was put into the lines, it just blew out through the discharge lines into the chamber, and only warm, moist air entered the chamber.

Master Diver Jordan was a retired Navy chief in charge of the chambers and all ancillary equipment at the Naval Submarine Medical Research Lab. I casually mentioned it to him in question form. "Gee, Chief. I wonder if they hooked that thing up the other way around, if it would work?"

The next day, I heard him telling project supervisor Lcdr. George Adams that they were going to reverse the input lines. There was another problem I wondered about. When blood was drawn, a needle was stuck in the "patient's" vein and on the other end of the little hose was another needle. This was stuck into a vacuum test tube. That works great on the surface, but I was wondering what would happen if they did that in the chamber. The equivalent vacuum would be around thirty PSI plus what the tubes were charged with. I asked one of the physiologists if PSI issue might cause a problem. He said it might, but they would cross that bridge when they came to it. Well, the first time they took blood using those vacuum-type test tubes, the guy's vein almost collapsed and the blood shot into the test tube so fast, it turned to a red froth and the platelets were damaged. After that, they just drew blood with large syringes and put it into tubes with the tops taken off. On the way "up" in the medical lock, the tops would be left slightly ajar, so the air could escape as it expanded. Things work differently under pressure.

Soon after the experiment began, Ray and Gary were in the chamber and pressed down, and the other guys started going out, drinking and smoking, and staying up late. Each morning, we were required to sit for a blood sample taken by Roger A. Williamson, M.D.[†] After about a week of being jabbed with needles, our arms all were black and blue from wrist to elbow. It looked as though we were junkies. Our blood gases were all screwed up because the topside guys were smoking, and the urine volume was high because of the beer. I was the only one who tried to stick to the regimen. I wasn't a goody-goody; I just wanted the damned experiment to be a success. We ate the food that they guys inside ate, and were supposed to note what we ate in addition to that. An old black woman came in and cooked for the guys. I can imagine she had trouble getting her kids to leave home. It was great chow.

Feeding the crew required the use of the medical lock: a small protrusion on the end of the chamber. The operator would call into the chamber and tell them to secure the inner door. After this was done, we

† Roger is now a professor at the University of Iowa Medical College.

depressurized the lock through a valve on the outside, then opened the door. Food, books, and whatnot were loaded into the lock, and the outer door was closed and dogged. We repressurized the lock by opening a valve inside the chamber. The "divers" would open the door and remove the items, then close and dog the inner door. Sometimes, a couple of us would lock in and eat breakfast with the chamber team. This required the large outer lock door to be opened. We entered the lock, closed the door, and the outside tenders pressurized the outer lock until the inner door could be opened. Then we would go inside, sit down, and eat the breakfast we carried in with us. The doctors took our blood and did whatever else was required as part of the day's procedures. Dr. Claude Harvey, MD was not especially adept at taking blood. He always had trouble hitting a vein. One morning when I was in the chamber, after we had eaten breakfast, Dr. Harvey was trying to get a blood sample from Ray "Superfine," who was lying down on his bunk. The Doc missed the vein about three times. Ray looked up at him and said, "Doc, you've got one more shot at hitting that vein before I tear your fucking head off."

Claude backed away and had the corpsman do it. The corpsman hit it first try. After that, he let the corpsmen draw all the blood from the guys in the chamber.

Dr. Ben Weybrew, the resident headshrinker, was a short man. He had a good sense of humor—a basic requirement for psychiatrists working with Navy divers. We used to take him out on the town with us, and he'd often have a beer with the guys before they went into saturation. We took the Minnesota Multiphasic Personality Inventory test (MMPI), along with some other personality profile exams. Mine came back that I had a "fighter pilot" personality. Dr. Weybrew administered an I.Q. test, too, and all the guys came back with above average scores. Mine was good enough to join MENSA, to which I belonged for many years.

In addition to the psychological exams, we had to take color vision, respiratory capacity, coordination, math skills under stress, and other tests. On the day we were taking the color vision test, I mentioned to Doctor Saul Luria, Ph.D., that I thought this test would not provide proper data because it was being given under abnormal conditions. He looked at me funny and asked me what I meant. I pointed up at the lights.

"What is the color temperature and composition of the spectrum of light coming from those?" I questioned.

He slapped himself on the forehead. "Shit, that's right. There's excess green and not much red in there. All the tests we've given so far have been done under incorrect conditions."

Saul mounted one of those little Tensor reading lamps over the table, and after that, all of us got nearly perfect scores. Being a photographer helped me understand about light color temperature.

The coordination and math tests were fun. For the coordination test, we sat in chairs using joysticks, trying to keep one green dot on top of another green dot. The dots were the same size and color. The faster we went the faster the first dot moved, so we could never win. The math test was interesting, too. There was a column of three three-digit numbers. We had to add the top two three-digit numbers together, subtract the bottom three-digit number, then punch in the answer from left-to-right, instead of right-to-left as normal. The more times we were right, the faster the machine went, until we made mistakes. The machine kept the pressure on, and even though we knew it didn't count for anything, most of us tried to do our best.

We shot color slides of each others' retinas so that the doctors could detect any rupturing or abnormalities in the blood vessels inside our eyes from pressure or decompression sickness. To do this, we used a special fundoscopic camera—a 35mm camera connected to a long tube. We looked at a bright light in the end of the tube; stared into it until the photographer on the other end could see the retina. Then he fired the shutter and the camera captured a flash picture of the inside of the eye. Well, Ray and Gary created their own version of a "retina." When the first batch of photos came back from the processor, one of the naive doctors couldn't understand why the retina had hair around it. Either Ray or Gary had photographed the other's rectum. Some of the doctors had a sense of humor. Others, we found out, did not.

On some days, the program required the men in the chamber to make "excursions." These were normally kept at the pressure equivalent of sixty feet, but sometimes the men were taken down to well over two hundred feet. Common sense dictates that, at sixty feet, a man will perform better mentally and physically than at deeper depths, where pressure and an increase in nitrogen narcosis might impair his mental capabilities. Not so Ray Fine. He did better on the math test and the coordination at over two hundred feet than he did at sixty feet. Nobody ever figured out why.

When I took the respiratory volume test, there was a problem. The test consisted of taking all the air into your lungs that you could hold. You would then blow it out into a bellows arrangement that was calibrated in liters of volume. This would measure your tidal respiratory volume. A little rod on the side of the bellows would pass by a gage so the corpsman could read the capacity your lungs. When he did mine, the needle kept going off the scale. The corpsman had me repeat the test until I thought I was going to pass out from hyperventilation.

"Hey! Get in here, Doc," he called out to a physician passing by. "There's something wrong with the wedge spirometer."

The doctor came into the room and had me do the test once again. "Hell, there's nothing wrong with the equipment. This guy just has huge lungs."

It turned out that I have about an eleven-liter lung capacity. Normal is from five to seven. They started giving me the third degree on where I grew up and if I'd had any diseases or anything as a child.

"Oh, shit," I thought, "here goes my diving career down the tubes." About this time, one of the doctors spoke up and told me whatever they learned here stayed here and would not be part of my medical record. "I had asthma when I was a kid," I told them.

The doctors decided that might be the reason for the large lung capacity and said I wouldn't be able to be a subject in the chamber. If nothing happened to me and did to others, it might have been because of childhood asthma, or the other way around.

The SHAD project lasted two months, with Gary and Ray in the chamber for weeks four through seven. The eighth week, the doctors conducted studies on the men who had been in the chamber.

I didn't believe there was a good baseline for the project, either on the outside or the inside of the chamber. Gary's wife, Mona, was staying in the area, but he had marital problems. Using the headset, Mona bragged to Gary about her sexual exploits with men she'd meet at night at bars and clubs. And Ray was a mean, cantankerous bastard most of the time. I just couldn't imagine any reliable results from this study upon which to base further experimentation.

One day, I decided to go to the base at Groton to see if I could find a classmate from Second Class Diver's School who had been transferred to the NR-1, the Navy's smallest nuclear submarine. The Top Secret sub was used for "black projects" and had a very small crew for a submarine. I walked down the pier to the NR-1, where it was tied off by itself. I was a bit nervous about going aboard, as my clearance level was only *secret*. I walked closer and shouted, "Hello aboard NR-1." No answer. I stepped onto the brow, walked onto the deck, and up to the conning tower. I called out again. No answer. I walked inside the conning tower and over to the hatch, which was open. I could hear machinery noises coming from below and could see into what I figured was the control room. Another shout from me and still no response. By now, I was quite nervous, given the capability and purpose of this sub, so I walked off it, went back to my car, and left. I was amazed at the slack security around that "black" boat.

At noon on April 12, 1974, Ray and Gary came out of the chamber not much the worse for wear, but not smelling very good. And the shower in the outer lock just didn't do the job. Later on, I heard that they were both weak for quite some time because, while in the hyperoxic environment of the chamber, their bodies hadn't created new red blood cells necessary to provide oxygen.

The next year, they ran another SHAD dive. This time, Burton was one of the men in the chamber. I heard that he was sick for almost a year afterwards. It was decided to cut back the partial pressure of oxygen to about what a person would be breathing on the surface. The last week after the chamber run, there was not much to do, so we straightened out our gear and checked out of the NSMRL.

Mary rode the bus to Groton so she could help with the driving on the way home. I had been shooting Kodachrome so all my film and camera gear were packed and ready to go. We stayed a couple of days at the motel where I had been living, then drove back to Virginia Beach. As we were going through New York, I decided we should stop somewhere to get some food, so we pulled off the highway at an exit. As we drove through an underpass, we spotted a large station wagon pulled to the side of the road. The hood was raised and there was a woman standing there as if waiting for assistance. I drove by and we managed to get something to eat at a convenience store. On the way back to find the freeway, I got lost as usual. We passed the disabled car again. The woman was no longer with the car. It had not been twenty minutes since we last passed by this vehicle. We couldn't believe it, the car was now up on cinder blocks and all the wheels were gone, the seats had been stripped out of it, and it was nothing but a hulk.

Mary was working at Haynes Furniture in Norfolk as a layout artist. Her job was laying out ads using the artwork produced on site by a man named Paul Boatwright. Paul had a degree in fine arts from Yale, and he and his wife, Kitty, became good friends of ours. Paul had a sailboat. It was a Cheoy Lee twenty-eight-foot sloop. I had never been sailing on a real sailboat before, but I'd had my share of time on the water, lobster fishing and, in one way or another, being on the water my whole life. Paul asked us if we wanted to go sailing. I figured, why not. It might be fun. So we went to where he kept the boat at the Rebel Marina on Willoughby Spit, and we cast off for an afternoon on the Chesapeake Bay.

It didn't take me long to catch the bug, and before I knew it, I was reading *Sail Magazine* and *Cruising World Magazine*. Mary and I decided to buy a WestSail 32 sailboat and live on it. Lane Briggs, owner of Rebel Marine Service and Rebel Marina, told me I would be able to keep the boat at the marina and, to pay for the slip, be a night watchman and do some diving. It would be a good deal. I went to the bank and talked to the manager, a retired Navy captain by the name of Lee Mather. I asked him if they would finance the boat as a residence if I were to live aboard. He said they would and asked me where I was going to buy it. I told him I didn't know yet. He said it just happened that a good friend of his, Rear Admiral Jim Cobb, was the local representative and I should give him a call. He kept his boat over at the Norfolk Shipbuilding and Dry Dock yard, and was one hell of a good guy. I was an E-6 and quite nervous about hobnobbing with a retired admiral. I hadn't had much experience with anybody above the rank of lieutenant commander, but I called Cobb up and asked when I could look at a WestSail. He told me he'd be there on the weekend, so Mary and I went and had a look. We immediately knew that was the boat we wanted. It didn't look like a racer, but it looked bullet proof and was modeled after a Norwegian pilot boat, so I knew it was seaworthy—probably more so than we were.

Cobb turned out to be one of the nicest guys I'd ever met.[†] I couldn't imagine a better person to do business with. The first day we met him, he invited us for lunch. He was eating sardines and peanut butter crackers, washing his down with beer. I drank a Coke with mine. He didn't want to use the head in the boat, so he had a plastic bottle to urinate in, and he'd dump it overboard later. The guy was a real person and Mary and I both liked him a lot. He became a surrogate father to us.

We came up with the thousand-dollar down payment to lock in the order and discussed the features we wanted on the boat. I chose the teak decks and a few other extras that would be easier to get from the builder rather than add on later. Jim took us sailing on many occasions and told us many sea stories about his forty-six years of naval service. He had quit high school—or been thrown out—and joined the Navy. An officer he worked for had seen potential in him and counseled him to get his GED and to try for the Naval Academy. Jim did and got accepted.

† Rear Admiral Jim Cobb, USN, (Ret.) died at the age of 97 in August 2008.

He was accepted to flight school and flew PBY amphibious airplanes during WWII. He was stationed at Pearl Harbor during the attack and had made a bombing run on a Japanese submarine off Diamond Head the day before. He told me that, on the day of the attack, he'd jumped out of bed and pulled his socks on so hard he drove his feet right through the bottoms of them. He went into the yard and shot at the Japanese planes with his .45. He never hit any, but it made him feel as if he was doing something to help.

Later on, he was flying the first plane to ever bomb an enemy ship by radar contact alone. PBYs didn't have bomb racks, so they would open the door in the side and throw bombs out by hand. He always tried to get the strongest and biggest men on his flight crew. Jim had flown a PBY under the Golden Gate Bridge and gotten away with it. He was a wild man in his younger days. To get into the Navy, Rear Admiral Jim Cobb had lied about his age and about having asthma. Years later, he called his friend, an admiral who was chief of the Bureau of Naval Personnel (BUPERS), and told him there was an error in his service record. Jim said that a mistake had been made in his age and that he was one year younger than was recorded; that he'd lied to get into the Navy. The admiral laughed and told Jim he'd made up for it by serving more than forty years on active duty. Jim was not one to shirk hard work. He rebuilt the stone walls on his property in Virginia and ran his first marathon at the age of sixty-eight.

Not long after ordering the WestSail, Mary discovered she was pregnant, but we still wanted to get the boat. We decided to go back to Maine for a few days of leave, so we climbed into the old Datsun pickup and pounded our way up the coast. When we got there, we found out my neighbor's house was for sale. It had been built by my great-grandmother's brother in 1898, and had a great view of the Mussel Ridge Islands. I could look out from the kitchen window and see Dix Island where my great-grandmother had been born in 1866. Her father, Cyrus Rackliff, had been a member of the granite-cutting crew who worked on these small islands a couple of miles off shore.

I had approached my neighbor previously about selling it. He had been reticent about putting it on the market, but gave me first refusal on it. He'd inherited it from his best friend and didn't want the capital gains tax burden right away. Now he was ready to sell. We told him we'd take it. I hated to go back to Jim Cobb and tell him about the house deal, but when I did, he understood perfectly and said, "I don't blame you for buying a house instead. They'll be making fiberglass sailboats a long time after they've quit making shorefront property in

Maine." He smiled and wrote me a check for my one-thousand-dollar deposit. Jim told me that in the time since I'd ordered, the price of the boat had gone up and he had people who would take it.

I began working for Cobb on weekends, taking people out sailing, and generally being the guy who kept the boat squared away. He gave me a hundred bucks a month and I could go sailing whenever I wanted to. That fall, I went to the Newport Boat show and helped sail a new WestSail 43 to Annapolis, Maryland with Jim Cobb and an old friend of his, retired Navy Captain Buck James.

Before cancelling the boat order, Mary and I had been looking forward to getting the boat and had stuffed every cent we could into the bank. Between getting rid of Mary's car payments and paying off our bills, plus our frugal life style, we were rapidly building up a cash reserve. By now, we had ten thousand dollars in savings.

I called Rockland Savings & Loan in Maine and they told me there would be no problem financing the house, so I transferred our savings into the checking account so my check would be good when I got to Maine. My sister, Heather, drove me to the Greyhound Bus station. She had joined the Navy after finishing college and was now the Classified Material Officer at the Naval Weapons Station in Yorktown, Virginia. Mary and my other sister, Cheryl came along for the ride.

We arrived at the bus station. I grabbed my bag and walked inside. When I got to the counter to buy a ticket, I broke out my checkbook and asked the ticket agent how much it would cost for a round trip to Rockland, Maine. She noticed I was starting to write a check and informed me that I would have to speak to the manager before they would take my check. I thought nothing of it and walked back his office. From his glass enclosure, he looked out through the little round window and asked me if he could help me. I said I was going to Maine to close on a house and needed to write a check for the ticket. He asked me where I worked. I told him I was in the Navy. His exact words were, "Sorry, pal. We don't take checks from servicemen here on weekends."

I went apeshit, to put it mildly. I started raving about how the whole goddamned Tidewater Area of Virginia depended on us—low-life servicemen—to stay alive, and the sons-of-bitches wouldn't even take a check from us! I made some remark about dragging his narrow ass through that little round window and stomping the shit out of him. I decided to back off when he reached for the phone, I assumed to call the police. A bus driver was standing at the back of the room. He just grinned as I stormed out the door.

Heather hadn't left yet, so I threw my things in the car and we drove away. I had a couple of dollars in my pocket, but it was the principal of it— that jerk not accepting my check. I told her to step on it, as I assumed he would be calling the Norfolk Police. She drove me to the Chesapeake Bay Bridge Tunnel and I got out at the bus stop at the end of the bridge. In a while, the bus came by and I got on board. The same driver who saw my tirade earlier was behind the wheel. He grinned and told me that I could pay for the ticket at the first stop. I had calmed down by now and I just put my brain in neutral until I got home. Mary flew up later on and we closed the deal. Now, we were making payments on a house in Maine as well as paying rent on the Lauderdale Avenue house in Virginia Beach behind the Little Creek Amphibious Base.

Our neighbors in Virginia Beach, Duke and 'Chele Leonard, were some of our closest friends. Duke had been a second-class mineman (MN2) in SEAL Team 2. He had served in Vietnam extensively and had been awarded the Silver Star for saving a Vietnamese troop. Duke and his men were pinned down in a river when he saved the troop, then loaded him into a hovering helicopter during a firefight in the middle of the river. Not a good place to be. Duke had recently left the Navy and was attending college to get a degree so that when he returned to the Navy, he could become an officer with the SEALs. Duke needed a job to relieve some of his financial strain. I called Beldon Little to see if he had anything going. Beldon didn't have any steady work, but managed to throw Duke some work now and then.

'Chele worked full time at a bookstore. The only "kid" they had at the time was a large, black Great Dane named Whiskey. He must have weighed two hundred pounds and was ferocious—at least that's what they wanted people to think. He would ride around town in the front seat of 'Chele's yellow VW convertible. When she had the top down, Whiskey could look over the windshield if he wanted to, he was so tall. People rarely gave her any trouble. We had a lot of good times and parties. There was a party almost every night.

Mary and I were also friends with Slator Blackiston, and Bill Barth. These two had gone through UDT Training with Duke. Slator and his wife, Diane, had a new brick house in a development that was not close to the beach. We went there a few times for parties, and they came to our houses on the beach. 'Chele's parents and brother came by and visited us quite a lot. Mike, 'Chele's father, was a hard working, ex-enlisted sailor who had served on submarines in combat during WWII. Mike retired from the Navy as a LCDR. 'Chele's mom, Olga—whom we called Ogie—was one of those people everybody wants for a mother. 'Chele's parents were great people who would do anything to help any of us. Peter, 'Chele's brother, had a job riding around a railyard on a bicycle to check for fires and bums lying on the tracks. He was really intelligent, and it took him a while before he finally found his place in life—working on computers.

The next house over from Duke and Chele's was occupied by Guntis "John" Jaunzems, a member of SEAL Team Two who had emigrated from Germany when very young. He was born in Latvia and had spent his teen years in Germany. John, as we all called him, was a great guy, superior operator, and had an I.Q. off the scale. One night, a group of German UDT guys (Kampfschwimmers) were over at John's house getting drunk, and before the night was over, Mary was over there speaking German with them. She had thought she'd forgotten her German, but the beer made it come back.

Another time, I was at a bar called the Casino, just a couple hundred yards up the road. Another of my neighbors and former frogman, Howard Blaha, was there drinking beer. Somehow, we ended up arm wrestling. I beat him every time, but just barely. We went back and forth, alternating arms until I had won ten times. It was very close each time. The next day, I couldn't raise my arms. I was so damned sore. Howard was killed in a car wreck some years later.

My sister, Cheryl, by now a lieutenant in the Medical Service Corps, lived in the house on the other side of ours. She was stationed at the Portsmouth Naval Hospital. Cheryl had worked her way through college using some government loans for her internship, so she had to serve her time in the Navy. She put in a total of twelve years active, and made commander in the Naval Reserves. Our younger sister, Heather, had joined the Navy after college. Cheryl swore her in, and I photographed the ceremony while Mary, my wife, took pictures of the whole thing.

Later on that year, I took a crew of underwater photographers up to Newport, Rhode Island to worked for the Underwater Sound Lab on Gould Island where we'd be doing more missed-distance testing on the Mark 48 torpedo exploders. My sister, Cheryl, had been transferred to the Newport Naval Hospital. She had a large apartment, so we borrowed two sets of Navy issue bunkbeds, converted one of her rooms into a bunkroom for the four of us, and had the use of the kitchen and bathroom. This saved us from renting motel rooms. We paid her for the duration of our stay as well as buying all the grub.

Joe Parker, an engineer from the Naval Ordnance Lab in White Oak, Maryland, was the man in charge of the torpedo project. We worked for him while on the island. Frank Deriso, a mechanical engineer from the Underwater Sound Lab, was our direct boss. Each morning, we went to the pier and rode out to Gould Island aboard a Navy utility boat. We left our diving gear on the island, so we only needed to take our lunches and dry towels back and forth.

We dived in wet suits, but mostly stood around waiting for the crew to fire torpedoes. One of the guys brought a .22 target pistol, so we set up a range outside and practiced shooting at cans and pieces of roofing that had blown off the buildings. The place was in a rundown condition. The huge compressor still worked. We used it to fire the torpedo tube and had a whip rigged up to fill out scuba tanks with this same air. Our job was to rig up an underwater housing in which a Hasselblad camera was mounted. The camera was mounted on an H-beam that was part of the target past which the torpedo would be fired. The torpedo had a row of lights in its right side. When the crew had everything set, they would turn the lights on in the fish; we'd open the shutter on the camera, remotely, and fire the torpedo—in that order. The torpedo would flash past the camera leaving a streak of light on the film, then float up a distance from the target. A torpedo retriever boat from the base was standing by to pick up the dummy torpedo and bring it back to the dock where it would be used again. The purpose of this drill was to determine exactly how far away from the hull of a ship the torpedo could be and still trigger the warhead. Of course, there were no explosives involved here, and the electrical charge that would have fired the torpedo made a mark on the engineer's oscilloscope instead.

This job was not exciting. Newport was a stuffy place with a mild to strong dislike of enlisted sailors, so on weekends, we would pile into the rental car and drive up to Maine. We ate lobster and generally messed around like sailors on liberty did. When the job was completed, I turned in the rental car and we all flew back to Norfolk. It was now nearly June 1974.

Chapter 19

Italy

When we weren't on the road working at our trade, things got a little boring around the diving locker. We had some make-work projects like helping out in the pool, going to leadership school, attending meetings, and pulling maintenance on our air compressor and the two inflatable outboards. All of our underwater motion picture cameras had rechargeable batteries and had to be constantly monitored to insure they didn't discharge and ruin the insides of the housing. So I put in for a slot at the Naval School of Deep Sea Diving, where I would become a diver, first class. My request went through the chain of command and was approved. School would start sometime in April 1975. In the meantime, I needed to stay busy.

Not much was happening and we were getting a little antsy and wanting to get out and operate. I looked around for more work, but found none. Then one day Chief Dick Johnson asked if I had a passport. I told him I didn't.

"What's the deal?" I asked.

"They need somebody to fly over to Naples, Italy to do a job and you're the only one I trust to do it right. I'll check and see if you can get away with just a Navy I.D. Card." He checked and found out that I could as long as I was traveling on Navy orders.

The USS *Cascade* was a destroyer tender that had been hauled out and painted in an Italian shipyard. The yard had been hired to paint the bottom with a special tin-tributylin paint that was supposed to be extremely effective in keeping the marine growth to a minimum. It hadn't been working. Reportedly, the workers had sprayed the paint on from distances of up to ten feet, and that there was no way they could have done a proper paint job from that distance.

The *Cascade* was tied up in Naples and was due to be towed home for scrapping. It seems the Navy wanted to sue the yard and recover some of the costs of the bad paint job. My job was to go to Naples and shoot underwater stills of the growth on the hull, which would be used in court to prove that the paint hadn't been applied per specifications.

I packed my diving gear. All I needed was a regulator, fins, mask, and my UDT life jacket, as the water would be warm and the tender had plenty of weight belts and tanks. My choice of a camera was a Leica M-2 body in an underwater housing built by E. Leitz of Canada. This housing was specially built for the Navy, didn't require any focusing and the lens was the sharpest one I have ever seen. The camera body was mounted onto the lens in the housing and the flash synchronization cord was connected, the back cover was dogged on, and I was in business. It was small and light. I packed a sub-sea strobe and some film and was ready to go. I would travel and work in civilian clothes.

Mary drove me to the airport and I took off for New York, where I would change planes en route for Naples. The flight was as boring as one can be. We change planes again in Rome. The sight of a group of nineteen-year-old Italian cops in uniform carrying machine guns as they wandered around the airport did not instill much confidence.

PH1 Doug Keever, of the AFCCG Naples Detachment, picked me up at Naples Airport and took me to a house where I would be staying with him and another man from Combat Camera's Naples Detachment. I unpacked my things and he gave me a ride to the *Cascade*. I told him I'd arrange a ride to the photo lab; he had set it up for me to process my film there when I finished the job.

I walked up the brow, showed my I.D. to the officer of the deck, and was escorted aboard. The *Cascade's* diving officer was a warrant officer. When I entered the diving locker, he was sitting at his desk. He looked up and then stood and shook my hand.

"Welcome aboard, Waterman. So you're the guy who's gonna try to shoot underwater pictures of our hull?" The smirk was not hidden in the tone of his voice.

"No, Sir. I *am* going to shoot underwater pictures of your hull," I countered.

He smiled and sat down again.

"Tell me what you need for gear and I'll get you a swim buddy."

I told him I only needed a set of tanks and a weight belt as I already had my vest, regulator, mask, and fins. I changed into my trunks and we went out on deck. We carried our gear down to the pier where some of the deck crew had rigged a ladder down to the water. My swim buddy was going to use a Jack Browne mask instead of scuba so that he'd have a lifeline and communications to the surface. He had a mask that was fitted with a communications microphone so he could talk to the tender. I had the camera loaded with Kodak Tri-X film and had made sure the battery was charged in my strobe unit. We jumped into the water—the ladder was for getting out—and made our way over to the side of the ship. I had not gone very far down the hull when I started seeing huge amounts of marine growth. It looked like a damned garden. There were anemones the size of small apples sticking out from the hull. I shot some photos of them and continued under to the keel. My swim buddy had a flashlight that he used to point at where he thought the worst of the growth was. But there really wasn't any "worst." It was all bad. The Mediterranean is a great place for marine growth, and without the protection of the bottom paint, the hull was like a fertile garden.

We returned to the side of the ship and climbed the ladder onto the dock. Just then, a young officer walked up to me and asked if I could get some photographs of the underside of his destroyer. It was moored outboard of the *Cascade*. I told him I could. He asked if I could shoot them in color as they had put some red lead on something and wanted to show it in color to see if it was corroding. I had a few rolls of Ektachrome with me that could be processed at the lab. I usually shot Kodachrome, but that has to be sent to Kodak for processing and takes a few weeks to get back. I wanted to be able to get results right away. Back in the diving locker, I dried off the camera and changed film, putting in the roll of color.

"Do you have any idea where this thing is we have to shoot?" I asked my swim buddy.

"Yeah, I can put you right on it." he answered. I wasn't sure that he could.

We returned to the pier and the water and then swam under the *Cascade*, out the other side, between the two ships, and then under the destroyer. Once we passed the turn of the bilge, the visibility turned to zero. During the swim, my buddy's flashlight quit working and we moved along in the darkness by feel. After a while he grabbed my arm and put my hand on something on the hull over my head. With the other hand, he squeezed my arm twice. I understood the thing I had my hand on was what they needed photos of. I pointed the camera up where my hand was, moved my hand quickly, shot the photo, put my hand back and did this several times, varying the F stop. After the last shot I turned and gave him two squeezes on the arm and he led us out from under the destroyer.

Now for the good part. I wondered if I had just made an ass of myself for being so cocky in front of the diving officer. My swim buddy and I changed our clothes and he gave me a ride over to the base photo lab. He didn't have to be anywhere, so I told him to hang around and I'd process the film and see what I had. I souped the black and white and looked at the negatives. Everything came out perfect! You could even see the little hairs in the sea anemones' structure. Every little detail was there. While the negatives were drying, we went to the gedunk and got a hamburger and Coke. Then we went back to the lab and I made five prints of each shot. Meanwhile, one of the guys in the lab ran the color film for me. I couldn't believe it. All of the photos were right on the money. Most of the exposures were correct, and I had correctly framed the fitting I was photographing.

It was hard to keep the grin off my face when I laid those black-and-white photos in front of the diving officer. He had the damnedest look on his face, as though I'd hit him with a bat.

"I'll be damned," he said. "I can't believe you got pictures of the bottom of this tub in that sewer down there."

I remained humble and withheld any smart-ass remarks. "Well, Sir, there's a good reason why they sent me over here clear from Norfolk."

"Oh, yeah? What was that?"

"'Cause they couldn't find anybody else," I laughed.

He thought that was funny and started putting the photos into piles, separating them into stacks according to where they would be sent.

"I think you don't need me any more," I said.

"No, but thanks a lot for doing this job. It will mean a lot to the skipper and the admiral."

The diver who had been working with me took the roll of color slides and said he would get them to the officer on the destroyer. He must have done it, as we received a letter of thanks at Combat Camera Group from the captains of both ships.

I caught a ride back to the Combat Camera Detachment with the diver and went up to the office. There were only about a dozen people stationed here in the Naples Detachment, and it was more of a boondoggle than anything. The standard of living was high.

Art Cutter was the officer in charge—the guy I'd bad-mouthed previously when he made warrant officer. He wasn't really a bad guy, I had just been spouting off that day when I made that remark.

Sometimes, people just took me too seriously. Art took me out and showed me his house, and we drove around a little through Naples to see some of the sights. When we came back to the unit, I called Norfolk on the AUTOVON network (military and government phone network) and had the operator patch me though to Mary. She was pregnant with our first child and I wondered how she was doing. The connection was clear and I talked for a few minutes on Uncle Sam's nickel.

Later that afternoon, Doug Keever and I went back to his apartment. We cleaned up and got ready to pull some liberty in Naples. The car Keever had was a real junker. The passenger seatback kept flopping backwards and wouldn't stay up, so I had to lean forward if I didn't want to lie down. He said it was good for some things, but not much for riding around. On a corner, we passed by a couple of good-looking women, or at least I thought they were. I asked Doug what the story was. He told me they were cross-dressed men. I didn't believe him, so we slowed down when we came to some more of them.

Doug leaned out the window and said, "Quanta costa?" or "How much" in Italian. One of them walked over to the car. I got the message; "she" had a slight five o'clock shadow. That took care of my questions. We drove to the Silver Dollar, a local bar where many of the Combat Camera types hung out. The bartender's name was Jerry and he spoke excellent English. We stayed there and had a few beers, then drove back and hit the rack.

The next day, I rode to the base with Doug and made the rounds of the Exchange and some little shops nearby. I purchased a mandolin for about fifteen dollars that seemed to be a good instrument for the price. I bought a pair of silver earrings for Mary, then hung around the Combat Camera spaces for the rest of the day. We shot the bull and talked about photography, the Navy, and women, as usual, but probably not in that order.

My flight was due to leave the next day, so I collected my gear (what little I had) and crammed it into a small bag. My camera was in a small case that looked like a woman's compact kit. That's what I liked about that Leica housing. I wish I had one of them today. It was the best underwater camera I have ever used. Most of the underwater photos in this book were taken with one of them. Doug ran me to the airport and we shook hands good-bye. I told him I'd see him in Norfolk soon, as he was getting ready to rotate back to the States.

I went through the usual routine to get on the plane. Security was fairly tight, but nothing like it is today. The same kids were running around with machine guns and looking like they were trained for anything. I checked my bag and carried my mandolin and camera case onto the plane with me. My seat was up against the bulkhead, so I had a lot of legroom. As I got comfortable in the seat, I looked around and noticed that everybody around me was a lot taller than me, and I am six feet, three inches. After a while, I asked the guy sitting next to me how tall he was.

"Seven-foot-six," he answered.

I glanced back at the three guys sitting behind us. They were all about the same.

"You guys play a little basketball?" I asked.

"Yeah, we're semi-pros and play for a corporate league, we were over here playing another company's team."

I can't remember the guy's surname but his first name was Ron. He told me he'd been drafted by the Chicago Bulls, and was a schoolteacher from somewhere in Illinois. He was worried about not making the team because of an old knee injury he had suffered. We talked for a while and the flight attendant announced that tax-free liquor could be purchased. I looked over at Ron and asked him if he drank scotch. He replied that he did so we purchased a liter of Johnny Walker Black Label from the stewardess for five dollars and I asked for two cups of ice. She gave me a little talk about it being against regulations to drink on the plane unless she served it. I told her I understood the rules and we would make every effort to comply. When she turned her back and waited on others, I cracked the cap and Ron and I poured a couple of large slugs of the fiery liquid into our plastic cups. We managed to consume the entire bottle crossing the Atlantic. I can barely remember getting off the plane.

When I passed through customs, the inspector asked me where I had been, how long I had been there, and what I had brought back. I told him: Italy, three days, a mandolin, and half a bottle of scotch, and that it was inside me. He was only slightly disgusted as he passed me through. "Three days in Italy and all you brought back was a bottle of booze? Get out of here."

My next flight left from Kennedy Airport. I had landed in La Guardia, so I took a helicopter shuttle from La Guardia to Kennedy. At JFK, I called Mary and told her what time the flight landed in Norfolk, then got aboard and ordered a drink—something I really needed. By the time I arrived, I was in good shape—I thought. When it came time to get off the plane, I staggered down the ramp and walked to the gate. Mary was waiting for me, terminally pregnant with our first kid, and had to help me walk to the baggage claim and then to the car. We got a lot of stares.

Ron had given me a package on the plane. He had bought some things in Italy and wanted me to have something to take to my wife. It was a small ceramic vase. It seems we'd become good friends in our drunken state.

Mary poured me into the VW and drove me home. I went to bed and slept soundly for the remainder of the night.

When I returned to the unit the next day, there was a message to our command from the staff in the Mediterranean thanking them for the great job I did. The skipper called me up to the office and told me he appreciated me taking care of that job. I told him that I would be willing to take any off-the-wall job that nobody else either would or could do. It was a good feeling to be appreciated.

My next big adventure was attending Race Relations Training. Once again, I went over to Little Creek Amphibious Base for the school. It was supposed to last one week, and make us aware that we were probably racist, bigoted, unthinking sons-of-bitches.

The first day of the class, we had to stand up in a circle and tell everybody our name. The class met in a circle of chairs, so that nobody got to sit at the end of the table and feel somehow superior as a result.

The petty officer who ran the class was a light-colored black guy with blue eyes, who was wearing a second-class diving patch on his uniform. He also drove a Jaguar XKE. The first thing I did was to ask him about his background.

"Looks like you're from the guts of the ghetto," I joked. "What does your father do for a living?"

"Oh, he's a thoracic surgeon out in L.A.," he answered.

"Yeah, and you bought that Jag on a second class's pay, right?" I asked. "Something tells me you ain't exactly what the Navy had in mind for this course, being a typical black guy and all that," I kidded.

He got the message. I knew that being the "race relations" counselor was a tit job and I wished I had something as good. As a matter of fact, I did, so I backed off and got along with the guy very well, as we were both divers.

When they got to the part about being prejudiced, I stood up and made my speech.

"Well," I started, "where I come from, we don't have any black people, except a few that came to Maine on the underground railroad during the Civil War. But they've been watered down by white people, and we don't even consider them to be black any more. When I was growing up, they had to pick on somebody, so they picked on the Finns because they spoke a foreign language and drank a lot. Pretty soon the Finns lost their accents and became lawyers and doctors, etc., so nobody could tell who they were any more. We still needed somebody to pick on, so I pick on people who are assholes. They come in all colors."

That got a round of cheers and laughter, which is all I lived for in these stupid politically correct schools. At the end of that class I returned to Combat Camera Group and more underwater photography adventures.

One of the people I had met over the years was Jack Chappell. I haven't mentioned him up to this point, because we never did anything together, just talked. Jack was an ace underwater and topside photographer and one of the smartest people I had ever met. He could also sell ice to the Eskimos.

Jack, and Buck Rousie, a commercial and salvage diver, had teamed up with Hyrum Mulliken. Hyrum owned the dive shop where most of us bought our gear. One day, a fisherman from the Eastern Shore of Virginia dragged up a piece of gold bullion in his net and marked the spot on the chart. Somehow, Jack and Buck became involved and wanted me to be on the crew that followed up on the find. They felt the gold bullion had come from the steamer *Merida*, a 6,207-ton passenger freighter that was struck amidship and sunk by the SS *Admiral Farragut* on May 12, 1911. While steaming in a fog on a voyage from Mexico to New York, *Merida* was rumored to have had a large amount of silver and copper on board. Others had tried to recover the treasure, but if they managed to pull it off, they certainly had kept quiet about it. The earliest attempt recorded was in 1917.

Jack and Buck came over to the house and we formulated a plan. There would be several teams. The Salvage Team would be in charge of setting up the diving operation and removing the metal from the wreck. The Support Team would get the diving equipment, the food, tools, and the rest of the equipment, like radios, etc. The Photo Team would do no salvage or support work, but would only document the entire operation. This sounded like it had the makings of a successful operation, but Murphy is always lurking in the background.

We planned to go up the Eastern Shore, take a boat out to the site and make a preliminary dive on the wreck. I would go along for the ride and Jack, Buck and Hyrum would be there as observers, and to oversee a dive that one of Hyrum's men would make to survey the wreck.

This ship lay in two-hundred-ten feet of water, so the working dives would require a serious diving operation and we'd need to have a chamber topside and medical personnel standing by.

The lot of us drove to the Eastern Shore, climbed aboard the old fisherman's boat, and steamed out to the Loran A bearings he had marked when he found the bullion. We got on-site and watched for the indication on the recording fathometer that showed us we were above the ship. The ocean floor in that area is mostly flat mud, so anything sticking up from it would have to be a ship. The skipper of the fishing boat was right on target and we hooked into the wreck with our anchor. Our diver, a Navy first class diver taking time off, strapped on a set of double tanks and jumped overboard. He followed the anchor line down to the wreck, and stayed to his maximum bottom time. When he came up, he assured us that it was the *Merida* and that it had been blasted flat. He was eager to make another quick dive so, against our better judgment, he strapped on another set of tanks and went down for a quick look.

Apparently during World War II, the navy had depth-charged this vessel until it was nothing more than a pile of scrap metal on the bottom. German U-Boats had traveled off the coast up and down the Eastern Seaboard, and any underwater metal was hammered by the surface craft. We also heard unsubstantiated rumors that the silver had been removed by one of several salvors attempting to get the riches off the vessel.

We went ashore and headed back to Norfolk. Later that evening, our diver was stricken with decompression sickness and had to be treated in the recompression chamber at the dive school at Little Creek. That did not bode well for us, and we never followed through on this adventure, although Jack and Buck's company, DiveScan, was well-equipped to do it.

Chapter 20

Naval School, Diving, & Salvage

Mary was getting big with our first kid, and had arranged to go to the Portsmouth Naval Hospital to have the baby when the time came. We had made friends with her doctor, Lcdr. Lee Artman, who would deliver the child. Lee came over to the house quite frequently and had beers with us. He felt the need to be around "real people" instead of the medical crew he was tied to. While she was pregnant, Mary had quit drinking (not that she had been a big consumer of alcohol), and cut her smoking way down.

On March 14, 1975, quite late, Mary went into labor. I drove her to the hospital and went up to the "labor deck" with her. A nurse assigned her a bed, and Mary got rigged up and climbed into it. I was nervous of course, but tried not to show it. As I wandered about the room, I grabbed the chart from the foot of the bed and opened it up to read it. The nurse, using the tact I would expect, snatched it out of my hand saying, "You can't look at that."

I felt my blood pressure go off the scale. She caught me at the wrong moment and I was really pissed off. "She's my wife so I think I can look at the fucking chart if I want to," I shot back. That was the wrong answer.

"We'll have you removed from here if you don't behave," she replied.

"I'll take care of that myself," I said, and walked out the door. Over my shoulder, I shouted, "Call me when she has the kid."

I stormed out of the hospital and drove home. At about 0630 in the morning, I got the call from the hospital that I had a little girl. We had decided to name her Emily Olga. Emily was my great-aunt's and my great-great-grandmother's name. Olga was from two of Mary's favorite people: one of her friends, and the mother of her best friend. Emily was a healthy little girl. The date was March 15, 1975, just two weeks before my twenty-ninth birthday. A nurse that helped with the delivery, Nora Miller, NC, Royal Navy, became a long-time friend.

We were going to be making another trip to Andros and Paul Whitmore got wind of it. He was one of our underwater photographers who had been discharged from the Navy, and had taken a job as a diver with Atlantic Undersea Test & Evaluation Center (AUTEC) on Andros Island in the Bahamas. The divers working there were all ex-military and one of their jobs was jumping out of helicopters and picking up torpedoes that had been fired from submarines in the Tongue of the Ocean. This was an excellent place to have a torpedo range. The torpedoes were all live except for having warheads, and the nuclear subs could operate in the area as the water was a thousand fathoms deep.

Whitmore wanted a new outboard motor. He had a boat, but the engine on it was pretty old. He asked if we could smuggle one through customs so he could avoid having to pay the thirty percent duty on it to the Bahamian government. I told him we could probably handle that. He sent me a large amount of money in a cashier's check and I went to an outboard shop on Shore Drive, not far from Little Creek and bought what he wanted. I told the salesman that it had to be in a crate that would stand up to some abuse. He took a motor, checked it out, ran it, and had it repacked in a very heavy cardboard box. I also told him I didn't want any labels or names on the box. He understood where it was going and cooperated fully with my requirements. Then we borrowed a pickup truck and manhandled that big box back to the diving locker in Norfolk. We put a label on it that designated it to be photographic gear, contents we knew they wouldn't mess with. The Bahamians were used to us coming down to Andros and carrying lots of gear. We usually carried spear guns, too, which were illegal in the Bahamas. As the Bahamian customs guy liked to go spear fishing with us, he didn't bother to look too closely at our equipment.

We managed to get all of our equipment packed and ready for the trip. It took a couple of trucks to get our inflatable boats and all the rest of the gear, including Paul's motor, to the airport. We loaded it on a C-9 jet and blasted off for West Palm Beach. There we would have to change to a C-1A, a small, twin-engine prop airplane that belonged to VRC-40. The C-1As were used for COD, Carrier On-board Delivery. They had a lot of power and could carry a large amount of cargo.

The C-9 landed us in Palm Beach and the smaller plane was ready to take us across to Andros airport, a dirt field where only small aircraft could land and take off. By the time we had everything jammed into the plane, I was trapped in the back by the door and the pilot had to climb in through the overhead emergency escape hatch to get in. He was a young lieutenant, junior grade and was up for the adventure. We made it over to Andros in a few minutes and landed on Andros at Fresh Creek International Airport, as I called it. Once there, we called AUTEC. They sent a truck to get us and our equipment. We made it through customs, and invited the customs guy to come and have a beer with us when he had the chance. The equipment was taken to the torpedo shed where the diving locker was located. We used a forklift to get Whitmore's crate off the truck, and he was quite happy to see his new outboard. Later that night, we went out to eat at Papa Gay's in Fresh Creek, which is just across the Fresh Creek Bridge in Andros Town. Paul Whitmore bought us a beer, but the cheap bastard didn't spring for the meal, even though we saved him several hundred dollars, not to mention the risk we took smuggling an expensive piece of gear into the Bahamas.

The trip was partly mission-oriented and partly training. One of the projects we had to do this trip was test an underwater light and camera array that, I found out years later, was used to find a sunken Russian submarine. Then we had a short job photographing the hull of a ship as it went by overhead. We used 16mm motion picture cameras set at a high frame rate to do this. This took us part of a morning. Then we stayed about a week and did some spear fishing and scuba diving. A writer from Maryland by the name of Ellsworth Boyd† came down to do a story on us for Skin Diver Magazine. He was a decent guy and a lot of fun. The first day out on the water, Chief Johnson asked him if he was ready to dive with us. He just about choked and asked what he meant by that. Dick told him to saddle up and get ready. It turned out that in all the time he had been writing about Navy diving units and other military service divers, he had never been allowed to dive with them for an "official" reason. Dick figured this guy had as much time in the water as most of us and there would be no reason for him not to be able to dive. Screw the regulations.

We even let Ells use some of our underwater photo gear to shoot some of his pictures, although the guys from the Underwater Photo Team ended up having all their photos in the magazine with the story. It came out in the August 1975 issue of Skin Diver Magazine, if I remember correctly.

† Ells Boyd and I remain in contact to this day.

We speared a few fish, filleted them for the freezer and then put our spear guns away. A vice admiral was visiting the AUTEC facility and wanted to dive with us. He was not a navy diver, but he was close enough, after all, he had made vice admiral. So we took him out in one of the Zodiacs to a place with a lot of coral and fish. We got to the area and I bailed out of the boat face first, without checking. I landed right on top of a branch of staghorn coral that jutted up from the bottom some twenty feet below. It hit me in the shoulder and cut me some, but not badly enough to require medical attention. I still have the scar.

On another dive, one of the new guys, PH3 Ike Johnson, was feeding a small grouper with scraps of fish. The grouper he was feeding probably weighed fifteen pounds. Ike was holding the bag off to the side and out of his field of vision. Next thing he knew, a larger grouper had swallowed the bag of scraps along with his hand clear to his wrist. In a panic, he jerked his hand out of the fish's mouth, raking his teeth across the back of his hand. When we finished laughing, we took him up to see Dottie, the nurse at the AUTEC sick bay. She fixed him up with some antibiotic cream, but had trouble seeing with all the tears in her eyes from laughing.

I would be reporting in at the Naval School of Deep Sea Diving soon. In 1974, there were probably only three or four photographer's mates in the entire Navy who were first class divers. I caught a flight back to Norfolk and packed for the trip. I loaded my gear into my old VW bug again and headed for Washington, D.C. This time, I took an additional piece of equipment that I hadn't needed to carry before, an automatic pistol. I had heard horror stories about the D.C. area and how unsafe it was, so I carried my Heckler & Koch HK-4 .380 pistol in a shoulder holster. I only wore it once before I got tired of lugging the damn thing around. I figured I could talk my way out of just about anything, so the first weekend I went home, I took it back.

In the Navy, there are several different levels of diving qualification. The absolute lowest on the food chain is the scuba diver. He is qualified to dive with open-circuit scuba. This is the same equipment used by the sport diving world. The next level is diver, second class. These men are qualified to dive any scuba-or surface-supplied equipment that uses compressed air. Additionally, they are trained to some degree in salvage and underwater burning and welding.

The diver, first class has to have all these levels behind him before he can attend school. At the Naval School of Deep Sea Diving (NSDS), the training involves air diving, mixed gas diving, submarine rescue chamber operation, salvage, decompression chamber operation, diving medicine, treatment of decompression sickness, diving supervision, burning and welding, explosive demolitions, and waxing and buffing acres of tile floors. This level is the step that brings the Navy diver closer to becoming a diving supervisor.

Some first class divers went to Point Loma to qualify as saturation divers. These men had to learn much more diving physiology, mixed gas techniques, and a different set of equipment. A lot of them worked in black projects diving from nuclear submarines on spy missions.

If a diver is a chief petty officer and has met certain requirements, he can then go on to become a master diver. There are lots of politics involved in becoming a master diver and the Navy only has billets for about fifty of them at a time. A master diver has an enormous responsibility on a diving ship.

There are a couple of other specialized diving ratings. One is EOD technician and the other is Combat Swimmer (UDT/SEAL). The EOD men were second class divers, plus they were trained in the non-magnetic version of the Mark 6 semi-closed circuit scuba. The UDT/SEALs took the standard scuba course and then went on to learn the Mark 6 and the pure-oxygen rebreather, the Emerson. The master diver rating also included a saturation master diver. There were very few of them ever made.

Now back to the story. I checked in at NSDS in Washington and was assigned to a room on the ninth floor of one of the barracks on Bolling Air Force Base some five miles away from the school. We were paid com-rats (commuted rations), which meant we could eat wherever we wanted and if we ate in the chow hall, we would have to pay. I could live with that, but had been hoping I would be able to draw per diem and live off base in an apartment like many of the men in other classes did.

My building had three elevators, but at least one of them was always broken. The place was noisy and the air conditioning usually didn't work. I was in a room with two other guys who were in the class ahead of me. One was Bruce McLawhorn, from SEAL Team 2, and the other was a man named William Spurling, who would be returning to a ship when he graduated. Bill was a PADI Scuba Instructor and gave me an Advanced Scuba card in exchange for a couple of rolls of Kodachrome. I had other civilian certifications that were gleaned in a similar manner. My NAUI card had cost me a color 8" by 10" photo of one of the SDVs we worked on in Puerto Rico. A Chinese guy from Canada gave me my ACUC (American/Canadian Underwater Council) card in a Mexican

Restaurant in Orlando, Florida. I had several. To me, the only one that counted was the Navy one, but some scuba shop owners would only accept a civilian certification if someone wanted to buy compressed air or scuba gear.

Class began and MM1 Barefoot was assigned the role of class leader. Even though I was the senior person in the class and should have been leader, Barefoot told the administration officer that he had made chief before he left the Navy. When he rejoined, he was told he would be advanced once some things were straightened out in his record. In the meantime, I was standing watches and doing all the other duties of regular sailors. A couple of weeks after class started, the administration found out that Barefoot had not made chief, so I was appointed class leader. That meant I didn't have to stand watches anymore, but now I had to run the class. There I was, an aviation rating in a diving school with bosun's mates, machinist's mates, enginemen and hull technicians. My job in the real Navy had nothing to do with fixing broken ships or salvage. I had done all that work on my own time. The fact that I was a photographer's mate did not affect the way my classmates treated me. The skipper of the school was Lieutenant Commander Tony Esau,[†] an Annapolis graduate and former football player. I had heard stories about how he used to take care of problems with sailors on his ship, and I didn't want to experience this first hand.

Sometimes McLawhorn and I would travel home on the weekends in his camper pickup truck. One afternoon, we got ready to go, picked up the usual six-pack of beer to nurse on the boring drive, fueled up the truck, and headed down the road. We had passed the halfway point and were cruising down a deserted road in the boonies somewhere near A. P. Hill Training Area when the left rear tire blew. Bruce started to panic and hit the brakes. I yelled at him not to hit the brakes, just let it roll to a stop. He was out of control and had the damned brake pedal all the way down. We were slowing down from forty-five miles per hour, but I could tell we were about to overturn. The ditch was fairly deep and the road was narrow. There were trees to our right and a field on the left. In a matter of seconds, the truck flopped onto its left side and scraped noisily along the pavement. Bruce began screaming that we were going to die. We slowed to a stop fifteen feet in front of some trees. I looked through the back window and into the camper. I could see flames.

"We're on fire, Bruce! We better get out of this thing fast," I shouted.

† Tony is now deceased.

I stood on the inside of the driver's door and lifted the passenger's door open, then climbed up and sat on the side of the cab, holding the door open for Bruce. He scrambled up and out of the cab, stepping on my hand in the process. He kept going until he was across the road and a few yards into the field. I went to swing my legs out of the cab and the door dropped on one of them. I freed my leg and jumped to the ground. By now, the flames were following the trail made by the spilled fuel. Sparks from the left rear tire rim scraping the road had ignited the gasoline.

I ran across the road where Bruce was having a fit. All of his uniforms, electronic repair tools, and a couple of guns and some ammunition were in there, and his insurance wasn't enough to cover everything.

The flames shot higher and higher. An old black farmer who lived in a house in the field came out and told us that he'd called the fire department. I thanked him. He said we could use his phone when things settled down. Before long, an old fire truck showed up being driven by one fireman. We were so far out in the sticks, the community only had a volunteer fire department and an old pumper truck. I grabbed the hose off the truck and the fireman started the pump. He couldn't figure out which valve to turn to start the water, so I went to the truck and we finally got it set right. I started spraying water on the trees and the bushes to extinguish the flames while he made sure the water pressure stayed up.

"What about my truck? Save it!" Bruce shouted.

"Screw the truck! If these woods catch on fire we're gonna have bigger problems than your truck." I figured it would wipe out half of the state if the forest caught on fire.

By now, aluminum was melting and running down the side of the road and ammunition inside the camper was cooking off like firecrackers. I left my wallet with two hundred dollars in it on the dashboard after we stopped for gas and beer. It was gone. Each time I made this trip, I stopped at a shop on the way home and purchased an outrageous sandwich for Mary. This one went up in flames with Bruce's truck. I wanted to kick the windshield in to rescue my wallet and the sandwich, but the flames were just too high to get close to the car.

After the fire was out, Mac went across the street and called someone who gave us a ride home. They dropped me off at my house. Mary's parents were visiting and I didn't want to upset them. "How was the ride down?" Mary asked.

"Not bad, but I don't have your sandwich."

"What did you do, forget to buy it?"

"No, it burned up along with the truck and my wallet." She thought I was kidding. Then she saw the black charcoal stains on my pants and shoes.

On the way back Sunday night, Bruce and I stopped at the garage where the wreck had been towed. I shot a roll of film for the record. Later on, Bruce managed to get some insurance money from his homeowner's policy and reimbursed me for the money I had lost.

One afternoon, as I was driving back to the barracks in my old tan VW with three other classmates, I stopped at a four-way stop on Bolling Air Force Base. I looked to my right and saw an official Air Force sedan rolling up to the stop sign. I was already stopped, so I just pulled forward and made a left turn. I drove along at my usual pace of twenty miles per hour on base and noticed that the sedan was behind me. I wondered if it was coincidence or if it was following me. I cut through the parking lot of the commissary and he was still behind me. Finally, I pulled over to see what he wanted, and an E-8 Air Force sergeant came up to my window.

"The colonel would like to see you, sailor," he said.

I hated being called "sailor," even though that's what I was. I got out and walked back to where the colonel was sitting behind the wheel of his blue sedan. He never looked up at me once, but only talked to me like there was a microphone in the steering wheel.

"Sailor, it is people like you who make military life difficult. People (he didn't say men) like you who don't obey the rules, and cause problems for others." He went on with some more of his diatribe, but I don't remember any of it.

I was getting really pissed off. Finally, he asked me, "Sailor do you live here on Bolling Air Force Base?"

"Yes, Sir, I do."

"Well then, sailor, do you like living here on Bolling Air Force Base?"

"As a matter of fact, Sir, I don't."

He chuckled, "I think we can do something about that. Sergeant, get this sailor's name and see that he doesn't have to live on Bolling Air Force Base any longer."

"Yes, Sir," was the sergeant's response.

That was the end of our conversation. I climbed back into the car. I thought, what an asshole! At least when I get reamed by a Navy man, the son-of-a-bitch looks me in the eye.

The following afternoon I was lying on my bunk in my skivvies in the sweltering, non-air-conditioned heat of July in Washington, D.C. Two

Air Force men walked into the room. One was a captain and the other an E-6 sergeant.

"You Waterman?" the sergeant asked.

"Yeah, that's right."

"We have orders to escort you from the barracks."

"I figured that might be why you're here. Any idea where I am going?"

The captain replied, "The Navy has found you a place over at the Anacostia Naval Station in the barracks where the misfits are housed until they are discharged."

Great, I thought to myself. This should be good. "Oh, did the colonel tell you to rough me up or try to kick the shit out of me or anything like that?" I asked.

The two Air Force guys cast sheepish looks at each other, and then the captain answered, "Well, the colonel did say we might expect some trouble."

The sergeant had been looking around the room. He saw my dress blues hanging on the locker door with all my Vietnam ribbons, jump wings, etc. on them.

"Oh. You been to Vietnam, I see," he offered.

"Yeah, I was there for one tour with Underwater Demolition Team 13. And you can tell that little pissant colonel that if he had come to throw me out of the barracks personally, there would have been trouble. I would have given that sawed-off cocksucker flying lessons right out of his goddamned Air Force barracks ninth-floor window. By the time he got to the ground, he would be even shorter than he is now. And you can tell him I said that."

Bill Spurling and McLawhorn helped me carry my bags down to my car. The Air Force guys apparently had orders not to lay a hand on my gear or in any way assist me. They escorted me to what used to be Anacostia Naval Air Station to the front of a two-story brick building, then they drove off. It did not look like a typical barracks to me. I humped my bags up onto the top step where I could keep an eye on them from inside and walked in the door. I went to the office next to a communications center and walked in.

"You must be Waterman," the petty officer behind the desk said.

"Gee, how'd you guess?" I replied.

"News travels fast around here. We have a room for you upstairs with a chief cook. He's never here, lives in Norfolk, but leaves his gear here. There's a television, and the air conditioner works. I think he's even got a refrigerator."

"Ain't this the barracks where the misfits and homosexuals are housed until you discharge them?" I asked.

"Yes, but that's in the other wing, and the two are not connected. This wing is where the Navy men who are in the old guard live. They're a pretty squared away bunch, all young boots and gung ho."

"So you told the Air Force this barracks was for guys who were gonna be shit canned?" I replied, smiling.

"I didn't, but when they called the chief and asked where they could put a first class petty officer who had wised off at the base commanding officer, he knew that guy had to be okay, so he stretched it a little. He wanted to make them think they were really shafting you."

"Well, tell him thanks a lot. I am not gonna give you guys any trouble, that's for sure."

The petty officer helped me carry my things to my room on the second floor. The room had two beds in it, the chief's TV, large lockers, and a table on which I could put my typewriter. When I walked in I had to turn the air conditioner down a little as it was too cold in there. I unpacked my things and put them in the locker, then went back downstairs. The communications room was at the bottom of the stairs. I walked in and asked the kid at the desk what sort of work they did there. He told me they routed calls all over the base. I asked if it was hard to make a call to Norfolk on the AUTOVON System. He said not at all, and that the operators there probably patch me through to a local number if I wanted. I thanked him and, later on, made good use of the system.

Just down the hall was a small Navy Exchange where I could buy things such as soda, candy, some canned goods, shoe polish, toiletries, and other odds and ends. It was open a few hours a day, and in the morning on Saturdays. Hell, I wish I'd gotten kicked off that damned Air Force Base sooner. I even had a parking space! I thought of the story of Br'er Rabbit. "Please don't throw me in the briar patch!"

A few days later, I was doing something in the chamber room, when the skipper opened his office door and motioned for me to come. I walked over and entered.

"Have a seat, Waterman," he said. "Rumor has it you got thrown off Bolling Air Force Base."

"No rumor, Sir. That's a fact."

"And did you make some remark about throwing the colonel out of the ninth-story window?"

"Yes, sir, I did. I also added a few more phrases after that."

Esau grinned, "I figured that. Listen, I don't like that little son-of-a-bitch any better than the rest of you guys, but we have to get along with those Air Force pukes. We can't afford to pay per diem to everybody, so tone it down a little. Got it?"

"Yes, sir, I'll work on it. I like where I am now," I said, and left his office.

During the training phase when we dived, we did all of our diving in the wet pots. These were chambers inside the building that were full of water and were capable of being pressurized to three hundred feet or so. We split and mixed helium-oxygen gas, and made up our own mixes based on percentages. We learned the theory and practice of using inert gases other than nitrogen and had plenty of practice rolling heavy gas cylinders around the building to place them in the racks and remove them again for use.

One of the training evolutions we took part in was the "narc run" in the chamber. A half dozen of us at a time would be placed in the chamber with one of the instructors and we would be pressed down to two-hundred-ninety feet on air for a ten-minute bottom time. The idea was to give us a feeling of what it would be like to be at that depth and the resultant effects of nitrogen narcosis, or "rapture of the deep." We took our shoes off to prevent dirt and oil from contaminating the chamber, and crawled into the chamber, taking seats along opposite sides. The instructor was near the speaker so he could talk to the outside tender.

"Ready to leave the surface," he said into the speaker.

The air started hissing into the chamber as we were pressurized to the depth equivalent of two-hundred-ninety feet. It got very hot in there and everybody started sweating profusely. The air was thick like syrup and we could not whistle. They had told us we wouldn't be able to, but we all tried anyway. Most of the class started laughing uncontrollably and I just sat there staring at the depth gage and tried like hell not to crack up. Eventually I joined in the laughter, but I had been trying to make myself think clearly in preparation for when I would actually have to make a dive to this depth. We knew we would make a training dive in the pressure pot to two-hundred-ninety feet on air. We made our way back to the surface at the standard ascent rate of sixty feet per minute. I think we had a decompression stop at ten feet. Now the chamber got really cold and vapor formed in the air from all the sweating and then the lowering of the pressure. It covered us in a cold, clammy, wet fog.

The chamber door clanked open and we all crawled back out and into our shoes. We stayed around until the rest of the class had completed their "narc run," then went across the street to the classroom, which was located on the top deck of a floating barge. There was a machine shop on the first deck where repairs were made to equipment and where suits and helmets were stored.

As we sat in the classroom filling out the routine dive report that would be sent to the Naval Safety Center, I noticed that when my hand went toward the right side of the paper, it disappeared. I closed my left eye and did a quick peripheral vision check. I could not see anything to the right of me, only straight ahead.

"Chief, I think I have a central nervous system (CNS) hit in my right eye," I spoke up.

"What makes you think so?"

"I am losing peripheral vision in my right eye."

That was all he needed to know.

"Hey, Hill! You and Mills grab "Curly" here and walk him over to the chamber, I'll phone Doc and tell him he's coming."

Hill (my swim buddy) and Mills walked me over to the chamber. By the time I got there, which was three minutes or less, they were standing by the chamber with their hands on the valves. The doctor and a corpsman were inside the chamber waiting for me. I kicked off my shoes once again, crawled inside and lay down on a foam mattress on the floor. As soon as I did that, we left the surface to level off at sixty feet. I was immediately placed on one hundred percent oxygen by mask, and the doctor was shining his flashlight into my eyes, alternating between them. The doctor asked if I could see anything. I told him that my peripheral vision was clearing up. When I looked with my right eye, flashes of vision occurred closer together, as though somebody kept turning the lights on and off, and then finally they stayed on.

"I think we had better extend this table five for one oxygen-breathing period, just to be safe," the doctor said.

"Yeah, it ain't gonna cost any extra and it might help," the corpsman agreed.

It seemed like hours when I was finally out of the chamber, and the duty driver drove me to the Naval Ophthalmology Clinic at Bethesda Naval Hospital. I found the correct desk and checked in. An ophthalmologist administered a vision test that would detect any blind spots in my eye. My vision turned out to be normal, so we drove back to school and I finished out the rest of the day.

Another classmate, a Seabee by the name of Alley, got the bends in a jaw hinge on the same chamber dive. After that, the master diver drew a line through that particular dive on the decompression tables and they went to the next greater depth for the decompression schedule, but used the same bottom time as before, ten minutes at two-hundred-ninety feet.

One of the more exciting parts of the class was when we went down to Indian Head to the Explosive Ordnance Range to do the demolition phase. As we were sitting in the classroom, smoking and joking, the instructor came in and gave each of us a stainless steel soupspoon and a sock of C-4 plastic explosive. Then we drew some shaped-charge canisters from a box in the front of the room and started making shaped charges by shaving the C-4 from the block and packing it into the little metal housings. Later that day, we took our Play-Doh projects down to the range and learned all about the Monroe effect: the science behind the way shaped charges work. With a very small piece of C-4, about the size of a 35mm film can, one could make a shaped charge that would blow a hole straight through a piece of railroad track. The hole, except for some spattering around the edges, would look like somebody had drilled it.

We shot holes in some steel plate and through the sidewalls of some empty, out-of-date scuba bottles. We learned how to tie in a trunk line and set up cratering charges in a road. It was a welcome respite from the smoke-filled classroom and heat of summer in Washington, D.C.

One morning, the word was passed that the diving detailer, Master Diver BMCS "Red" White, would be coming to the school to talk to us about our diving careers. It would be our chance to see what was out there and maybe snag some choice assignments. The small group filed into the classroom and "Red" White walked in. He was a large senior chief bosun's mate and had an imposing appearance. A lot of master divers are small, ratty looking guys, but not he. Red told us that if anybody got caught smoking dope or doing any drugs, we would be history forever in the diving community—there were no second chances. He also said that there were some billets here and there, and told us a few things about dive pay and how they were going to raise it, etc. We had heard all that a million times and read it in Navy Times, but it never seemed to materialize.

I spoke up and asked Red how I could get to go to Saturation School. He looked up at me and said, "Volunteer to go to the USS *Ortolan* and you can get it."

The USS *Ortolan*, ASR-22, was a ship about two-hundred-fifty feet long, had a catamaran hull, two Mark 2, Deep Dive Systems, was equipped to do saturation diving, and was supposed to support the new Deep Submergence Rescue Vehicle (DSRV). It was home-ported in Norfolk and didn't go to sea much. I asked if he was sure I would be able to go to saturation diving school if I volunteered to go to the *Ortolan*. He looked me in the eye and said, "No problem. Just talk to the XO when you get there. He'll take care of you."

I thought about it some more and told him I would call him at his office. I called Mary that night and asked her what she thought. She figured saturation school would be a good thing to have under my belt, and to go ahead and take the billet. I called Red White and told him I would take the job. I felt a little bad about jumping ship from Combat Camera Group as they had obtained this billet for me at school, but I had bailed out before on them when I went to Vietnam with UDT.

During some of our training in the "wet pot," we got to attend some of the officer's classes. It was there that I met a man I would end up being friends with and stationed with later on. His name was Edward Miller. He had graduated from the Naval Academy and had been instrumental in finding the USS *Monitor* during Operation Cheesebox. Ed had been part-way through college when he received an appointment to the Naval Academy. He took the appointment and found that he didn't have to take some of the courses he had already completed, so he had the time to get involved in the search for the *Monitor*. When the USS *Monitor* sunk off Cape Hatteras while being towed, there had been a red lantern hanging from the turret as a signal. Ed was in the submersible when that lantern was recovered. Ed wrote the book, *USS Monitor: The Ship That Launched a Modern Navy*.

One day, he was in the tank doing his underwater cutting project. This was a timed project. The object was to clamp a piece of half-inch-thick steel plate to the workbench, and burn off a piece of it. Your time started when you struck the first arc and it stopped when the plate was broken off. Sometimes in underwater burning, the cuts are not complete and you have to take a hammer and break the steel off because "spider webs," as they're called, hold the plate together. In this case, we had a large crescent wrench in the tank to snap the piece off. When the students would have the sheet cut all the way across, they would take the wrench, put it on the edge of the steel, and use it as a lever to snap off the burned off piece. Ed burned the piece most of the way through, but there were some spider webs holding it together, so the instructor got on the comm box and said, "Ensign Miller, finish it off with the crescent hammer." Ed picked up the wrench and instead of fastening it on the steel and bearing down, he started pounding away on it with the crescent wrench. The class was nearly rolling on the floor with laughter. It took Ed a while to live that one down. He had a good sense of humor, though, and didn't let it get to him.

Two of the other officers I met were from the Middle East. One was in the Israeli Navy and one was in the Egyptian Navy. I could not imagine the administration that would put these two guys in the same general area. One day, I was standing on the comm box outside the wet pot while the Egyptian guy was diving. The Israeli officer came up to me and said. "Hey, you let me tend him and he not come up." We acted as though he was joking, but he probably wasn't.

A few weeks passed and we were ready to go down river to do our salvage project, which involved the actual salvaging of a ship sunk in the river. The steel vessel, one-hundred-twenty-five feet long, was scuttled in forty feet of water alongside another of the same type. The classes alternate between the ships, so that the class before us could not tell us where all the holes were that we would have to patch in order to raise the ship. We loaded all the gear and clothing we would need onto the training barge and got under way. This project would take two weeks and I was warned that the class leader always received the lowest grade in the class.

Each day, we headed down river on a crew boat at about 0600 and came back to the dock near the school in the afternoon just before dark. The days were long, but went quickly as we had a mission at hand.

The first day, we had to set up the diving station on the wreck and begin the process of determining where the leaks were. All the diving would be done in the Mark V deep sea rig, and the visibility was either zero or very close to it. The school had plywood, old fire hose for gasket-making material, and nails, hammers, saws, canvas, and anything else we would need for this project. As class leader I had to send in a Situation Report (SitRep) every day after school. I wrote it up and gave it to the instructor to place in the file.

On the second day, one of the instructors, BMC Bamberger, walked out of the wheelhouse of the training vessel and started ragging on me out about being behind schedule. He had done this a little on the first day, but now he was really putting it onto me. He said his ten-year-old kid could do better than we were and we would never get the damned thing afloat, etc., etc.

I piped right up. "Chief Bamberger, if your kid is so damned smart, why don't you bring the little bastard down here and we'll work for him.

Maybe you can get your wife to come down, too, and cook us some decent chow while you're at it." He shut up and walked back into the pilothouse.

"Shit, you've had it now, Waterman," one of my classmates said.

"Yeah, I guess I got a little carried away. He's probably going in there right now to write me up or drop me from the school."

Bamberger acted as if nothing happened. He would come out, chewing on one of his unlit cigars, watch us from the deck of the training boat, and go back in and suck down more coffee.

We found all the holes and patched them using toggle patches, where we would make a wooden patch with plywood and run a bolt through the center of it, push it through the hole, and then place a strongback (with the bolt running through that) on the inside and tighten it with a nut. Some holes required Tucker patches. These were similar to a toggle patch, but they would fold in the middle so we could get them through a round hole. Any other hole but a round one, we could make a toggle patch to fit.

Some places needed the doors or hatches shored up with timbers and wedges. We had the ship all tightened up and ready to pump by Friday morning of the second week. Now I had to come up with a pumping plan. I had the blueprints to the ship and took them back to my room. I measured each compartment with a yardstick, as that's all I had, converted it to scale, and figured the cubic footage of the spaces, which I converted to gallons of water. There are seven and a half gallons of water per cubic foot. I knew the capacities of the pumps we would be using, and dynamic head, the pump's height above water, would not be a consideration, as the pumps would be sitting almost at sea level.

I had the plan down pat. I figured the time and then threw in a little "Jesus factor" in case something screwed up.

The next day, we rigged the pumps and started pumping. Sure enough, one of the electric submersible pumps failed and we had to alternate between two compartments with one pump. When we had pumped her dry and secured the pumping operation, I was ten minutes from the time I had estimated. I was actually ten minutes early. I was more shocked than anyone that I was so close. We stripped out the remaining water with buckets and climbed inside the wreck to see what it looked like. We were a group of happy sailors to see that test over with. Later that afternoon, we pulled the patches and sank her back to the bottom again for another class to raise.

Before we left the project for good that day, Chief Bamberger called me up into the wheelhouse of the training boat.

"Waterman," he asked, in a somewhat gruff voice, "what grade do you think you got in this class?" I started to feel a little weak.

"Gee, Chief, I don't know, but if I passed, that's close enough."

He was standing with the grade book open and he had his hand over where my grade was written in the book. He slid his thumb down and uncovered it. I scored a ninety. Then he spoke up.

"I never give anybody a ninety, especially the class leader. You drove me off the job that first day and showed that you were in charge. That's what I wanted you to do. On a salvage job, there can only be one boss, otherwise people start second guessing each other and men get hurt and gear gets destroyed. Good job." Another situation where I couldn't get the grin off my face.

I needed to return to the barracks and write an after-action report. I was pretty tired and had decided not to go home that weekend. Besides, they had steaks on special at the Petty Officer's Club on the base. I gathered my copies of the daily SitReps and formulated a salvage report using my old typewriter. It may have taken me half an hour to write it, but I included details about having to abandon the wreck before the tugs came to tow it, taking small arms fire from the East Bank of the Anacostia River—things such as that. I noted we had to scuttle the boat to avoid it from falling into "enemy hands." In reality, some boys were firing BB guns at us from the shore, and they were hitting the ships around us.

Monday afternoon, one of the instructors told me the skipper wanted to see me in his office. "Shit, what have I done now?" I thought. I walked through the door of his office. Lcdr. (Big Tony) Esau was standing behind his desk with a coffee cup in his hand. He was an imposing sight, standing six-foot-six and weighing in at around three hundred pounds.

"Have a seat, Waterman. I read your salvage report." Silence.

"Best one I've seen. How long did it take you to write it?"

I answered. "Oh, I don't know, about a half hour, I guess."

He gave me a quizzical look and continued.

"I'm going to use it as an example of what these reports should look like and put it out to the salvage officers' classes. Those guys could use some improvements in their reporting."

"Well, thanks skipper, I was afraid you were calling me in here to chew my ass for something." I joked.

"Not this time." Esau laughed.

The rest of the week was spent making some deep helium/oxygen dives in the wet pot and preparing to go down river to Dahlgren to make our deep-qualifying dives. A master diver candidate, Chief Jim Starcher, would be along to mess with us. There were two or three other master divers who would be there to evaluate his performance. We rode the boat down river and would be staying in barracks at the Dahlgren Naval Weapons Station. It was a run-down place, bare of essentials, but we were only going to be there for a week and, after one more week of school, we would be graduating.

Each day, we went aboard the boat and steamed to a point near the bridge that crossed the Potomac River near Dahlgren. There, the boat would anchor in about one-hundred-eighty feet of water. We had made our qualifying dives in the wet pot, but had to get one more to satisfy a requirement for open-water dive.

Each dive would be made with only one diver on the stage. We would dress in the Mark V Mod I rig using the helmet with the Baralyme canister, etc. When I was fully dressed in that gear, I weighed over five hundred pounds with the eighty-pound belt and the eighty-pound set of shoes. The helmet and canister alone weighed one-hundred-thirty pounds. When a diver was dressed to dive and waiting to go, a rope was threaded through a becket in the top of the helmet. It went through a pulley arrangement so the weight of the helmet and breastplate could be lifted from his shoulders.

When it came time for me to dive, one of the evaluating master divers came up to me and started whispering in my ear. He told me that when I got to the bottom to get off the stage, but when they told me to get back on, to say I was on, but not to get back on the stage. They wanted to see if Starcher, the master candidate, would be watching the gages to see if I was actually coming up with the stage.

The tender closed and dogged the faceplate and the hissing of the helium/oxygen mixture was all I could hear as I climbed, with the help of tender on each side, clumsily onto the diving stage and prepared to be lowered to the bottom of the river. I felt the stage hit bottom.

"Red Diver on the bottom." I reported, in the high-pitched nasal tones of someone breathing helium.

"Roger, Red Diver. Get off the stage."

"Red Diver getting off the stage."

"Red Diver off the stage." I reported in a moment.

"Roger, Red, get back on the stage and stand by to leave the bottom. Let me know when you are on the stage and ready to leave the bottom."

I waited a few seconds. "Topside, Red Diver ready to leave the bottom."

At this point, I was up to my thighs in the muddy bottom of the Potomac River in total blackness, my helium suit blown up to the point where, if I relaxed, my arms would extend out from my body. The Michelin man was only a thin version of me. The Mark V Mod I helmet requires that gas be blown through a venturi in the back of the helmet where the canister of Baralyme is mounted. In order for the gas to flow correctly and the carbon dioxide to be scrubbed out, there has to be constant over-pressure in the suit and this causes the diver to be almost blown up all the time.

The stage started to lift, and I kept my hand on it until it went out of reach. "Red Diver, are you on the stage?" came the voice over the comm speaker.

"Negative, topside, I fell off the stage. Lower it again." I knew that I would have a problem if that damned stage came down and drove me farther into the mud. I was already having enough trouble moving around. They lowered the stage and, sure enough, it landed on top of me, even though I hadn't moved. Now I was almost up to my waist in the mud.

"All stop! The stage is on top of me," I reported.

"Roger that. Taking the stage up."

"Just lift it up slowly about three feet," I ordered. I tried to hang onto the stage as they pulled it up a few feet so that I could pull myself out of the mud. It didn't work so I had them lower it down. This time, I guided it down so that it came down right in front of me. I bent over and put the top half of my body, which wasn't in the mud, onto the stage and then had them lift it up a few feet. Once I was clear of the mud, I stood up and hung on as they raised me up. I arrived at the surface and climbed off the stage. I was undressed quickly by my tenders and got dressed to take my turn topside. Jim Starcher came over and asked me what the hell happened to me. I told him that I had done what the guys told me to do. He understood then that it had been a drill. Starcher made master diver and went on to his next command.

We finished the week making qualification dives and were tied up alongside the school at the Navy Yard by Friday afternoon. The next week, we would do the course on the McCann Submarine Rescue Chamber and then graduate.

On Monday, we started classroom sessions for the McCann Rescue Chamber. This device was used for rescuing trapped submariners from a submarine on the bottom in water more than six hundred feet deep.

The bell had an upper and a lower section and was one atmosphere, meaning it was not pressurized internally. The lower section is open at the bottom, and a watertight hatch is in the floor of the upper section of the chamber.

The McCann Submarine Rescue Chamber requires two operators and can carry six passengers per load. There is a hatch in the top of the chamber, also, that enables the persons operating the chamber to climb into it once it is sitting in the water. The inside piping system had twenty-two valves that controlled various ballast tanks and the air supply. The umbilical to the surface carried air down to the bell and allowed the chamber to be exhausted to the surface.

When the bell was mated to a downed submarine, the operators of the bell could vent the sub and give it enough fresh air to last between runs to the surface with rescued submariners. By the time we went into the chamber to make dry runs we had to understand the operation of the bell and be able to explain what all the valves did.

On an actual chamber run the scenario is as follows:

The submarine releases the sub rescue buoy, which is attached by a cable to a bail on the submarine's hatch. There used to be a telephone in the emergency buoy, for talking to the men in the submarine. The buoy-phone has been replaced by the UQC wireless underwater communication system.

When the buoy is released in an actual emergency, smoke grenades can be remotely released to show the buoy's location to the rescuers. The Auxiliary Submarine Rescue (ASR) finds the buoy and runs a race track pattern around the buoy while setting out the four mooring spuds, huge steel buoys with wooden chafing gear on them. They are anchored to the bottom with chain. When all four are set, the ASR sends out its boat to secure mooring lines to the spuds and the ASR is maneuvered alongside the sub's emergency buoy. At this point, the word is passed to the submarine that they are cutting the cable and attaching it to the air powered winch on the McCann Submarine Rescue Chamber. When this is done, the crane on the ASR lowers the bell over the side and the operators climb in. The bell's umbilical (hose and safety line combination) is faked down on deck so that it will run out freely. This umbilical is about six inches in diameter and takes every free hand in the diving gang and a few others to handle it. In the water, it is nearly neutral, but it is damned heavy to handle on deck.

The chamber operators begin flooding the ballast tanks until the chamber is slightly positive. Then the winch is activated and they start winching the chamber down to the submarine. Once they get to the sub and make the "Kittredge Seal," they equalize the upper and lower chambers at atmospheric pressure by venting the pressure in the lower chamber to the surface through the exhaust hose (part of the umbilical). Then one of the operators opens the hatch in the bottom of the upper section of the chamber. He taps on the submarine hatch with a small hammer, and the submariners slowly open it. Lead pigs are handed down into the disabled submarine to offset the weight of the men soon to be taken aboard the chamber. As soon as that is accomplished, the rescued submariners are allowed to climb into the chamber. The sub's hatch is closed, the lower chamber hatch is closed, and the chamber is flooded by allowing sea water to come into it through a valve. The operators allow the winch to free-run slowly back to the surface. Once on the surface, the chamber's ballast tanks are blown full of air and the upper hatch is opened. The submariners climb out and more lead pigs take their place. The whole evolution is repeated until the remainder of the sub's crew is taken off.

The school had a McCann Submarine Rescue Chamber sitting outside the classroom on a concrete pad. A ladder was rigged up to it and permanently attached as each class used it for "chamber week." The only operating we did with the chamber was to go inside and talk our way through what each valve did and why we were turning it. During one of our classes on that piece of gear, it was mentioned that a certain procedure when docking the chamber to a bottomed submarine was called the "Kittredge Seal." I asked how it came to have a name like that. Was it a procedure, or a piece of hardware? The instructor said it was a procedure and was named after an old submarine skipper who had perfected it.

I told the class that I knew Captain Kittredge and that he was my neighbor. "Aw, bullshit, Waterman," was the only answer I got. I really do know him, he grew up about two miles from where I lived in Maine and retired from the Navy two years before I joined. Kittredge was a WWII sub skipper and built midget submarines after he retired.[†]

The next time I went home on leave, I asked him exactly what the "Kittredge Seal" was, as I hadn't paid close attention in class. Captain Kittredge explained it to me:

> "The chamber has ballast tanks in it to give it positive or
> negative buoyancy. The old system required you to put a strain
> on the downhaul cable, and that would pull you down to the
> sub's escape hatch. Then you tried to hold the chamber down
> with the downhaul winch while you blew the water out of the

† Captain George W. Kittredge turned 90 in May of 2008 and still rides his two horses every day.

lower part chamber where the bell mated to the submarine. It did not work. What we did was get down as tight as we could. Then we would open the valve between the lower chamber and the ballast tank. That would instantly suck the chamber onto the seat around the sub's hatch and make the "Kittredge Seal." We set the record for the deepest operation of the *McCann* Submarine Rescue Chamber while I was COMSUBDIV 11. The USS *Coucal*, ASR-19 was the ship we used and the USS *Tang*, SS-563 was our "victim." The sub lay on the bottom and we took the chamber down to it. We made the seal and I went aboard the submarine for the ride back, and a torpedoman first class from the *Tang* rode the chamber back to the surface in my place."

During the week, I had gradually been packing up my clothes and gear so I could bail out of there after I graduated on Friday. We were going to have a small party at the Club afterwards, but most of us wanted to get on the road and get out of D.C. The traffic would be bad and the heat even worse.

On Thursday afternoon, we took the written test on the rescue chamber and all passed with flying colors. There was no final written exam as we passed through each phase as the course progressed. They probably didn't think we would be able to remember the material that long, anyway.

By noon, we were ready to graduate. The diplomas were handed out and the base photographer took our picture on the front steps of the school with Lcdr. Tony Esau and Lt. Duignan, the training officer. According to my final grade, I was number one in the class.

After the little ceremony, we went over to the club and had a couple of beers. Then I headed down the road for home, as I had put all my gear in the car that morning. I was beginning to rethink my decision to volunteer for the *Ortolan*.

Chapter 21

USS *Ortolan*, ASR-22

When I checked in at Combat Camera Group, I didn't tell anybody I had volunteered for the *Ortolan*. I knew it would come out in due time. Perhaps the orders would just appear out of the blue and the unit would think that it was just my turn in the barrel. As I did more checking into what sorts of things went on aboard the *Ortolan*, I realized I had made a mistake. However, perhaps getting a chance to attend Saturation School would make up for all the negative things.

We had a few interesting jobs, but nothing out of the ordinary came up at Combat Camera Group. The regular guys were still at the unit. Bill Curtsinger had been discharged some time back and was now a contract photographer for *National Geographic Magazine*. Frank Stitt was out in Hollywood, ostensibly making documentary films or something. Whitmore was still in the Bahamas working as a diver for AUTEC, jumping out of helicopters to snag practice torpedoes. Harry Kulu[†] was back in Hawaii, and Trotter was either in jail or in some trouble that might land him there.

We made it through the winter in the usual fashion. We worked at getting things lined up in the islands so that we would be able to dive where it was warm. It didn't always happen. By spring, we had some small jobs going and managed to wangle a training trip to Andros Island for a couple of months. I was hoping that my orders would not come through for the *Ortolan* before the trip was over. The *Ortolan* was in the Philadelphia Naval Shipyard getting some work done and I had heard horror stories about that place.

† Harry Kulu made chief and moved home to Hawaii where he had a heart attack and lived.

About a week before we were scheduled to go back to Norfolk, the message came down that I had a set of orders to the *Ortolan*. The command told me that I had a month to get there and if I wanted to take any leave, I would have to come home right away. I told them I would finish out the trip and not take any leave. That was met with approval.

We ended our trip in Andros and loaded up the equipment to fly back to Norfolk. This time, we caught a ride from West Palm Beach to Norfolk in a Navy P-3 submarine hunter. The plane had to stop in Brunswick, Maine first to drop off some torpedoes before it circled back to Norfolk. We were wearing our summer clothing, as it had been warm when we left West Palm Beach. When we landed in Brunswick, it was cold with snow on the ground, so we didn't spend much time off the plane. The aircraft made a quick turnaround and soon we were in Norfolk with the gear: compressor, boats, outboards, underwater cameras, diving equipment, and personal items.

I cleaned out my lockers at the gym and at the Underwater Photo Team. It wasn't as if I was leaving forever, just going on another adventure to another command. It didn't turn out that way. I didn't know it then, but I would never come back to Combat Camera Group except as visitor. This was a turning point in my life based on a decision I have long since regretted.

The *Ortolan* was home-ported in Norfolk at the Destroyer & Submarine Piers, only about two miles from Combat Camera Group, or Atlantic Fleet Audio-Visual Command, as it was renamed. None of us ever called it that, except when we answered the phone.

I checked out of the unit and went home to our place on the beach behind Little Creek. Using a sea bag and a duffel bag, I packed my Navy-issue wetsuit and other gear that I might need while Mary helped me pack clothes. I made arrangements to get a flight from Norfolk to Philly, or Filthydelphia as we called it, to get on board the *Ortolan* in the Philadelphia Naval Shipyard. Perhaps I should have had a better attitude, but I just couldn't make myself look forward to going to the this ship. I had been hearing more and more horror stories about what a piece of junk it was, and now I was going to be able to see it first hand.

I had the phone number of the quarterdeck at the *Ortolan*, so I called the officer on duty and told him when I would be flying in to Philly. He said he'd send somebody down to pick me up. I got off the plane and walked to baggage claim. I was in uniform, so not too hard to spot. A small senior chief petty officer walked over to me and asked if I was Waterman.

"Sure am, Chief. Is that good or bad?" I joked.

"I don't know. I'm Senior Chief Apodaca," he said. "I'll give you a ride to the ship. Where's your gear?" We made small talk while I waited for my bags to come around on the conveyor.

"How's the work going on the ship?" I asked.

"Not too bad, but as usual, we are behind schedule. The sand crabs are too busy buying cigarettes in the ship's store and taking breaks to get the work done, but we should be out of here in a couple of weeks. You can square away the photo lab and get supplies while we do this."

"How many duty sections are we in?"

"Four, but it's pretty slack. It's fairly easy to get somebody to take your duty on weekends or Friday night if you want to go back to Norfolk. I go down every weekend if you need a ride."

"Gee, Chief, that would be great."

I rode home a couple of times with Apodaca and chipped in for gas.

Apodaca drove me to the shipyard and dropped me off at the brow. He said he had some errands to run. I thanked him again for the ride and walked up to the brow.

The Philadelphia Shipyard was a giant, gray steel, ghost town with hundreds of ships in mothballs. It was like visiting a graveyard where all the bodies are above ground. The *Ortolan* was moored under a huge hammerhead crane that jutted out over our ship where it was berthed alongside a pier. Steam lines were hissing and blowing all over the place and the smell of rotten food in the dumpsters reminded me of every Navy base I had ever been on.

One of the seamen on watch helped me carry my gear to the photo lab, which was on the O2 level and right at the stern of the large catamaran. The low part of the ship under the huge bridge crane used to move the Deep Submergence Rescue Vehicle (DSRV) around on deck. As I walked across the bridge crane deck, I noticed the it was slick with oil. I asked the sailor about it.

"Oh shit, that's always like that. The damned bridge crane leaks hydraulic oil all the time. Sometimes, you practically have to wear a raincoat on the deck."

"Great," I thought to myself. "Now I will have the added pleasure of falling on my ass in the oil if I forget it's here."

The photo lab consisted of two rooms. The outer room was the "finishing room" and the inside was the darkroom. The outer room had a large, Navy-issue, stainless steel refrigerator where the film, paper and other "essentials" were kept. I found plenty of room for sodas and containers of yogurt. There was also a large Pako drum print dryer in the corner and a Polaroid camera on a stand for doing I.D. photos. Roll-up background paper on one wall served as a backdrop for shooting "official" portraits. There were several cases under the finishing table and some more in the darkroom under the large stainless steel sink, the only places for storage in the compartment. There was a standard, hinged, household-type door between the darkroom and the finishing room and the outer door was a watertight, steel door with a central dogging lever. It had a place for a padlock. The lab was kept locked whenever nobody was there.

The entire space was clean and neat, and well-lit. The kid who had been running it, Seaman Rivera, had an interest in photography and had been put in charge of the lab pending somebody taking his place. He was not a diver and had no designated rating. I wondered why he had not changed to airman so that he could strike for Photographer's Mate. I didn't asked him why once found out he was not the most popular person on board.

My first duty was to check in with the administration officer, the XO, and the skipper. I went to the admin office and walked in. YN1 Sherby Hart stood up to greet me. He was a short guy, somewhat older than myself. Hart shook my hand enthusiastically and introduced me to the other man in the office, PN2 Hosea. I'd always thought Hosea, usually spelled José, was strictly a Spanish name, but not so. Sherby took my records and orders and called the XO on the phone and asked if he was busy. Then he turned and motioned for me to follow him up to the next deck.

The XO's office was up in officers' country where all the officers lived and worked. It was a small room on the port side of the ship. I walked in. The XO, Lcdr. Dix was an ex-enlisted man. The commanding officer was Commander Ramsey. The XO made some small talk about how it was good to finally have somebody to run the lab and to have another diver on board. On the way to meet the CO, he said, "Welcome aboard the *Ortolan*, Waterman. We're glad to finally have a real photographer on board. Well, there's not much I can tell you about this ship, one of the divers will show you around. Sherby will get your diving pay started, and it will take you a few days to get squared away with a rack and learning your way around the ship. Good to have you aboard."

I thanked him and started for the XO's office. I turned back to him and said, "By the way, Commander Dix, "Red" White† told me that I
† "Red" White is now dead.

294

could get a set of orders to saturation school if I volunteered to come aboard here."

Dix turned around and smirked. "Shit, Waterman. He tells everybody that." I suddenly had the feeling that this tour of duty was not going to be much fun at all, but decided I would try to make the most of it.

As I walked down the passageway, Ltjg. Ed Miller came out of his room. "Well, I heard you were coming aboard. Glad to see you." He smiled while pumping my right hand. "When you get settled in, come up to my room and I'll bring you up to speed."

"Good to see you, Sir. I imagine I'll run across you again before long," I joked. "You're probably not too hard to find.

Two other officers, Lt. Wolfgang Knueppel and the engineering officer, Lt. Moen, were also there and greeted me warmly. Both of them were former enlisted men.

"These guys are alright. I may be okay here," I thought. "After all, we *are* in this together."

It didn't take me long to get squared away and get my gear stowed. I left my diving gear and personal camera equipment in the photo lab and got a rack two decks down with the guys from the engineering division. It was there that I met HT2 Drew Ruddy. Drew was a hull technician and saturation diver. He had a college degree in biology and had eyesight much worse than mine, but wore contact lenses. They made him squint and that made him look like a mole. He was good friends with Ed Miller. The two of them used to go diving on weekends when they could get away. Both of them were interested in underwater archaeology.

One of my first duties on the *Ortolan* was to inventory all the gear and all the film, chemicals and paper. I knew that we had a tight budget, but I wanted to be able to stock up the lab so that it would not be a constant hassle to get consumable materials later on. According to Rivera, there was a great camera store that did business with the Navy and we could to get whatever we needed there if we had the proper paperwork.

In looking over the gear and checking it against the custody cards, I found two items not on the cards. One was a twenty-thousand-dollar DBM-9 Milliken Underwater Camera, and the other item was an underwater Leica housing built by E. Leitz of Canada. If only I had known then what I know now, maybe they'd be in my inventory today. When I put them on the custody list, it turned out that the Naval Supply System had no record of them, either, and these items could have just walked off the ship and nothing would have ever come of it. I was just too damned honest—or too scared of getting in trouble.

The levels of consumables were getting low, so I drew up a list of what I thought we needed and ran the paperwork through supply. The warrant officer who ran supply had been a storekeeper when he enlisted. He helped me with the forms and before long, the proper requests were completed. Rivera and I took the duty vehicle, drove to the camera place and bought it all. We used bulk film that we reloaded into cassettes for the thirty-five millimeter cameras, and bought photographic paper by the five-hundred-sheet box. We took out only the number of sheets that fit into a paper safe. That way, all the sheets in the box wouldn't be ruined if some curious person opened the paper safe, on the cover of which was written in large letters, *DO NOT OPEN IN WHITE LIGHT.*

In addition to the black-and-white materials, we also had some chemistry and film for color slides. At the time, the Kodak process for Ektachrome was the E-6 process. We had a large stainless sink and a thermostatically controlled faucet, so I knew we would be able to process color film. I ordered a Sen-Rac roll-film dryer, the kind we'd had in the Naval Special Warfare photo lab, and it fit nicely onto one of the walls of the lab.

We got under way a couple of weeks after I arrived, and steamed back to Norfolk. The photographic work on the *Ortolan* was nothing exciting; many grips and grins, and broken parts—lots of broken parts, and groovy graphs (unofficial pictures of about anything) that I shot just to hand out to the crew and the other divers. Photographers are usually welcome wherever they go, provided they produce pictures for others to send home. I made sure I took many photos for the boys.

My station aboard was as a telephone talker on the bridge while getting under way or docking. I was to pass the word between the bridge and the damage control stations, and other stations on board. During docking maneuvers, I would pass the word between the wings of the bridge and the helm if the weather was windy and the helmsman couldn't hear the OOD. When Lt. Moen had the conn, I would often help him maneuver the ship, especially at sea when we were making four-point moors. He had taken me aside and told me that he had very little experience above decks as he had been an engineer his entire career. Many times when we were maneuvering on a four-point moor or to pick up one of our mooring spuds, I would give him the proper engine and helm commands. My experience on fishing boats before joining the Navy helped a lot. I would say the commands in a low voice and he would then say them back to me loudly and I would pass the word over the sound-powered phones. Afterward, he'd give me a thumbs-up and wink.

One extremely windy day, I was on the bridge when we took a new pilot aboard for the docking. Being a friendly guy, I asked him if he had ever docked this ship before. He said he hadn't, so I asked him how many tugs he had for the docking. He said he had two. I then advised him that he should have three or four if he could get them. He looked at me as if I had tits on my forehead and made some remark about knowing what he was doing. I simply grinned and remarked, "We'll see, won't we." I hated being a smart-ass, but this guy deserved it. Before the day was over, he wished he had listened to me.

You see, I knew something that he didn't. This ship was about as seaworthy as a shoebox. It stuck up out of the water and offered as much windage as a kite. The northwest wind was blowing through the channel past the D & S piers at a minimum of fifteen to twenty-five knots and the tide was coming. We started our swing into the dock. We would be mooring port side to the dock and I felt the wind would tend to keep us off the dock. As we made the turn toward the dock, the tugs didn't have enough power to keep us from drifting toward a destroyer tied up on the opposite pier to our starboard side. I knew what would happen next. One of the tugs went forward and started pushing on the inside of our port hull (remember, the *Ortolan* was a catamaran) to move us against the dock, but to no avail. The wind had picked up and we were now rubbing against the old destroyer. With a metallic grinding sound, we broke off boat davits and scraped along, tearing lifeline stanchions down. No major damage was done. Petty Officer Sabat, one of the divers, had a home-movie camera, and came out on deck and started shooting pictures of the collision. The skipper of the destroyer shouted up to him. "Hey, Sailor. Rig some fenders."

Sabat shouted back, "You are our fenders."

You can rest assured that went over well. Fortunately for Sabat, the captain of that ship never figured out who he was. Sabat was the one who had stolen a brand new Mark V helmet up in Washington D.C. in Diving School. They searched our cars every day when we left the base. We all suspected he had taken it, but never found out how he got it off base. One day, I asked him how he did it.

"I just moved it ten feet from where it was normally kept and stuck it in a closet under some diving suits stored in there. Nobody thought to look around the area for it. They all figured it had been carried off the base. They searched all the vehicles at the gate for about a week.

When things cooled off, I just put it in the trunk of my car and took it out the gate."

He had also jumped off of the barracks over at Bolling with his hang glider. He didn't get caught or he would have probably been thrown off the base, too, as I was.

Meanwhile, at home, Mary and I realized the house we were living in was getting too small. We had one kid and two dogs. We were paying rent in Virginia and making a house payment in Maine. A friend of ours told us about some new town houses that were being built on Pleasure House Road, named so because a whorehouse had been there years ago. We checked the places out and I talked with the builder. He was an Italian guy who looked and talked like somebody out of The Godfather.

Elton Lee, a real estate broker representing the developer, was a real southerner from Hopewell, Virginia. He lined us up with financing through the Veterans' Administration and told us to forget we owned the property up in Maine. We signed the papers and moved in. It had two bedrooms, a full bathroom upstairs, a half bath downstairs, a kitchen and living room, and a backyard with a chain link fence where we could let the dogs out without tying them up. The place had central heat and air conditioning. We paid thirty-six thousand dollars for it and the payments were three hundred dollars a month with no money down. We had some good neighbors there, mostly either military or retired military. One of them was a Marine captain and his wife, but we didn't hold that against them. I was always getting junk mail addressed to "Occupant" so Elton Lee gave us a door knocker with "The Occupants" on it for a name. We put it on the door and left it there the entire time we lived in that house.

When I didn't have anything else to do on board ship, I hung out in the diving locker and shot the bull with the divers. We all had sea stories to tell, some of us more than others. One friend of mine, Kulzicki, was tired of people making Polish jokes about him so he changed his name to Culley. He was an easy-going guy and an excellent diver. The other men were of varying personalities and dispositions. Many of them were saturation divers and some had worked in Vallejo, California on Special Projects. We knew their job involved working on nuclear subs and locking out of them, but they were not permitted to talk about their adventures, and we didn't ask.

Occasionally, we would get a new guy aboard who was already rated and had served on a submarine. One man in particular was in a rating that was very much in demand on subs. He tried to get a transfer off his sub, but the skipper wouldn't let him go. Instead, he got caught smoking pot. Once that happened, he was automatically disqualified as a submariner, but could serve on board surface ships. So the submarine squadron commander transferred him to the *Ortolan*. The acronym "ASR" was sometimes said to stand for Assholes and Submarine Rejects, and it lived up to its name on occasion.

As a catamaran, the *Ortolan* had two hulls, with two engines in each hull. The two engines clutched together, in line, to drive one propeller on each hull. The ALCO Diesel engines were made by the American Locomotive Company. They were massive and made a loud rumbling sound that reverberated throughout the ship whenever we were under way, which wasn't very often. Many times we went to sea and came right back in because some piece of gear broke down.

I had heard stories about the ship being designed to carry a certain amount of weight, and berth a limited number of people. After the model tests were completed at the David Taylor Model Basin in Maryland, the engineers changed the plans and added one hundred tons of weight. We could only turn about ten knots, much less than the design called for. The ship was scary in heavy seas. The waves pounded under the flat portion between the hulls and it sounded as if the ship would break in half.

When the ship was new, it was out for sea trials and the forward chain locker had flooded. The ship had to be taken to the shipyard to sister up the frames on the inboard sides of the hulls. In a serious weather situation, the twisting motion of the two hulls working against each other combined with the added weight made the ship a floating coffin for two hundred men. I think the Navy knew that. They were supposed to build ten of these white elephants, but only built two before spending the money allocated for the remaining eight on something else. The other ship was named the *Pigeon*, ASR-21. It was stationed on the west coast in San Diego. I envied the guys on the *Pigeon* compared to what we had to put up with. At least they had warm weather.

I didn't stay in the berthing compartment very long. I decided I would move into the photo lab. In the compartment, there was a head and shower on the same deck, but when I moved up to the lab, I had to go down two decks for the conveniences. This was not a problem. I grabbed an extra mattress, some sheets, a pillow, and a blanket, and made a bed on the floor of the darkroom. I rolled up the mattress and stuffed it under the cabinet during the day. If I had to take a leak at night, I just went in the darkroom sink and rinsed it down, or stepped out to the rail if we were under way. Also, I kept my wetsuit in the darkroom in a parachute bag. There were times when I thought I would be better off wearing it. The ship pounded badly and shuddered throughout. I just tightened up my guts and wait for the next one. The seas would slam against the flat underbody of the catamaran and almost shake the teeth out of my head. It woke me up numerous times while I slept. Some nights, it scared the hell out of me.

The men in the compartment next to the photo lab were all electricians. Tim Noble was one of them. The ship was so crowded that Noble and another man found some material and built a couple of bunks in the electricians' shack. The ship had been designed to berth about one-hundred-twenty men and we had nearly two hundred on board. Noble's father was a retired Navy diver and now worked as a diving supervisor with the Taylor Diving Company of New Orleans. Tim planned to get out of the Navy and work in the Gulf or somewhere in the oil patch when his time was up.

I had no plans to get out. I had taken the chief's test several times and always made the board, but never got my "hat," so I decided to apply for the Warrant Officer Program again. I had tried twice, but each time had not been selected, in spite of high recommendations. This time, I would go up for Warrant Photographer and Warrant Boatswain. I asked Admiral Cobb to give me a write-up in the boatswain field and had a couple of photo officers recommend me in the photographer rating. I thought I could get one field or the other.

As time passed, I became familiar with the operation of the ship and got to know the Deep Dive System to a degree. As a first class diver, I was not required to know every valve and nut and bolt on the system, as that was not part of my area of expertise, but it helped to know some of it. When we put people in the chamber for dry runs, all the divers had to stand chamber watches. Usually, I was in charge of temperature and humidity. These areas are critical if the dive is on helium/oxygen. The temperature has to be kept in the nineties or it is too cold. There is a very narrow temperature range that is bearable when diving on helium, due to its thermal property of sucking heat away from the body. On deep dives, the breathing gas has to be heated, or the divers will get cold too quickly.

We made training dives once in a while, but I figured out that the master diver was gundecking the diving log. Master Chief Winter was a damned good master diver and a good chief, but he was under the gun to make it look like we were diving more than we were. The ship was always broken down, and we just could not get to sea to get our qualifications. A couple of us, who hated that damned *Ortolan*, went to the Naval Investigative Service with this information, and we might as well have pissed into the wind. It went nowhere. At that point, happy that our rat-fink status had not been compromised, we just fell in with the status quo and kept drawing our unearned diving pay. Men were taking their discharges or volunteering for "the Projects." A couple of them even dropped their diving qualifications to get off the ship. I wasn't ready to throw away one-hundred-fifty dollars a month. I asked the skipper what would happen if I did that. He said he would guarantee that I would get a set of orders to an aircraft carrier that never saw land. I told him, "Never mind."

I asked again about Saturation School. Each time, I was told there were only so many billets and that I was way down on the list. Hanging out in the diving locker, I learned about all sorts of jobs on the outside. BM2 Chuck Penn was going to work for some "oil patch" diving company. Culley was getting out. Milnes was going to take his discharge until he found out he had made chief, then he decided to stay. They were all good men and really knew what they were doing, but the Navy was wasting them on this rattrap of a ship.

I heard horror stories about the lack of "oxygen clean" procedures. When equipment that will be used with pure oxygen is installed or overhauled, strict protocols MUST be adhered to. Any hydrocarbon, oil, or other materials that contacts pure oxygen can cause an instantaneous fire. One man, Chief Dan Dodd, had saved the ship by crawling on his hands and knees through fire to shut valves to the O_2 storage tanks after an oxygen-transfer pump had blown up and caught fire. He received a medal for that. His burns healed and he was back on the job. I saw no reason for this fire not to reoccur. The clean room was not "oxygen clean" and rumors went round and round.

We were off of Hampton Roads doing some training and laying a four point moor one day when the supply officer, who was the designated aft safety officer, got the hell knocked out of him by a spud mooring line that surged, tore a P-250 fire pump out of its storage rack, and nailed him with it. He and a seaman got sucked around a bollard by a line and ended up in the Portsmouth Naval Hospital. Neither was hurt seriously, but it showed the lack of training and knowledge was rampant on this ship. A supply officer had no business being safety officer on deck. Due to lack of experience, he could not see an unsafe situation in the making.

Some time later, we were out in the Chesapeake Bay making training dives. We made Heliox dives on the first day. When I made my mixed-gas dive that day, Ltjg. Ed Miller was my partner. We left the open bell and traveled all over the bottom gathering up as many scallops and clams as we could find. We stuck them in a mesh bag we'd tied to the bell so we could take them up and cook them later. We were down at one-hundred-eighty feet, so it was not a deep dive, but we still had to spend some time decompressing on the way back to the surface. The open bell made it a fun trip. If your Band Mask failed, you could go back to the bell, take off your mask, stand up and breathe in the bubble that was trapped there. We were diving hot water suits, so we weren't cold. The hot water suit is a loose wetsuit with little capillary tubes throughout the inside. Hot water is pumped down through the suit from the surface and keeps the diver very warm in even the coldest water. I told the topside crew that if anybody shut off my hot water as a joke, they would suffer some physical injury when I returned topside. That was a little trick they would do to some divers. They didn't pull it on me, though.

On a dive later that day, one of the chiefs passed out on the stage at about one-hundred-sixty feet. He regained consciousness and we didn't have to do anything to help him or treat him, but it was scary for a while. Later, he said that he'd had too much to drink the night before. I always wondered if the gas mix was screwed up as it was a Heliox dive. The other diver had no trouble, so it probably wasn't that.

The weather was calm, so the skipper decided to stay out and make some air dives in the Mark V rig the next day. The first few teams went down and made their dives without incident. ET2 Singer was a new guy fresh out of school and hadn't dived yet aboard ship. I was one of his tenders. As we brought him up to the thirty-foot decompression stop, I heard him say to the tender on the comm box, "Topside, my legs are tingling like they are going to sleep."

The master told him to go ahead and just move around and keep breathing normally. I detected a tone in Singer's voice and knew that he was scared.

A few minutes later, after he had been brought up to the twenty-foot stop, Singer said, "Topside, I can't feel my legs. They're numb." I knew what was happening. He was suffering from a central nervous system hit in his spine and could end up paralyzed.

I couldn't stand it any longer. I was only a first class petty officer, but I understood decompression sickness and probably had as much or more knowledge than many of the divers on the ship.

I walked up to the chief corpsman and spoke to him. "Doc, I know it is not in the protocol, but you have to shift him to straight oxygen." I looked him right in the eye. "Fuck the protocol. We'll all back you up if anything goes wrong. His life is at stake here."

"Can't do it without approval from a medical officer," was his answer.

There might have been the consideration that the air hoses were not oxygen clean and there might have been a fire, but I doubt this would have happened.

"Jesus Christ, Doc. If that were me down there, I would be begging you to do it. He's not that deep now and there is no problem with O_2 toxicity."

They would not shift him to oxygen, which might have alleviated the symptoms and enabled us to treat him on the surface with no permanent damage. By now, Singer couldn't stand up on the stage. He was sitting down crumpled up, and the other diver, who didn't didn't have a problem, was making sure Singer didn't fall off the stage.

The master diver and the corpsman decided to skip the ten-foot stop and bring both divers up and treat them together. When the divers were brought to the surface, the tenders hurriedly stripped off their suits and helmets. They walked his partner to the chamber on the port side of the vessel, and carried Singer to it. The two men were immediately pressed down to sixty feet on oxygen. The other diver had no symptoms. He was only treated for the first part of the table, and was locked out of the chamber before extending the table.

The deck crew cast off the lines to the four-point moor and left the spuds anchored. The navigator noted the spot on the Loran and the *Ortolan* got under way as soon as we had the divers in the chamber. We treated Singer on extended tables with extra oxygen breathing periods, to no avail. His legs did not regain their feeling. When we reached Norfolk, an ambulance took him to Portsmouth Naval Hospital where they put him in the neurology clinic. We went to sea again for a few days and when we came back, a couple of the divers went to see him. They said he was still paralyzed from the waist down and was wearing diapers. He'd only been married a couple of weeks, so this was a great way to start a marriage. I heard later that he had recovered nearly completely, but the Navy still gave him a medical discharge with retirement.

When the ship was under way, the seas came sloshing up through the center well of the ship. This was the open space between the hulls where the DSRV would be lowered, if we had one. The rumors were that the DSRV had been redesigned with new fuel cells, and that it would no longer fit the ship as it was about another fifteen feet longer. I wondered why they didn't get to work right away extending the area where it should be stored. The divers used to talk about this all the time. Finally, one of them came out and said that we were just fluff and hot air and that the *Ortolan's* real mission was to make the parents and relatives of submariners think that their loved ones could be rescued if they ran into trouble. We all knew this was true, as the realities of the operations of nuclear submarines were quite apparent in the limited conversations we had with these elite sailors.

The submariners laughed at the prospect of being rescued. One of them told me, "Hell, if we are in a depth where you guys can help us, we can just blow and go with the Stanke Hoods." A Stanke Hood is a flotation device that looked like an inflatable life jacket with a hood attached. It had a clear plastic window in the hood. The submariners would get into the escape trunk, and inflate the hoods by compressed air. The trunk would be pressurized to ambient depth and they would simply float up to the surface. The air escaping from the jackets would dump into the hood and then blow out around the bottom of that. There was no need to breathe as they would be exhaling all the way up due to the expansion of the air in their lungs. I am not sure how deep they used these in training, but the Brits used a modification of this. On Project Upshot, they encompassed the Stanke Hood in a suit that allowed them to escape from depths down to around a thousand feet.

Rivera, my assistant in the lab, became a problem. I suspected he was stealing from other members of the crew. One day, I was going through some clothing that was hanging on the hooks in the lab when I found a pea coat with another sailor's name in it. I went to the personnel office and asked what department the guy was in. Sherby told me and I looked the guy up.

"Do you have a pea coat?" I asked him.

"I did have, but I lost it somewhere while we were in the shipyard," he told me.

"Well, I found it up in the photo lab. Why don't you come up and ask Rivera how he came to have it."

Nothing ever came of it. Rivera gave it back and made up some story about thinking it was his or something, so nothing was ever done. He started wising off to me whenever I asked him to do something that should be done. His time was up soon after that and he was discharged. On the rest of the ship the seamen did the swabbing and waxing of the passageways. Outside the photo lab, I was the one to do that. Junior petty officers and non-rated men would come by and chuckle at the sight of a senior petty officer having to swab and wax the deck.

In the summer of 1976, Cdr. Tony Esau relieved Cdr. Ramsey. I thought things would improve. Tony was a hands-on guy and took no bullshit from people. He liked to get things done and I thought he would be able to get some operating money and fix things that were wrong with the ship. Wrong again. I think he realized that it was a career buster. The change of command ceremony took place in the hot sun of June in 1976. I was now thirty years old and a significant number of men my age in the diving Navy had made chief and some had been advanced to warrant officer.

Before I had left Combat Camera Group, Eddie Dotson, Doug Keever, and Dave Harris had been promoted directly to ensign in the LDO (Limited Duty Officer) program. This would enable them to serve only in their specialty, photography, so they would be stationed in photo labs or on board aircraft carriers as the photo officer in charge of the photo lab at that installation. I, of course, was not on the list. My wife may have been correct. Perhaps my bout with the shrink at Naval Special Warfare was affecting my career. I didn't think so, but it was always in the back of my mind. Eddie had been in a court martial for attempted murder at one time, and Doug was famous for being a wild man when he was drunk. I had none of that in my record and had excellent write-ups, but I hadn't taken courses to get an associates degree, and the others had. That may have made the difference.

The change of command went off smoothly and nobody passed out from standing on the hot steel decks in the blazing sun. There was not a breath of wind that day, and we couldn't wait to get the hell out of there. Tony Esau made a speech about how he was happy to be there and looked forward to serving on board. His speech was the same one I had heard at every change of command ceremony I'd ever attended.

We broke from there, ate some cake and punch on the mess decks, and secured for the day, except for the duty section.

In August, it was time for the promotion examinations to be given. I was eligible, as were a number of others on the ship. John Cantale, and I sat together for the test, which was given on the base at the Educational Services office. He was an electrician's mate. We blew right through the test, as all of us had been studying. When you are a chief on a ship, you have your own quarters with the other chiefs. Up to that point, you are just meat along with all the other sailors on board, at least that's how it was on the *Ortolan*. We knew it would be a few months before we got the results.

BMC Raesman, one of the divers on board, had put in for warrant officer. We all knew he would be selected, as he was a sharp chief and everybody liked him. I had some connections and decided to see if either one of us had made it. I made the call and learned that he was on the list, and I was not. Oh, well. I hadn't had my hopes up very high, anyway.

I went to the uniform shop and bought a set of warrant officer bars and the appropriate insignia for his specialty. We were due to go back to sea for some more training. I had told the skipper that Raesman had made it and asked him not to tell the new chief boatswain's mate. I gave Raesman the bars and told him he would probably need them soon. He didn't think he'd made it and I didn't let on that I knew he had. I think he just didn't believe he *had* made it. He was already a chief, so if he was advanced, all he had to do was pin the bars on his collar after he removed the chief's insignia. We didn't have a hat for him, but I got the insignia for his "piss cutter" (as we called the Boy Scout-looking hat that chiefs and officers wore aboard ship). When the word was officially out, the skipper called Raesman into his office, gave him the hat insignia that I'd withheld, and told him to pin it on. Raesman was really surprised and happy.

By the time Christmas rolled around, we were still in port with no mission. The list came down and I found out I had passed the test with a high score and would be advanced to chief petty officer. About three hundred had taken the test for PHC and only about sixty had made it. I was number thirty-two on the list.

I was working in the photo lab on December 31, 1976 when I got a phone call from HMC Shirley, one of our diver-corpsmen. He told me he needed to see me in sickbay right away. I walked in and he told me to lock the door. I did and, when I turned around, he handed me a tin cup full of some orange liquid. He and HM2 Andy May were sitting there sipping some already.

"Drink this," he commanded.

I took a drink and it about killed me. It was a mixture of pure medical alcohol and Navy-issue canned orange juice. Once the fire went out a little, I liked it. After we had a few more, the dicksmiths† said Happy New Year and I left for home. The drive home wasn't bad. I didn't have any symptoms of being drunk. I knew I had a slight buzz on, but otherwise seemed okay. By the time I pulled into my yard and parked my VW, I was hammered. The spiked juice had taken hold and was really nailing me hard. I made it through the door and started taking my shoes and jacket off. I went up to the bathroom and the next thing I knew, I heard this little far away voice saying, "Steven, are you all right?"

† Dicksmith is the divers' name for corpsmen who are qualified divers.

Mary didn't know that I'd been drinking, as I had been in decent shape when I came through the door. I lay there for a while before got up and went to bed. Jesus! That grain alcohol was very powerful. I never had occasion to drink any again.

The *Ortolan* was like a fire department, except we "firemen" knew there would never be a fire. The morale was low and divers were getting out one after the other. We had no purpose there other than to draw our pay and hope that somebody would either decommission the ship or find a use for it. There were plans for a cruise to St. Croix in the Virgin Islands for some real diving. They were going to use the Mark II Deep Dive, the Personnel Transfer Capsules (PTC), and all the gear. Divers would get into the chamber and transfer to the PTC. We'd lower them down to a deep depth of four hundred feet or so, have them make an excursion, then return in the PTC, mate it up to the chamber, and decompress them in the Mark II.

Mary and I talked about the future, and I decided to get out of the Navy when my time was up in June 1977. I would have to turn down chief to do this, so I waited until the last possible moment to tell Sherby Hart in the admin office that I would be leaving. Mary and I spent lots of time talking about it. She was pregnant with our second kid, and Emily was growing quickly. I really wanted my kids to grow up in Maine, where they belonged. The crime rate was bad here compared to South Thomaston, Maine, and there were too many distractions. I'd been around Navy brats and saw some who turned out well and some who turned out badly. Also, I was afraid that if I stayed in for twenty years, my ambition, what little I still had, would be stifled by getting a sure-thing retirement check every month. I'd probably end up working at the Post Office, or selling insurance or used cars like so many retired military personnel. No, I would get out and jump naked into the civilian world, somewhere I had never been before. I had been corresponding with Captain George Kittredge, USN, Ret., the man who had invented the "Kittredge seal." He offered me a job running sub schools. He was starting a school to teach people how to operate his one-man dry subs.

One of my friends in the diving locker was MR1(DV) Jim Hutchinson, a saturation diver. Hutch was not too happy about some of the safety considerations on board the ship and we used to have long discussions about them. He had been at Special Projects in Vallejo, but I'd heard that he had become a conscientious objector or held other beliefs that wouldn't allow him to take part in what could become combat situations. I didn't ask him about it as I knew missions at Special Projects were highly classified. Anyway, Hutch and I were both going to leave the Navy, so we decided it was time to do something about the conditions on the ship. I knew my congressman, David Emery, because we had gone to high school together and he had gone on to become the youngest congressman in Washington. Hutch was from Wisconsin, so he figured that Senator William Proxmire would be his best bet to get some results. We formulated a plan, I called Dave Emery on Friday and asked him if Saturday morning was okay for him to meet with us. He said to call him at home when we got there and he'd come down to the Cannon Office Building to meet us, to make ourselves at home until he got there.

On Saturday morning, Hutch and I donned our "dress canvas" with all our ribbons and pins and drove up to Washington, D.C. We wondered if we were doing the right thing. We knew that the guys on the ship were really looking forward to going to St. Croix, and to enjoying the warm water and liberty that they would have there. We were going with them, but it just made us nervous knowing everything we had heard. We knew the facts about the safety of the ship and that it could kill some of us. We told Ltjg. Ed Miller and Lt. Moen that we were going to talk to the senators. They both wished us luck, but said they couldn't get involved as it would wipe out their careers. Jim and I understood their situations; we had already committed to getting out. Hutch had the same time in the Navy as I did, so between us, we had more than twenty years.

We arrived at the Cannon Office Building and walked through the door. The guard asked us who we were, and what we needed. I told him we were there to see Congressman David Emery from Maine and that he was expecting us. The security guard called Dave's office, received the okay, and told us how to get to the congressman's office.

We entered the office, and one of Dave's assistants was there. He pointed us to the coffeepot and we made small talk while we waited for Dave. In a half hour, he walked in wearing blue jeans and a flannel shirt, much as he might be dressed if he were in Maine.

We shook hands and I introduced Dave and Hutch.

"Well, you guys have some things to tell me. I've been catching up on some of it through the assistant you've been talking with. Now, fill me in."

Hutch and I took turns rattling off the points we were trying to make about the safety, morale, and uselessness of the ship. He sat there with his chair tilted back and his fingertips pushed together in front of him. After a while, he spoke.

"Steve, you know how to type. There's a ream of paper and a typewriter, the coffeepot is over there in the corner, and if you need anything to eat, let my assistant here know and he'll run out and get it for you. I'll talk to you next week."

Dave left and I started pounding the IBM Selectric. Hutch would make a point and then I would. We hammered away until I had created a ten-page document listing all the defects and dangers that we were aware of aboard the USS *Ortolan*. We tried not to make it sound like we were whining or just complaining, as both of us were professionals and had a genuine concern for the welfare of our fellow divers and friends. When we finished, I handed it to Dave's assistant and he put it in an envelope. Hutch and I drove back to Norfolk with the feeling we had just stepped into a huge pile of dog shit with both feet.

The next day on the ship, there was no sign anything happened. We told a select few of our friends what we had done. They agreed that it had been the correct thing to do.

A week went by and word came down through ComSubLant. The Admiral had asked Cdr. Esau who were the two sailors on the ship that had jumped the chain of command and gone to a congressman. The skipper never said anything to us about it, as he may have been advised not to. I called Dave's office a couple of days later and found out that the Secretary of the Navy had been extremely upset over the report. Of course, there had been a rebuttal. No attempt was made to write this off as disgruntled sailors just whining, as we were both what they considered career Navy men. I was very surprised that they didn't try to "kill the messenger" on this one. We fully expected to get court-martialed for not following the chain of command. The skipper never even referred to the report and everybody treated us pretty much the same as they had before. However, we ran into Lt. Moen in the passageway one day when Hutch and I were going the other way. He smiled and gave us a vigorous thumbs up, and as he walked by us, he said, "You guys sure have bigger balls than I do. Good job!" That was the only time he made reference to it.

The *Ortolan* took on stores to get underway for the Virgin Islands. We had plenty of breathing gas on board for diving as we had hardly used any since I had been there. We set sail for St. Croix and the whole crew was looking forward to going there if only just to get out of Norfolk for a change.

The ship was about eight hundred miles from our destination when a message came. We were to turn back and go to Charleston Naval Base and tie up alongside the tender. They had the capabilities for inspecting our oxygen system and rendering it oxygen clean and up to standards. Hutch and I quickly became quite unpopular with the crew and suffered many dirty looks. Both of us were over six feet and rumors had circulated that I was nobody to piss off, so we had no physical confrontations. The divers didn't treat us badly, as many of them had the same concerns, but failed to voice them to the proper authorities. Ltjg. Ed Miller was my friend and he said that we had done the right thing. He never said that in front of the other officers. None of the officers ever talked to us with other officers within earshot.

The ship pulled into Charleston, steaming past a nuclear submarine that had run aground on the side of the channel. The technicians from the tender came aboard and, with the help of some of our divers, started tearing the system apart and inspecting it. I didn't have much to do here as no photography was needed, so I painted the walls in the photo lab and generally cleaned things up, logged some negatives that I had been meaning to get to, and generally kept busy.

One afternoon, Hosea from the admin office called me on the phone and asked if I was going on liberty that evening. I told him that I might go to the bowling alley and get a hamburger and a few beers. I told him to come to the lab when he was ready to go and we'd walk over together. We spent a few hours at the bowling alley, had supper, and drank a few beers. On the way back to the ship, in total darkness, I stepped in a hole in the pavement and wrenched hell out of my right ankle. I hobbled back to the ship and it got worse and worse. In the morning, I couldn't put any weight on it at all, so I called sick bay and asked Doc Shirley to come and take a look at it. He came right up and, after examining it, told me that it should be x-rayed.

One of the guys in the duty section drove me to the hospital where I sat around until they had a chance to x-ray my ankle. When that was finished, the doctor called me into the examining room. He looked at the x-ray and said, "Well, there is a break here, but it is an old one. This time it's just a bad sprain."

"Well, Doc, I am on a ship and the head is two decks down and the chow hall is all the way forward. The frigging decks are always covered with hydraulic oil and we are heading for the Virgin Islands to do some diving. Can you put a cast on it and tell them I am unfit for shipboard duty?"

He looked at me for a minute. "Are you Cheryl Waterman's brother?" he asked.

"Yes. How did you know that?"

"We were stationed together at Portsmouth and she talked about you being a diver on some ship, I just figured it out when you told me about the ship. Yes, I think that ankle will heal a lot faster if it has a cast on it."

He sent me to the cast room and a corpsman put the cast on. He told me to have it removed in a few weeks to make it look good and go easy on it for a while after that. I thanked him and made sure I had his name to give to my sister when I talked with her again.

When I went back to the ship, I told Sherby Hart that there was no way I was going to be able to handle any of my shipboard duties. By now, they all knew that I was getting out, as had I refused to extend for the obligated service required to be advanced to chief.

"I'll have the XO transfer you back to the squadron and you can do light duty there until we get back," he said.

"There is a God," I thought.

Sherby prepared the necessary paperwork, got me lined up with a travel request (TR) for a plane ticket and I flew back to Norfolk. The next day, my neighbor, who had the day off, drove me to the squadron. The office was in the process of being renovated and all the desks and equipment were in a trailer. I hobbled in on my crutches and talked to the chief. "Go ahead home, Waterman," he said. "Just call us every morning around 0800 and let us know you are still alive."

I went home. Mary was going to have our second child soon and I would be there when it was born. Also, I was getting ready to take the tests for licenses for ham radio and Coast Guard captain. This little "vacation" would give me the chance to study for them. Things went along quite well. I called in every morning for muster, took the ham radio tests up to the advanced class and passed them. I even got my Coast Guard "six-pack" license. Admiral Cobb, my employer in the yacht business, had signed off my sea time and the rest of it was bookwork and practical knowledge.

On March 18, 1977, Mary went into labor. The cast was still on my leg and I couldn't drive, so my sister Cheryl, by then a lieutenant commander, drove her to Portsmouth Naval Hospital. A few hours later, Mary delivered our second daughter. We named her Nellie Marie after my great-grandmother, who had helped me learn to read before I was old enough to attend school. Later on, she went blind and I read to her—recipes when she was cooking and letters when she received them from her friends. She died in a nursing home at the age of ninety-four.

When the *Ortolan* returned to Norfolk, I reported back aboard. I only took clothes with me, as I had left all my gear on the ship. Rivera had long since been discharged, so Sherby Hart was the only one with a key to the photo lab. I had given it to him when I left, even though there was a spare locked away in the key cabinet in the office. I told him to help himself to the Coke and yogurt and other things I had put in the *official* photo lab refrigerator.

On board the ship, I was invited to move into the chiefs' quarters or "goat locker" as it was called. Word had spread that I was leaving the Navy. The guys in the admin office didn't believe I would to through with it. One of the chiefs, EMCS Powell, had heard the rumors and called me into the goat locker one evening when we had the duty together. He was a black guy and one of the real professionals on board the *Ortolan*. He wasn't a diver; he was in charge of the electrical gang. Powell was a class act all the way.

"Waterman, I hear you are getting out of the Navy," he started. "I want you to know that you are doing the right thing. It's not the Navy we joined. You're a smart guy and you'll make out all right in whatever you decide to do. Don't let them talk you out of it. I know you've given it a lot of thought."

Powell continued to tell about how he had to "bust his ass" to get where he was today and that the young black kids coming into the service figured that the world owed them a living. They looked at Powell and thought he'd had it all handed to him because he was black.

"I don't need that shit any more," Powell said. "My wife has a good job as a teacher and I own a farm down south. I want my kids to grow up in one place. I'll have twenty-two years in when my time is up. I'm going home."

We had a good conversation there in the chiefs' quarters, and I appreciated him taking me aside and speaking with me. I'd had some trepidation about getting out with almost thirteen years in service. I had made chief—a major stumbling block to many people. Now I would have the respect and perks that were accorded chiefs, even though some of them didn't rate it. I might still have been able to pick up a commission, but doubted it. I was too much of a rogue and had a tendency to put the men before the mission. Lately, the mission seemed to be get your ticket punched and never take chances.

The *Ortolan* was due to go to sea again the third week of May and would be away during the dates Tim Noble and I were to be discharged. We were transferred to the transient barracks at the Norfolk Naval Station. Hutch had already left the Navy and had procured a job designing anesthesia equipment for a medical supply company.

I cleaned out all the equipment that I owned and all my clothing from the photo lab. Then I said goodbye to the XO and the captain. Cdr. Esau said there were no hard feelings about what we did to the ship and that he hoped all would go well with me in civilian life. I thanked him and wished him luck with the *Ortolan*. Then I walked down to the office, got my records, saluted the fantail, and walked off the ship for the last time.

My new assignment was counting heads in the chow hall. Tim Noble's job was running road crews that picked up trash along the road to the base. We attended some meetings where we were told how to convert our military life insurance to a civilian policy, how to take advantage of G.I. benefits, and the procedure to follow to join the Reserves. I got my discharge, and Tim and I said goodbye to each other. I didn't expect to see Tim, or any of the other people I had served with, again.

I drove to Little Creek, Virginia on the way home, and signed up to join the Naval Reserves. A few weeks earlier, I had told the chief at the Reserve Center that I would be going home to Maine once I got out, and after my house sold. He advised me not to tell him that, and said he would sign me up the day I got discharged, after which time I could tell him that I was going home to Maine. I assumed he needed the numbers for his recruitment quota. That day, Friday the 13th, May 1977, was the end of my active-duty naval career.

I had a job lined up working for Captain Kittredge teaching people to operate dry subs, and working as the skipper of his sub tender, the *Aquatic*. I didn't think it would last, but it would get me started working in the private sector.

Glossary

AFCCG – Atlantic Fleet Combat Camera Group

ASR-21 – Auxiliary Submarine Rescue 21 (USS *Pigeon*). This ship was home-ported in San Diego and was the sister ship of *Ortolan*

BM2 – Boatswain's mate, second class

BMC – Chief boatswain's mate

BNAO – Basic Naval Aviation Officers School

BOQ – Bachelor Officers' Quarters

BUD/S – Basic Underwater Demolition/SEAL Training

Cdr. – Commander

CO – Commanding officer

Cumshaw – Many sailors thought this was a Chinese term for beach time in Hong Kong. We used the term to mean trade or barter for materials and supplies we needed.

DSRV – Deep Submergence Rescue Vehicle

EMCS – Senior chief electrician's mate

EOD – Explosive Ordnance Disposal

ET2 – Electronics Technician, Second Class

Gedunk – a Navy expression for junk food. I think it stands for God-damned junk.

Hanoi Hilton – the prison in Hanoi where American P.O.W.s were held.

HM2 – Hospital corpsman, second class

HMC – Chief Hospital Corpsman

JOOD – Junior Officer on Deck

Ltjg. – Lieutenant, Junior Grade

Lcdr. – Lieutenant commander

LCPR – Landing Craft, Personnel Reconnaissance

LCVP – Landing Craft, Vehicle, and Personnel

LPSS – Amphibious Transport Submarine (retired)

Lt. – Lieutenant

Master-at-Arms – the man in charge of the barracks. This job was usually rotated among people in the commands. We never had to do it as we were on sea duty. I don't know why that made a difference, except that we were subject to deployment.

MM1 – Machinist Mate, First Class

NAO – Naval Aviation Officers (non-pilots)

NAS Pensacola – Naval Air Station, Pensacola

NASDS – National Association of SCUBA Diving Stores

NATTU – Naval Air Technical Training Unit

NAUI – National Association of Underwater Instructors

NSMRL – Naval Submarine Medical Research Laboratory

NSWG – Naval Special Warfare Group

OCAN – Officer Candidates

OIC – Officer in Charge

OOD – Officer of the Day

PADI – Professional Association of Diving Instructors

PBY – A twin-engine amphibious aircraft, the type Admiral Cobb flew.

PH1 – Photographer's Mate, First Class

PH2 – Photographer's Mate, Second Class

PHCM – Master Chief Photographer's Mate

PLF – Parachute Landing Fall

PR2 – Parachute Rigger, Second Class

RDT&E – Research, Development, Testing, and Evaluation

RFPFs – Regional Forces and Popular Forces, commonly called Ruff Puffs, Vietnamese troops like National Guard, not regular army.

SDVs – Swimmer Delivery Vehicles or SEAL Delivery Vehicles

SERE – Survival, Evasion, Resistance, and Escape.

SHAD – Shallow Habitat Air Dive

SMC – Chief Signalman

STG2 – Sonar Technician Second Class

UDT – Underwater Demolition Team

UDT/R – Underwater Demolition Team Replacement

UQC – Underwater Communications System

WESPAC – West Pacific (a.k.a. WestPac)

XO – Executive Officer

YFNB – A non-self-propelled, covered barge, we called it *your friendly navy barge*. YFNB-17 housed the Second Class Diving School at Little Creek Amphibious Base.

YN1 – Yeoman, First Class

About the Author

Steven L. Waterman was born in Maine and raised on a chicken farm in the mid-coast area. He started SCUBA diving at the age of thirteen against his mother's better judgement. While in high school, Steve became interested in photography, and he built a darkroom in the dirt basement of his home in Spruce Head. After joining the Navy on June 24, 1964, three months after his eighteenth birthday, Waterman served his country on active duty with the Navy for thirteen years as a Photographer's Mate, First Class and Diver, First Class, and was HALO Parachute qualified. Steve served a tour in Vietnam with Underwater Demolition Team 13 as a combat/intelligence photographer. He retired from the Reserves with a total of twenty-one years of service.

In 1972, Steve married Mary Ware, his high school sweetheart. After his May 13, 1977 discharge from the Navy as a Chief Petty Officer, Steve moved back to his home town in Maine with Mary and their two daughters. The couple had two more children, a son and another daughter.

Waterman boasts a diverse working career, from dry-submarine instructor to dive shop owner, lobster fisherman to commercial diver, and as a photographer and author. Among his accomplishments, Steve attained his private pilot certificate, gyroplane, and built an aircraft, a two-place gyroplane .

Steve may be reached at *JustASailor@mac.com*.

Fearless PRESENTING

Fearless PRESENTING

A Self-Help Workbook for Anyone Who Speaks, Sells, or Performs in Public

Eric Maisel, Ph.D.

BACK STAGE BOOKS

AN IMPRINT OF WATSON-GUPTILL PUBLICATIONS

New York

FOR ANN
and for
DAVID, NATALYA, AND KIRA

Copyright © 1997 by Eric Maisel, Ph.D.
All Rights Reserved

First published in 1997 in the United States by Back Stage Books, an
imprint of Watson-Guptill Publications, a division of BPI Communications,
Inc., 1515 Broadway, New York, NY 10036-8986.

Library of Congress Cataloging-in-Publication Data for this title can be
obtained by writing to the Library of Congress, Washington, DC.

Manufactured in the United States of America

ISBN 0-8230-8834-0

1 2 3 4 5 / 01 00 99 98 97

Editor: Dale Ramsey
Designer: Jay Anning
Production Manager: Ellen Greene

Acknowledgments

I would like to thank the many people in the arts, in business, in academia, and elsewhere, with whom I've worked as a psychotherapist and creativity consultant, for the opportunity to learn from them about their struggles and triumphs with presentation and performance anxiety issues. I would especially like to thank those courageous souls who have volunteered to come forward at my workshops and, despite their anxiety, have role-played presentation situations.

I would also like to thank those of my colleagues who have supplied me with material especially for this book. I am thinking in particular of psychologists Dr. Julie Nagel and Dr. Susan Raeburn, pianist and conservatory teacher Peggy Salkind, singer and arts administrator Reneé Hayes, actor and acting teacher Ed Hooks, and psychotherapist Metece Riccio.

Additional thanks for his fine editing job to Dale Ramsey of Back Stage Books and, for her continued attention and interpersonal skills, to my literary agent, Linda Allen. I would also like to express my appreciation to my children, who already know about having to present themselves: to David, Natalya, and Kira, with love. And to someone who has been presenting herself and wonderful literature to high school students for some time now, a kiss for my wife, Ann Mathesius Maisel.

Contents

1

The Language of
Performance Anxiety

As a therapist working with people in the arts, I see clients struggling with performance anxiety, a problem of which they themselves are often unaware. This may seem surprising at first glance, and in the beginning it surprised me, too. Now, a decade later, I'm convinced that the typical view of performance anxiety is far too limited. Many more people suffer from it than know it, in and out of the arts, and many more life situations elicit performance anxiety than we generally realize.

For every actress I know who is aware of her anxiety before an audition, there are a dozen more who flounder as they attempt to select an audition piece and who do not recognize their floundering as a special case of performance anxiety. They don't identify as symptoms of performance anxiety the feelings they're experiencing—agitation in the bookshop as they face the row of monologue books, queasy feelings of indecisiveness, fear that they'll choose a too-popular monologue or a too old-fashioned one, "spacy" feelings as they read monologue after monologue without focusing, and even a powerful desire to flee. Embedded in such moments, and even though they are

safely in a drama bookshop or in their own living room, is the experience of the audition and the anticipatory anxiety that comes with that particular performance.

These "hidden" cases of performance anxiety abound. A dancer may assert that she never experiences performance anxiety, but it turns out upon investigation that she can neither ask her teacher to recommend her to a local dance company director, nor ask a prominent choreographer, whom her sister knows as a next-door neighbor, for a special audition chance. The dancer can certainly produce reasons why it would be best not to ask for the recommendation or for the audition chance, but when these reasons are explored they are seen to be rationalizations masking performance anxiety.

The dancer may argue that she's "not ready" to audition, that her body isn't "really in shape," that her teacher "probably" doesn't think she's ready to dance with a top company, that the choreographer "will be annoyed" if approached in that way, and so on. But her arguments do not stand up even to mild scrutiny. Something else is going on—and that something else is performance anxiety.

As I grew more attuned in sessions with my clients to the signs of performance anxiety, I began to see that creative artists in all the disciplines—painters, poets, screenwriters, and composers—were bothered, and sometimes even plagued, by this problem. The painter who couldn't recontact a gallery owner who'd already expressed interest in him, the poet who couldn't pick up the phone and ask for a few days' extension of the application deadline for a writers' colony residency (a deadline she had missed through procrastination), the playwright who sabotaged himself at dinner with his agent by announcing that their conversation was boring him—all were victims of this hidden anxiety.

It dawned on me that many instances in which people are blocked are actually better conceived as instances of performance anxiety. This point was driven home to me in the course of a conversation with a publisher of one of my previous books. He was describing himself as a frustrated writer—a writer manqué. I remarked that I was currently working on a book about anxiety that addressed the fears and inhibition of artists and others when they must make presentations of themselves or their creative products. I suggested that many writing blocks were in fact cases of performance anxiety. Without needing me to elaborate further, he replied that that was true in his own case; he'd simply never realized it before. Creative blockage and performance anxiety actually felt different in the body, he continued, and it was the latter that he experienced when he attempted to write.

When we begin to understand that a painter may be holding the act of painting as a certain kind of performance, we better understand why he or she may come to a blank canvas with a preformed idea, which is quite different from a willingness to encounter the canvas and apply paint without knowing what will appear. This is analogous to the difference between a speech for which one can prepare and the question-and-answer period after the speech (which for many public speakers is the most frightening part) or the difference between a theatrical performance for which one can rehearse, reducing the anxiety, and an improvised performance.

The following questions, along with the numerous others that appear in this workbook, are provided to guide you in your exploration of any performance anxiety that you experience in your life and of the ways you can confront and resolve any problems you have in making presentations. Although some space is provided for your response to each question, you may want to keep a separate notebook as you actively engage in exploring the issues addressed in this book.

*Do you have the sense that performance anxiety may be affecting you in "hidden" ways?*_____

_____

_____

Playing detective, can you identify some of these hidden cases of performance anxiety?

_____

_____

Performance Anxiety Territory

The territory that interests us here is a very large one. It includes, of course, the performance anxiety we associate with musical, theatrical, and dance performances. But also it encompasses business situations, cases of creative blockage, and many other presentation situations. It is a territory that includes the performers named below (see box), but also tens of millions of people—professional and amateur performers and nonperformers alike. Indeed, when the general public is surveyed about their fears and phobias, invariably heading the list, before a fear of flying or of snakes or any other simple or complex phobia, is a fear of public speaking.

IN THE SPOTLIGHT

Getting up in front of an audience and having the spotlight turned our way is apparently one of our greatest fears—even for those who have an exhibitionist streak in them. Consider these names from the performing arts who have wrestled with stage fright.

Richard Burton

Enrico Caruso

Franco Corelli

Frederic March

Laurence Olivier

Luciano Pavarotti

Maureen Stapleton

Maria Callas

Pablo Casals

Gertrude Lawrence

Anna Moffo

Estelle Parsons

Carly Simon

As Fred Silver explained, in *Auditioning for the Musical Theatre*: "There is a vast difference between the mild anticipatory nervousness that is a healthy part of the performance process and shows you care enough to want to give it your best shot, and the debilitating paroxysms of fear that can immobilize a performer." Yet it is also fair to say that the experience is more than mildly disturbing for a great many people. To take just a pair of examples, in a 1987 survey of 2,212 professional classical musicians, 24 percent complained of suffering from significant performance anxiety; and in a more recent survey of ninety-four classical musicians, fifteen reported suffering from severe performance anxiety.

The territory, then, includes people whose experience of performance anxiety ranges anywhere from mild to severe. It also includes a great number of people who regularly avoid performing—including professionals in whose best interests it is to perform. Because they want to avoid the experience of anxiety, these individuals make it their business to avoid performance situations. It is especially for them that the issue of performance anxiety remains a hidden one.

Some performances are easy to avoid, others very difficult. It is easy not to telephone a literary agent or a talent agent. It is much more difficult to cancel your Carnegie Hall recital. It is easy not to attend a writers' conference, where you might engage an editor in a one-on-one conversation. It is much harder to refuse to return your editor's call if you are under contract. Thus, the territory we must explore includes both the performance anxiety you feel before making a presentation and that you *would* feel if you faced making the appearance you are avoiding.

*Do you tend to avoid presentation situations because of performance anxiety?*_____

_____

_____

Do you avoid them only sometimes, or do you avoid them as a rule? _____

_____

_____

As we begin habitually to avoid making presentations, we may not feel anything like anxiety anymore; we have no need to grow anxious because we know that we mean to avoid the situation. There is no performance anxiety to speak of, and if we looked for symptoms we wouldn't find any. So, paradoxical as it may seem, what follows from this observation is the fact that some of the severest cases of performance anxiety may produce no symptoms at all. That is, people simply avoid that presentation of themselves: They don't write a novel, don't learn an instrument, don't act a role, don't choose work requiring a presentational function, don't date, don't state opinions at work. They may look calm and confident, but only because the anxiety has been perfectly kept within bounds by avoiding. In this regard, they resemble the person with a fear of flying who is perfectly calm on the ground and can even talk about flying with insight and enthusiasm—knowing he or she will never, ever board a plane.

Have you mastered your performance anxiety by avoiding most performance situations?

_____

_____

You may even be an actor and avoid performing. You may read about a particular audition, experience anticipatory anxiety (without realizing that you're growing anxious), and decide not to audition, rationalizing your avoidance behavior by saying, "Oh, I don't think I'm right for that role," "I'm sure that part's pre-cast," or "That director's never liked me."

It bears repeating in connection with avoidance tactics that few people realize to what extent performance anxiety operates in the creative areas of their lives. Not only are they regularly unaware of how it prevents them from approaching talent or literary agents, editors, supervisors, directors, producers, and gallery owners, but they may be equally unaware of how it prevents them from discovering their full creative powers in their work.

For example, many artists work more mechanically, with an emphasis on technique, correct ideas, formula, and general safety, than they really want to. They do this because doing otherwise would feel too dangerous and would produce too many anxious feelings. Thus an actor may be reluctant to get too deeply into a role, or a musician may be reluctant to interpret a piece too personally, out of fear of losing control, gaining unwanted attention or provoking criticism. Likewise, safety-minded visual artists may discover that they can't move toward abstraction, even though they feel pulled in that direction, and a safety-minded sales manager may avoid presenting a novel sales strategy, out of fear that the new idea may look foolish.

In the creative work you do, is there a connection between the inhibitions of performance anxiety and a failing to delve deeply or go in a new direction? _____

_____

Some Case Histories

The following case histories, culled from my clinical practice, help illuminate this intricate territory.

• An artist-therapist began to see that her reluctance to show her paintings to gallery owners and even to friends and her reluctance to present art-therapy case material at conferences were related phenomena — related by the performance anxiety she felt in both situations. Slowly she began to recognize the symptoms of that anxiety, especially the shallow breathing that accompanied each episode. She also began to recognize the sorts of internal messages that contributed to the anxiety, especially "It's not good enough" (about her paintings and her presentations) and "I'm not good enough."

• An actress grew aware in therapy that her hypochondria, fear, and general irresolution were anxiety manifestations. She began to notice that free-floating anxiety was also manifesting itself at auditions, in acting classes, in her interactions with directors, and in her unwillingness to audition for certain roles.

• A teacher, who regularly worked until midnight preparing her lessons and always came into class overprepared if anything, nevertheless still never *felt* prepared. It turned out that because she held teaching as a performance for which she needed a complete and perfect script, she never felt free to improvise, relax, or "just let kids discuss things" in her class. Once she realized this, she began to make more modest preparations, to interact more with her students, and to enjoy teaching more.

• A musician procrastinated for many months about selecting the music she wanted to sing in her cafe act. What, she wondered, was exactly the right mix of ballads and up-tempo tunes? What songs would her accompanist handle best? Would her choices have the right mix for the club owner who'd expressed an interest in her? And if the set was crafted for just that club, would it be right for any other club? And if it wasn't, did that mean that she needed two different sets right from the beginning? And was she really doing justice to her interest in Latin fusion music if she excluded it, just because it didn't fit in with her pop choices? And so on. . . . It gradually became clear that her many doubts represented not a set of actual problems to be solved, but rather her anxiety about performing—despite the fact that she did not experience anxiety in the performance situations themselves. Given the chance to doubt herself beforehand, she freely did so; but faced with an audience, she stopped doubting herself and performed with great confidence.

• A photographer, bold enough to pose her subjects in the nude outdoors without a bit of worry, nevertheless experienced performance anxiety in her sales clerk job with respect to personnel reviews and even in anticipation of innocent conversations with her supervisor. Toward society and its norms she felt rebellious and confidently rebelled, but toward her critical supervisor she felt meek and incompetent, and on the job she developed the equivalent of a social phobia. In exploring the contours of her Southern upbringing, it became apparent that she had overlearned deference, politeness, and other social niceties. She had also acquired a keen sense of her family's inferior position in the world. As an artist, she had somehow managed to shed that baggage and could act in socially nonconforming ways. But as a department store clerk she could not. There, she was a "girl" again, anxious to please, worried about appearances, and nervous about being found wanting in her "performances" by her boss.

• A singer expressed puzzlement that she sounded so much worse when she publicly performed than when she practiced—and worse yet when she auditioned. She blamed these shortcomings on several factors: starting out later in life as a singer than her peers had, having studied under a teacher who harmed her with his ideas and harshly criticized her, not having enough time to devote to her singing career, which remained very much a part-time affair, and so on. Still, none of these rationales quite explained why her singing actually deteriorated in moving from private practice to public performance situations. And deteriorate it did. When asked to examine concretely the differences between her singing in private and in public, she discovered that she was actually losing two to three notes at both ends of her range in her public performances. Identifying this fact helped locate the problem in the territory of performance anxiety, where it properly belonged.

• A painter in his late sixties who, after forty years of professional painting, was still not satisfied that he had found a personal and distinctive style, presented as one issue his inability to do an abstract painting. He claimed to love abstraction and had in the Forties shared a studio with one of America's preeminent abstract painters, whose work he revered, but could himself only produce paintings based on preconceived images. In one of my sessions with him I invited him to attempt a quick, abstract sketch, and the attempt—the failed attempt—was revealing. Instead of playing with the crayons as a child might and enjoying himself, or attacking the canvas without directing himself consciously (as a bold abstract painter would), he instead peppered his tentative gestures with questions like "What's the point?", "What are you looking for?", and "Is this what you want?" It became apparent that, to him, painting without an image to work from felt like an improvised performance whose rules he didn't understand and whose displeasing results reflected poorly on him. Because he "didn't understand" and because "he couldn't do it well," he experienced real anxiety. In no other session did he manifest such evident anxiety, and no other session disturbed him as much as this one.

• A playwright, screenwriter, and actor learned over time to identify his ineffective ways of "performing" in artistic business situations. Together we identifed four such ways:

1. Often he would disparage himself and his work, so that if asked how his new play was going he would inevitably reply, "Oh, you know, terribly."

2. Sometimes he would turn himself "inside-out" in order to please the other person. For example, he would be all too ready to accept without question the deadline suggested by a theater director on a play commission or his agent's opinion that one or another of the characters in his latest screenplay "wasn't working."

3. Other times he would act seductively, with men and women alike, and "play little games."

4. Most often he would simply withdraw, as when a well-known director visited his roommate and he, instead of "networking," retired to his room to read the newspaper.

Identifying these interactions as anxiety-producing performance situations helped begin the process of improving his art business effectiveness and, more generally, reducing the anxiety in his life.

• A singer-songwriter who also worked as a psychotherapist claimed to experience little anxiety when he performed—the bigger the crowd, the better. But among his presenting issues were periodic panic attacks and an inability to choose between the two women in his life, which indecisiveness could be construed in part as anxiety about "making the right choice." His difficulties made me wonder if performance anxiety might also be present. As it happened, one morning we both attended a psychotherapists' meeting, at which all the participants had to "check in" and introduce themselves to the group. Mild anxiety is natural in such circumstances, but it was clear to me that my client was experiencing more than a few jitters as he stammered his introduction. I resolved to investigate with him again the effects of performance anxiety on his singing career, a career which was currently stalled.

• Another musician, a former professional horn player who was on the verge of turning to alcohol after ten years of sobriety behind him, understood his own susceptibility to bouts of severe performance anxiety. Such bouts had plagued him throughout his career, causing him to dread performing; these had been a great enough problem that, when he resolved to stop drinking, he also resolved to stop playing professionally. He feared that the anxiety associated with performing would jeopardize his sobriety. Yet performance anxiety still manifested itself in many ways, especially in his inability to socialize with his wife's friends (which made the anxiety a relationship issue as well) or to attend parties with co-workers. He nowadays played a synthesizer for his own enjoyment and sometimes considered performing for his office mates at their annual Christmas party. Indeed, he missed performing and really wanted to perform for them a certain Russian Orthodox Christmas song that he loved.

But here, too, anxiety proved too great an impediment. He entered therapy wondering if it might be safe to purchase a horn again and play it just for himself. (He had crushed his "working" horn in a drunken rage one night when he hit bottom.) Over time, we developed the following plan: that he would rent and not buy a horn; that he would think of himself as a "person who played music" and not a "musician"; and that he would have permission from himself to return the horn if the anxiety grew too great. In fact, he rented a horn, developed mouth sores, and experienced significant anxiety in just handling the horn. He returned it quickly. This experiment convinced him again that he should avoid horn-playing, but it also relieved his mind, since wondering about whether or not to play had become something of an obsession for him.

Have any additional instances of "hidden" performance anxiety in your life come to mind? _____
_____
_____
_____
_____
_____

It should be clear from these examples that to understand performance anxiety we must first recognize the many situations that can rightly be thought of as performances. Is *dating* often held by the participants to be a sort of performance? Certainly. Are a hundred different *workplace situations*, from presenting at a business meeting to speaking with a new client on the telephone, sometimes viewed by the participants as important performances? Indeed they are. Can *sculpting* in the privacy of one's studio sometimes be held by the sculptor as a sort of performance? Absolutely.

It is consequently preferable to define *performance* broadly and not narrowly, because that is how we human beings actually experience life. Indeed, it is often advantageous to frame an event or activity as a performance, even if it could be framed in some other way, because by calling it a performance we may better understand how to handle the situation effectively. Sometimes just remembering that a certain situation *is* a performance—that one doesn't have to reveal one's true thoughts and feelings, but can instead play a role and reveal as little or as much as one likes—can significantly reduce anxiety.

Describe one situation that you previously hadn't thought of as a performance. Might it be usefully relabelled a performance? _____

_____

_____

_____

_____

_____

The Performance Situation

What is so anxiety-provoking about presenting oneself or one's creative products to others? What is it about giving a performance that can strike fear in a person's heart? Does it have more to do with the ideas we hold about performance or more to do with the

realities of the situations themselves? What, to begin with, is a performance?

A client entering a psychotherapist's office may or may not view the next fifty minutes as a performance. One week, worried that he or she has nothing to say, the client may sweat and feel dizzy on arrival, and then experience no symptoms the next week feeling unselfconscious and eager to speak.

A cool, calm biology teacher who never experiences performance anxiety as long as she is speaking about science may stammer and sweat if forced to discuss some matter in the humanities. A recent experiment demonstrated this. Science teachers and English teachers were compared as to their rate of hemming and hawing as they lectured. Presenting their own subject matter, English teachers, having to deal with opinions and imprecise material, were considerably more likely to stumble over their material than were science teachers in presenting theirs. But given the same sort of imprecise material to discuss, the study showed, both groups stumbled at an equal rate.

A boy who is bouncing a ball off a wall and catching it is not performing. But the second he says to himself, "If I make this next catch, we win the World Series," he suddenly transforms his situation. Just like that, he is performing. The importance of the event to come—the next throw, the next catch—is magnified out of all proportion to the reality of the situation. There is, after all, no audience, no one who cares, no penalty if he drops the ball. In an important sense, the boy himself does not care, for he knows that he can do it again and win the championship on the subsequent throw, or stop the game, or say that he caught it even if he muffed it. Nothing is really hanging in the balance, and whatever he does he can undo. Still, all reality-testing notwithstanding, the moment he says to himself that his next catch will win or lose the World Series, he has created a vivid performance situation whose reality we all understand. Out of nowhere, with a single thought, in the absence of an audience, a performance has been initiated that not only is real but provokes real anxiety. The moment matters in an entirely new way. Suddenly the boy *cares* whether or not he catches the next ball. Even something about his identity and self-esteem become wrapped up in the moment.

Many a child has "choked" in such circumstances. Because of performance anxiety, they fail to make a play they have succeeded at a hundred times in a row. Apparently this is the way we are constructed as human beings. We can transform any innocent moment into a performance moment, simply by thinking a thought. A man and a woman are chatting easily, but then the man thinks, "Shouldn't I ask her out now?"—and the situation is transformed. An employee and her supervisor are chatting casually, but then the employee thinks, "I wonder, could this be the right moment to ask for those extra days off?"—and the situation becomes a different one.

*How do you define "performance"?*_____
_____
_____
_____

There is more to say about this performance-situation phenomenon—consider the following. You have an instrument in your hands and an audience in front of you. What exactly are you trying to do? Play the notes, of course, and the right ones at that, at an appropriate right tempo, and so on. That is the very least the audience is expecting of you (and even this "very least" is hard to do).

But much more is expected. It is expected that you will please them by giving a performance. That is, you will really "make music," interpret the composition, turn musical phrases into alluring bits of magic, and give the audience enough of your talent, intelligence, technique, wit—without pause and without hesitation—so that they'll be absorbed, mesmerized, transported. You are to excite them when the music calls for them to be excited and communicate all the poignancy of the music when poignancy is the message. You will not interrupt the music, and you will "act" even your entrances and exits so that everything appears seamless and controlled.

And more besides. Everything that happens while you are onstage is part of this thing, your performance. Occurrences that you cannot be held responsible for, like a plane buzzing low over the concert hall, are nevertheless part of your performance. How many or how few people attend the concert is part of your performance. Empty seats, water stains on the walls, coughs and sneezes in the audience are part of it. Your choice of music must itself be just right, for didn't you choose to play it? Didn't you choose this late Beethoven quartet, this piano sonata of your own composition, this jazz standard? Your choice of material is part of the performance, and you will be held responsible for it and judged on that score as well.

In all these matters, you stand ready to be judged as either successful or unsuccessful. It seems that to be considered successful the performance must be a special feat, something extraordinary enough to applaud at the end, something exemplary—even heroic. Anything less is an "unsuccessful" performance.

Is this a premise with which you agree? ____
_____
_____

*How "good" must a performance of yours be for you to judge it as a success?*_____
_____
_____

*How many mistakes are you allowed per performance?*_____
_____
_____

*Is anything less than perfection acceptable to you?*_____
_____
_____
_____

We will vigorously applaud a young piano student at the end of her mistake-ridden, labored first recital because she is nine years old and a beginner, but if we are to applaud *you*, you must do exemplary work—dare we say even perfect work? For we do believe that a successful performance

is something more than and different from a merely correct one. It is compelling and convincing, like a powerful argument. It is something that must be created, for the notes that appear on the musical score, if followed only mechanically, will lead to nothing but a lifeless performance, which we will judge as inferior.

How do you look as you perform? And how do you compare to other performers? How do you compare to yourself at other times and in other places? To say that a performance need be "perfect" is not just in a performer's mind. It is in all of our minds— even if we know better and do not want to sit in judgment of another person.

A situation hypnotizes us as soon as we label it a performance situation. As soon as the theater darkens, as soon as the overture commences, as soon as the interview begins, we are arrested and sit in judgment. The world closes around us, whether we are bouncing a ball off a wall or playing at Lincoln Center, and in that closed world we await our own judgment or the judgment of others.

*How do you judge other performers?*_____
_____
_____
_____
_____
_____
_____

What about the way you judge them affects how you judge yourself in your own performances? _____
_____

———————————————————
———————————————————
———————————————————

The truth of the matter is that performers will be judged. Singers, for instance, will be held responsible for the songs they choose to sing. But is that really so large a matter? Should the fear of that particular judgment become paralyzing? There is a gap between the reality and the perception of the situation. Could we label such anxiety "irrational"? This brings us to a new point. It is hard to call a performer's fears irrational in this regard because, undeniably, some of these performances really can matter. Consider:

• Would effectively speaking up for your agenda at a business meeting really make a difference in how you are perceived at work and whether you're promoted?

• Would a series of successful speeches really enhance a candidate's chances of election?

• Would success in even a single performance—in an audition that leads to a breakthrough role in movies; or in a minor role, if just the right person happens to be in the audience; or in a meeting where you get the opportunity to pitch your script to a studio executive—have life-altering consequences?

The answer to all of the above: Without a doubt. That makes it significantly harder to call a person's worries about such moments out-sized or irrational.

Some presentations are very important. Among the many we may give, some carry more weight than others. But some of us get agitated about every minor performance situation. For a major competition, anxiety is appropriate—but speaking to an agent? For a major audition, yes, fear makes sense—but in chatting with a director at a party? *And yet which really is the more important performance situation? Can you be sure?*

How do you go about judging which are the really important performances in your life and which the not-so-important ones? _____
———————————————————
———————————————————
———————————————————
———————————————————
———————————————————

Because of our lack of clarity as to which are the truly important performances in life, it is easy to begin to unconsciously redefine "presentation" or "performance" as "important event." This redefining can begin in childhood with a child's very first recitation or appearance in a school play. The pressure to perform well in that moment may be internal, external, or both, but the result in any case is that the child learns to associate such a moment with "important event." His or her own vital signs cause this, because the moment is exciting, and parents are nervous with and maybe demanding of him or her. Indeed, the household may be in an uproar as the child and the rest of the family get ready to attend the recital or show. The young performer is dressed up and brought to a room filled with expectant others, and without anyone meaning it to happen, the child begins to redefine "performance" as a noun with the adjective "important" always secretly attached.

So, while at first glance it may seem irrational to worry greatly about presentations of all kinds and to experience fear that, at its severest, can even incapacitate one, at second glance it is easy to account for the anxiety.

Have you attached the adjective "important" to all the situations in which you must make a presentation of some kind? _____

_____

_____

It is made even more understandable when we remember that in many important presentation situations we do not know what responses we should prepare to make when given feedback or directly questioned. Former theatrical agent Ann Brebner explained in *Setting Free the Actor*:

> In my work as a casting director and agent, I was always amazed that people expressed surprise or panic when I said, "So, tell me something about yourself." It was the most predictable question in the world. They knew it would be asked, but it was often so intimidating that they seemed to draw a complete blank.

When I make this point in session with actor clients, they regularly flush. They hate the question and often have little idea how to respond to it. But in what sense can this question still come as a surprise to an actor? Why are they avoiding preparing themselves for this familiar ritual interrogation? Why, as Brebner puts it, do they hold this question as dangerous rather than as an opportunity to present themselves to a casting director or agent? One answer is that they are uncertain as to whether they are supposed to perform or to act naturally. Are they really supposed to have prepared an answer to that question beforehand? Are they to rehearse it, memorize it, and then act a role when the question is popped? How strange that seems! But perhaps that's exactly what's required.

What, to your mind, is the difference between performing and acting naturally?

_____

_____

_____

_____

_____

Is there a sense in which one can both perform and act naturally at one and the same time? _____

_____

_____

We think it strange to prepare for informal, unstructured performances, especially those that just pop up in life, yet we also understand that they are performances and need to be handled "just right." This helps explain why, throughout life, we can react so strongly (and negatively) to unexpected, impromptu presentation situations. We feel that we should have something rehearsed—

that, in a sense, we should have prepared our whole life for just this moment—and yet we also feel that we should be able to handle such simple situations in the moment, easily and effortlessly, as the "no big deal" they ostensibly are.

These contradictions, which we encounter again and again in life, teach us to worry about the *possibility* of a presentation situation arising.

Do you customarily worry about
presentation situations suddenly arising? ___

_____

_____

_____

_____

Think about the following situations. If you're sitting in a meeting with the assurance that your opinion will not be solicited, you take in the meeting one way, with little anxiety. If the matter of speaking or not speaking rests entirely with you, you may internally debate throughout the meeting whether you will or won't voice your opinion at some point—that is, whether you will present your ideas to the group—and sit with mounting anxiety. But that anxiety can be alleviated as soon as you say to yourself, "No, I don't need to speak, the point I wanted to make has been made already." However, if you don't know whether you will be *required* to speak, but know that some real possibility exists that you will be, you are likely to attend to the proceedings with an anxiety that can't be fully extinguished. The anxiety will wane when you are distracted by the proceedings, forgetting

that you may have to present yourself soon, and return full force if your opinion is solicited. But whether waxing or waning, it is likely to remain present throughout, beneath the surface, simply because of the possibility of a "performance." It is as if we carried over our anxieties about *important* presentation situations to all similar but lesser situations and even to those in which a presentation is only a possibility.

Once we've unconsciously defined all presentations as important ones, we can expect that the phenomenon of performance anxiety will generalize itself. The painter complaining about the difficulty of facing a blank canvas—who doesn't know what to paint—is also likely to admit that he avoids talking to collectors and gallery owners at artists' openings. The actress who is unable to make a choice about how to play a character in an audition is also unlikely to ask her acting teacher, who happens to be a well-known director, to consider her for a part in his next production.

Finally, the way we hold the idea of "performance" is intimately related to some of our most abstract ideas, like "art," "beauty," "truth," and "quality." As the musician Stephen Nachmanovitch explained in *Free Play*:

> I found myself plunged into considering a whole set of questions that I think we must ask but cannot answer: What is quality? What is good? The enigma of quality in art brings up another word, which is to some extent out of date and therefore a bit quaint-sounding,

namely, *beauty.* Our Pandora's box pours out yet more enigmas: grace, integrity, truth. . . . What is it that calls forth the aesthetic response, and how do we test it? How do we point our gyroscope? I will not and cannot define quality; yet I insist that there is such a thing and that it is of vital importance.

If we did not care about the quality of our performance, it is hardly likely that we would experience much performance anxiety. If we did not care about the quality of our response to a question like, "Tell me a little about yourself," or "What is your opinion on a new product design?" it is hardly likely that we would experience anxiety in otherwise innocent presentation situations.

To put the matter another way: In ordinary moments, we are not vitally concerned about the quality of our actions. In performance moments, we are. Whenever an ordinary moment is transformed into a performance moment, we demand a movement in ourselves from the ordinary to the extraordinary. And, in thinking about it, would anyone say that the transformation from ordinary to extraordinary in the blink of an eye is an easy feat?

Are you very concerned about the quality of your actions as performances? _____

_____

_____

What do you suppose that you mean by the word "quality"? _____

_____

_____

_____

_____

Do you sense that you demand of yourself a movement from the ordinary to the extraordinary in presentation situations?

_____

_____

What Performance Anxiety "Sounds Like"

We can grow more aware of the presence of anxiety in others and in ourselves simply by listening carefully and learning to decipher the message behind their or our own words. This is a skill that for most people must be honed, for we generally do not listen well, either to others or ourselves. Since utterances are often circumspect and evasive, what is really being said can easily elude us.

Even in a paradigm of performance anxiety—a teacher, an announcer, or an actor who knows that he or she suffers from stage fright, is aware of the symptoms, and has consciously tried to manage the anxiety—what she says to herself before a performance is unlikely to be "I'm suffering from performance anxiety again." Her statements to herself are more likely to be, "My mind's a blank," "I can't go on," or "I'll die." Even when this person knows she is experiencing performance anxiety and is making no effort to hide it from herself or anyone else, the language she uses does not reveal her meaning literally. What does she mean when she says she'll die? Is she having a heart attack?

She, too, as she listens to her own words, can easily forget what is really going on. Instead of working to manage her anxiety, she may attempt to "fill her mind," since it has "gone blank"; in the case of the actress, she may try feverishly to remember her lines, which seem to have vanished. She may tell herself she will never perform again, since performing is "killing her." In this way she becomes caught in the trap of her own self-statements.

Each of the following expressions is likely to point to the presence of performance anxiety. They sound so innocent to the ear that it takes effort to recognize them as possible warning signs of performance anxiety. Each is presented here as a main theme and several variations.

"I'm not ready."

1. I'm not quite ready to ask for a raise.

2. I need another few weeks before my audition piece will be ready.

3. I don't feel ready to sing a Mozart aria.

4. I'm not ready to ask her out yet.

5. It's too early for me to direct a panel discussion.

6. I'm not ready for the sales conference.

As Neil Fiore writes in *The Now Habit*, "procrastination is a mechanism for coping with the anxiety associated with starting or completing any task or decision." It is vitally important to remember that procrastination is an anxiety state. Whenever someone says that he or she is not ready to tackle a pre-

sentation of some kind, check to see if performance anxiety is the real roadblock.

*Do you use phrases like "I'm not ready" when you want to avoid a situation that makes you anxious?*_____

_____

_____

Can you distinguish in your own mind when "I'm not ready" is the literal truth and when it reflects your anxious feelings? _____

_____

_____

_____

Can you envision doing something even though you're "not ready" to do it? _____

_____

_____

In what circumstances would it make sense to go ahead and do something, even though you're "not ready" to do it, and in what circumstances might it be better to wait? ___

_____

_____

_____

_____

_____

"I don't feel like it."

1. Everybody else at the AA meeting spoke, but I just didn't feel like it.

2. I don't feel like working on a new lesson plan right now.

3. I don't feel like fronting the band; Bob's much better at that sort of thing than I am.

4. I don't feel like doing interviews for my new book, the questions they ask are always inane.

5. Yes, there were a few producers at the party, but I didn't really feel like meeting them.

6. I don't feel like auditioning for that.

In polite conversation (including polite conversation with ourselves), we often use euphemisms and accept without argument the euphemisms of others. A *euphemism* is an inoffensive expression substituted for one that suggests something unpleasant, and in each of the above cases, "I don't feel like it" is a euphemism hiding some unpleasant truth, like the fear of fronting the band, of going on a book tour, or of speaking to producers. If, say, as an actor you're convinced that it's in your best interests to speak to producers at parties, but instead find yourself saying when you arrive at one, "Oh, I just don't feel like talking to them tonight," alert yourself to the possibility that you're hiding an unpleasant truth from yourself and couching evasion in one of the euphemisms we all regularly use.

*Do you use the phrase "I don't feel like it" to avoid presentation situations?*_____

_____

_____

*When you say to yourself, "I don't feel like it," what exactly are you saying?*_____

_____

_____

_____

*Do you sometimes use the phrase "I don't feel like it" to inappropriately assert your independence?*_____

_____

_____

*What strategies do you employ to help yourself do the things you "don't feel" like doing?*_____

_____

_____

_____

_____

_____

"I don't feel well."

1. The stuffy air in the audition room will make it too hard to breathe.

2. I ate lunch before my matinee and that always gives me these stomach pains.

3. I always throw up before I go on the air.

4. I can't believe how sore I get when I practice before a concert.

5. Between my day job and classes and rehearsals at night, I get very sick and run-down.

6. I always get a little dizzy before a symposium.

Somatic complaints are often the symptoms that announce the presence of anxiety. An upset stomach and diarrhea are two simple symptoms; a more complex example is the syndrome of hypochondriasis, the essential feature of which is a preoccupation with one's bodily sensations and the fear that those sensations indicate a serious disease. Coming to understand at least a little the intricate relationship between our physical complaints and their organic and/or psychological sources is part of learning to manage performance anxiety.

Do you tend to use the phrase "I don't feel well" in presentation situations? _____

_____

_____

Can you distinguish between a complaint with a real underlying physical problem and a symptom of performance anxiety? _____

_____

_____

_____

Are you alert to the possibility that any given somatic complaint might indicate anxiety?

_____

_____

Does your anxiety generally tend to manifest itself in physical ways? _____

_____

_____

_____

"I can't think straight."

1. I'm finding it harder and harder to concentrate.

2. He asked me how I thought the character might walk, but I just stood there like a dummy.

3. I met with my agent for lunch yesterday, but then I couldn't remember any of the questions I wanted to ask her.

4. I always feel spaced out in marketing meetings.

5. Like any painter, I guess I'm a little crazy.

6. I missed the audition because I couldn't figure out where I'd parked my car.

Anxiety manifests itself in both body and mind. People with severe performance anxiety may feel as if they're losing their minds. Even mild anxiety can produce disorienting effects: strange, or disturbing, or obsessive thoughts; a sense of inner chaos; memory loss; dissociative feelings; and so on. When we say, in one way or another, that our mind is not working, we should look to anxiety as the culprit before we point to madness, dementia, or some other severe mental disorder.

Do you often fear that you are losing your ability to "think straight" in presentation situations? _____

_____

_____

What characteristic language do you use to signal that problem to yourself? _____

_____

_____

_____

_____

When you feel you can't "think straight," what do you do? _____

_____

_____

_____

*How would you describe the relationship between mind and anxiety?*_____

_____

_____

_____

"I can't do it."

1. I can't go on tonight.

2. I can't ask such a talented musician to stop drowning me out.

3. I can't do my routine in a noisy club.

4. I just can't seem to ask my agent to send out my work more often.

5. I couldn't possibly play Hamlet.

6. I know I won't get the regional managers to listen to me in a late Friday meeting.

"I can't do it" often means "I might be able to do it, but it makes me anxious to think about trying it." It may also mean "It's not my preference," "I don't have that skill," or "I can do it, but there will be consequences." Whatever it means specifically, it's also likely to signal the presence of anxiety.

For instance, suppose you are a stand-up comic. Naturally, you prefer presenting your routine before an attentive and loving audience—who wouldn't? But when you assert "I can't do my routine in a noisy club," even though you and every other stand-up comic must sometimes do that, you may simply be reminding yourself that things at this club will not be ideal or even adequate—a self-talk reminder that is sure to provoke anxiety.

*Do you tend to use the phrase "I can't do it" to avoid situations that would provoke your anxiety?*_____

_____

_____

_____

Does your use of the phrase "I can't do it" often mean "It's not my preference" rather than "It's beyond my capabilities"? _____

_____

_____

_____

*Can you distinguish between the "I can't do it" of sheer inability and the "I can't do it" of fear and anxiety?*_____

_____

_____

_____

*What might you do or say to help yourself do that which you say you can't?*_____

_____

_____

_____

"I don't know what to say."

1. I couldn't talk to the Attorney General at the party—I didn't know what to say.

2. The agent I met last week said to give her a call, but what would I say?

3. I have this story about a dinosaur that I've been wanting to write, but I don't know how to begin it.

4. Some people have a knack for saying exactly what they mean, but I always hem-and-haw and beat around the bush.

5. I wanted to tell the band they weren't taking rehearsals seriously enough, but I didn't know exactly how to put it.

6. I never know what to say when people tell me they love my voice.

In most circumstances, we allow ourselves to speak even if we aren't perfectly sure what words will come out of our mouths. When the phone rings we pick it up and answer it without experiencing much anxiety, even though we don't know who is on the other end or what the contours of the conversation will be like. When we greet our mate after work, we each find something to say, or else we experience our communal silence, in either case without experiencing much anxiety. In these and most other situations we never know what to say beforehand and feel no need to rehearse something. When we assert that we "didn't know what to say" in a certain situation, therefore, we are announcing that the situation has struck us as unnaturally difficult and that the effort to find the right words has brought on a bout with performance anxiety.

Do you tend to use the phrase "I don't know what to say," or some variation, to avoid presentation situations? _____

_____

_____

What do you mean when you say that to yourself? _____

_____

_____

_____

In what circumstances would preparing "something to say" be a useful thing to do?

_____

_____

How do you help yourself speak when you "don't know what to say"? _____

_____

_____

_____

_____

_____

_____

"I can't see the point."

1. I can't see the point in auditioning for that—I'm just not the type.

2. I can't see the point in approaching that gallery owner cold—he'd just show me the door.

3. I can't see the point in publishing my research—everybody and his uncle is publishing research.

4. What good would one more video presentation do?

5. I can't see the point in trying to call my agent—I never get through to him.

6. I can't see the point in trying to get my own band together—I'm a drummer, not an organizer.

"I can't see the point of trying to climb Mt. Everest in the shape I'm in," one weekend hiker might say. That would mean for the moderately active person that he or she expected—and was right to expect—dire consequences from mountaineering in Nepal. But what are the dire consequences a painter is dreading when she says to herself, "I can't see the point in approaching that gallery owner cold—he'd just show me the door"? What she means is something more like, "It would be nice to approach the gallery owner I have my eye on, but I don't feel prepared enough and he might say or do something to hurt my feelings." The expectation of negative consequences in this situation appears to be, first, an experience of performance anxiety and, second, a threat to the painter's self-esteem. When people face presenting themselves to others and say that they "don't see the point," it is often these two threats they are meaning to avoid.

Do you find yourself using the phrase "I can't see the point" when a presentation situation arises that, on balance, you would prefer to skip? _____

_____

_____

_____

When you say you "can't see the point" in presenting yourself in some way, do you take into account how performance anxiety may be implicated? _____

_____

_____

_____

When you say you "can't see the point" in doing something, do you tend to forget what your ultimate goal is? _____

_____

_____

Can you articulate what threats are involved when you conclude that there's "no point" in attempting a given performance? _____

_____

_____

_____

"It feels too difficult."

1. It's really hard to interrupt my agent and ask him a question when he goes on and on in that fast New York way.

2. Memorizing this speech is more than I can handle.

3. This dance is just too difficult to learn!

4. It's impossible to write if you've waited as many years as I have to begin.

5. This sonata is too technically demanding.

6. This is a tough room to lecture in!

We understand what it means to say that it's too difficult to lift up the front end of a Chevy or solve complex algebraic problems in one's head. But we also regularly act as if we understood what it means to say that it's too difficult to talk to one's agent or to audition for a choreographer. Rather than acting as if we understood, we might instead quizzically shake our head and ask questions (of ourselves especially) until we really did understand.

Do you often hold that your upcoming performances are "too difficult" to handle?

_____

_____

What has "too difficult" tended to mean in the context of a presentation? _____

_____

_____

Is your answer to these "difficulties" more often doing something arduous or something relaxing? _____

_____

_____

What other language do you use to tell yourself that something is "too difficult" to do? _____

_____

_____

_____

"What's happening here?"

1. Oh, I didn't know *she* was one of the auditors!

2. What did the director mean by *that* look?

3. Am I coming down with a cold?

4. Is that the overture already?

5. Is there a smudge on my forehead?

6. What's that commotion in the audience?

Hypervigilant, highly self-conscious individuals—the kind who startle easily, who notice every wart on themselves and others, who are aware of every temperature change in the room—are anxious people whose anxiety naturally leaves traces in their language.

Do you consider yourself a hypervigilant person? _____

_____

Do you tend to be too aware of external circumstances and events? _____

_____

_____

Do you tend to be too aware of your own physiological processes? _____

_____

_____

Do you tend to be too aware of your own mental processes? _____

_____

_____

Are you too self-conscious? _____

_____

_____

"I do better with . . ."

1. I give a much better presentation if I don't eat for two hours beforehand.

2. I do better the second week of a show than the first.

3. I do better when just the casting director's watching me, rather than a room full of auditors.

4. Our quartet always give a better performance when the audience really understands the music.

5. I'm sure I would give a better speech if the room were better ventilated.

6. It's better for me to practice when my roommates are out and it's quiet.

"I do better with . . ." is one of many sorts of phrases that represent a longing on the person's part. But since the problem, as often as not, can't be corrected—the audience may simply not understand the music, and the room may simply remain overheated—all you are left with is the worry, unresolved and with little hope of resolution. Longing breeds worry; the more longing, the more worry.

What sorts of phrases do you use when you perceive some problem and wish that things were "better"? _____

_____

_____

_____

In what circumstances do you try to change things and in what circumstances do you try to let go of the worry? _____

_____

_____

_____

_____

Do you neither try to make things better nor try to let go of the worry, but just stew instead? _____

_____

_____

Do you hold that conditions need to be, or can be, perfect, for you to make a presentation? _____

_____

_____

_____

"Yes, but . . . "

1. Yes, I should get ready for the conference, but there's lots of time left.

2. Yes, I know I should practice at least three hours every morning, but I have friends visiting this week and next week I've got to do my taxes.

3. Yes, I probably should enter that competition, but the best musicians from around the world will be competing.

4. Yes, I should invite my agent to the play, but she came to see me just three months ago, and I don't want to be pushy.

5. Yes, it's probably my turn to chair a meeting, but John likes doing that and does such a fine job of it.

6. Yes, I'm probably ready to do a little music teaching, but aren't there just too many teachers out there already?

Transactional analysts and gestalt psychologists first elaborated on the idea that the "Yes, but . . . " response to an internal or external suggestion is a special and important sort of "No!" As Eric Berne explained, in *What Do You Say After You Say Hello?*: "The most important single word in script language is the particle 'but,' which means, 'According to my script, I don't have permission to do that.'" In our context every "Yes, but . . . " should be examined to see if it is a case of "Yes, it is in my best interests to do that, but the thought of it makes me too anxious."

Do you tend to use "Yes, but" constructions to avoid situations that would provoke anxiety? _____

_____

_____

*Do you have the sense that when you utter the "Yes" in a "Yes, but" sentence you do not mean "Yes" at all?*_____
_____
_____

*Is the particular attraction of this way of avoiding situations the fact that you get to say "Yes," sparing yourself guilt, while at the same time really saying "No," sparing yourself anxiety?*_____
_____
_____

*Can you begin to say either "Yes" or "No" more directly and begin to eliminate the defensive "Yes, but" from your vocabulary?*___
_____
_____

Not every time you hear one of these characteristic phrases is performance anxiety the issue. But these phrases *should* be considered warning bells alerting you to the possibility that something worth investigating is lurking beneath the surface of some innocent-sounding expression.

A Word on Written Responses

By now you have had a chance to do numerous brief writing exercises as you've read this book. It is my experience that writing is an invaluable complement and supplement to reading. I hope that even if this self-examination makes you anxious you will try to answer the questions I pose. This examination in writing, rather than in the mind's eye only, will ultimately prove of great value to you.

Before starting this book, what were your thoughts about performance anxiety? Did you consider it a significant problem in your life? A modest one? No particular problem?
_____
_____
_____
_____
_____
_____

*What are your thoughts now?*_____
_____
_____
_____
_____
_____
_____

*Which presentation situations seem to provoke the most anxiety?*_____
_____
_____
_____
_____
_____
_____
_____

*Which presentation situations seem to provoke little anxiety?*_____
_____
_____
_____
_____
_____
_____

What differences can you distinguish
between these two sorts of situations? _____
_____
_____
_____
_____
_____

Do you experience less anxiety when you are
better prepared?_____
_____
_____
_____
_____

Do you experience less anxiety the less
important you consider the performance? ___
_____
_____
_____
_____
_____

Do you experience less anxiety the
technically easier the performance is (the less
there is to memorize, the less demanding the
material, and so on)? _____
_____
_____
_____
_____
_____

Do you experience less anxiety the more you
understand "what's wanted" from a given
performance?_____

_____
_____
_____
_____
_____
_____
_____

What elements seem to contribute to making
a presentation a pressure-filled situation? ___
_____
_____
_____
_____
_____

What performances—defining the word
broadly, in the spirit of our discussion on
page 16—do you engage in? Can you make
a list of these different performances? _____
_____
_____
_____
_____
_____
_____
_____
_____

What strategies, effective or ineffective, have
you employed so far to manage performance
anxiety?_____
_____
_____
_____
_____

The Look and Feel of Performance Anxiety

2

In the last chapter, we investigated what performance anxiety "sounds" like. Now let's examine what performance anxiety looks and feels like—its symptomatology and the experiences of performance anxiety sufferers. First, we need to further define performance anxiety by exploring the concept of anxiety, for our definition of performance anxiety necessarily turns on our understanding of anxiety.

What exactly is *anxiety*? Is it any or all of the following: fear, dread, stress, panic, nervousness, wariness, uneasiness, apprehension, or worry? Is it primarily a physical condition? Primarily sociological? Primarily psychological?

*Define "anxiety." How is it different from or the same as words like fear, nervousness, stress, and worry?*_____

_____

_____

_____

_____

"Anxiety" as a concept certainly hasn't eluded examination. Hundreds if not thousands of books and articles have been written about it. Its placement as a centerpiece of psychoanalytic theory is one of Sigmund Freud's strongest achievements. Among theories about human nature, human development, and personality, those that ignore both the reality and significance of anxiety are much weaker and less true-to-life than theories that affirm them. Perhaps because the existence and centrality of anxiety *have* so often been affirmed and written about, or perhaps as a reaction against the labeling of the middle decades of this century as "The Age of Anxiety" (the title of W. H. Auden's Pulitzer-Prize poem of 1947) anxiety has recently receded somewhat as a concept worth investigating—even as anxiety states like agoraphobia, multiple personality disorder, obsessive-compulsive disorder, and post-traumatic stress disorder are discussed every day in the popular media.

From the observations of some noted writers on the subject—featured on the following pages in excerpts from their writings—we can make these points:

• We rightly fear crossing a saber-toothed tiger's path, but what is it that we fear when we enter a crowded party or get ready to perform a recital? As Karen Horney explains, the danger is "hidden and subjective." She echoes Freud's thought that the threat about which anxiety warns us may arise as much from within ourselves as from outside ourselves.

- We may *say* that we fear nothing about calling our agent, but our *reaction* as we anticipate making that call, such that we put the call off for weeks (if not indefinitely), proves that we feared something. As Ernest Becker puts it, anxiety is a reality-tester par excellence.

- Why can't musicians or actors simply talk themselves through their performance anxiety, calmly and reasonably dismissing it through simple, good, truthful arguments? Because anxiety is pressure in the face of danger, and, as Harry Stack Sullivan suggests, it is "a sign that something ought to be different *at once*." The pressure to take some anxiety-binding or anxiety-reducing action *at once* makes rational thought difficult.

- According to Freud, anxiety is a signal of danger in a context of pleasure and unpleasure. Without an awareness of this context it would confuse us to hear a musician say that he or she plays well, loves music, is able to give an audience pleasure, but gets no personal pleasure from performing. *If anxiety is present, pleasure is not* (relatively speaking).

- Silvano Arieti reminds us that it is the *complexity of the cognitive mechanism* that distinguishes anxiety from fear. Our

intelligence, our ambitions, our secret desires and secret dreads—all the workings of our personality and our consciousness—are bound up in the concept of anxiety. The complexity alarms us and exacerbates those "feelings of incomplete knowledge of the situation" to which D. T. Suzuki refers.

- Charles Frankel suggests that particular episodes of anxiety—episodes like bouts of performance anxiety—may constitute threads in the fabric of a *larger, more encompassing anxiety*. It is important, therefore, to learn just how encompassing that anxiety is for a given person. In other words, we need to look at performance anxiety not only as a kind of anxiety but also within the broader context of anxiety.

- Christopher McCullough remarks that anxiety is the state of looking forward to an uncertain event—a state of orientation in a certain direction. One can be upwind or downwind of a danger, so to speak, and in only one of those two orientations may experience anxiety. Additionally, McCullough points out that an anxiety reaction may well have a learned component.

- Herbert Benson explains that human beings simply may not have the biological resources to maintain "physiologic equanimity" without experiencing stress. Are people built to perform perfectly before a thousand people without severely stretching their biological resources and experiencing anxiety? Are they meant to speak brilliantly and charismatically in a meeting, or create breakthrough works of art

A SIGNAL OF DANGER

The ego has the task of self-preservation. It is guided in its activity by consideration of the tension produced by stimuli, whether these tensions are present in it or introduced into it. The raising of these tensions is in general felt as *unpleasure* and their *lowering* as pleasure. It is probable, however, that what is felt as pleasure or unpleasure is not the absolute height of this tension but something in the rhythm of the changes in them. The ego strives after pleasure and seeks to avoid unpleasure. An increase in unpleasure that is expected and foreseen is met by a *signal of anxiety*; the occasion of such an increase, whether it threatens from within or without, is known as a *danger*.

SIGMUND FREUD, *An Outline of Psycho-Analysis*

without experiencing stress? These questions alert us to the possibility that performance anxiety may be quintessentially a natural reaction to a given set of unusually trying circumstances.

We may now incorporate these different points into our definition of performance anxiety: Performance anxiety is a special case of anxiety, to be considered in the context of a person's everyday experience of anxiety, which:

1. Occurs when a person is consciously or unconsciously oriented toward a given performance.

2. Is experienced as unpleasure.

3. Strains the biological resources of the person.

4. Causes the person a psychological pressure that he or she wants to reduce or eliminate.

5. Has roots that are likely complex.

6. Serves as a reality-tester.

7. Can be conceived of either as a normal or abnormal reaction to a set of circumstances.

8. Warns the person that the performance situation is a dangerous one, for reasons that can be hidden or apparent, subjective or objective.

As we have seen, the artist about to saturate an expensive sheet of watercolor paper with a wash and the writer listening doubtfully to characters' voices in his or her imagination can each experience the moment as a *per-*

THE UNWANTED EXPERIENCE

Under no conceivable circumstance that has ever occurred to me has anyone sought and valued as desirable the experience of anxiety. No series of "useful" attacks of anxiety in therapy will make it something to be sought after. This is, in a good many ways, rather startling, particularly when one compares anxiety with fear. While fear has many of the same characteristics, it may actually be sought out as an experience occasionally, particularly if the fear is expected or anticipated. For instance, people who ride on roller coasters pay money for being afraid. But no one will ever pay money for anxiety in its own right. No one wants to experience it. Only one other experience—that of loneliness—is in this special class of being totally unwanted. And not only does no one want anxiety, but if it is present, the lessening of it is always desirable. Anxiety is to an incredible degree a sign that something ought to be different at once.

HARRY STACK SULLIVAN, *The Psychiatric Interview*

formance just as surely as the cellist or stand-up comic on stage does. We can equally imagine a limitless number of social, interpersonal, and business presentations that qualify as performances also. Performance anxiety, then, is the anxiety that wells up in a person before or during a presentation of any sort, causing physical and psychological distress.

In extreme forms this distress is a disabling ailment that may prevent performers from pursuing their careers, or it may curtail a career already in progress. As the violinist Kato Havas observed about musical performance: "There are few activities in life which can produce tension and anxiety as rapidly and thoroughly as playing a musical instrument in public."

What does it mean to be "oriented toward a performance"? _____
_____
_____
_____
_____

Can you describe in some detail how you experience "unpleasure"? _____
_____
_____
_____
_____

When your biological resources are stretched, what happens? _____
_____
_____

*When you feel a psychological pressure that demands to be reduced, what do you do? Light a cigarette? Have a drink? Physically flee the room? Mentally flee from the thought? Or something else?*_____

_____

_____

_____

If you are unable to reduce that pressure, what happens? _____

_____

_____

_____

_____

Clinical Categories of Anxiety

It will help us now to take a brief look at the ways in which anxiety symptoms seem to constellate into recognizable patterns, or syndromes. We explore this territory not because performance anxiety is an abnormality, but rather because syndromes, defined in clinical studies, remind us that anxiety complaints not only can appear as discrete, simple symptoms—a dry mouth, a queasy stomach—but may also come in "packages" that are surprising in two regards: First, it may surprise us to learn which symptoms tend to appear together; and second, it may surprise us to learn that certain symptoms are signs of anxiety. The psychologist Philip Zimbardo explained in *Psychology and Life*:

> When an individual feels chronically threatened by life's hazards

THE SUBJECTIVE NATURE OF ANXIETY

I used the term "anxiety" before as synonymous with fear, thereby indicating a kinship between the two. Both are in fact emotional reactions to danger and both may be accompanied by physical sensations, such as trembling, perspiration, violent heart-beat, which may be so strong that a sudden, intense fear may lead to death. Yet there is a difference between the two. Fear and anxiety are both proportionate reactions to danger, but in the case of fear the danger is a transparent, objective one and in the case of anxiety it is hidden and subjective. That is, the intensity of the anxiety is proportionate to the meaning the situation has for the person concerned.

KAREN HORNEY, *The Neurotic Personality of Our Time*

A PERCEPTION OF HELPLESSNESS

"Anxiety" refers to that troubled state in which we find ourselves looking forward to an uncertain event with apprehension or fear. Anxiety can be sudden and acute, as when we hear a skid nearby and wait for the sound of a crash, or when our child doesn't get off a school bus as expected. Anxiety can also be chronic; for instance, when we worry daily about whether our new boss will treat us with respect or how much longer we will be able to keep our job. Anxiety is the way we have learned, based on our past experiences, to respond to situations in which we perceive ourselves to be helpless.

CHRISTOPHER MCCULLOUGH, *Managing Your Anxiety*

and inadequate to the task of coping with them, the ordinary ego defenses we all use are not enough. Gradually such a person may come to rely excessively on one or more neurotic defense patterns.

These patterns have in common the search for *relief* from anxiety. Characterized by an absence of joy in living and by actions aimed at lessening pain rather than at positive accomplishment or the constructive solution of objectively real problems, neurotic defense patterns provide enough temporary relief from anxiety that many individuals cling to them desperately even though they do not solve their basic problems, and they may even worsen them. Clinicians, drawing on work with clients over the past century, have come to believe that anxiety symptoms, as they grow severe, tend to cluster together

into recognizable syndromes. For example, the trauma of war can result in long-term effects which taken together form a pattern that clinicians call posttraumatic stress disorder; in some individuals this syndrome is characterized by nightmares, dissociative flashback episodes, irritability, outbursts of anger, an exaggerated startle response, and other symptoms.

An excursion into this clinical arena would help us better understand several points about anxiety, and by extension about performance anxiety. These points include the following four:

1. Anxiety can manifest itself as physical symptoms, psychological symptoms (including disturbances of identity, memory, and consciousness), and/or disturbances of mood. Thus one person before an audition might say, "My palms are sweating"; a second, "I have a pain in my

chest"; a third, "I can't remember anything" or "I don't feel like myself"; and a fourth, "I feel blue," and each would be reporting his or her personal (and different) experience of anxiety.

2. Anxiety in general, and performance anxiety in particular, can significantly disturb a person's thought processes. The sufferer may have a clear understanding that a bout of "butterflies in the stomach" is symptomatic of anxiety, but may not realize that the inability to think clearly or the sense of detachment or unreality is also symptomatic of performance anxiety (and not evidence of stupidity or madness).

3. Symptoms can and do come in "packages"—in complexes or syndromes—that may reflect something about the source or cause of the anxiety. For instance, recurrent distressing dreams about a past performance, internal efforts to avoid thoughts about that traumatic performance, and irritability or outbursts of anger might all appear together in a posttraumatic stress disorder–like package.

4. Many of a person's symptoms or complaints, linked to anxiety and the effort to reduce it, may not easily be recognizable as such. Would we look to anxiety as the issue if a pianist complained of hand or finger pain? And yet we might be in the territory of clinical pain disorder. Would we look to anxiety if a model complained that the mole on her neck was costing her work? And yet we might be in the territory of a hypervigilant body awareness associated with clinical body dysmorphic disorder. Would we look to anxiety if a painter complained that he or she couldn't resume painting until a favorite brand of watercolor paper had been obtained? And yet we might be in the territory of obsessive thinking. An understanding and appreciation of the clinical categories of anxiety just alluded to help us become better detectives as we sift through our own complaints and the complaints of others.

Other disorders have anxiety as a significant contributory factor, disorders ranging from substance abuse to sexual dysfunction and problems like insomnia. To be fully educated about how anxiety looks in all its aspects, we would need to educate ourselves about the various "symptom pictures" to which anxiety may significantly contribute. But for our purposes it is more useful that we narrow our focus rather than expand it.

The following symptom picture scale is based upon one compiled by Marilyn Gellis and Rosemary Muat, authors of *The Twelve Steps of Phobics Anonymous*. It includes the symptoms associated with mild bouts as well as with moderate and severe bouts of performance anxiety, on a scale of 1 to 10.

Functional

1. "Butterflies"; a queasy feeling in the stomach; trembling; jitteriness; tension.

2. Cold or clammy palms; hot flashes and all-over warmth; profuse sweating.

3. Very rapid, strong, racing, pounding, or irregular heartbeat; tremors; muscle tension and aches; fatigue.

Decreased Functional Ability

4. Jelly legs; weakness in the knees; wobbly, unsteady feelings; shakiness.

5. Immediate desperate and urgent need to escape, avoid, or hide.

6. A lump in the throat; dry mouth; choking; muscle tension.

7. Hyperventilation; tightness in chest; shortness of breath; smothering sensation.

Very Limited or Completely Nonfunctional

8. Feelings of impending doom or death; high pulse rate; difficulty breathing; palpitations.

9. Dizziness; visual distortion; faintness; headache; nausea; numbness; tingling of hands, feet, or other body parts; diarrhea; frequent urination.

Complete Panic

10. Nonfunction; disorientation; detachment; feelings of unreality; paralysis; fear of dying, going crazy, or losing control. (Frequently people experiencing their first spontaneous "panic attack" rush to emergency rooms convinced that they are having a heart attack.)

Where do your experiences of performance anxiety fall on this scale? _____

_____

_____

_____

If you experience some symptoms from the various levels on the scale, how would you characterize your experience of performance anxiety on average? Is it mild, moderate, severe? _____

_____

_____

_____

_____

Under what circumstances do the more drastic symptoms tend to occur? _____

_____

_____

_____

_____

A Mental Disorder?

Our look at clinical views of anxiety in the last section may have planted the suspicion that performance anxiety is to be thought of as a mental disorder. This is not the case, and there are good common sense reasons not to make this connection. Displaying a little nervousness before or during a performance is entirely normal, *natural* behavior. Such a reaction means, in part, that the person is acknowledging the importance of the event and wants to do well. It also means that the person is alert to the difficulties (or dangers) associated with, say, remembering a prodigious amount of material and pre-

INSECURITY

All forms of anxiety come from the fact that there is somewhere in our consciousness the feeling of incomplete knowledge of the situation. This lack of knowledge leads to a sense of insecurity and then to anxiety, with all its degrees of intensity.

D. T. SUZUKI, *Zen Buddhism and Psychoanalysis*

senting it with technical acumen and artistry. Surely we hold the presence of nervousness in a concerned presenter attempting to perform well as healthier than the absence of nerves in an ill-prepared one who presents poorly and then blames an ineffective showing on the restlessness of the audience or the vagaries of fate.

In fact, there are good reasons to be more suspicious of an absence of anxiety in such situations than of its presence. Such an absence might mean that the person is exceedingly well-defended against the realities of the situation and of his or her part in the proceedings. That is, a defensive structure shields this person from anxiety but also prevents an openness to the situation and an authenticity in making the presentation. Thus, an absence of performance anxiety in a presentation situation does not signify mental health any more than a lack of anxiety in a person's day-to-day life does.

Indeed, according to one model of personality development, the complete absence of anxiety is a likely sign of a personality *dis-order*. In this model, the "normal" range of mentally healthy people is placed not at one end of a continuum but, instead, in the middle, producing two "directions" of mental disturbance. In one direction we encounter, first, the anxiety disorders and, eventually, severe disorders such as obsessive-compulsive disorder and schizophrenia. In the other direction we encounter, first, the behavior disorders and, eventually, personality disorders such as are found in the antisocial or sociopathic personality. Individuals in this second direction would be marked by their lack of anxiety; in the extreme, they are willing to say and do anything, because they do not experience the pangs of a guilty conscience, because they are not "in it" with the rest of humanity and will not let others judge them. These people have perfectly bound their anxiety. Thus, in this model, we would fully expect anxiety to affect people in the middle, "normal" range. It further follows that the goal of the presenter is not to attempt to eliminate anxiety but rather to embrace it, reduce it, and manage it.

Performers' Experiences

The experience of mild performance anxiety is well known to each of us. At such times we might experience butterflies in the stomach, the need to urinate, and a slight sense of disorientation. We would tend to react with more anxiety before more important or difficult events, perhaps moving from butterflies to a feeling that approaches nausea, or from slight disorientation to a considerably more "spacey" state. Each anxious person, whether experiencing the anxiety as mild, moderate, or severe, has his or her own individual "package" of physical symptoms and distressing thoughts. It is instructive to hear what professional performers have to say about their own experiences of performance anxiety. The following reports involve performers whose anxiety is in the moderate-to-severe range.

The actress Maureen Stapleton explained about herself:

> When I work, the anxiety starts about six-thirty at night. I start to burp. I belch—almost nonstop. I keep burping, right up to the curtain, and then I'm all right. If a truck backfires, I jump. I can hear everything. I get scared that something is going to fall down or that there's going to be an explosion. I'm nervous every night, but opening night is more of a nightmare, there's so much at stake that it just overpowers you.

Among the most common symptoms of performance anxiety are sweaty palms, a dry mouth, increased heart rate, shaky hands, weak knees, shortness of breath, butterflies in the stomach, and an increased need to use the bathroom. As Stephanie Judy attested, in *Making Music for the Joy of It*:

> It's as if some Bad Fairy visits each one on concert day and bestows the most aggravating symptoms possible: a trembling arm to the strings, a dry mouth to singers, clammy hands to pianists, scant wind to the winds, and a foundering memory to us all.

THE STRESS OF CHANGE

We live in very difficult times, when man is constantly faced with anxieties caused by rapid change. Man simply does not have the biological resources to maintain physiologic equanimity, certainly not without experiencing the effects of so-called stress that may have led to the recent prevalence of the disease hypertension.

HERBERT BENSON, *The Relaxation Response*

Psychological symptoms include feelings of confusion, disorientation, powerlessness, and loneliness. A few performers report going deaf or blind. On the anxiety scale appear such additional psychological symptoms as the desire to escape or to hide, feelings of impending doom or death, and feelings of unreality or craziness. The singer Rosa Ponselle explained:

> I actually prayed that a car would run me over so that I wouldn't have to die onstage—a prayer I was to repeat before every performance for twenty years.

The operatic soprano Anna Moffo said:

> I've never started a performance without thinking, "It's only the first act—I'll never live to see the final curtain."

John Bonham, the drummer for the rock band Led Zeppelin, admitted:

> I've got terrible bad nerves all the time. I just can't stand sitting around, and I worry about playing badly. Everybody in the band is the same, and each of us has some little thing they do before we go on, like pacing about or lighting a cigarette.

The cellist Pablo Casals wrote in his autobiography, *Joys and Sorrows*:

> I gave my first real concert in Barcelona when I was fourteen. My father, who had come to Barcelona for the occasion, took me on the tramway. I was terribly nervous. When we got to the concert hall, I said, "Father, I've forgotten the beginning of the piece! I can't remember a note of it! What shall I do?" He calmed me down. That was eighty years ago, but I've never conquered that dreadful feeling of nervousness before a performance. It is always an ordeal. Before I go onstage, I have a pain in my chest. I'm tormented.

The actor Paul Lynde confessed:

> I have never gotten over being terrified in front of an audience. Oh, I know most performers get the jitters before they go on. My reaction is more like nervous collapse.

The actress Estelle Parsons explained:

> I get this feeling that I just can't go on. And sometimes I've had to stay in bed all day in order to get to the stage.

Dr. Stephen Aaron in his book *Stage Fright: Its Role in Acting* provided the following examples:

> A British actor in his late sixties still becomes so nervous before each performance that he must be dressed and made up by an assistant. First of all, his body is so out of control that he is unable to perform these functions for himself. Second of all, left to his own devices, he often forgets what play he's in and will sometimes appear costumed

for another piece in the repertory. An American actress throws up before going on stage; buckets have to be placed by each of her entrance positions. Another actress, who has played many leading roles, says, "Most people are really very frightened. Getting out there on stage is like walking a tightrope. It's like walking on stage naked—naked and looking awful."

Performance Anxiety over Time

The experience of performance anxiety often changes for an individual over time, the anxiety either increasing or decreasing, and it can even change from performance to performance for no discernible reason. Today's audition may seem no more important than yesterday's, but today a severe bout of performance anxiety strikes. You've played this music a hundred times before and experienced moderate performance anxiety before going on each time, and today you feel no anxiety at all—absolutely none. In such cases we must presume that a "warning bell has rung" or, conversely, that a "switch has turned off" our awareness, increasing or decreasing the sense of danger independent of any external factors.

In each of these cases, a single instance of talking to oneself quite possibly makes the difference. Without noticing it, we may remark to ourselves, "I'm really not ready today" or "This feels easy today." We hear our own entirely casual remark, take it for gospel, and react accordingly.

One significant example of how the experience of performance anxiety can change over time involves performers who stop abusing themselves with alcohol or other drugs and begin to perform "clean and sober." Before they begin the process of recovery from substance abuse—that is, while they are still "using"—they are able to mask from themselves their own feelings and bind their anxiety by medicating themselves. As the musician Don Henley explained:

> I think the only reason I ever used drugs was to overcome shyness or self-doubt. I didn't use drugs actually to create, but simply to buffer feelings of inadequacy.

The performer may be in denial about the dimensions of his or her drug use and may even romantically affirm that drugs are a necessary part of the creative life. But as the jazz saxophonist Charlie Parker remarked:

> Any musician who says he is playing better on tea, the needle, or when he is juiced is a plain straight liar.

Most performers, even those who continue to use drugs, know that this practice is mainly an anxiety binder. Performers who take the step of abstaining from drugs and alcohol remove this primary anxiety binder from their lives, thus demanding of themselves that they go ahead and experience whatever it is they must experience without the buffering effects of chemicals. This pledge they *know* will mean that they'll experience more performance anxiety than they did when stoned. Especially in the early months and years of sobriety, such performers may well experience the performance anxiety that was always there but which they "managed" previously with drugs.

The musician Eric Clapton remarked:

> To play sober, to play straight, is like going to the dentist, I suppose. You're very, very nervous until the actual thing is taking place, then you call on some reserve inside you which is just waiting.

Another example of the sort of performance anxiety that is experienced in a recovery program is described by "Henry" in the article "Stage Fright: Recovery for 12-Step Sharing" (*Recovering*, no. 35, Nov. 1991):

> Sharing at meetings is a valuable part of all 12-step programs. Yet, despite the loving, accepting atmosphere, some of us feel too much "stage fright" to share until we've been in the program a long time. Or we share but feel ashamed of what we shared. . . . Sharing is not a performance. Aside from cross-talk, gossip, or religion, nothing you say is wrong. Get out of denial. Admit you are afraid. Feel the fear. Stop isolating. Ask for support. Tell someone you're scared to share. Ask for a hug. Begin by admitting you are scared. Stop trying to control your body. Turn it over to your higher power. It's OK to blush, shake, stutter, etc. It's OK to be nervous. It's OK to risk. It's OK to be a human being.

A performer may miss the relief that drugs afforded but may still abide by a pledge to stop, even when not knowing how to pro-

THE ENCOMPASSING ANXIETY

We do have substantial causes for anxiety. But many of these genuine problems remain unmet because we blanket them in a larger, more encompassing anxiety. This is the anxiety that the cards are simply stacked against us, that the universe is such that our knowledge and our powers must inevitably be on one side and our hopes and our ideals on the other. It is the anxiety of our "Age of Anxiety," which, certainly, many in our age appear to cultivate and to love.

CHARLES FRANKEL, *The Love of Anxiety and Other Essays*

ANXIETY AND ANTICIPATION

If anxiety's importance has been firmly established, its definition, however, has not been so widely agreed upon. Freud himself changed his early view of this emotion. At first he felt that anxiety is the state of not being gratified. He later abandoned this definition and described anxiety as the emotional response to a situation of danger. To my way of thinking, anxiety is the emotional reaction to the expectation or anticipation of danger. It is the complexity of the cognitive mechanism that distinguishes anxiety from fear.

SILVANO ARIETI, *The Intrapsychic Self*

ceed. The singer Bonnie Raitt, for example, remarked:

> I think too much and judge too much, and alcohol suspended that for a while, so it actually freed me up. Now I have to tap into a wellspring I haven't seen yet.

At such times the experience of performance anxiety may increase tremendously. But then, after time, it may finally abate, as the performer learns more functional ways of handling the anxiety that remains. He or she may even simply grow less anxious over time. As Ringo Starr explained:

> After I stopped drinking and taking drugs, I realized I wasn't frightened of the dark and I wasn't an insomniac.

A severe case of performance anxiety can curtail the performer's career. The follow-ing is an excerpt from a brief therapy counseling session, conducted in a public workshop, between therapist John Weakland and an "anxious violinist." Recorded in Fisch, Weakland, and Segal's *The Tactics of Change*, the session provides a striking picture of one person's severe performance anxiety. A few of the musician's characteristic responses are reproduced here:

> I am a music teacher, and I'm a very, very, very poor performer—to the extent that my hands shake, they sweat when I perform, which they do not do at any other time. . . . When I came back [after ten years of not performing], I tried to perform on several occasions, and it was as dismal as I remembered it back when I was eighteen, when it made me quit to begin with, because it was so bad. And the rewards I got for performing were so

small that I gave it up to begin with back then. . . . I'm willing to be a little anxious, willing to be a little nervous, but I'm not—I'm concerned about it being incapacitating, *ridiculously* incapacitating. . . . [In my second year at the conservatory I had to perform a piece and] I forgot a great deal of the piece, my left hand was shaking so much that I couldn't execute a simple scale with any efficiency at all. It was very, very upsetting to me at the time. . . . It was the decisive factor in making me quit.

Weakland adds that the violinist eventually went into the real estate business, became successful in that business, and gave up his professional career in music. But he still played the violin for his own enjoyment.

Therapy

In psychotherapy sessions with my own clients on performance anxiety issues, we investigate together the situations that provoke anxiety and all the factors—internal and external; historical and in-the-moment; psychological and practical—that contribute to their anxiety. As we investigate these matters I see clients manifest in different ways their discomfort at having to wade into these troubling waters. Clients regularly appear self-conscious. Actors are embarrassed, for instance, not to have mastered such "simple" performance situations as calling their talent agent with a question or bringing their embryonic solo perfor-

mance piece to an open-mike night. They feel they "should" be equal to these "simple" tasks. That they in fact are not up to it causes them to feel ashamed and guilty.

Does thinking about your own performance anxiety make you feel self-conscious or embarrassed? _____
_____
_____
_____
_____

Does talking about it make you feel even more self-conscious? _____
_____
_____
_____
_____

Might it be possible to "surrender" to the fact that you experience performance anxiety and not treat that fact as an embarrassing secret?
_____
_____
_____
_____
_____

Clients also regularly appear confused. The confusion is often the result of a lack of recognition or identification of the problem, as discussed in Chapter 1. It can take some time to recognize that performance anxiety is the issue. Sometimes it is only accidentally, by seeing how difficult it is for a client to role-play a presentation situation in a session, or by noticing that a client is regularly passing up auditions for suitable roles, that an understanding of the nature of the problem dawns on us.

The confusion a client displays can also be the result of the anxiety being experienced in session, anxiety that arises from thinking and talking about performance anxiety. Then the anxiety is right there with us in session, not an abstract problem, but in the flesh, so to speak. When this happens we have to work to reduce the anxiety in order to proceed—without, however, stopping everything to reduce that anxiety. Part of the work is finding a breathing rhythm together that is calming and providing verbal cues that suggest to the client that he or she slow down, relax, take it easy, and so on. Until the anxiety and its attendant state of confusion can be reduced, directly examining performance anxiety issues proceeds only with great difficulty, if at all.

As you experience it, what is the relationship between anxiety and confusion? _____

_____

_____

_____

*If anxiety makes you feel confused, how can you become clear-headed enough to manage anxiety, even as your anxiety is muddling your thoughts?*_____

_____

_____

_____

What is your solution—or tentative solution—to this paradox? _____

_____

_____

_____

_____

Clients are regularly defended. A client may acknowledge performance anxiety as a problem but may keep it at arm's length, intellectualizing about it, disconnecting it from real life, making excuses, blaming others, or blaming circumstances beyond his or her control. These, of course, are defensive behaviors familiar to all of us that warrant taking a beginning stab at describing your own defenses.

*What defensive maneuvers would you say you usually employ to ward off feelings of anxiety?*_____

_____

_____

_____

_____

Anxiety and Personality

Stella, an actress, enters an agent's office and doesn't appear visibly nervous. Indeed, she appears confident, even cocky. If asked, she says that she doesn't feel nervous in the least. But the agent soon feels that Stella has an "attitude problem": She's a little sarcastic, and acts as if she's doing the world a favor by being in show business. She disparages a prominent director, acting as if she and the agent secretly agreed that the director's work reeked, and offers in parting the recommendation that the agent secure an office with a more convenient location.

What is Stella's problem? Is she dense? Immature? Or should we conceive her attitude as a particular mix of defensive reactions meant to ward off the anxiety she would feel if she interacted with the agent

ANXIETY THE TEACHER

The flood of anxiety is not the end for man. It is, rather, a "school" that provides man with the ultimate education, the final maturity. It is a better teacher than reality, says Kierkegaard, because reality can be lied about, twisted, and tamed by the tricks of cultural perception and repression. But anxiety cannot be lied about. Once you face up to it, it reveals the truth of your situation, and only by seeing that truth can you open a new possibility for yourself.

ERNEST BECKER, *The Denial of Death*

"stripped" of her ego defenses? The latter is the more psychologically acute answer. An important element of personality is the defensive structure built up by each of us to handle life's stresses and to protect us from anxiety, shame, or guilt. These ego defense mechanisms include all the following examples, based upon James Coleman's *Abnormal Psychology and Everyday Life*:

Denial of Reality

Here, the individual protects the self from unpleasant reality by a refusal to perceive or face it, and often by escapist activities like getting "sick" or being preoccupied with other things.

Let's continue using the actress Stella as an example: In denying reality she busies herself internally with thoughts and externally with activities that distance her from rehearsing and preparing properly for an upcoming performance. She does not allow the fact of the impending performance to enter conscious awareness, but instead "denies" that she has a performance for which she ought to prepare.

To what extent, if any, do you employ denial as a defense against anxiety? Can you think of any concrete examples? _____
_____
_____
_____
_____

Fantasy

Through gratification of frustrated desires in *imaginary* achievements, Stella avoids preparing herself for a given audition or networking event by drifting off into fantasies about her meteoric career, her future Emmy and Oscar victories, and so on.

To what extent, if any, do you employ fantasy as a defense against anxiety? Can

PERFORMERS IN DENIAL

Denial is a primary ego defense, and its use sometimes strikes us as remarkably strange (except when we use it in exactly the same way ourselves). How, for instance, can an actor deny that he will have to speak the words written for the character he is about to play in an audition scene? And yet actors do this all the time, so much so that acting teachers must remind them that they will have to speak the words written in the script. The actor and acting teacher Ed Hooks, for instance, explained in *The Audition Book*:

> The best way to approach an audition is to take a long, cool look at what the scripted character is saying and doing in the scenes you will be reading—and accept whatever is going on there as your behavior. Don't waste time denying that you would behave or speak the way that he does. Immediately embrace it. . . . "But, I would never, not in a million years, talk and behave like the person in the script!" you complain. Oh, yes you would, and yes you will, just as soon as you get into the audition room. Those very words are going to come right out of your mouth, so you might as well motivate them. There is no gain in denial.

you think of any concrete examples? _____
_____
_____
_____
_____
_____

Compensation

Compensation is the covering up of weakness by emphasizing desirable traits, or making up for frustration in one area by overgratification in another.

Here, Stella practices her best audition piece over and over again, past the point of needing to and at the expense of the pieces she still needs to learn, because it gratifies her to hear that one piece excellently done.

To what extent, if any, do you employ compensation as a defense against anxiety? Can you think of any concrete examples? ____
_____
_____
_____
_____
_____
_____

Identification

The individual increases feelings of worth by identifying him- or herself with a person or institution of illustrious standing.

Stella, in this case, claims to be intimate with well-known actors, directors, and producers, on the basis of brief professional interactions with them and even of glimpsing them at publicity functions.

To what extent, if any, do you employ identification as a defense against anxiety? Can you think of any concrete examples? _____

_____

_____

_____

_____

_____

Introjection

Introjection is the individual's incorporation of external values and standards into the ego structure so that he or she is not at the mercy of them as external threats.

Stella has learned at the feet of her parents and teachers that intense practice, even to the exclusion of other activites of value, is virtuous, that mistakes are to be eliminated, and that perfection is the goal. These values are now her own values — even though she gets no particular pleasure from performing.

To what extent, if any, have you introjected values as a defense against anxiety? Can you think of any concrete examples? _____

_____

_____

_____

Projection

Placing blame for difficulties upon others or attributing one's own unethical desires to others is a common ego defense.

Stella blames other cast members for upstaging her and stealing scenes she appears in, not recognizing that she herself has avoided directly asking for a chance to take center stage in her biggest scene (asking for the heightened anxiety such an opportunity would bring).

To what extent, if any, do you employ projection as a defense against anxiety? Can you think of any concrete examples? _____

_____

_____

_____

_____

Rationalization

Attempting to prove that one's behavior is "rational" and justifiable makes the individual feel worthy of self-affirmation and of social approval.

Stella, arguing that the sites on a projected tour of her one-woman show are acoustically inadequate, informs everyone that she is contemplating cancelling the tour, not realizing that doing so — which will eliminate her mounting performance anxiety — is her secret desire.

To what extent, if any, do you employ rationalization as a defense against anxiety? Can you think of any concrete examples? ___

_____

_____

_____

TALKING CIRCLES AROUND ANXIETY

Intellectualizing and rationalizing are regularly employed by intelligent, fluent men and women who keep anxiety at bay by "talking circles" around the issues at hand. In *Setting Free the Actor*, Ann Brebner described the following interview with a young actor:

> My first question to him was, "So, tell me about yourself." He responded by talking a mile a minute about the universe, life, goodness, truth, the universe again. I soon lost track of what he was saying, unable to get any sense of who he was. I pointed out that I had asked him to tell me something about himself, and that he hadn't done that at all. Later he said he knew that he had blown many interviews with casting directors because he had tried to appear as he thought a good actor should appear—tortured and riddled with anxiety—only he didn't really know how to do that. Because he didn't feel adequately anguished, he would jump into his intellect as the next best thing.

Here we have an elegant example of an actor providing rationalizations—that he is just not as naturally anxious as actors are supposed to be—to support his penchant for intellectualizing, which is his defense against the anxiety he claims not to be experiencing.

Repression

Preventing painful or dangerous thoughts from entering consciousness, Stella avoids thinking about her last audition, which she knows she handled poorly and the pain of which is still with her. But because she prevents the memory of that audition from fully entering consciousness, she also can't fathom what really happened or learn the lessons that would allow her to excel at future auditions.

To what extent, if any, do you repress painful thoughts as a defense against anxiety? Can you think of any concrete examples? _____
_____
_____
_____
_____
_____
_____
_____

Reaction Formation

The individual prevents dangerous desires from being expressed by exaggerating opposed attitudes and types of behaviors and using them as "barriers."

Stella, who secretly wishes she could give herself permission to bring spontaneity and freshness to her performances, not only compulsively adheres to a repetition of the same well-rehearsed inflections and gestures from night to night but snidely disparages actors who vary their performances.

To what extent, if any, do you employ reaction formation as a defense against anxiety? Can you think of any concrete examples? _____

_____

_____

_____

_____

_____

Displacement

Here, the individual discharges pent-up feelings, usually of hostility, on objects less dangerous than those which initially aroused the emotions.

Very anxious about the demanding nature of the role she's agreed to play and deeply unhappy with the director's interpretation of the role, Stella, instead of noticing the anxiety or communicating with the director, finds fault with and shows hostility to her lover.

To what extent, if any, do you employ displacement as a defense against anxiety? Can

you think of any concrete examples? _____

_____

_____

_____

_____

Emotional Insulation

Withdrawal into passivity protects the self from hurt. Thus, Stella, whose last performance was roundly criticized, argues that she needs time—which becomes a very long time—to recover from the experience. Rather than face the possibility that what she fears is the new wounding and heightened anxiety that a future performance might bring, she dwells on her last bad performance and withdraws, finding relief in that insulation.

To what extent, if any, do you employ emotional insulation as a defense against anxiety? Can you think of any concrete examples? _____

_____

_____

_____

_____

Isolation

Isolation is a cutting off of feelings from hurtful situations, or separating incompatible attitudes by logic-tight compartments.

Stella appears "not to care" about performing poorly at an audition for a role she seemed to want. On the one hand, that "not caring" protects her from the pain of failure and allows her to leave the audition in an almost jaunty mood. But it also protects her from the anxiety she only dimly understands would have been hers to experience if she had "cared" enough, gotten the role, and been forced to publicly perform.

To what extent, if any, do you employ isolation as a defense against anxiety? Can you think of any concrete examples? _____

_____

_____

_____

_____

_____

Regression

Retreating to an earlier developmental level involving less mature responses and usually a lower level of aspiration, Stella appears as helpless as a child when it comes to choosing a selection of songs to perform for her first cabaret appearance. Suddenly she seeks out mentors whose advice she does not necessarily trust, instead of stopping and realistically saying to herself, "This club gig is making me really nervous."

To what extent, if any, do you regress as a defense against anxiety? Can you think of any concrete examples? _____

_____

_____

_____

_____

Sublimation

Stella receives a substitute sexual gratification from the attention she receives as a performer. The need for attention keeps her performing and helps mask from her the fact that she is severely anxious each time she performs.

To what extent, if any, do you employ sublimation as a defense against anxiety? Can you think of any concrete examples? ___

_____

_____

_____

_____

_____

Undoing

Atoning for immoral desires or acts is another defensive strategy. Here, Stella counteracts her past behavior. She attempts to make up with an actress with whom she fought during the run of a play, writing her explanatory letters, asking to meet with her to air their grievances, and in other ways obsessing about how to repair this "broken" relationship—all the while not noticing that she has stopped auditioning for future work, which is the real motive behind her "undoing" maneuvers.

To what extent, if any, do you engage in undoing as a defense against anxiety? Can you think of any concrete examples? _____

_____

_____

_____

_____

_____

Sympathism

Striving to gain sympathy from others, the

individual bolsters feelings of self-worth despite failures.

Anxious about her advancement to a featured performer's role and fearful of failing, Stella complains to her friends in the dressing room—who are already doing their best to deal with their envy of her—that her scene partner can't act, that the costumer isn't fitting her properly for her new role, and that becoming a featured performer is hardly all it's cracked up to be.

To what extent, if any, do you employ sympathism as a defense against anxiety? Can you think of any concrete examples? ___

_____

_____

_____

_____

_____

Acting-Out

Reducing the anxiety aroused by forbidden desires by permitting their expression, Stella, who is anxious about the role she has, acts out her desire not to come to the theater at all by arriving just a little late to rehearsals. When the director takes her to task for this, she stops it and switches to another ego defense.

To what extent, if any, do you employ acting-out as a defense against anxiety? Can you think of any concrete examples? _____

_____

_____

_____

_____

_____

Conformity

A complex defense mechanism built out of social identifications and socially acceptable activities, conformity blends the individual into the herd. Anxiety is reduced by "just following orders" or "just doing as everyone else does." Stella contains her anxiety by always looking good, acting cheerful around the cast and crew, and giving "correct" performances—at the cost of never risking real feelings or stretching her characterizations.

To what extent, if any, do you employ conformity as a defense against anxiety? Can you think of any concrete examples? ___

_____

_____

_____

_____

_____

A Life Beyond Defenses

This long list of ego defense mechanisms is hardly complete. We might also include humor and anger as an additional pair of defenses. As the comedian Mel Brooks explained, "Humor is just another defense against the universe." Many people respond to anxiety-provoking situations by making lame jokes that in fact heighten the anxiety of all involved. And, as the actor Alan Rich explained, "Anger permeates a room. When you walk in with anger, everyone feels it. Lose the anger and you may win the part."

The important thing is this: To understand how you deal with performance anxiety you will want to look not only for symptoms of that anxiety but also to examine your characteristic defense mechanisms. For just as avoiding presentation situations will spare you anxiety—but at the cost of lost opportunities and a diminished life—so approaching these situations in a guarded fashion will protect you from anxiety, but at the cost of diminishing or ruining your performance. You may be duller in presentations than you really are, because you've isolated, insulated, and distanced yourself from experiencing the moment. You may be less passionate, spontaneous, and adventurous than you can be, because of your introjected values and protective coloration of conformity. You may be angrier than you need be—angrier at the artistic director, the regional sales managers, the oral examination committee, whomever—because you are using anger to protect yourself from experiencing the anxiety simmering underneath.

Thus what we see when we look for performance anxiety is not just sweaty palms: It is also inappropriate distancing, inappropriate conformity, inappropriate anger, and all the rest. The performer who is actually sweating may be in much better touch with the moment—less guarded, more present, more ready, more available—and better able to give a lively, human performance than the person who looks perfect but whose artistry and real being are unavailable behind a defensive wall. With these thoughts in mind, the ill-tempered behavior of the actress Stella becomes more comprehensible. We are witnessing a person defending herself in the face of danger. We

do not know from one event what defense mechanisms she always employs, what her personality style usually is, or how her attitude changes from situation to situation or from year to year. But we do know that she isn't terribly aware of how defensiveness is harming her in her performing career. She would be better off experiencing the performance anxiety she is avoiding, and then learning to manage that anxiety, than sabotaging herself through inappropriate defensiveness.

We can rightly conclude that in stressful presentation situations a person may manifest not anxiety symptoms but a defensive attitude instead. This defensiveness binds anxiety, protects the person, and is the way the person "handles" the situation. Whereas giving a strong performance is typically the main desire of the person who experiences performance anxiety, for the defended person the primary goal is avoiding the experience of anxiety and maintaining integrity of the self. The person prefers to deny reality or to aggressively act out, rather than invite the anxiety in and deal with it head on.

To masterfully handle a presentation situation you may have to first suspend your defensive attitude and experience the anxiety. You must embrace and invite the anxiety in. The director André Antoine remarked, "The audience has no idea of the labor that goes into a play it has just applauded"; and we, too, often have no idea how much labor we expend erecting psychological mechanisms to defend the integrity of the self. The look of performance anxiety may not involve sweaty palms or shortness of breath but the look of our characteristic ego defenses instead.

Would you characterize your own performance anxiety as mild, moderate, or severe? Describe your sense of its severity as carefully as you can. _____

_____

_____

_____

_____

_____

_____

What symptoms of performance anxiety do you experience? What physical symptoms? ___

_____

_____

_____

_____

_____

What psychological symptoms? _____

_____

_____

_____

_____

_____

Can you give a detailed symptom picture or report with respect to one specific bout of performance anxiety that you remember? ___

_____

_____

_____

_____

_____

Are the symptoms different in different situations? How? _____

_____

_____

_____

_____

_____

_____

_____

Can you tell what characteristic fears are present as the anxiety mounts?
Fear of forgetting the material? _____

_____

Fear of making mistakes? _____

Fear of doing an inferior job? _____

Fear that "something will go wrong"? _____

Fear that you will be found wanting? _____

Fear that you will be recognized as an "imposter"? _____

Fear of not knowing what to do or say? _____

Fear that "so much" is riding on your performance? _____

Fear that you won't appear to be "an expert" or "a master"? _____

Some other fear? _____

_____

_____

Sophia Loren once confessed, "I am scared to death of a live audience. I don't feel prepared spiritually to face the public." How would you describe your relationship to "the public"? _____

_____

_____

_____

_____

Would you say that you regularly avoid certain performance situations? _____

_____

_____

_____

_____

If we sat down together and discussed the presentation situations that make you anxious, how would you appear? Embarrassed? Self-conscious? Confused? Defensive? _____

_____

_____

_____

_____

Look again at the section on ego defense mechanisms. Which of them, if any, do you regularly employ to ward off anxiety? _____

_____

_____

_____

_____

_____

_____

What are the results of employing these defenses? Do the presentation situations go as you would like them to go? _____

_____

_____

_____

What sort of attitude—for example, aloof, angry, superior, scornful, cheerful, meek, and so on—do you carry into various presentation situations? _____

_____

_____

_____

What are the strong points or advantages of this characteristic attitude of yours? Does it help you feel in control? _____

_____

_____

_____

Does it feel comfortable and familiar? _____

_____

_____

Does it help you mask some other, more unacceptable attitude? _____

_____

_____

Is it "just revealing enough" without making you feel "too revealed"? _____

_____

Is it proper and acceptable? _____

_____

_____

*Does it elicit positive feedback?*_____

_____
_____
_____
_____

*Does it allow for some flexibility on your part, so that you can follow directions and make quick decisions?*_____

_____
_____
_____
_____

*What are the weak points or disadvantages of your characteristic attitude? Is it inappropriate?*_____

_____
_____
_____
_____
_____
_____

Is it offensive? _____

_____
_____
_____
_____

*Does it prevent you from doing your best work?*_____

_____
_____
_____
_____

Is it restrictive or constrictive? _____

_____
_____
_____

Does it elicit negative feedback? _____

_____
_____
_____

Are you too secretive in that posture? _____

_____
_____
_____

*Are you too revealing in that posture?*_____

_____
_____
_____

Are you too uncompromising in that posture?

_____
_____
_____
_____

On balance, does it seem to be important to alter your characteristic defensive posture? __

_____
_____
_____

*Can you say what you've learned about your particular experience of performance anxiety as a result of thinking about the first two chapters?*_____

_____
_____
_____
_____
_____
_____
_____

3 *Contributing Factors*

Is there one single something that causes performance anxiety? Could that single factor be our youth or inexperience? Maybe after we've performed a hundred times and learned the ins and outs of performing, our performance anxiety will abate. But neither performers' anecdotal reports nor studies confirm this hypothesis. For some performers the experience of performance anxiety even intensifies over time. The actress Gertrude Lawrence, for one, complained, "These attacks of nerves seem to grow worse with the passing of the years. It's inexplicable and horrible and something you'd think you'd grow out of, not into."

Certainly we can understand why this might happen. As a performer's career progresses, the real and felt importance of her performances may also increase dramatically. Many people depend on her success, playing before very large audiences becomes the norm for her, and a great deal is expected of her band, dance company, repertory theatre, or ensemble. The publicity that precedes her performance now touts her as the funniest woman alive, the greatest Blanche DuBois or Juliet of recent memory, a splendid interpreter of Beethoven's piano sonatas, or the best jazz singer around. The pressure to live up to such billing can easily produce increased anxiety.

She may also be asked to act as a spokesperson for her work, giving interviews, appearing on television and radio shows, helping to raise money for projects, helping to promote and advertise her work. Performers are increasingly encouraged to undertake these tasks, each of which is a performance in its own right. While some performers relish these moments, others number them among their most anxiety-producing.

So we can't single out youth or inexperience as the cause of performance anxiety. Perhaps, then, it's the magnitude of our worries? If we fear that we'll be utterly ruined by a bad performance, certainly that thought is disturbing enough to provoke a bout of performance anxiety. Is it, perhaps, that only negative thoughts of that magnitude precipitate performance anxiety?

Unfortunately, thoughts much less dramatic than those produce very great performance anxiety. A momentary doubt about the location of a piece of costume or a momentary doubt that the lighting in the hall is adequate can produce sudden, violent symptoms. It is as if a small breach in the insulation that protects us can prove just as dangerous as a large breach: In either case, we feel jolted. If momentarily misplacing our best reed or momentarily losing sight of our speech text can bring on sweats and tremors, it can't be that the cause of performance anxiety is the magnitude of the signaling thought.

Is performance anxiety, then, a gender-related issue that has to do with the feeling of feelings? Is it that women, insofar as they allow themselves to feel their feelings more than men do, are more susceptible to bouts of performance anxiety?

Not only is performance anxiety not exclusively a women's affliction, it doesn't appear to be even more a women's than a men's affliction. Studies and anecdotal reports support this, as does my clinical experience. It might be argued that male artists have a more fully developed "feminine"side — more sensitivity and better access to feelings — than do men who are not in the arts, and therefore feeling emotions may indeed play an important role in the process. But since men from every walk of life experience performance anxiety, it is probably safe to assume that anyone, no matter how "masculine" or "feminine," is equally a candidate.

We could continue attempts to isolate factors in a hunt for the cause of performance anxiety. We could ponder issues of upbringing, childhood trauma, lack of self-esteem, introjected messages about one's

self-worth, and many other important ideas. But by analyzing these various ideas we still wouldn't be able to put our finger on the cause of performance anxiety.

Many factors contribute to performance anxiety. Childhood experiences, hereditary factors, a lack of preparation, the importance of the event, or even the presence of a particular person in the audience can and do contribute to the *gestalt* of a given presentation situation. This gestalt interests us very much, since it is the whole person, living through a real presentation, who experiences the anxiety and who must manage that anxiety.

The Gestalt Model

Fritz Perls wrote, in *Gestalt Therapy Verbatim*:

> What is first to be considered is that the organism always works as a whole. We are not a summation of parts, but a *coordination* — a very subtle coordination of all these different bits that go into the making of the organism. The old philosophy always thought that the world consisted of the sum of particles. You know yourself it's not true.

The model the gestalt psychologist uses is important for us to consider. In that view, each moment in a person's life is a complex configuration involving the person and his or her circumstances. We bring all that we are — character, instincts, experiences, personality, armor, memories, rigidities, motives, and in-the-moment perceptions to the moment, which is itself an infinitely complex field. How rich and complicated is any particular "now"! It may look so innocent—a person absorbed in thought under an apple tree—and in that moment Newton is receiving the laws of motion and inventing the calculus. About this "now" Perls wrote:

> Let me tell you of a dilemma which is not easy to understand. The *now* is the present, is that moment in which you carry your so-called memories and your so-called anticipations with you. The past is no more. The future is not yet. Nothing can possibly exist except the now. And I say it's *not possible* to live in the here and now, and yet, nothing exists except the here and now.

If the demand that you live in the here and now is a demand that you be free of the past and the future, free of your personality and free of your circumstances, that is an impossible demand and an impossible hope. But it is also impossible to be anywhere *but* in the here and now.

These two ideas taken together are the central ideas of existential psychotherapy, of which gestalt therapy is one branch. What we see when we look at a person is someone embedded in his or her circumstances, embedded in life right at this moment. We do not see the individual as he or she *is*, no matter how great our powers of empathy, for not an object but a subject looks out at us, seeing us. Buffeted by many internal and external forces, and not buffeted by forces which are (though they may look powerful) mere background noise, this other person, through his or her eyes, sees the audience as a lion or a lamb, or as a lion one second and a lamb the next. The gestalt may change; and he or she may effect change. For the individual is embedded in the gestalt but is also an actor in and an architect of the gestalt, able to change figure and ground and to focus his or her own senses and mind. In the blink of an eye he or she can change everything.

Internal Contributing Factors

A fear of dogs is internal. This particular large dog, off its leash and growling, is external. That you were absorbed in your own thoughts and did not see the dog is a personal fact; the dog growling and alerting you to its existence is a matter of circumstances. That you've had little contact with dogs and have always avoided dogs are historical facts; the presence of this dog is a vivid in-the-moment experience.

Thoughts, doubts, memories, lessons learned, habits of mind, flights of fancy, are all internal phenomena. The character of this audience, the nature of this performance situation, are external phenomena. The gestalt is this presentation on this evening at this stage in your career with all this happening in the universe and all this going on within you and going on within your audience, and more. The gestalt is the relationship between perceiver and what is perceived, a relationship that can include distortions, misperceptions, projections, even hallucinations. While triggers of anxiety can be considered internal or external, they are in another sense always internal. Even if the trigger is "out there," it still must be perceived, taken in, and considered. It must become figure seen against ground if it is to become a contributing factor in a specific case of performance anxiety.

What follows is an examination of a score of these contributing factors. It is important that you not feel overwhelmed by this long list. Rather, remember that even if many of these factors contribute to your anxiety, the solution remains the same: to learn anxiety-reduction techniques and use them.

The purpose of this investigation is to help you pinpoint particular contributing factors. If you discover that one or two factors are especially relevant, you can then better tailor your anxiety-management program to your specific needs.

Hypervigilance

When we are "in a state," our body—our physical system—is activated. Depending upon the intensity of our bodily reactions and also upon our *awareness* of them, we become more or less aware of the "state" we are in. Thus we treat a large bodily reaction as small and not worrisome insofar as we do not pay attention to it; likewise, a small bodily reaction looms large and frightening insofar as we notice our bodily reactions acutely—that is, with hypervigilance. Not only may we watch ourselves too closely; we may also mislabel what we are experiencing. We may feel aroused, excited, enthusiastic, or even exhilarated, and mistake the

adrenaline rush that accompanies such states for the telltale signs of anxiety and danger. In an even more likely scenario, we look to a future presentation with a mixture of excitement and apprehension, arousal and anxiety, but label all the things we're feeling as symptoms of anxiety—that is, as warning signals that the presentation is to be avoided.

When we mislabel butterflies of excitement as butterflies of anxiety, or when we notice mild butterflies of anxiety and announce to ourselves that we are *really* anxious, we reinforce our sense of danger and provoke further bodily reactions. Now there aren't just butterflies—our palms begin to sweat and our breathing becomes affected. Indeed, this whole body reaction to a heightened sense of danger is a profound one. As the psychologist Jeffrey Gray described it:

> The body's emergency reaction functions to mobilize the body's resources for swift action that may be needed. There is an increase in the rate and strength of the heart beat, allowing oxygen to be pumped round more rapidly; contraction of the spleen, releasing stored red blood cells to carry this oxygen; release of stored sugar from the liver for the use of the muscles; redistribution of the blood supply from the skin and viscera to the muscles and brain; and a deepening of respiration and dilation of the bronchi, to take in more oxygen. All this takes place in a matter of seconds or minutes.

The young dancer who is hyperaware of even the mildest symptoms, which may mean only that she is excited by an upcoming performance, risks taking her body to full alert by hypervigilance. She may begin to doubt her ability to function and fear that the situation is worsening quickly, thus turning mere arousal or a mild case of performance anxiety into a severe one.

Indeed, some would argue that the primary benefit of beta-blocking medications that are used to control performance anxiety—they work primarily to reduce the somatic symptoms of anxiety—is not that they reduce the somatic symptoms *per se*, but rather that, by reducing them, they help reduce the workings of an insidious "feedback loop."

For some performers, an important factor in the experience of performance anxiety is their too-keen awareness of symptoms and the dire meaning they attach to those symptoms. In this regard performers can be made more anxious by *noticing* their body's reactions to threat and by *affirming* that the threat is significant.

A sales manager may take his sweaty palms to mean that something terrible is about to happen, or that he is falling apart, while his colleague, sweating just as much, is able to ignore her symptoms and to normalize the situation. In a manner of speaking, then, this contributing factor may be likened to a hypochondrial reaction to one's own symptoms.

Can you distinguish between the physical manifestations of arousal and the physical manifestations of anxiety? If they feel the same to you, how can you tell which are which? _____

_____

_____

_____

When even mild symptoms of anxiety appear, are you very quick to spot them? ___

_____

_____

Does your quick and keen awareness of your own symptoms further your anxiety? _____

_____

_____

_____

What thoughts go through your mind when you notice that you've grown anxious? Can you identify the things you characteristically tell yourself and reproduce it here? _____

_____

_____

_____

_____

Is your "self-talk" realistic and balanced, or unrealistic and charged with catastrophe? _____

_____

_____

Is hypervigilance a problem for you? _____

_____

_____

*What might the roots of such hypervigilance be?*_____

_____

_____

_____

*If hypervigilance is a problem for you, what might you do to lessen its impact on your life?*_____

_____

_____

_____

Fear of Lack of Preparation or Loss of Memory

It's hardly possible to meet the goals we set for ourselves without considerable preparation, and that applies to making presentations of all kinds. If we don't prepare enough—if we don't overlearn our material and really master it, and overlearn how to handle the presentation situation itself—we're likely to have our fears realized. We may fall prey to technical mishaps, to cues missed, passages played too quickly or too slowly, notes missed, marks missed, and so on. Or we may play correctly but stiffly, as energy that might have been used for interpretation is used instead to keep everything "hanging together." We may stumble through our speech, or read it in a monotone. Worst of all, some, much, or all of our material may be forgotten entirely, which of course is a presenter's worst nightmare.

With respect to this necessary preparation, we may realistically understand that we haven't prepared adequately for the performance. Or we may fear that we haven't prepared *enough*, even though, objectively speaking, we have prepared adequately. We may feel well-prepared in general, but ill-prepared for certain sections of our presentation. Letting that feeling generalize, we begin to feel ill-prepared altogether.

Our objective lack of preparation may precipitate a bout of performance anxiety; but anxiety already contributed to that procrastination, to that unwillingness to do what was required. This is a vicious circle: Because of anxiety, we do not prepare, and, because we are not prepared, we feel anxious. If we are to succeed, this circle must be interrupted.

Consider Andrew, the captain of his college debate team. No matter how adequately he prepares, he still dreads a memory loss. What person in Andrew's shoes hasn't felt that the most thorough preparation still won't ensure that a catastrophe won't happen? Nor is Andrew's fear "irrational." Think for a second about the feats of memory that presentations often demand of the presenter. An actor is to act in character, remember cues, blocking, and lines, which may number in the hundreds. An opera singer is to act also, and remember lyrics in a foreign language, the intricacies of hours of music, and even when and how to breathe. It's little wonder that people fear that their memory will fail them, that they will lose their place and not be able to recover, or worry, like Andrew, that they will blank out entirely. This danger confronts them all, and typically they meet it with "buckets of adrenaline."

Consider Paula, who was regularly criticized as a child and labelled as unprepared. Feeling anxious and subjected to chronic disturbances as a child, she in fact prepared poorly for exams, recitals, and the like. Labelled as unprepared, she now carries that label within herself and is likely to continue procrastinating, create vicious circles for herself, and experience terrible performance anxiety.

The fear that you are not adequately prepared will not be alleviated by more preparation *per se*, but by better preparation which may include learning your material in a new way; altering your relationship to your material (so that, for example, you love, respect, and "own" it more thoroughly); and, most importantly, engaging in a long-term anxiety-management program that allows you to grow in calmness as you learn to prepare more effortlessly and effectively.

Do you regularly fear that you are ill-prepared for your performances? _____

_____

_____

Where do you locate the basis of that fear?

_____

_____

_____

Do you adequately prepare for your performances? _____

_____

_____

_____

In which areas are you usually best prepared? _____

_____

_____

_____

In which areas are you usually ill-prepared?

_____

_____

_____

What happens when you are ill-prepared? What are the negative results? _____

_____

_____

_____

_____

Do you feel yourself to be inadequately prepared even when well-prepared? _____

_____

_____

Do you regularly fear failures of a technical kind? _____

_____

_____

_____

Do they typically happen? _____

_____

_____

Do you regularly fear memory losses? _____

_____

_____

_____

Do they typically happen? _____

_____

_____

Are the technical failures and memory lapses you experience more related to the adequacy of your preparations or more related to other factors? _____

_____

_____

_____

Do you think that there are issues from childhood contributing to these particular fears? _____

_____

_____

_____

Do you currently create a preparation schedule before performances? _____

_____

_____

_____

_____

What strategies have you tried to insure against technical failures and memory lapses that have proven ineffective? _____

_____

_____

_____

_____

_____

What has worked best for you as insurance against technical failures and memory losses? _____

_____

_____

_____

_____

_____

The Burden of Responsibility

You may be someone who takes personal responsibility for the actions of others, even when those actions aren't in your control and aren't really your business. This, for instance, is a characteristic of some people who grew up in families in which one or both parents were alcoholic.

Suppose you are a musician. You may get nervous backstage if a person near you is having trouble with an instrument. You may offer to help, forgetting your own preparations in the process. You may feel responsible for everybody's feelings and try to make things "nice" between people who are feuding backstage. You may grow anxious when you can't resolve the conflict and suddenly realize that it's time to go on. As a soloist or featured performer you may feel a special and painful burden of responsibility for the performance, arguing to yourself that a muff will not only embarrass you but will cast everyone around you in a bad light.

This "caretaker" identity is burdensome and anxiety-producing but is sometimes the identity we adopted in our family of origin. And we may naturally, but unfortunately, play that role in performing.

This sense of responsibility, which often comes with a moral component—if you fail to take responsibility for everything, then you think of yourself as a bad person—can also be thought of as a tyranny of *shoulds*. In the event that your fellow musicians are unprepared you feel yourself inexorably saddled with that burden, rather than possessing the freedom to decide in the moment whether you should shoulder the responsibility for the evening's performance.

Do you hold as an important part of your identity the idea that you must be responsible for what happens? _____

_____

_____

_____

_____

What are the positive consequences of that self-identity? _____

_____

_____

_____

_____

_____

What are the negative consequences? _____

_____

_____

_____

_____

Do you feel responsible for:
the actions of others? _____

_____

_____

the feelings of others? _____

_____

_____

events that you neither directly nor indirectly cause or control? _____

_____

_____

Are you burdened by a tyranny of shoulds?

_____

_____

If responsibility is this kind of problem for you, can you identify the family dynamics or childhood events that might have contributed to it? _____

_____

_____

_____

_____

_____

_____

What might you do to overcome this problem? _____

_____

_____

_____

_____

_____

Conflicts

Conflict raises a person's anxiety level. Just as a disagreement between two friends produces tension in a friendship such that each gets a little nervous just thinking about encountering the other, so a disagreement between the leading lady and the leading man, between two teachers doing team teaching, or between a soloist and an accompanist produces anticipatory tension.

The conflicts these people experience are as likely to be internal as external. Indeed, many performers are in conflict about even wanting to perform. They may not be doing it of their own free will, but rather because they wish to please others, or because they've been told that they're too talented not to be performers. They may have been more thrust into performing than drawn by choice, or they may have ended up in a performance career as the result of decisions made very early in life, decisions made either by themselves or others that may no longer be valid.

Dr. Julie Nagel, a psychologist and pianist, has studied these particular conflicts extensively. She found, among eighty students at the University of Michigan School of Music, that one group experienced significantly less performance anxiety than did subjects in three other groups. This first group, called the Identity Achieved group, she characterized (in *Medical Problems of Performing Artists*, Dec. 1968) in the following way:

> Identity Achieved individuals seek careers in music performance but also have tried or thought seriously about other options; they have weighed the pros and cons of their decision. Ultimately, they have arrived at their choice, perhaps despite parental objections, and, most importantly, are relatively conflict-free.

A musician, actor, or dancer who has not freely chosen his or her performance career is, in this view, a prime candidate to experience performance anxiety.

Conflict as a source of anxiety can hardly be underestimated. Because your parents yelled at each other, which yelling made you anxious, you may now grow anxious if someone raises his voice in a seminar room or drops her musical instrument case. The more you experience life as conflict—the more you see presenting as an unwanted battle between yourself and audience (or between yourself and critics), or the more you're burdened by unresolved inner conflicts—the more likely you will be to approach a presentation situation in a defended way. That is, you'll be more likely to experience performance anxiety.

Many inner conflicts hamper actors and render them anxious. A typical conflict is the felt discrepancy between the following two positions: "I want that role" and "I'm not good enough for that role." The actress burdened by this inner conflict may determine to audition for the role, but then approach the audition too meekly and too anxiously, not bringing enough of her skills, savvy, and strength to the moment. In Freudian therapy, a primary goal was the working out of inner conflicts through the insight gained through the dynamic relationship between psychoanalyst and patient and the ensuing analysis. For Sigmund Freud, neurosis in the individual resulted as much from painful unresolved conflicts as from any other psychological source. Today, the investigation of intrapsychic conflicts remains a vital component of depth-analysis psychotherapy. It is to the benefit of anyone stricken with performance anxiety to attempt to fathom what conflicts are simmering beneath the surface and how those conflicts may be affecting—or even creating—the anxiety.

Do you sense that you are harboring important internal conflicts with respect to performing? _____

_____

_____

*About what specific issues are you in
conflict?*_____

_____

_____

_____

_____

*If you are in conflict about wanting to
perform, is this a mild, moderate, or even
severe inner conflict?* _____

_____

_____

_____

*Consider how you currently handle inner
(intrapsychic) or outer (interpersonal)
conflicts. Do you deal with them
By attempting to deny their existence?* _____

_____

_____

By avoiding situations that provoke them? __

_____

_____

_____

*Through other defensive measures?*_____

_____

_____

*By airing them and examining them?*_____

_____

_____

_____

Or in some other way? _____

_____

_____

_____

*If you sense that some potent inner conflict is
troubling you, what might you do to attempt
to resolve it?*_____

_____

_____

_____

_____

Fear of Loss of Love and Approval

The actor Burgess Meredith once observed,
"If you're a hit, there's so much love
around, you can't stand it. And if it's a flop,
the audience is merciless and there's very
little you can do about it." The actress
Blythe Danner complained that after an
unsuccessful performance she felt that people stopped liking her.

A musician offered the following observation in response to a column of mine in
Callboard magazine: "Over the past thirty
years I've discovered that performance anxiety is largely due to being too eager to please
others rather than myself." If you are burdened by a too-keen need to have the audience like you, and if you believe they won't
like you unless you please them—by looking a certain way, presenting inoffensive
material, or coddling and cajoling them—
then you're looking at your presentation as a
special kind of popularity contest. If, however, you're loved in your everyday life, it
may be less important that your audience
also love you. It may be sufficient that they
respect or appreciate you. It may be sufficient that you move them, educate them,
interpret music for them, show them a mastery of your material, even thrill and astound
them, without also having to seduce them

or to feel emotionally uplifted or dashed according to their opinion of you.

But if you're missing that love and affection in your life, or if an expression of love or affection feels insufficient to make you feel fullfilled, then you may turn to your audience as an anonymous whole, or to individuals within it, to gain the love you lack. This is no easy matter to reconcile, for the desire to be loved by an audience and the fear of not being loved by them on a given occasion (a fear that provokes performance anxiety) very likely constitute hidden motives. The simplest probe is probably the question, "Do I need the love and approval of strangers to a high degree?" If the answer is yes, that answer should alert you to the possibility that your performance anxiety is connected to unmet love needs in your life—that you are looking for something more from your audience than just their attention and receptivity.

Do you look for love or affection in the wrong places? _____
_____
_____

Is your secret goal in making a presentation to win love and approval from your audience? _____
_____
_____

Are you too eager to please others? _____
_____
_____

Do you feel that people approve of you, like you, or love you according to how well you perform? _____

_____
_____

Do you hold performance as a kind of popularity contest? _____
_____
_____

Do you seek out and need the love and approval of strangers? _____
_____
_____

*Are you missing love and affection in your life and attempting to get them through a praiseworthy presentation of yourself?*_____
_____
_____

How might these issues relate to your childhood experiences? _____
_____
_____
_____
_____

*If seeking love and approval is a problem for you, what might you do to try to alter this dynamic?*_____
_____
_____
_____
_____

Activated Sense of Shame

In recent years we've grown more aware of the difference between guilt and shame, a difference highlighted by John Bradshaw in his work on the dynamics of families. Simply put, the difference is this: A person feels guilty about having done or thought a bad thing, but a person feels ashamed about *being* a bad thing.

The ashamed person feels inferior, damaged, small, and worthless. He or she feels only marginally entitled to be seen or heard and scarcely competent to do anything—except, perhaps, making music, acting, or dancing. Thus music, acting, or dance may have become a place of refuge in the midst of a difficult childhood, when the young person focused energies on performing and got proficient at it.

The time naturally came when public presentation became the next logical step, but this activated a sense of shame. However much the injured person may have practiced and possessed talent, he or she nevertheless expected to be humiliated or punished for the effort, and this expectation provoked performance anxiety.

In *Setting Free the Actor*, Ann Brebner has pointed out:

> For actors, shame as a constant companion can have deep consequences, endangering our dream of success. When an actor goes to an audition, the director is hoping to see the most intimate parts of his or her soul. If what comes up is shame, the actor is not going to get a lot of work.

Whether you are in the performing arts or not, shame may be contributing to a fear you experience when you appear and make a public presentation.

To what extent were you made to feel ashamed of yourself as a child? _____
_____
_____

To what extent do you feel ashamed of yourself in the present? _____
_____
_____

Do you feel inferior to other people (even if you also feel superior to them)? _____
_____
_____

If you are a performer, do you feel inferior to other performers? _____
_____
_____

To what extent do you expect to be punished for your efforts to engage an audience? What form might that punishment take? _____
_____
_____
_____

Do you recognize a relationship or connection between shame and performance anxiety in your life? _____
_____
_____
_____

If so, what might reduce or eliminate your sense of shame about yourself? What might constitute small steps, and what large steps, in feeling less ashamed of yourself? _____
_____
_____
_____

Anxious or Fearful Personality

Because of childhood experiences and/or constitutional makeup, some people are regularly more anxious than other people. This anxiety can be manifested as obsessive thinking and compulsiveness. In somatic ways, it can instigate hypochondrial worries and physical ailments such as headaches. Phobias, including stage fright, and even severe psychological disturbances are additional manifestations. The effects of this anxiety may not reach clinical proportions but may still significantly affect one. A person may, for instance, suffer from a chaotic inner life, from an inability to concentrate, or from difficulty in making decisions. He or she may procrastinate and be creatively blocked often, or may experience a state of relatively mild but ever-present generalized anxiety.

Performance anxiety is a predictable problem for the person who is highly anxious to begin with. The possibility of a genetic basis for this high anxiety level cannot be ruled out, for we have a very incomplete knowledge of the relationship between anxiety and heredity (just as we have of the relationship between anxiety and environment). Insofar as the anxious person has insight into and can tolerate self-examination for the causes of the anxiety, he or she already knows the extent to which anxiety is deleterious. For the anxious personality, implementing a long-term anxiety management program of the sort outlined in Chapter 5 is of vital importance.

Are you generally an anxious person? _____

_____

_____

If you are, what is the relationship between that general anxiety and the performance anxiety in your life? _____

_____

_____

_____

_____

_____

Are members of your family anxious people?

_____

_____

_____

Do members of your family complain of panic attacks, phobias, and the like? _____

_____

_____

_____

Have any members of your family who suffer from anxiety disorders been successful in treating their disorders? _____

_____

_____

_____

If you are a generally anxious person, what successful or unsuccessful measures have you taken to quiet your nerves? _____

_____

_____

_____

_____

What new measures do you think you might want to take? _____

_____

_____

_____

Fear of Negative Responses and Evaluations

Few people enjoy being judged or criticized. Performers, especially, set themselves up for scrutiny, judgment, and criticism with every appearance. Not only may any number of different people criticize them—parents, friends, peers, critics, teachers, and strangers—but they can be found wanting in many different ways. Consider orchestra players, who are judged in terms of their playing, in terms of their section's playing, in terms of the ensemble's playing, in terms of the pieces selected, and so on.

When performers actively hear, absorb, and brood about the evaluations made of them by others, they are susceptible to the vagaries of stage fright. While it's important to possess the analytical ability to understand how well or poorly one is performing, and while some critical feedback may prove constructive and even invaluable, it pays not to be *too* open to such evaluations or *too* available to be hurt by them. Those who habitually let criticism into consciousness or habitually fear it risk dreading rather than enjoying performances. As Julia Cameron explained in *The Artist's Way*:

> It is important to be able to sort useful criticism from the other kind. Often we need to do the sorting out for ourselves, without the benefit of a public vindication. Pointed criticism, if accurate, often gives the artist an inner sense of relief: "Ah, hah! So that's what was wrong with it." Useless criticism, on the other hand, leaves us with a feeling of being bludgeoned. As a rule, it is withering and shaming in tone; ambiguous in content; personal, inaccurate, or blanket in its condemnations. There is nothing to be gleaned from irresponsible criticism.

While no one likes negative evaluations and criticism, not everyone *fears* such moments to the same extent. A healthy goal is not to embrace all criticism, or to reach a point where criticism never hurts, but rather to reach the place of strength and calmness where one fears criticism only a very little.

To what extent do you fear criticism and negative evaluations? _____
_____
_____

Are your performances (in any kind of presentation) generally strong? If so, does your strength provide you with a basic immunity against the sting of criticism? _____
_____
_____
_____

If you don't feel a basic immunity, why do you suppose you do not? _____
_____
_____
_____

Are your performances generally less than strong? Do you need to improve the caliber of your work in order to develop a basic immunity against the sting of criticism? _____
_____
_____
_____

Have you had many negative evaluations of your performances, or some, or only a few?

_____

_____

Do you sometimes think you've had many when in fact you've had only a few? _____

_____

_____

Think back to a negative evaluation you received. What were the external and internal consequences, if any, of that negative evaluation? _____

_____

_____

Were you more anxious the next time you performed after that negative evaluation? ___

_____

_____

Have you developed some effective methods of dealing with criticism? _____

_____

_____

_____

Do you see a relationship between fear of criticism and the performance anxiety in your life? _____

_____

_____

If so, what might you do to reduce that fear and, in turn, your anxiety? _____

_____

_____

_____

_____

Fear of Diminished Self-Esteem

We hardly enjoy disappointing ourselves or tarnishing our self-image. If we're already fragile in the area of self-esteem — if we don't trust, respect, or like ourselves that much — then the risk of performing poorly may seem too frightening to take. A person with very low self-esteem may doubt that he or she can endure doing a bad job in making a presentation. A performer may wonder if he or she can survive a bad review.

Ego-defenses come strongly into play in the face of a threat to self-esteem. Take this year's keynote speaker at a fund-raising benefit: He may lose his voice or the ability to turn the pages of his speech text, or he may deny that the occasion is important and under-prepare for it. He may act hostile (see box), avoid the painful reality of the situation by drinking too heavily, or rationalize away a poor performance with a litany of excuses afterwards. With his fragile self-esteem at stake, it's no wonder that he must marshal his defenses in this manner.

The common way that the construction "self-esteem" is employed suggests that we think of it as a quantity which can be reduced or increased. If it is "low," we feel it too risky to lose more of it; if it is "high," we can even afford to squander some of it in bold and risky ways. It is to every performer's benefit to determine, even in a hazy, imprecise way, what self-esteem might mean and how it might be increased, such that a surplus of it can be squandered on wild, brilliant performances.

THE ANGRY ACTOR

You may well ask why an actor would express hostility at an audition. He doesn't intend to, probably, but his nervousness, his insecurity, his feeling that he is being put on the spot and judged and very likely rejected all combine to make him feel like the auditors are out to get him. I counsel all actors: Control your hostility. I have seen actors lose good roles that might have importantly furthered their careers because of a mistaken display of hostility or temper. You may get temporary relief about a situation you feel, perhaps rightly, is unjust, but it ain't worth it. You lose.

From *Audition,* by Michael Shurtleff

Are you able to gauge your own self-esteem? How would you measure or characterize it?

_____

_____

_____

_____

_____

To what extent is your self-esteem on the line when you must appear before an audience? Or, to put it differently, how much of your self-esteem is on the line with each presentation situation? _____

_____

_____

_____

Do you possess effective strategies that allow you to "get some distance" from how well you perform, so that your self-esteem isn't always on the line? _____

_____

_____

_____

What raises your self-esteem? _____

_____

_____

With respect to making a presentation or performing, what raises your self-esteem? A series of successful performances? Praise? New opportunities to engage an audience?

_____

_____

_____

Can you still maintain your self-esteem in the absence of praise or new opportunities?

_____

_____

If a fear of diminished self-esteem provokes anxiety in you, what might you try to do to alter this? _____

_____

_____

_____

Issues of Autonomy and Individuation

Fear of taking independent action contributes to performance anxiety. In the presentation situation, we must stand on our own two feet and accept responsibility for our performance. This *autonomy* may not come easily for the person who had poor role models in this regard, who learned to see the world as a terrifying place, or who was smothered and had little chance to practice independent behaviors. Autonomous action may not come easily to someone who grew used to hiding to avoid abuse or parental conflicts. Likewise for the person who, falling into drug or alcohol dependency, became practiced at avoiding and denying personal responsibility.

Individuation is a key task for the late adolescent and young adult. Nowadays it seems that issues of individuation persist for a great many people, performers included, even into late adulthood. Some observers believe that we are in the middle of a "dependency epidemic" manifesting itself in different ways, from epidemic drug and alcohol use to "codependent" relationships like those between a battered woman and the batterer she continues living with. Additionally, training in a particular discipline—dance, for instance, where a talented youngster may start a professional training program at the age of eleven or twelve and stay in it through adolescence—can foster dependency and prevent the artist from learning to think independently. As the dancer Vera Zorina explained, "Dancers are very obedient people. Dancers

don't go around making a fuss. They are not like actors who will say, 'I don't feel this line.' We simply all stood around waiting for the choreographer to tell us what to do."

Conversely, a more independent artist, fighting to retain a sense of independence, may aggressively act out. This artist experiences anxiety in situations where he or she has no choice but to conform. This constraint prompts a desire to rebel. On the other hand, he or she may have self-control but may still fear an outburst of "attitude." Such artists may experience quite strange fears in a presentation situation, anxious that they will lose control and speak their own words and not the playwright's, offend the gallery owners who show their work, or in some way thumb their nose at their audience. All presenters, whether meek, "acting out," or somewhere in between, must sometimes act independently and sometimes bow to the will of others. These are perennial life tasks that provoke anxiety and require conscious resolution.

Are you inclined to fear acting independently? _____

_____

_____

Are you too obedient a person? _____

_____

_____

_____

Are you too emotionally dependent on others? _____

_____

_____

*Are you so keen on maintaining your
independence that you rebel inappropriately
and refuse to conform?* _____

_____

*Have you established effective ways of
dealing with people in authority, relating in
ways that are neither too obsequious nor too
rebellious?* _____

_____

_____

*Can you tease out a connection between
your performance anxiety and issues of
dependency and authority?* _____

_____

_____

*If such a connection exists, what might you
do to help yourself act both independently
and appropriately?* _____

_____

_____

_____

Fear of the Unexpected and the Unknown

Anybody who's ever watched a horror
movie knows what it feels like to anticipate
the monster's arm crashing through the
wall. We try to get ready for it, our body
starts pumping adrenaline, but when the
hairy arm crashes through the wall we still
feel the urge to scream. If we aren't expecting that hairy arm, if the filmmaker has
really caught us off guard, we can almost
experience cardiac arrest.

Performance anxiety can make a horror
script out of an upcoming presentation.
The operatic soprano, with visible sweat
stains appearing under her arms, will climb
toward the aria's famous high note, the note
that everyone came to hear, fearing that she
will not make it and that the audience will
head for the exits or start booing. Much of
what she dreads is unnamable.

This is the territory of monsters in the
dark and primitive fears. People who perform for a living may have, out of conscious
awareness, nightmares that are scaring
them half to death. For those who were
frightened as children by traumatic events,
or who experienced childhood as a fearful
time, the likelihood is great that nightmares
still plague them and that they will bring a
sense of dread to the performance arena.

But fear of the unexpected and the
unknown need not have anything to do
with events from childhood. It may simply
be that we are bothered by insufficient
knowledge of an upcoming event, which
can put anyone on edge. One client of
mine who was an opera singer came into
counseling identifying performance anxiety
as the issue she wanted to work on. She had
a benefit recital coming up at which her
singing teacher would be honored. Many of
the city's arts luminaries would attend.
While she suffered from performance anxiety generally, she anticipated that in this
case a really severe bout was likely. I gave
her a menu of strategies to think about, of
the sort we will cover in Chapter 6, and the
next week we discussed the strategies in session. One had struck her as particularly use-

ful (the one called "Bring a Friend," where the performer imagines that a supportive friend is in the audience) and we went over in detail how she would use it.

I then had her perform her recital, from entrance to exit, silently singing all the pieces. During her silent recital I would stop her and ask questions.

"What was going on then?"

"That's a part I worry about. It's a hard part."

"What do you need to do with it?"

"I need to get ready for it. When it sneaks up on me I get too nervous, and then I can't handle it."

"When do you need to get ready for it?"

She could pinpoint the moment when she needed to begin readying herself for the difficult passage, and that knowledge helped lessen her anxiety. We continued on to the end, identifying other moments of anxiety, and she expressed satisfaction with the knowledge she had gained. But I could tell that something remained unresolved.

"Did we miss something?" I asked.

"I'm supposed to give my teacher flowers."

"You mean you're supposed to bring flowers and present them?"

"No, someone else is bringing them. But I'm supposed to present them at the end of the recital."

"And say a few words?"

"Yes, but that's fine. I know what I want to say."

"But something about the flower part is making you nervous?" I asked. Slowly it dawned on her that because she hadn't stopped to *visualize* receiving the flowers and handing them to her teacher and that those moments thus remained an unknown to her, she had made herself anxious. It turned out that she had to prepare mentally for the bouquet presentation, just as she had for the singing. Once she could visualize what would happen, she visibly relaxed.

Are you inclined to dwell on what you don't know about an upcoming performance? ____

_____

_____

Do you sufficiently rehearse in your mind's eye how an upcoming event will proceed? Do you familiarize yourself with it from beginning to end in order to reduce your fears about the unexpected and the unknown? ___

_____

_____

Can you identify any family dynamics that promoted a fear of the unknown in you? ____

_____

_____

_____

_____

Is there a connection between a fear of the unknown and your performance anxiety? ___

_____

_____

What might you do to relieve this fear and break this connection? _____

_____

_____

_____

Guilt

Guilt and anxiety are intimate partners. A manager who is young, less experienced, or even less talented than older employees of the same firm may feel guilty about having been selected to address an annual meeting. A violinist may feel guilty for having a better instrument than the colleague sitting in an adjacent chair. A college instructor may feel guilty about getting a coveted Ivy League job through a social connection.

But what is this guilt? It is not at all easy to define. The psychoanalyst Karen Horney likened it most to a "fear of disapproval" and a "fear of being found out." In this view it is related to the fear of the loss of approval and to doubts about one's competence, rather than being a unique and separate emotion.

To the degree that we have been made to feel guilty in life—that is, made to feel fearful and anxious about issues with moral overtones—we are likely to approach presentation situations on the lookout for things to feel guilty about. Linda Schierse Leonard explained this in *Witness to the Fire: Creativity and the Veil of Addiction*:

> Guilt is a lack, a debt, but not one that can be made up or paid off, although traditionally guilt has been understood in this way. But our existential guilt does not stem primarily from committed or omitted acts. We are not the source of our own being, nor do we have total control. We are not able to be perfect.

In presentation situations, where nothing less than perfection seems demanded, a great number of "guilt possibilities" arise. Did you really prepare enough? Are you really right for the role? Can you really do justice to the music? In presentation situations, a person inclined to feel guilty can always find something to feel guilty about.

Are you regularly bothered by guilty feelings?

_____

_____

What do you feel guilty about—that is, what are the contents of your guilty feelings? _____

_____

_____

_____

To what extent are these pangs of conscience real, and to what extent do they mask, distort, or protect you from other feelings? For instance, do your guilty feelings about not preparing well enough for an important performance mask other feelings about (let us say) being an imposter, or fearing the consequences of a successful performance?

_____

_____

_____

_____

*Is there a connection between your guilty feelings and your bouts of performance anxiety?*_____

_____

What steps might you take in order to begin to feel less guilty? _____

_____

_____

The Imposter Syndrome

Many people who excel in their profession wonder if they deserve their high position. You may have arrived at a place in your life where your tone on the oboe is exquisite, where people praise you for that tone and pay you to perform, but still you may not really believe that you play all that well. You may focus instead on your flaws or compare yourself to the best oboist you've ever heard, and in the process begin to think of yourself as an imposter. Many people who reach the very top regularly experience such feelings of inadequacy; this is equally true in boardrooms and concert halls, law offices and theaters. The performer plagued by this powerful doubt can't help but wonder if this is the night the little boy will leap out of his seat and cry, "Mom, we came to see *him*? He's terrible!"

Some people who appear before the public are indeed quite sure of themselves (see box), but many are not. The director David Black remarked, "Fame, experience, and success do not necessarily mean that an actor knows what he is doing, or that he feels secure with his proven talent." Performers who are looked upon as successful professionals but who regard themselves as imposters are both assailed by the doubts themselves and burdened by the embarrassing "secret" of their minimal competence.

*Are you inclined to think of yourself as incompetent? As an imposter?*_____
_____
_____

THE CONFIDENCE OF A RUBINSTEIN

Part of [pianist Arthur] Rubinstein's image lay in the confidence he exuded. He was extremely sure of himself. I just wish some other musicians had his confidence. Some of them come across as tremendously self-assured, but with them it seems more of an aggression, and their aggression is just insecurity. I used to be frightened the whole time I was working at my music. Then Rubinstein told me that I must not be frightened; I must calm down. I was at a point before I met him that brought me to physical illness before I'd play, even in a student master class. I was frightened of people; I was frightened of everything. Maybe I still am, but I don't think so. Basically, I'm really not frightened any longer.

From an interview with Janina Fialkowska in *Great Pianists Speak for Themselves*, Vol. II.

Is that a fair, objective assessment? _____
_____
_____

If that is fair, what steps might you take to become more competent? _____
_____
_____

If that is an unfair assessment, what steps might you take to remind yourself or convince yourself of your own competence?
_____
_____
_____

Are feelings about a lack of competence implicated in your experience of performance anxiety? _____
_____
_____

If so, how will you help yourself either feel more competent or become more competent?
_____
_____
_____
_____

How can you begin to acquire the "confidence of a Rubinstein"? _____
_____
_____
_____
_____

A Sense of a Lack of Entitlement

Some individuals who feel worthy enough performing or making a presentation to an audience do not feel very worthy as people.

As one rock musician put it, "I believe in what I do, but not in who I am." Lack of self-worth, a factor of performance anxiety related to others already discussed (such as shame), is highlighted here to emphasize the fact that some performers dismiss their successes because they feel themselves to be imposters, while others doubt their reception in the world because they feel a general lack of entitlement. The two patterns of conflict may evince the same behaviors—bouts of anxiety, acts of self-disparagement and self-dismissal—but for the second the despair is deeper and more pervasive.

The possible reasons for these feelings of a lack of entitlement are many. Consider Janice, a school principal who confesses she is nervous appearing before school assemblies, PTA meetings, and the like. It may be that few, if any, members of Janice's family ever experienced real success, and a tarnished self-image results from the feeling that she comes from a family of "losers." She may come from cultural or socioeconomic circumstances that appear to dictate her station in life and doom her to second-class status. Usually, however, her lack of a sense of entitlement is related to the view held of her by her parents and the negative messages, overt or covert, she received from them. They may have characterized her as unwanted, unworthy, a burden, or incompetent, and as a result it is hard for Janice ever to feel that good things are about to happen.

It is each person's job to learn to feel entitled to a share of life's happiness. To perform joyfully and to give joy: Why shouldn't every human being feel entitled to these experiences?

*Do you feel yourself as entitled as anyone
else to share in the world's riches and
pleasures?* _____
_____
_____

*If you don't, can you trace the roots of that
sense of a lack of entitlement?* _____
_____
_____

*Do you suppose that there is a connection
between your sense of a lack of entitlement
and your experience of performance anxiety?*
_____
_____

*If so, how can you teach or persuade yourself
to feel more entitled?* _____
_____
_____
_____
_____

Fear of a Loss of Control

Actors, dancers, and other performers often
fear that their bodies or minds will slip from
their control during a performance. In one
study, this fear ranked as the number one
anxiety-producer for both male and female
performers. Performers fear that they won't
be able to control their bodily functions,
bodily movements, or behaviors. One writer
reported, for instance, that "an internationally renowned concert musician stayed off
the concert stage for ten years because of the
dread fear that he would accidentally expel
flatus during a performance," adding that
"the fear of urinating on himself has
prompted more than one performer to leave

a bottle just offstage, into which he could
relieve himself just prior to entrances."

Performers may also feel trapped before
going on, as if caught in a snare. Here, it is
not a fear of loss of control that disturbs
them, but rather the *reality* of a loss of a
specific kind of control: They have lost
their ability to flee from danger. As Stephen
Aaron explained,

> The actor, waiting in the wings, can
> resort to neither fight nor flight. He
> is physically and emotionally
> trapped, and there is an intimate
> relationship between such immobil-
> ity and passivity, on the one hand,
> and panic anxiety on the other.

Thus some cases of performance anxiety
can best be thought of as cases of *inhibited
flight*.

Paradoxically, a performer may feel anxiously eager to take flight and passive at the
same time. He or she is like the dog in laboratory studies who was given frequent electric shocks when it could not flee and, when
the door to its cage was opened, made no
attempt to escape. So, too, the person suffering from performance anxiety may feel both
panicky and defeated while waiting in the
wings. He or she may look calm but may
only feel resigned to fate. The fear of losing
control has become, over time, the feeling
of having actually lost control.

*Do you sense that a fear of loss of control
plays a part in your experience of
performance anxiety?* _____
_____
_____

What is it that you fear you will not be able to control? _____

_____

_____

Do you fear that you will lose control of your body or of some bodily function when you must make a presentation of some kind? ____

_____

_____

Do you fear that you will lose control of your mind or do odd or self-sabotaging things when you perform? _____

_____

_____

Do you think it makes more sense to attempt to maintain control of your body and mind than to work to let go of control and surrender to the moment? _____

_____

_____

Can you trace this fear back to some childhood experience or family dynamic? ___

_____

_____

What might you try to do to release the hold this fear has on you? _____

_____

_____

Fear of Imperfection

The need to achieve perfection can contribute to performance anxiety. Learning by trial and error—that is, by making mistakes—is not only a natural way to learn but universally acknowledged as the best way to learn. But for many people, as children, mistakes brought quick punishment, sometimes of an overt kind, like a beating, and sometimes of a more covert kind, in the form of a critical comment, a harsh look, or an impatient pregnant sigh. Children growing up in

THE PERFECTIONIST

The perfectionist fixes one line of a poem over and over—until no lines are right. The perfectionist redraws the chin line on a portrait until the paper tears. The perfectionist writes so many versions of scene one that she never gets to the rest of the play. The perfectionist writes, paints, creates with one eye on her audience. Instead of enjoying the process, the perfectionist is constantly grading the results. For the perfectionist, there are no first drafts, rough sketches, warm-up exercises. Every draft is meant to be final, set in stone. Midway through a project, the perfectionist decides to read it all over, outline it, see where it's going. And where is it going? Nowhere, very fast.

From *The Artist's Way,* by Julia Cameron.

ANOTHER FACE OF PERFECTIONISM

Throughout the early phases of my career, the mirror was my nemesis, seductive to the point of addiction. Stepping through the looking glass meant confronting a double who exposed all of my flaws and pointed out all of my physical imperfections. The physical side of the discipline does involve a certain degree of tedium, to say nothing of the pain. But the hours of practice are minor compared to the emotional terror that can sometimes haunt a ballerina when she studies her reflection in the mirror. This anxiety is not due to simple vanity or fear of professional rejection. As in the myth of Narcissus, the beautiful youth who falls in love with his own reflection, the relationship between the dancer and her mirror image is an intimacy of extraordinary power and potentially perilous consequence.

From *Dancing on My Grave,* by Gelsey Kirkland

such circumstances begin to feel that only perfection, whatever that might mean, will suffice, and that anything short of perfection should be judged a failure and bring criticism or punishment. People thus become critical of themselves and of others, because no one seems capable of doing the perfect job (see box, "The Perfectionist").

Naturally the thought of an upcoming presentation generates anxiety for the perfectionist, because he or she has never yet done well enough and no doubt will not be perfect this time either.

An actress may be able, after the final curtain, to applaud her performance a little; nevertheless she will rush to point out the blemishes and decide by the next morning that the performance really wasn't adequate at all. Unable to point to performances that she considers successful, she may rightly wonder if she's a victim of this need for perfection. She may also wonder how perfectionism affects her in other ways (see box), for the underlying dynamics that make her doubt the goodness of her performances will also make her doubt that she is good enough in other areas of her life.

Must you always be perfect? _____
_____

What do you see as the distinction between mastery and perfection? _____
_____

How would you define a "good performance"? _____
_____
_____
_____

How would you define a "good enough" performance? _____

_____

_____

_____

Do you feel that you have permission from yourself to be only "good enough" sometimes? _____

_____

_____

Do your definitions of "good" and "good enough" vary from situation to situation? ___

_____

_____

Do you need to be "perfect" in every presentation you make, becoming obsessed about even the least details? _____

_____

_____

Do you perceive a connection between perfectionism and performance anxiety in your life? _____

_____

_____

If so, what might you do to reduce that burden and redefine excellence in your presentation? _____

_____

_____

Fear of Strangers

An audience is a special set of strangers, and one may understandably feel some "stranger anxiety" before making a presentation. The audience is not usually the performer's peers, except in the case of student recitals, class demonstrations, company meetings, and the like. They are not the performer's friends, unless the hall is filled from one's own personal circle. Who are they then? Should one suppose that they are friendly or hostile? Supportive, indifferent, or antagonistic? Deeply knowledgeable about one's medium and message, superficially knowledgeable, or basically ignorant? As the choreographer Paul Taylor put it:

> I'm always puzzled by audiences. I really don't know who they are or why they're there or what they're thinking.

Fears about the audience parallel our primitive fears of hostile strangers and thereby contribute to the experience of performance anxiety. The audience becomes "the other" or even the enemy, and we are made anxious by the fact that we are about to enter into a kind of battle with these strangers. Even being seen by them or looking at them can be experienced as a threat. One actor who had to leave the profession because of stage fright explained:

> It occurred to me one night, while on stage and waiting for my cue, that if one looks at the two galleries in the dark, they remind one of an open mouth ready to swallow you up.

Some scholars have argued that actors performing in the ancient Greek theater wore masks in order to protect themselves from the evil eye of the spectator. That stepping onto a stage feels like going into battle is clear from the way actors typically characterize the audience as people to be tamed or slain. Richard Burton, for instance, described the perfect audience as "sheep." Laurence Olivier would stand behind the curtain before a performance chanting "You bastards!" at the audience. Burgess Meredith described the audience as "the dragon to be slain." And expressions like "Kill 'em!," "Lay 'em out in the aisles!" and "Knock 'em dead!" are among the most common pre-performance exclamations heard backstage.

As Brian Bates explained in *The Way of the Actor*:

> Like an animal, the actor allows himself to be cornered, and then he performs and does battle with the audience. This is a sense of living with danger which creates a tremendous vitality and energy. But there is no doubt that there are elements of hostility involved—it is indeed a battle. Simon Callow has identified the aspect of competition, even aggression, that exists between the actor and the audience. "There's no getting away from the fact that theatre contains an element of hostility. Every actor knows that. Standing on the stage is an aggressive act. It says: Look at *me*. Listen to *me*. It says, I'm interesting, I'm talented, I'm remarkable." Callow points out that the audience naturally responds to this as a challenge. "Oh yeah?" says the audience. "You'd better prove it."

It is one thing to assume that some audience members, among them critics and competitors, may not like what you do. It is a different and darker matter to see all strangers as threatening and every audience as standing in personal opposition. Here it may be that it is the presenter who feels hostility toward others, and who assumes that others feel toward him or her the hostility that he or she is harboring for them. But this "projection" onto an audience can create for the angry performer enemies where no enemies exist.

How would you characterize your relationship with your audience? _____
_____
_____
_____

Do you typically look upon them as hostile strangers? _____
_____
_____

To what extent do you fear your audience? __
_____
_____
_____

What about them do you fear? _____
_____
_____
_____

To what extent do you hate your audience?
_____
_____
_____

*What about them do you hate?*_____
_____
_____

Are you regularly anxious before meeting strangers at a party, reception, and the like?

_____

_____

Do you tend to worry what strangers will think or say about you? _____

_____

_____

Were you very often left with strangers as a child? _____

_____

_____

Have you been traumatized by strangers? ___

_____

_____

Would you say that stranger anxiety is implicated in your bouts of performance anxiety? _____

_____

_____

_____

If so, how might you revise your relationship with your audience? _____

_____

_____

_____

_____

Fear of Meaninglessness

Actors, musicians, and other performing arts professionals invest great meaning in their performances and are likely to characterize each appearance as a significant event, an event even of mythic importance. As the actress Maureen Stapleton put it, "There's so much at stake that it just overpowers you."

A bemused observer might ask, "What's at stake? That the audience has a pleasant evening? Relax a little!" But the performer, whose identity and reason for being are implicated in each presentation, has a much greater stake in it than the audience's enjoyment or even his or her reputation or career. For those two hours the actor is living meaningfully, making meaning for his or her life and for the audience, supporting the meaning in the playscript. Almost two thousand years ago Lucian of Samosata wrote:

> It is the dancer's profession to show forth human character and passion in all their variety; to depict love and anger, frenzy and grief each in its due measure. There is meaning in his movements; every gesture has its significance; and therein lies his chief excellence.

Artists believe there is significance in what they are doing beyond its entertainment value, because they are communicating something about the human condition. Through their images, words, music, movement, and colors that condition is compellingly revealed and even transformed. Thus, for many, the presentations of their vision of life have a great deal to do with heroism, on the one hand, and spirituality, on the other; these are held to be sacred tasks, and this naturally magnifies their importance. Such magnification easily heightens the experience of anxiety.

It is a benefit to consciously determine how a balance may be struck between the idealistic investment of meaning in each presentation and a wise disengagement from identification with each event. A performance ought to be meaningful, but not *so* meaningful that one's reason for being and self-worth hang in the balance.

*Do you invest "too much" meaning in every presentation you make?*_____

_____

_____

*Is "who you are" too tightly wrapped up in "how you perform" in these situations?*_____

_____

_____

Is there a way to care about your presentation while also remaining detached?

_____

_____

_____

_____

*How might you retain your investment in the meaningfulness of performances while at the same time detaching or divesting enough to reduce your anxiety?*_____

_____

_____

Fear of Success

At first glance, it may seem strange to imagine that a person might fear succeeding at what he or she has set out to do. But when we think about concrete presentation situations it becomes a much less strange idea.

For instance, Elaine is a radio announcer who plans to fly across the country to audition for a position with a major urban station, all the while doubting that she really wants to leave her friends and family behind

and move to a different climate, a big-city setting, and a whole new life. She quite simply fears the practical results of a move up. She may wonder if she really wants to outshine her senior partner at the station where she's now announcing, for she knows he has a fragile ego. She may wonder if she's equal to the demands that the next step in her career might bring: A more pressured schedule and heightened expectations on the part of a tougher listening public. She may fear that success will end up fitting her like a straightjacket, costing her personal freedom and saddling her with marketplace players who beleaguer her with ideas about what the public wants.

Indeed, there are many reasons why someone in the public eye might view success as something to avoid. Some of these reasons are rooted in childhood experiences and the parent-child relationship. In *Medical Problems of Performing Artists* (Mar. 1990), Dr. Julie Nagel has observed:

> As a child develops greater independence, the parent's apprehension of the child's potential to surpass his or her own accomplishments or the parent's need to keep the child close and dependent creates anxiety in both parent and child. It is believed that this tension is conveyed to offspring even if it is not realized on a conscious level by the parent. Therefore, lowered functioning and heightened anxiety mount in the child as success or professional goals become more and more feasible. Success becomes forbidden, and

defensive thoughts and behavior to decrease anxiety increase. These might include lowered self-concept, an obsession with being judged or evaluated by others, and self-sabotage when success appears imminent.

There are real as well as imagined negative consequences to succeeding, so it's little wonder we might cherish the simplicity and safety of a small career and a limited horizon. Anxiety may mount before important presentations because, possibly, we stand at the edge of a forbidden or unwanted ascent.

Is success somehow forbidden to you? _____

_____

_____

Can you identify any family dynamics that might have encouraged you to believe this?

_____

_____

_____

_____

Do you fear the practical consequences of success? _____

_____

_____

Do you fear emotions that might arise if you were to have a successful career? _____

_____

_____

Were you permitted to feel successful in your family? _____

_____

_____

_____

Do you permit and encourage yourself to feel successful? _____

_____

_____

Do you feel that a fear of success is implicated in your experience of performance anxiety? _____

_____

_____

If so, how might you air the issue and become friendlier with the idea that you deserve and are entitled to success? _____

_____

_____

Fear-Inducing Self-Talk

People often have certain *cognitive styles*, or modes of thinking, instilled in them, and these become habitual patterns of thought, even though they may be extremely flawed and detrimental to the individual. Cognitive therapists have identified many kinds of faulty patterns in people's self-talk—that is, the language of their stream of consciousness. Among those that can contribute to performance anxiety are the following:

- Fortune-telling
- Catastrophizing
- Mind-reading
- Discounting
- Overgeneralizing

You might, for instance, say to yourself, "I know I'll mess up this afternoon because I didn't get enough sleep last night," or "I never sing well after I eat a big lunch."

These are examples of *fortune-telling*. By predicting failure and acting as if a bad performance is a foregone conclusion, you help raise your anxiety level.

You are *catastrophizing* when you say things to yourself like "This is the worst I've ever looked," or "This is the most boring piece of music I've ever played in my life." By magnifying the badness of the situation you up the emotional ante and increase your anxiety level.

Mind-reading takes place when you say to yourself, "I know the conductor isn't happy with my playing" or "I know the audience can tell I didn't rehearse enough"—in the absence of proof that anyone is thinking any such thing.

Discounting happens when you minimize your estimation of your talents and successes. You may assert that you can't project your voice to the back of the hall or hold your own with the rest of the ensemble, even though you've projected well enough and held your own with this ensemble a hundred times already.

You *overgeneralize* when you leap from one or several negative events to some iron-clad rule about yourself. Here, you begin to say things like "I'll *never* audition well" or "I *always* blow my introductory line." People who think in these ways are naturally plagued by doubts as they get ready to make a presentation. Once a given doubt is put to rest, another pops up, because their very way of talking to themselves provides them with endless doubts. Matters of cognitive style and negative self-talk are vital, and we'll return to them in Chapter 5, when we map out a long-term anxiety-management program.

Do you engage in much negative self-talk?

_____

_____

What sorts of negative and self-disparaging things do you tend to say to yourself? _____

_____

_____

_____

_____

Do you foretell disaster? _____

_____

Do you catastrophize? _____

_____

_____

*Do you conclude, without any evidence, that others are harboring negative thoughts about you?*_____

_____

_____

Do you discount yourself by the self-talk you use? _____

_____

_____

Do you overgeneralize, leaping from a single instance—a single error, a blown line—to some general statement about your ineptness or unworthiness? _____

_____

_____

Do you see a connection between your cognitive style and your experience of performance anxiety? _____

_____

_____

If you do see such a connection, how might you begin to change your self-talk? _____

_____

_____

_____

Three Helpful Tips

I conclude this chapter by underscoring three points:

- *Isolating even one of the contributing factors discussed above may result in significant and even life-altering changes.* You may discover, for instance, that you never really chose to be a performer, but instead pursued a performance career because you were talented and because your art was a means of escape from a tumultuous childhood environment. Now, coming to grips with the psychological facts of the matter, you have the chance to fall in love with your art for the first time. You can recommit to your choice and thereby eliminate the anxiety attached to that long-simmering inner conflict.

- *If you do pinpoint a specific factor contributing to your performance anxiety,* that information can guide you to the kind of pre-event anxiety-reduction technique best suited to your circumstances. The techniques and strategies outlined in Chapter 6 cluster into twelve groups, and techniques from one group may prove more valuable to you than techniques from another. To give one example: Fear of memory loss may best be met by new preparation and rehearsal tactics. Strategies matched to the precise factors implicated in your personal experience of performance anxiety will yield the best results.

- *On the other hand, you may find it quite difficult to isolate the factors that contribute to your experience of performance anxiety.* Remember, however, that you can work to manage your anxiety even if you can't pinpoint the sources of that anxiety. While there are no magic bullets available to slay performance anxiety, it's nevertheless possible for you to put together a long-term anxiety-management program that works. Again, Chapter 5 outlines such a program; and Chapter 6 presents the practical techniques you'll need.

Presentation Situations

On any given day, Sharon, a professional singer, might take a class, call her agent, speak to schoolchildren about her life as a singer, be interviewed on radio, give a recital, and attend a reception. Her performance on this day is not only the recital; she has been performing steadily from morning till night.

Which one of Sharon's performances actually provokes the most anxiety in her? The answer is not obvious. For another performer like her, it might be the call to the agent, whom she suspects doesn't even remember her name. For yet another, it might be the "easy chat" with the schoolchildren, because she has no idea what young children might be interested in hearing about. For a third, it might be the reception, because of her almost phobic dislike of small talk. Only for a fourth performer might the recital be the greatest source of anxiety.

As we examine the range of presentation situations likely to confront you, do consider which are the really difficult ones for you, the ones that provoke the most anxiety in you. The question isn't which presenta-tion situations in the abstract "should" or "shouldn't" make you feel anxious, but rather which actually do—and why.

Practice and Rehearsal

Both private and public rehearsal are aspects of making a presentation that can easily provoke anxiety.

Many people experience practicing and rehearsing as negative, unpleasant events. Carl, a young politician, may feel incompetent as he learns to give speeches and muddles through the natural trial-and-error steps toward mastery in the learning process. He may not like the way he sounds, or grow upset at his forgetfulness as carefully phrased passages concerning his platform slip from memory. He may powerfully feel the pressure of an upcoming appearance as he sits with his advisers practicing his script.

Despite all his hard work, Carl may not seem to be improving sufficiently; he may, as he practices, compare himself to other politicians, either peers or historical greats, and feel inferior. Or he may grow bored with the process, and the boredom provokes existential anxiety as the meaning drains out of the practice session. To top it off, as a result of anxiety and in order to avoid anxiety, he may procrastinate and practice less than he should, which raises his anxiety level in its own right, as he begins to fear that he'll fail when the campaign really gets rolling.

To keep negative thoughts and disturbing feelings at bay, Carl may begin to practice mechanically, so as not to really have to be present. With his eye focused narrowly on memorization and the sound of his voice and with his mind shutting out negative thoughts, he binds his anxiety. He determines that he *will* learn all his prepared statements—but is he feeling the words he must say, so as to really connect with the voters?

In preparing to make an appearance, we can reasonably hope to get more out of practice and rehearsal sessions than the

PRACTICE

Our stereotypical formula "practice makes perfect" carries with it some subtle and serious problems. We think of practice as an activity done in a special context to prepare for performance or the "real thing." But if we split practice from the real thing, neither one of them will be very real. Through this split, many children have been irrevocably taught to hate the piano or violin or music itself by the pedantic drill of oppressively boring exercises. Many others have been taught to hate literature, mathematics, or the very idea of productive work. The most frustrating, agonizing part of creative work, and the one we grapple with every day in practice, is our encounter with the gap between what we feel and what we can express. "Something lacking," said the flute player's master. Often we look at ourselves and feel that *everything* is lacking! It is in this gap, this zone of the unknown, where we feel more deeply—but are most inarticulate. Technique can bridge this gap. It also can widen it. When we see technique or skill as a "something" to be attained, we again fall into the dichotomy between "practice" amd "perfect" which leads us into any number of vicious circles. Competence that loses a sense of its roots in the playful spirit becomes ensconced in rigid forms of professionalism.

From *Free Play*, by Stephen Nachmanovitch

mere mastery of technique and the memorization of material (see box). We might even hope to have a soul-satisfying experience; we might even hope to enjoy ourselves as we practice.

According to Martin Seldman, in *Performance Without Pressure*, a performer in practice sessions might attempt to obtain a clear, detailed picture of the desired performance; anticipate obstacles and areas where further preparation is needed; increase confidence by experiencing success mentally; reduce anxiety by making a mental "road map" and acquiring the "I've been there" feeling; and really achieve the benefits of practice and repetition. These added benefits, however, are only available to the performer who consciously chooses to accomplish more during practice time than "merely" mastering technique and material, as important as those goals also happen to be.

Public rehearsal—practice conducted with members of a team or, in any case, in the presence of others—is anxiety-provoking in additional and different ways. These rehearsals take place in a field of interpersonal and group dynamics. The individual agendas of the participants come into play, as do power, control, and authority issues among individuals. Therefore conflicts arise, both interpersonally and intrapsychically.

For instance, making mistakes is permitted during rehearsals, and mistakes in the service of interpretation are even encouraged. On the other hand, mistakes by their very nature are disturbing, especially as the public performance date nears. At each rehearsal, group members will have a different tolerance for mistakes and a different attitude about their permissibility.

Similarly, you are to stand wholeheartedly behind the material you are presenting, for the sake of the group, the production, and your own ego investment in the project; on the other hand, you may clearly see its flaws, not really like or respect it, be bored by it, or be upset by another's contribution to the effort. You find yourself in a company of your peers, perhaps pulling together to make a joint presentation a good one, so that each of you will prosper. But you are also among competitors and critics who are watching you, noting your strengths and weaknesses, judging you, rating you, and marking you as better or worse than themselves.

Each of these dynamics can produce simmering conflicts which raise everyone's anxiety level. In addition, there may be last-minute changes, new material added, the sense that the presentation is getting worse, not better, as the assigned day approaches, the sense that there won't be enough time to get ready in the remaining time, and much more. It turns out that everyone involved in a public rehearsal has the job of managing anxiety as well as crafting the event in question.

How would you describe your experience of practice? _____

_____

_____

_____

_____

ACTORS AND DIRECTORS ON REHEARSALS

Carole Rothman, director:
The first day of rehearsals is always a nightmare, yet you've got to be coherent and excited about the play. It's very nerve-wracking.

Gregory Mosher, director:
The whole idea of rehearsing a play in four weeks is a ridiculous convention; it has nothing to do with the needs of the play. Some plays need three weeks' rehearsal, some need three months.

Tom Hulce, actor:
What's really difficult is when something is changed or removed that was a vital step in the race you were running. It's as if they take out part of the track and you have to make this great hurdle in the middle of the race.

Hume Cronyn, actor:
Sometimes, even with work, you not only don't improve the piece, but can actually dig the hole deeper. You can't take something the playwright has conceived, tear it apart in rehearsals, and start all over again. You end up with a patchwork quilt, and it ain't very pretty.

Donald Moffat, actor:
Overnight, I was presented with a new poem. It took me some time to learn the poem and fill it out. It's always a shock to be thrown something on such short notice—especially the night before the critics come.

From *Creating Theater*,
by Lee Alan Morrow and Frank Pike

What anxiety issues arise for you with regard to practicing? _____
_____
_____

Do you practice and rehearse as regularly and as carefully as you would like? _____
_____

Are the number of practice sessions you engage in sufficient? _____
_____
_____

Is their quality high? _____
_____
_____

Do you make use of your practice time to enjoy yourself? _____

_____

Do your practice goals include more than the mastery of technical matters and the memorization of material? _____

_____

What thoughts help you rehearse effectively? For example, do any of the following help:

I love the work I do. _____

I love hearing my instrument/ expressing new ideas/etc. _____

I love interpreting Mozart/ Shakespeare/etc. _____

My practice is a kind of spiritual practice. _____

What thoughts hinder you from rehearsing effectively? For example, do any of the following?

This is a lot of work. _____

This is too hard. _____

I can't get it right. _____

I'm not equal to this. _____

Is procrastinating over practice an issue for you? _____

_____

Do you understand procrastination to be an anxiety issue? If so, in what sense? _____

_____

_____

What steps do you take to lessen anxiety so that you're less inclined to procrastinate? ___

_____

_____

Is practice a time when you are really permitted to make mistakes? _____

_____

What anxiety issues arise for you during public rehearsals? _____

_____

Can you identify recurrent or particularly troublesome ones? _____

_____

_____

_____

Are you generally in decent relationships with the people you practice with, or do conflicts simmer beneath the surface? _____

_____

_____

What ineffective or harmful measures do you take to relieve anxiety during the rehearsal process? _____

_____

_____

Do you use alcohol or drugs? _____

_____

Do you eat more? _____

_____

Do you sleep more? _____
_____

Do you lash out at others? _____
_____

*Do you experience health problems or
somatic complaints?* _____
_____

*Do you experience any specific thought
difficulties?* _____
_____

*What effective strategies have you developed
to make the rehearsal process less anxiety-
provoking?*

Does exercise help? _____

Meditation? _____

A routine of regular practice? _____

Visualizing a successful performance? ___

*Do you dispute negative with affirmative
self-talk?* _____
_____

*Can you pinpoint any specific strategies you
employ to manage your performance anxiety
during the period of practice and rehearsal?*
_____
_____
_____

Which of these strategies seem most effective?
_____
_____

Lessons and Classes

Performers often continue to take lessons
and classes even after their professional

careers are launched. The actor coming to
Los Angeles from New York is likely to
make a priority of locating a good acting
class. The soprano may return to a voice
teacher at any point in her career, perhaps
to prepare for a difficult role, perhaps
because something about her singing seems
off to her. The dancer may take classes every
day as part of the process of staying in shape.

By the same token, performers often
become teachers and give private lessons,
work in colleges, conservatories, or acting
schools, teach workshops and classes, and
provide master classes at festivals. Like
teachers in any setting, performers can experience performance anxiety from that side of
the student-teacher relationship as well.

Sometimes student–teacher relationships are among the most stressful relationships into which we enter. Performers bring
with them any of the contributing factors
discussed in the last chapter and may then
be met by a teacher who harshly criticizes,
who looks on indifferently or reads a letter
during a practice session, who offers dog-
matic or contradictory advice, who is both
unpleasant and exemplary of everyone who
is rejecting in the performer's life.

Margret Elson, a pianist and artists'
counselor, described several of these harmful student–teacher interactions. One she
calls the "move over, darling" tactic, where
the teacher makes use of your time and
money to satisfy his or her own need to perform. Elson writes:

> No sooner does a student play a few
> notes before a teacher whose heart
> lies in performing, not teaching,

than the teacher vigorously shakes his head and says sweetly while dusting the student off the chair: "Move over, darling." He then proceeds to show what music *really* sounds like in the hands of a master.

On the other hand, some teachers *never* demonstrate, refusing to expose themselves to scrutiny and judgment and thus remaining high on their perch of perfection, from which the performer's imperfections can be all the better highlighted. The teacher may interrupt repeatedly and give full vent to criticisms, making use of a vocabulary heavily laden with "nevers" and "always."

Teachers may demand that performers do things which they patently cannot do, like sing beautifully in an unsupported falsetto, or demand that they follow rigid instructions and yet never copy anyone. Envious of their students' talent, teachers may seek to subvert them. As the pianist Rosina Lhevinne put it, "There are no jealous students, only jealous teachers."

Critical, powerful, and controling teachers are often injured themselves and may have as a central item on their agendas the desire to put and keep students in their place. Conversely, teachers may hold to certain beliefs which are appropriate but which also put real pressure on students. They may, for instance, believe that performers should practice only the very best music, even if it is also the most difficult. The pianist and teacher Leon Fleischer articulated this point of view in the following way:

As far as my ideas on degree of difficulty are concerned, the music must be difficult both physically and musically, like late Beethoven sonatas, Rachmaninoff's Third Concerto, and Brahms's B-flat Concerto. I think you should study them at a young age, because if you learn something and then drop it, during the dropped period whatever you tried to learn begins to grow, ripen; it matures, so that in a year or two when you pick it up again, you see it in a different way and it becomes part of you in an almost genetic sense.

People not in the arts also encounter teachers and enter into student–teacher relationships more often than might be supposed. Psychotherapists in training, for example, engage in supervision and for an hour each week present cases and client material, often in the form of tapes of actual sessions, to a seasoned therapist who asks questions and wonders aloud about the appropriateness of the trainee's actions.

The situation for the trainee is very like the situation for the performer. What exactly is the supervisor's agenda? Does he or she need to show off, keep the trainee subordinated, or push a personal theoretical position? Trained as a psychotherapist and not as a supervisor, are his or her methods of supervision effective, appropriate, or fair?

Each such situation, for the singer or counseling trainee, for the actor or employee put under a mentor at work, demands that the student keep good boundaries and maintain a healthy objectivity about the teacher. Part of the maintenance of boundaries involves asking oneself questions when made anxious by a teacher's comments, questions like "Is the teacher being fair here?", "Is what I'm being told good for me to do?", or "Is this the best way to help me learn?"

Similarly, one needs to listen to criticism, but with enough detachment to hear it without feeling too wounded by it.

Classes, in contrast with private one-on-one lessons, can be both less intense and more intense: When you are not on, you can be invisible, but when you are on, many people are watching you. Additionally, classes in the performing arts often demand that students access feelings, "open up," and in other ways allow themselves to be vulnerable—demands which provoke anxiety.

In both individual lessons and classes, the focus most often is on technique, so questions of technique may loom very large in both the teacher's and the performer's mind (see box).

You may not be worried about your bowing at this precise moment in the lesson, but isn't there something about your fingering to brood about? Or if not your fingering, what about your tone? Or if not the tone you produce, what about the way you handled the fast passages? Or if not the way you handled fast passages, what about the way you handled the slow passages? Were they slow enough, beautiful enough? Like an iron filing in a shifting magnetic field, anxiety can jump from one technical issue to another, turning lessons and classes into torture sessions for the too-anxious performer.

WHY AREN'T ACTORS' VOICES BETTER?

People sometimes ask me why by the third year of drama school all our actors' voices aren't of a very high standard, or why in the professional theater not all voices are what they should be. If I were to list all the things one is actually up against, one would wonder how most actors do as well as they do. It takes many years to overcome obstacles and get to a state of equilibrium. So when people say, why isn't the standard higher, I say I have been working on my voice for twenty years and I am just beginning to be able to tolerate it. It's very difficult to get the voice to do what you want it to do. As it is, drama schools are working miracles—and so are all the students who commit themselves to working on their voices.

From an interview with Julia Wilson-Dickson
in *Masters of the Stage*, by Eva Mekler

Are lessons sometimes, often, or usually anxiety-provoking experiences for you? _____

Can you pinpoint what exactly about the experience produces anxiety? _____

Is one of the following a more important factor than the others?

Fear of criticism _____

Fear that you'll be found lacking _____

Fear of unjust or unwarranted criticism _____

Fear of the teacher's "hidden agenda" _____

Mistrust of the teacher's style or actual expertise _____

Dislike of the teacher's attitude _____

Do you usually come prepared for lessons? _____

If not, can you identify the factors contributing to your lack of preparation? _____

Are you less assertive during lessons than you would like to be? _____

Are you too eager to please the teacher? _____

Are you too quick to take every suggestion and criticism? _____

Would any of the following make the student–teacher experience a less anxious one for you?

Better teacher selection _____

A different attitude with respect to "authority figures" _____

More serious preparation _____

More ease about "being seen" _____

Better ways of accepting criticism and dismissing criticism _____

Are classes sometimes, often, or usually anxiety-producing situations for you? _____

Are you worried more about how your classmates perceive you or about how the teacher perceives you? _____

Do you see class as a place to learn, experiment, and enjoy, or as a place where you will be scrutinized and judged? _____

_____

_____

How does your anxiety manifest itself with respect to classes? _____

_____

_____

_____

Do you fail to prepare for them adequately? _

_____

Do you cut them or get sick on class nights? _

_____

Do you hide, never volunteer, and hope not to be seen? _____

_____

Do you experience physical and mental symptoms of performance anxiety? _____

_____

What one thing might you do to help make class a less tense experience? _____

_____

_____

_____

_____

Interviews

An interview is a special presentation of yourself. It might be a formal job interview; an informal job interview at a party or conference, where you find yourself chatting with someone in a position to hire you; an on-the-air interview where you try to sell your ideas, your current film or your upcoming concert; or that special interview, the audition, which we'll cover next. In each case, the task of presenting yourself in the best light, in circumstances that really matter with regard to your career, naturally provokes performance anxiety.

Informal interviews are often a part of the networking (and auditioning) processes. When someone in a position to help your career casually talks to you and asks seemingly idle questions about your recent work or future commitments, you are being interviewed, and your mental preparation for and presence of mind during such interviews are important ingredients in your recipe for success—especially if you are in the performing arts.

Performers are at least partially aware that this is the case and often experience performance anxiety before and during social situations where informal interviewing is likely to occur: at receptions, benefits, opening nights, galas, fund-raisers, and at work sites like production studios and talent agencies. Indeed, most of us have felt similarly anxious before a party or gathering that will put us together with others in our profession.

Are you prepared to be informally interviewed right now? _____

_____

_____

Are you prepared to give a compelling answer to that terrible, unnerving, innocent-sounding question, "Tell me a little about yourself?"

_____

_____

Do you have a good sense of:
What to present and what to withhold at
such times? _____

_____

What questions to ask? _____

_____

How assertive to be? _____

_____

_____

Studying up a bit on the interview process (see box on being interviewed on radio or television) and making the effort to find opportunities to do interviews will help you better understand how to handle yourself in any interview situation, whether formal or informal and whether expected or a complete surprise.

As a participant in a play or concert, you know what the next line or bit of melody will be, but in interviews, you're in the territory of improvisation. For example, I've found myself in the following situations:

- Just as she goes into a commercial, an interviewer in an in-studio radio interview says that she'd like to cover a certain question after the break. That is the question I think about during the break. After the break, she asks an entirely different question.

STEVE ALLEN'S FIVE ON-THE-AIR INTERVIEW RULES

Rule 1. *Act naturally.* If talking on the air doesn't come naturally, then try pretending that the interview is taking place on a park bench or in a rowboat.

Rule 2. *Listen carefully to the questions.* Do not make the common mistake of starting to respond to what you think the questioner will ask. Interrupting, if repeated, will make you appear rude.

Rule 3. *Don't ramble.* You are well advised to give your answers in short sentences.

Rule 4. *Think ahead.* If you can't think fast, then do as much preparation beforehand as possible.

Rule 5. *Rehearse.* Do an interview in the privacy of your own home or office, just to see how well you respond. Do you digress unnecessarily, or forget the point of the question? The time to find out about such problems is before you appear on the air.

Adapted from *How to Make a Speech*, by Steve Allen

- On the other end of a phone interview, five people—two co-hosts and three in-studio guests—ask me questions. The questions come from "different directions" with lightning rapidity.

- An editor and I are discussing manuscript changes. At the end of the conversation he asks, "What do you think your next book will be about?"

- I meet with a publisher in his office for an hour. This is a social visit, but at a certain point I present a book idea, and he in turn asks me questions about the book's structure, contents, and audience potential.

These and scores of similar situations arise. We can be carefully prepared for some of them, and *generally* prepared for all of them. General preparation includes expecting the unexpected, remaining cognizant of our agenda, and being prepared at all times to speak confidently about ourselves and our work.

Can you identify which aspects of the interview process are the most anxiety-provoking for you? _____

_____

_____

How does the anxiety manifest itself? _____

_____

_____

Do you regularly search out interview possibilities, either of a formal or an informal sort? _____

_____

_____

If not, are you avoiding them because of anxiety? _____

_____

If you presently avoid them, is it in your interest to seek them out? Might you actively seek out interview opportunities? _____

_____

_____

_____

Might you prepare answers for the sorts of questions that are likely to arise and rehearse those answers? _____

_____

_____

Might you rehearse or role-play interview situations with a friend? _____

_____

_____

During the next week, find someone to interview you. Prepare the questions, but not the answers. Tape record the interview, listen to it, and think about it. If it went as may be expected—rockily—think about what you need to do to become better prepared at speaking confidently about yourself and your work goals.

Auditions

Auditions, which are performers' primary job interviews, are especially grueling for several reasons. Among them are the following:

- The work the performer is hoping to get is not just a job or a career step but an event tangled up with his or her deepest hopes and dreams.

THE EXPERTS ON AUDITIONS

If you were to tell an actor that he or she would be auditioning for a Broadway musical in the next few days, you would probably swear, from the reaction, that this was a fate worse than an IRS audit. Successful actors with credits ranging from *Antigone* to *Zorba* become petrified at the thought of having to give a vocal audition. I have seen stars dissolve in tears at the prospect of having their work judged and found wanting. The terror of having to put oneself on the line and face rejection can cause mental distress varying from mild stage fright to total emotional and physical collapse. Some performers give up in despair and vow never to be put in that thankless position again—while a few who have done their homework can't wait for the chance to show off their talents and skills.

From *Auditioning for the Musical Theatre*, by Fred Silver

Most actors come into the interview situation wearing a thick mask, spending their energies protecting themselves. It's rough interviewing someone who is determined to keep himself hidden. Try to give. Try to open up. Try to see who the interviewer is. I've had many occasions to interview actors all day—thirty, forty of them—and then at lunch or at the end of the day run into the same actors. I say hello and they look blankly at me, as if I were a mugger. I remember them, and they never saw me. I've interviewed thirty people, and they've had *one* interview, and they don't know what the guy who interviewed them looks like.

From *Audition*, by Michael Shurtleff

The interview is a business meeting, but it is also very personal. It's our best opportunity to let the casting director know who we are. Instead, we sometimes spend it looking up fearfully at the ceiling, clearing our throats, coughing, muttering, or otherwise acting as if we've been asked to talk about something we know nothing about. In some ways, the interview represents everything that is frightening about being a creative person. It demands a great deal of self-revelation, it requires that we be present in the moment and respond to changing circumstances, and it reminds us that we have to sell ourselves over and over again in ways that people with "regular" jobs never have to do.

From *Setting Free the Actor*, by Ann Brebner

• The performer is to come in with memorized pieces and perform them "perfectly" and "without anxiety."

• Many audition situations are not strictly about the talent of the performer. It may be that an actress with a certain look is wanted, or one with a certain twang or lilt to her voice. Band members holding auditions for a lead singer may be looking for a singer who has a certain presence, who can be a leader, who has good connections, who can project an image, who's reliable, who can contribute money for studio time and, only incidentally, who can sing. Given these many difficulties and uncertainties, it's no wonder that performers number auditions among their most stressful experiences—a fact that acting teachers know intimately well (see box).

Do auditions regularly make you anxious? __
_____
_____

If so, how does that anxiety manifest itself?
_____
_____
_____
_____

Do you regularly avoid auditions because of the anxiety? _____
_____
_____

Do you see auditions as job interviews? ____
_____
_____

Would you say that you've learned how to

effectively manage anxiety before and during job interviews? _____
_____
_____

Do you know what is required of you at job interviews? For instance, do you have clear ideas about what your auditors want and need? _____
_____
_____

Do you have clear ideas about how best to present yourself at a job interview or audition? _____
_____
_____

Do you have some clear ideas about what constitutes inappropriate behavior or self-defeating behavior at a job interview or audition? _____
_____
_____

Have your most successful job interviews or auditions been ones where you felt most confident and relaxed? _____
_____
_____

If so, what steps do you take to bring those feelings to all of them? _____
_____
_____

Have your most successful job interviews or auditions been those for which you were most prepared? _____
_____
_____

If so, is it the case that preparation is your best anxiety-reducer? _____

_____

_____

If you could change one thing that is in your power to change to make job interviews or auditions less anxiety-producing, what would that one thing be? _____

_____

_____

_____

_____

Presentations

Most presentations have structural elements in common. They happen on a certain predetermined date at a certain predetermined time in front of a group of people who have chosen to be there—in the case of an artistic performance, they have usually paid to be there. In the period before the lights in the hall dim, the person slated to appear anxiously waits in the wings. The technical preparations commence, the audience begins to settle down and, finally, he or she (and fellow performers) begin the ritual countdown.

It is at such times that the very worst bouts of performance anxiety occur. In the few minutes between "Places!" and "Curtain!" actors can feel as if they're about to die. Speechmakers feel trapped and unprepared. Dancers hold their breath, frightened. It is to quell this anxiety that performers especially have been known to resort to drugs (see box).

Adding to the anxiety one may experience with respect to a given appearance is the makeup of that particular audience.

DRUGS AND PERFORMANCE ANXIETY

Stevie Nicks described how in the past she used drugs and alcohol to assuage her fears of performing. "In the beginning," she explained, "stimulants made you brave. You're scared to walk onstage in front of a bunch of people. In the old days to get away from that you had a drink, or whatever everybody was doing, so you didn't have to experience that terrible fear. The last ten minutes before I go on, my hands are really shaking. I'm almost sick to my stomach. But I've learned that the second I'm onstage I'm not nervous anymore. The second I walk out, it just goes away, and I'm totally confident. If you can't depend on yourself without chemicals, you might as well stop doing it and go on to something else."

From *Musicians in Tune*, by Jenny Boyd

There are nights when the critics come, nights when the audience is small and the atmosphere dull, nights when every seat is occupied and the atmosphere electric. There are times when a particular person attends, a person whose approval the performer desperately wants. As ballerina Gelsey Kirkland explained:

> This particular night at the New York State Theater held a special significance for me: My father was in the audience. This was the first time he was to see me perform. In the past, some pretext had always kept him away from the theater. For me to realize that he was there induced emotional terror that went beyond stage fright. I knew I would be judged by the only person other than myself whom it was impossible to please.

How does your performance anxiety manifest itself in the day or two before an appearance? _____
_____
_____
_____

What changes take place in you? _____
_____
_____
_____
_____

What symptoms do you manifest? _____
_____
_____
_____

Does the approaching performance seem to become more real to you or less real? _____
_____
_____

Do you rehearse and prepare more often or less often? _____
_____
_____

Does your mastery of the material seem to deteriorate or improve? _____
_____
_____

What is your experience of performance anxiety on the day of the presentation? _____
_____
_____
_____
_____

What symptoms do you experience? _____
_____
_____
_____

Do you seclude yourself away, medicate yourself, pace restlessly? How do you spend the time? _____
_____
_____
_____

What worries, if any, occupy your thoughts on that day? Can you identify your self-talk?
_____
_____
_____
_____

What is your experience of performance anxiety in the period just before going on (say, during the last fifteen minutes or so)?

_____

_____

_____

_____

*What symptoms of anxiety do you begin to manifest?*_____

_____

_____

_____

Does the anxiety intensify markedly during this period? _____

_____

_____

Do you employ some strategy or strategies to reduce the anxiety or do you "white-knuckle" it? _____

_____

_____

What do you tend to focus on during this period? _____

_____

_____

_____

_____

What external factors seem to affect your experience of performance anxiety during this period?

The size of the audience? _____

The makeup of the audience? _____

*How often you've performed the material before?*_____

The quality of the material? _____

Whether critics are in attendance? _____

What is your experience as you begin the presentation? Does your anxiety peak and then begin to abate? _____

_____

_____

_____

Does your anxiety tend to completely disappear once you begin? _____

_____

_____

*If you are still anxious once you're into it, how does the anxiety manifest itself? What symptoms are present?*_____

_____

_____

_____

_____

If the anxiety is still present, about what in particular are you worrying? _____

_____

_____

_____

_____

Does your anxiety level rise and fall during the presentation, depending on whether, say, a difficult passage is upcoming? _____

_____

_____

Are you relatively aware or unaware of the audience? _____

_____

*Does becoming aware of them make you
more or less anxious?* _____
_____
_____

*Does your anxiety increase markedly
according to external circumstances, say if
someone forgets a cue or fumbles a passage?*
_____
_____

*Do you feel in control or out of control
during the presentation?* _____
_____
_____

*What strategies, if any, do you employ to
reduce anxiety?* _____
_____
_____

*How do you feel once it's over?
Happy or unhappy that the presentation has
ended?* _____
_____

Greatly relieved, even giddy with relief? ____
_____

Still anxious? _____
_____

*Worried about what people are thinking,
about meeting people at the reception, about
your next performance, etc.?* _____
_____

*Do you analyze the performance or tend to
forget about it immediately?* _____
_____
_____

*Recalling an important presentation
situation, how would you like to have
handled it differently?* _____

_____
_____
_____
_____

*What can you do to better manage your
performance anxiety before, during, and
after these events?* _____
_____
_____
_____

Public Speaking

Most people fear public-speaking situations. This same fear may prevent you from, say, teaching workshops or fronting the band, even though such activities might be soul-satisfying career ingredients.

To prepare a worthwhile speech, lecture, or workshop, we must develop the material ourselves (unless we are in the unlikely position of hiring a speechwriter or other professional). This preparation is a creative rather than a recreative or interpretive task and puts fresh demands on us. New negative self-talk may intrude and new fears and doubts may encourage procrastination. Just as an audition book can help illuminate the audition process, so a book on public speaking can clarify the realities of speech-making. For instance, James Robinson, in *Winning Them Over*, outlines the following ten steps to effective speech-making:

1. Speak with a strategy.

2. Spy on the audience and setting.

3. Always write it—never wing it.

4. Keep it brief.

5. Simplify your speech.

6. Add humor.

7. Create a fireworks finale.

8. Don't be afraid to be afraid.

9. Triumph over adversity.

10. Win them over!

The actor, musician, or other performing artist—whose job and whose goal is, after all, to be seen—will benefit from creating public-speaking situations, accepting them when they arise and mastering the anxiety that accompanies them. A performer may, for example, profitably invent lectures to give and workshops to teach, as a change of pace from regular performances and as new performance experiences in their own right.

Confidence is bred in the person who manages to speak successfully in public, a confidence likely to spill over into artistic performance and into everyday life.

Do you currently have occasion to lecture, teach, or give speeches? _____
_____
_____

Have public-speaking possibilities presented themselves, in any setting from an AA meeting to a benefit dinner, which you've avoided because of anxiety? _____
_____
_____

Have you thought about lecturing or teaching, but avoided that path because of anxiety? _____
_____

FOUR RULES FOR "SPEAKING EASY"

The Speakeasy approach revolves around four basic concepts: **Energy, Awareness, Strength** (or **Self-Esteem**) and **You.** Together, the first letters spell EASY—the way speaking should and can be. Energy: To make an audience listen, a speaker must have energy. The energy necessary for effective speaking can best be defined as intensity or involvement. Awareness: If you stop thinking about yourself and pay attention to what is going on out there, your gut will respond to your audience. Strength: Strength, or self-esteem, means having a strong, secure sense of self which you will not allow your audience to threaten. You: Like it or not, it all comes back to you and how much time and effort you are willing to devote to improving your spoken image.

From *Speak Easy*, by Sandy Linver

Before speeches, lectures, or workshops, how does your performance anxiety manifest itself? _____

_____

What ineffective or harmful strategies do you use to reduce this anxiety? _____

_____

_____

What effective strategies have you learned to use at such times? _____

_____

_____

If you perform for a living, what one thing might you do to begin to add public speaking to your repertoire of performances?

_____

_____

Business Situations

Professional relationships are typically presentation situations that are charged and complicated. An actor walking into an agent's office or returning an agent's call may experience severe performance anxiety. As the talent agent Lester Lewis puts it:

> Most actors when they come into the office are so damned nervous they can hardly respond. I've had actors read for me and their hands are shaking. I tell them, "Look, we're not the enemy . . . yet! Just relax."

Can you confront the boss, director, business colleague, or fellow band member when confrontation is called for, without experiencing anxiety? Can you casually speak to your agent without anxiety or listen to criticism from your coach, your choreographer, or your faculty chairman without anxiety? Generally not. At such times, there may be so much at stake or going on between the lines that, while ordinarily cool under fire, you begin sweating through your shirt as you attempt to fire the drummer, speak to the head of the firm, or return a record company executive's call.

Many business negotiations are enacted through subtle, nuanced rituals in which a great deal is said in a few words (see box). Most people are made anxious by these rituals; they don't engage in them often enough to really understand them, and they feel too invested in the outcome to maintain the distance kept by other players in the game. For instance, a practiced literary agent and a practiced editor in a book contract negotiation are likely to present the points important to them clearly and quickly, for they have done this many times, know the shorthand of the business, and don't have the kind of personal stake in the outcome that an author would. But a writer involved in such a negotiation with an editor, first of all, is likely not to understand fully what is going on and, second, will probably feel a great stake in the outcome. Both circumstances naturally produce anxiety.

On the other hand, you may begin to approach these interactions with a keen sense of excitement, which is often inextricably mixed up with performance anxiety in such situations. A senior partner of the firm is buying you drinks at the fanciest place in

AN AGENT AND AN EDITOR DO LUNCH

Sometime around ten-thirty or eleven, your host or hostess calls you with the traditional phrase, "Are we on for today?" The time and place are then agreed upon. But not always easily. To wit: "How does Italian sound to you?" "Had it last night. Mexican?" "I'm on a diet. There's a great fish place around the corner from my office." "But that's all the way on the other side of town from me." And so it goes. Sometimes there is more to these negotiations than two busy people trying to find common ground. Nothing serious, just a subtle game of chicken: *I am more powerful than you because I made you come to my side of town at an inconvenient hour and eat a cuisine that gives you heartburn.*

From *How to Be Your Own Literary Agent*, by Richard Curtis

town: Isn't this wonderful? The touch of the high-powered agent on your shoulder is electric: Does charisma rub off? The recording contract your manager sets before you outlines in legal language a future of compact discs and major city tours: If this is business, then heaven must have boardrooms!

We are challenged to normalize these professional relationships as best we can, so that we neither fall in love with nor fear people simply because of the position they hold in the world. The power that once resided in the person of kings now resides in those able to provide roles, promotions, contracts, lucrative deals, and all the rest, and we must somehow maintain our own counsel in the throne rooms of this new kingdom.

Do you regularly experience performance anxiety with respect to business situations?
_____
_____

Since many of these situations can be avoided, does your anxiety manifest itself in procrastination and avoidance? _____
_____
_____

Which business situations cause you the most anxiety?
Phone conversations? _____
Face-to-face meetings? _____
Money talk? _____
Small talk? _____
Hiring and firing situations? _____
Choosing projects and making commitments? _____
Those in which you'd benefit by taking a stand or exerting leverage? _____

Do you regularly practice or rehearse such situations beforehand? _____

What ineffective or harmful strategies do you employ to reduce the anxiety before or during business situations? _____

_____

_____

What effective strategies have you learned to employ at such times? _____

_____

_____

_____

What one thing might you try to do to help you reduce your anxiety about such situations?

_____

_____

_____

Blank Page, Blank Canvas

The creative artist experiences anxiety whether he or she is making or not making art (as when blocked), selling or not selling art. These various anxieties are examined at length in a previous book of mine, *Fearless Creating*, and for our purposes a single example will hint at the issues involved.

A client of mine who is a successful playwright was working on many projects at once but not effectively working on any of them. She had two play commissions overdue, one for a Chicago theater and one for a San Francisco theatre, a very personal but probably uncommercial "second stage" piece in its early stages, and several screenwriting ideas that intrigued her and on certain days even obsessed her.

It seemed reasonable to attribute her creative block to the fact that her plate was too full and that she was finding it hard to settle on any one project. But the situation turned out to be much more complicated than that. With each piece of work she felt torn between her own ideas about how to create the piece, ideas which themselves were not perfectly clear, and contradictory ideas about what the audiences for each piece—the artistic directors of the two theaters, the subscribers to those theaters, and her fellow playwrights—were expecting of her.

Once an artist begins to wonder about what reception her work will receive and what people will say about it, once she makes the distinction between what she wants to do and what she believes she is permitted to do, her art-making is bound to take on the flavor of performance. At such times the creative blockage she experiences is really a special case of performance anxiety.

Creative artists are well-advised to think through whether they view their work as performances and to what extent performance anxiety may be implicated in their experience of a creative disablement. If they find that they are holding their work as performance, their remedies are exactly the same as any other performance-anxiety sufferer's: putting into place a long-term anxiety-management program and learning calming techniques to use as they approach the blank screen or canvas.

As a creative artist, do you tend to think a lot about who the audience is for your work and what they're expecting? _____

_____

_____

_____

Do such thoughts lend an air of performance to your art-making efforts? _____
_____
_____

Do you experience much creative blockage?
_____
_____

Thinking about that blockage now, is it really more like performance anxiety? _____
_____
_____

*If this is true, how might you handle your creative blocks differently?*_____
_____
_____
_____

Do artistic business situations, like calling a literary agent or gallery owner, regularly provoke performance anxiety in you? _____
_____
_____

Does that anxiety cause you to avoid such situations or tackle them only very infrequently? _____
_____
_____

Which sorts of artistic business situations provoke the most anxiety? _____
_____
_____
_____

Do you regularly rehearse or practice for these situations beforehand? _____
_____
_____

What ineffective or harmful anxiety-reduction strategies do you use in connection with these situations? _____
_____
_____
_____
_____

What effective strategies have you learned to use? _____
_____
_____
_____
_____

The Gamut of Presentation Situations

Countless other situations provoke performance anxiety in performers and nonperformers alike. Everything from dating to Thanksgiving dinner with the family, a company softball game to asking for a raise, socializing after work to sexual relations, can be and often are held to be presentation situations. As a concluding note on this subject, let's look at two special presentation situations: opening nights and role changes.

Here, let's use the opening night as a metaphor for *all* those occasions when a presentation is made for the first time "for real" to its intended audience. The occasion might be a first kiss with your newest flame or the first time you perform a certain violin concerto in public. Such opening nights tend to generate an inordinate amount of performance anxiety, and for that reason the performance often doesn't go quite as intended or expected. As the stage manager Thomas Kelly observed in

The Back Stage Guide To Stage Management: "Often performers throw a lot of curves at the stage manager during the first performance in front of an audience. Actors have a tendency to either speed up or go slower, and speak louder or softer than they had at rehearsals." Each of us should be alert to these opening night dynamics, for the extra adrenaline that is naturally present is bound to affect both the performance and our experience of anxiety.

A second situation that heightens performance anxiety is the changing or exchanging of roles. The actor who takes on directing, the musician who begins to conduct, the middle manager who gets promoted to executive—they are likely to experience the performance anxiety that comes with added responsibilities, new tasks, and a step into unknown territory.

The performer who is relatively free of anxiety when she performs may suddenly experience it when she fronts her own band or opens in her first solo performance piece. The performer who has always wanted to step forward in some way but who has never taken a shot at it may not realize that it is the anxiety associated with changing roles and adding responsibilities that is preventing her from trying. If she does try to front her own band, she will have to choose among the musicians who audition for her—and on what basis will she choose? Will she choose the most versatile performer, the one who best understands her concept for the band, the one not on drugs, the friendliest one, or the one who comes with a little capital to invest in the band? These are questions that she did not need to tackle at this heightened

level of care and responsibility when she was one player among many.

We can easily avoid the "hassles" of stepping up or out and assuming the difficulties associated with supervising, directing, producing, and so on, but then we will also fail to reap the rewards. We are then unlikely to understand that our decision not to lead may be based not on the arguments we present to ourselves, but on a desire to avoid a certain amount of new anxiety.

Can you list the various presentation situations that provoke performance anxiety in you? _____

_____

_____

_____

_____

*Is there a common theme among them, a theme that distinguishes them from presentation situations that do not provoke anxiety?*_____

_____

_____

_____

_____

Do you attempt to handle the anxiety that arises in these diverse situations in the same way? _____

_____

_____

Do you experience "opening nights" as particularly nerve-racking? _____

_____

_____

If so, do you use certain special strategies—either effective or ineffective ones—to handle anxiety at such times? _____

_____

_____

Can you identify those times when you've changed roles or "switched hats"? _____

_____

_____

Have such changes—from performer to creator, from follower to leader—increased your experience of performance anxiety? ____

_____

_____

Do you avoid making such changes in order to avoid the experience of anxiety? _____

_____

_____

If you undertake to make such changes and find them anxiety-provoking, what measures do you take to reduce that anxiety? _____

_____

_____

_____

_____

In thinking about the many different kinds of presentation situations that confront you, what new things have you learned? _____

_____

_____

_____

_____

_____

5 Long-Term Anxiety Management

I recently happened upon a TV documentary about a stand-up comic. For years this young man had worked the comedy clubs. Then, one day, the phone call that all comics pray for arrived, from a *Tonight Show* producer. The documentary follows the comic as he prepares for his debut. Then his appearance is rescheduled at the last minute—or has it been canceled? Neither he nor we feel anything but anxiety as he realizes that his big chance may have gone up in smoke. But it turns out that his appearance has indeed only been rescheduled, and now it's on again. We watch him discussing his palpable fear with the comic Jerry Seinfeld, who says matter-of-factly, "First time on the *Tonight Show*? Terrified? Of course!"

We watch him as the day arrives, as his makeup is applied, as he waits to go on. To watch him, the real person that he is with his particular history and basic anxieties, facing that crucial career situation, is to be convinced all over again that performance anxiety cannot be entirely eliminated from the lives of human beings, not even from the lives of those fortunate few who feel genuinely good about themselves.

Some performers evolve complicated methods of binding their anxiety, but these complications do not necessarily add up to a successful plan. One client, a highly anxious stand-up comic who attempted to reduce his feelings of anxiety by using alcohol, marijuana, food, and prescription drugs, also contrived to create a super-nervous stage character, so as to make good use of the anxiety he believed he couldn't eliminate or disguise. He argued that by using this character he could provoke laughter—albeit nervous laughter—just by walking on stage. But of course this approach failed him in several ways. First, when the quality of his performance really counted, and especially at competitions, he could not deliver his act. He forgot bits, missed on the timing, even dramatically shortened the set. Second, much of the material he wanted to write and deliver could not be delivered by this character; it would have been out of character. The shaking, sweating character onstage turned out to have a very limited range. Third, maintaining this stage character exacerbated, rather than lessened, his general feelings of anxiety, which played themselves out in alcoholic binges and sudden flights from his day job and everyday responsibilities.

What should these two comics have done to better manage their performance anxiety?

Certainly they were trying already. All human beings already have ways of dealing with anxiety as a part of survival. If every fear, stress, worry, or doubt incapacitated us, our species would have precious little hope of survival. My client was already managing his anxiety—but *reflexively*, not in ways that either reduced his experience of anxiety or served him as a human being and artist.

Reflexive methods of handling anxiety begin early in life, and if we have a great deal of it to handle—if we are not helped to feel safe and wanted, if we are criticized or abused, if we experience our parents as absent, untrustworthy, or dangerous, or if we are made to feel frightened in any of the countless ways that a small child living among towering adults can be made to feel frightened—we not only reflexively manage anxiety but we take that task as our primary mission. Our personality forms around the job of handling anxiety, and that formed personality is who we are and who we remain, unless and until we remake ourselves.

As the psychologist Karen Horney explained:

> Although the range of manifest forms of anxiety, or the protection against it, is infinite and varies with each individual, the basic anxiety is more or less the same everywhere, varying only in extent and intensity. It may be roughly described as a feeling of being small, insignificant, helpless, and endangered, in a world that is out to abuse, cheat, attack, humiliate, and betray.

Horney argued that personality forms in one of three different ways as a response to excessive anxiety in childhood: A person withdraws, or learns to be submissive or compliant, or attempts to look powerful. These responses "work" insofar as the experience of anxiety is made bearable in the moment. But there is a cost to the person in a lack of inner security and in the formation of a neurotic personality less free than the ideal to experience or effectively cope with reality.

Thus the factors that contribute to the experience of anxiety—all the factors considered in Chapter 3—a lack of a sense of entitlement, an exaggerated fear of strangers, or a hypervigilance about bodily sensations, and so on—become rooted in that formation of personality. They are built right into the structure, as it were. So, too, are our basic anxiety management strategies: our avoidance tactics, defensive maneuvers, hand-washing compulsions, and psychogenic pain complaints. We produce our own anxiety, manage it, produce more anxiety, and are forced to manage it all over again.

To glance ahead to what we will want to say shortly about the effective management of performance anxiety, we can begin by saying that excessive performance anxiety must be rooted in personality formation; and that the goal of a long-term anxiety-management program is not the manage-

RESPECTING YOUR EFFORTS

Stop everything for a few minutes. Get up and take this book with you to a new location, perhaps to a seat by a window or to a garden spot. As you move to this new location, allow yourself to feel all the many ways you are not pleased with yourself. Allow yourself to suffer. But even as you honorably experience those feelings, remind yourself that *in a core place* you are worthy. You are worthy of your own attention, worthy of respect, worthy of love. You are important; you count; and thus you will *seriously and adamantly* respect the attempt you are about to make to reconstruct your personality and make yourself into a calmer, stronger, more confident person. Not only will you make such an effort, but you will make it lovingly, with an attitude of self-regard and self-respect. Try saying out loud, "I will respect my own efforts." Do you feel that it is possible to care about yourself? Do you feel that it is possible to take yourself seriously? Sit in this new location awhile and enjoy the sensation of being alone with yourself and kind to yourself. Revel in the prospect of becoming your own best friend and advocate.

ment of anxiety per se, but the remaking of personality. This is a formidable task but also a beautiful one: To become new, to become the person who is so confident and strong that he or she neither experiences a self-created, unnecessary anxiety nor inappropriately manages the reduced anxiety that sometimes persists.

A Long-Term Approach

The following is the first part of a two-part plan to help you manage performance anxiety. The second part—arming yourself with specific techniques to use before and during a presentation—is described in Chapter 6. If you follow both parts you'll enjoy pre-

sentation situations more, experience less performance anxiety, and better weather the anxiety you do experience.

Our previous discussion should have made clear that the time to begin to deal with performance anxiety is not fifteen minutes before the event—but let me recapitulate here: First, the techniques you'll want to employ as the hall fills up and your anxiety mounts are ones you needed to rehearse beforehand. Whether you're going to use the Sarnoff Squeeze, the Alexander Technique, a certain breathing exercise, a certain walking meditation, or another of the techniques described in the next chapter, you'll need to practice it beforehand so that you really own it in the moment of truth.

Second, you'll need to take the time to learn about the psychological root causes of your performance anxiety and how they are hidden from view. No anxiety-reducing technique is likely to work very well if you fear success, or if your sense of shame is activated every time you appear before an audience, go to an interview, and so on. Nor are you likely to effortlessly handle the stress of presenting yourself if you are anxious in the other areas of your life. It's crucial that you have in place a general anxiety-management program to help you with *all* the stressors in your life.

The following long-term plan is designed with these considerations in mind:

1. Awareness training

2. Experiential learning

3. Awareness of creative issues

4. Cognitive restructuring

5. Stress reduction

6. Interpersonal analysis

7. Counseling and therapy

8. Discipline practice

9. Discipline understanding

10. Preparation

Awareness Training

Very little in the typical school curriculum helps a child with self-examination, and very little in the typical home does either. Even in homes where children are financially advantaged and are sent to weekly piano or dance lessons, it is unlikely that children will be helped to know themselves. Chil-dren are taught instead to do and not to do things, but they are not encouraged to reflect on their thought processes and feelings or on the world's complex realities. Thus it becomes hard for people to know what their thoughts really are—which are the important ones and which the merely habitual or pre-programmed ones—and to manifest their own creativity or choose values different from society's values. These tasks require a willingness to look at oneself and listen to oneself, followed by real practice in doing such things.

As a consequence of growing up in a society and a home where self-awareness is not valued, the child, and later the adult, is relatively unresourceful when it comes to meeting *inner challenges*. The clarinettist may meet every challenge her music conservatory places on her, but not in the grounded, secure way that she might were she regularly pausing to evaluate and understand her thoughts and feelings. She may graduate and join a good orchestra and still not possess the skills to determine what is in her best interests to do, or even what is in her best interests to think.

If we were to define self-awareness, we would want to include both presence of mind and understanding of mind in the definition. *Presence of mind* is related to genuine self-esteem and self-confidence, which, if not fostered in youth, may still be fostered by the self-caring adult. The person who feels inwardly secure, who looks out for him- or herself, who is unafraid of the opinions of others, who maintains personal integrity and affirms the right to be can manifest this presence of mind.

BREATH OBSERVATION

As the patient attempts to concentrate on his own inhaling and exhaling, activities of mind become very apparent. This exercise, if carried out faithfully for several minutes, will serve to make a patient aware of his own mental preoccupations, for some patients notice a predominance of thoughts about past events (memories) interrupting their breath observation, while others notice that they are most frequently interrupted in breath observation by thoughts pertaining to the future. The patient will quickly discover a rather complicated, but comforting, situation: one aspect of his mental "self" is calm and psychologically strong, and can watch, label, and see the melodramas of the other "selves," selves which get so involved in painful memories or beautiful and escapist fantasies of the future.

From "The Clinical Use of 'Mindfulness' Meditation Techniques in Short-Term Psychotherapy," by Gary Deatherage (*Journal of Transpersonal Psychology*, vol. 7, no. 2, 1975)

Understanding of mind is based on certain habits and practices like introspection, reflection, self-analysis, self-evaluation, and the working through of denial and other ego defenses. We can define self-awareness as the practice of identifying and understanding one's thoughts, feelings, and behaviors, the practice of which is in the service of self-esteem and helps a person be present and self-confident in all situations.

How is this self-awareness to be achieved? Learning "mindful meditation" is one possible starting point. Every style of meditation has its own premises and rituals; some traditions stress point-focus concentration and have the meditator focus on a flame, part of the body, or an object such as an icon. Oth-

ers stress openness and the freeing of attention. All teach breath observation, which is an excellent beginning tool for gaining self-awareness (see box).

The meditator learns to discriminate between what is inside and what is outside the self (see box, page 123). This ability to discriminate is of vital importance to the performance anxiety sufferer, whose pain is in such large measure a product of his or her own thoughts.

Gaining self-awareness is no easy matter, because to practice it one must *volitionally* produce uncomfortable feelings (see box, page 124). Most of us prefer to deny, ignore, or ward off feelings we don't like, rather than let them into consciousness and experience them. If the number of people willing to let them in is small, the number of people who will *produce* them for the sake of examining them is even smaller. No matter how intelligent or sensitive a person may be, no matter how great a performer, artist, scientist, or citizen of the world, this task may feel beyond his or her capabilities.

At different points throughout this book we have talked about the consequences of a lack of self-awareness. To take one example, the person who is made very upset by an experience of mild performance anxiety is in a real sense simply unaware that the experience is a mild one. That he or she has "butterflies" or feels the need to urinate means nothing beyond its obvious meaning: a mild anxiety.

Mild performance anxiety is a normal, natural, and perhaps even inevitable by-product of exposing our abilities and our being to public scrutiny—of that we should be aware. Neither the arousal nor the anxiety need frighten us. To internally label this state as "dreadful" or "unnatural" is to make an awareness mistake. The pianist Glenn Gould, for instance, once explained: "I used to take my pulse rate just before a concert out of scientific curiosity, and it was always very fast. So there was obviously a kind of unnatural excitement." That he called this excitement unnatural is interesting and may help explain his preference for the recording studio over the concert hall. By framing his modest anxiety as unnatural,

DISCRIMINATING STIMULI

The phrase *discrimination training* is used to describe the process by which an organism acquires the ability to discriminate one stimulus from another. In one hour of meditation, a practitioner may have hundreds of experiences of being identified with thought, then returning to a more attentive state. The process can be regarded as discrimination training, since the meditator is learning to discriminate thought from other stimuli. Being skilled at discriminating thought from other events puts the meditator in a particularly strong position of mental health. In fact, it could be argued that since nearly everyone has a certain number of neurotic thoughts, mental health is dependent upon the ability to recognize that they are "just thoughts." The author has found that clients who learn to discriminate thought from other kinds of stimuli characteristically regard the discovery as a revelation.

From "Meditation as Discrimination Training: A Theoretical Note," by C. G. Hendricks (*Journal of Transpersonal Psychology*, vol. 7, no. 2, 1975)

he may have lent it greater weight than he ever realized.

Similarly, a person with a social phobia (as stage fright is often conceptualized) is typically unaware of the grounds for that fear. This, again, is an awareness problem. To put the matter in a different context, if you panic on a wilderness walk and, when questioned, reply "I saw a snake, and I'm afraid of snakes," your fellow trekkers will tend to accept your answer. But they could legitimately continue, "Why? Was it poisonous? Was it near you and ready to strike?" If you continued, "I just have an irrational fear of snakes," or "I'm just very anxious, and snakes are one of the things that make me anxious," you might satisfy your companions. But your answer does not amount to an explanation. Certainly seeing the snake produces anxiety symptoms. The snake is clearly a "source" of anxiety. But why? The question is not so much "What are you afraid of?" as "Why are you afraid of what you're afraid of?" To find the answer you will have to analyze yourself. Until you do, you remain at the mercy of snakes—or heights, elevators, mice, or public speaking engagements.

Take the case of Wynn, an actor who regularly sabotages himself at auditions. What is so striking is the obviousness of his attitude—everyone concerned can't help but recognize his cynicism and flippancy. And the actor, too, is aware that he is bringing an "attitude" with him, but he is not aware *enough*. He is not able to ascertain

---

PRACTICING SUFFERING

Why do people keep suffering even when they "know they are the ones who are doing it"? It seems that people are unconscious or ignorant of what they are habitually doing. They do not know how they "make" pain, discomfort, sadness, etc. The purpose of practicing suffering, then, is to bring the method of making discomfort into awareness. The focus is on how discomfort is made, rather than on the external attributes (i.e., content) of a situation. Patients who are unable or unwilling to shift their focus from the content of suffering to its process are not successful in this therapy. The therapeutic task is to change the direction of attention and interest toward the discomfort rather than toward avoiding it.

From "Application of Awareness Methods in Psychotherapy," by Edward Wortz (*Journal of Transpersonal Psychology*, vol. 14, no. 1, 1982)

his real motives. If he could, he might understand that his attitude is the result of the following piece of self-protective logic: "If I am ironic and casual about the whole thing, I can't experience failure. I may fail to get the role, I may look like a jerk, I may alienate the casting director, but I won't *experience* failure, because I won't have stooped to playing their stupid little games."

The performer who magnifies her experience of anxiety, the person who has never examined his phobia, the self-sabotaging actor—all are insufficiently self-aware. To become more aware, they must *agree* to become more aware. They can't simultaneously grow aware and fight off self-understanding. They must contract with themselves to experience the anxiety of learning about themselves. If they can leap that hurdle and contract with themselves, they can begin to gain self-awareness.

How will you work to gain self-awareness?

_____

_____

_____

_____

Why do you suppose that we act slavishly with respect to our thoughts, even though we ourselves produce them? _____

_____

_____

Is there a single aspect of your inner life about which you would like to grow more aware? _____

_____

_____

_____

How will you practice self-awareness, so that you have the opportunity to learn about your thoughts—and dispute the ones that need disputing—on a regular basis? _____

_____

_____

_____

_____

What prevents you from understanding yourself? _____

_____

_____

What do you fear you would learn if you were to gain self-awareness? _____

_____

_____

_____

_____

Is that perhaps an old fear, no longer felt today? Are you perhaps better equipped to look at yourself today and deal with what you find? _____

_____

_____

_____

_____

Experiential Learning

The most useful and powerful way to gain self-awareness is to learn from our own experiences. I regularly teach a college course called "Personal and Professional Assessment" to adults returning to college after a long absence from school. In it students must write five experiential-learning essays in which they demonstrate that they have *learned something* from their experiences.

To have had experiences is not enough to gain them credit. They must demonstrate, by reflecting on their lives and analyzing and evaluating their experiences, that they can think and write intelligently about a given field of inquiry. They may write about alcoholism, divorce, office management, cancer, personal finance, or a hundred other topics, but in each case they are obliged to do more than anecdotally recite their personal experiences. They must reflect on alcoholism or office management and make use of their personal experiences to illuminate the larger concepts. This is exactly what a performer must do with respect to performance anxiety.

You may want to give yourself the same assignment I gave my class. Ask yourself: What have I learned from my firsthand experiences of performance anxiety? Write your answer freely and at length, for several pages at least, with an eye to answering just this question.

Possibly we learn a little something from all our experiences, even if we do not stop to reflect on them. But this is an open point. If we are strongly defended against the feelings we would feel if we really experienced life, it is likely that we learn very little from those experiences. Learning involves reflection, but even more fundamentally it involves our willingness and readiness to let down our guard and acknowledge the truth of our experiences.

This idea is at the heart of any long-term anxiety-management program. You already have enough presentation situations behind you from which to learn. You already have a wealth of data and the skills of mind to analyze that data. What you need are the courage and willingness to look at experiences that are likely to feel painful and embarrassing. If you have that courage and willingness, you will learn that experience is the best teacher.

An excellent example of learning from experience is the excerpt (see box) from actor Ed Hooks, who describes an experience he had when filming a scene of a TV series on which he had a recurring role.

Stopping to learn from your own experiences is the best awareness-training tool available to you. Toward that end, I recommend that you keep a performance notebook in which you record what you learn from your experiences of performing.

Remember that we're using "performance" in the broadest sense, so that a visit to an agent, a call on a customer, an appearance at a conference, or a post-concert reception might also get recorded in your book.

In your notebook record the following:

1. Specific details about the performance: the nature of the audience, the circumstances of the performance, and so on.

2. Whether you experienced performance anxiety, and if so, details about the experience. The richer and more detailed your observations are, the better.

3. Your thoughts and feelings about what transpired. Focus here on the internal "whys"—more on why you reacted in a certain way than on what the circumstances were that provoked the reaction.

4. Your thoughts about what you might have done differently or might do differently in the future.

AN ACTOR LEARNS FROM EXPERIENCE

Suddenly, as the camera began to roll, I realized that I didn't have a reason in the world for speaking, no objectives, no purpose other than to say the words and collect a check. I then seemed to mentally disconnect from my own self, sort of standing aside and watching myself as I grew pale under the makeup. I began to sweat profusely and my heart raced. Thoughts raced through my brain. "What if I can't say the words?" "What will the producers think of me?" "What if they can't finish the show because of me?" It was a moment of sheer terror. . . . For several months after that, I was afraid that it would happen again. I went into auditions trying to avoid negatives rather than pursuing positives, and I'm sure I lost some good jobs that way. Finally, I realized that I needed to reconnect with my roots as an actor, needed to get back in touch with what it is to play a pure action, to have a strong intention. I had become too accustomed to playing supporting TV roles that were frequently poorly written and merely relied on my personality to make them work. So, with my heart in my throat, I went out and got cast in a stage play. Knowing that I would be in front of an audience for prolonged periods of time each night and knowing that, if I was going to self-destruct there, it would be the end of acting for me altogether, I was nervous big-time. Fortunately, I stood toe-to-toe with the demon and won. The play was a success, I didn't fall apart, and I learned a valuable lesson. Now, no matter how trivial the role or acting challenge seems to be, I treat it like it is *Hamlet*, preparing myself fully, identifying my objectives and intentions as an actor. The terror has not happened since then.

Ed Hooks

5. Your thoughts about what activities or strategies you might incorporate into your long-term anxiety-management program. Does this particular experience tell you something about what you might do on a daily basis to reduce anxiety and feel stronger and calmer?

Begin this notebook as soon as possible. After a presentation of any sort has ended and you can spare a few minutes, find a private place and write in your notebook. The goal is to learn from your experiences.

Describe one experience in detail that reveals something about your anxious nature.

_____

_____

_____

_____

What have you learned from this experience?

_____
_____
_____
_____

What have you learned from your life experiences that you can put to use in rebuilding yourself as a less anxious person?

_____
_____
_____
_____

What specifically prevents you from learning from experience? _____
_____
_____
_____
_____

*How can you better train yourself to learn from experience? What techniques (like keeping a performance journal) might you employ?*_____
_____
_____
_____
_____

Awareness of Creative Issues

Performers face all the challenges that other human beings face, but because of their particular *personality* characteristics, the *nature of their work*, and the *world* in which they operate, they face many special challenges as well. For the performer—and perhaps for the nonperformer, too—the route to anxiety management includes understanding these three dimensions of a creative life.

On the level of *personality*, creative people are prone to depression, likely to feel alienated from the prevailing culture, and commonly desire solitude and time for introspection (even if they are also extroverted and exhibitionistic). They are likely to be intelligent (in a society that does not value intelligence), rebellious or nonconforming (even if also compliant), empathic (and so attuned to pain in the world), and honest (in a society that more values cunning and game-playing). Such personality traits present performers with significant questions that they must attempt to answer. How, for instance, is the actress to make use of her intelligence and creativity if the roles she garners do not inspire her? How is she to deal with her receptivity and empathic powers without experiencing too much of the world's suffering? To reduce anxiety and to find inner peace, she is obliged to bring these thorny issues into awareness and resolve them as best she can. The *creative work itself* requires a lot of technical and interpretive skill, and other anxiety issues develop. Can the soprano bring real heart to a Schubert song? Can she bring that heart and soul to repeated performances of the same set of songs on tour?

She must also learn to fathom her *place in society*. Is she essentially an entertainer? Is she looking for artistic success or commercial success? Does she mean to be popular and attract a large audience or work in an area of performance that she loves but which neither pays well nor attracts many fans? Does she happen to live in a society or a subculture that values performance as soul-nourishing and vital? Does she perhaps live in a society that scorns the "small" performance? What are her ethos, culture, and world like, and what is her place in them?

In a previous book of mine, *A Life in the Arts: Practical Guidance and Inspiration for Creative and Performing Artists*, I discuss artistic issues at length and provide scores of exercises that can help performers arrive at a better understanding of their personality, work, and world.

The special anxieties associated with the work that an artist does are also addressed—with suggested remedies—in my book *Fearless Creating: A Step-by-Step Guide to Starting and Completing Your Work of Art*. I especially recommend this book for the actor who dreams of penning a solo performance piece or the musician who also composes—that is, for the "creator" in each performer.

Indeed, one goal of a long-term anxiety-management program for any individual is to build up enough self-esteem and sense of security that he or she is able to launch creative projects—which themselves provoke new anxieties—and to bring performance anxiety into play.

The performer's person, work, and world must each be examined with discipline and courage, though the answers are unlikely to be perfect or even satisfactory ones. Making peace with the decisions that flow from this sort of self-analysis is a crucial step in gaining self-acceptance and inner calm. If you perform, you may remain conflicted about the sort of performer you mean to be; or angry at society for not valuing what you do; or at the marketplace for giving you so few opportunities to work; or unprovided with a

channel for your bristling intelligence. You may thus remain anxious and on edge. The challenges will not vanish by being ignored.

What is the creative side of your personality?

_____
_____
_____

What features or traits of your personality, by their very nature, cause you additional anxiety? _____

_____
_____
_____

Does anything about the work you do cause you day-in and day-out anxiety? _____

_____
_____
_____

Can you pinpoint what in the relationship of self, work, and world—your specific personality, the specific work you do, and the specific world you inhabit—is most anxiety-producing? _____

_____
_____
_____
_____

What techniques or strategies can you incorporate into your anxiety-management program that address the issues you've described? _____

_____
_____
_____
_____

Cognitive Restructuring

The literature on performance anxiety treatment suggests that cognitive-behavioral therapy is *the best way to treat performance anxiety*. It's therefore vital to understand the principles of cognitive-behavioral therapy and to implement cognitive techniques as part of your long-term anxiety-management program.

Simply put, cognitive-behavioral therapists believe that people can alter their experience of a situation by changing the way they think about themselves and the situation. They further believe that this cognitive restructuring is not only important but also achievable. James Coleman explains in *Abnormal Psychology and Modern Life*:

> Two main themes characterize cognitive-behavioral therapy: (a) the conviction that cognitive processes influence both motivation and behavior, and (b) the use of behavior-change techniques in a pragmatic, hypothesis-testing manner. That is, the therapy sessions are analogous to experiments in which the therapist and client apply learning principles to alter the client's cognitions, continuously evaluating the effects that the changes in cognitions have on both thoughts and outer behavior.

Recently I worked with a client, a painter, in this fashion. She wanted to attend an opening at a gallery because she admired the work of the painter exhibiting there. But she was afraid that the visit would depress her, because his array of paintings would remind her that she'd painted too little recently. She was certain that the experience of going to the opening would trigger the thought that regularly plagued her, namely: "I'm not good enough."

We worked on blocking or stopping that thought and on substituting new thoughts for it. This latter process required that she try out various thoughts in a hunt for ones that, when substituted for the negative thought, not only replaced it but even defused it. In her case there were two directions to take and many new thoughts to try out. First, she firmly believed that looking at the paintings was a necessary part of her process as a painter: that the experience would have value and meaning for her. The several thoughts that she would use when she attended the opening, created in session and meant to capture this idea of value, included the following: 1. "It's important that I be here." 2. "I want to be here." 3. "This is part of my process." 4. "This is an important part of my process."

She also felt that attending the opening would help her rekindle her love of art and, more broadly, serve to bring a measure of love into her life. While involved in an intimate relationship and while progressing nicely in a second career, she nevertheless felt that too little in her life had a loving feel to it. Visiting with art, like visiting with friends, had always helped take the chill out of life, and she wanted that experience again. She therefore tried out in session various thoughts to be used at the opening that might capture this idea, including the following: 1. "I love this." 2. "This makes me happy." 3. "It feels good to be here." 4. "I feel warm here." As she worked to find thoughts that could effectively be substituted for "I'm not good enough," she realized that the process of thought substitution involved one single, simple principle. It struck her that mental health was largely a matter of training herself—that is, training her thoughts—to dwell on *the positive and the present*. She realized that the words "positive" and "present" could themselves be used to block out unwanted thoughts or substitute for unwanted thoughts, and could even be used to inoculate herself beforehand so that unwanted thoughts didn't bubble to the surface.

According to Aaron Beck and other cognitive therapists, the negative self-talk that plagues people constellates into a certain number of characteristic "cognitive distortions" (see box, page 132).

At this point, you should stop and carefully consider these cognitive distortions.

Do your thoughts tend to pattern themselves in any of these ways? _____

_____

_____

Do you have a sense of how these cognitive distortions may have arisen? _____

_____

_____

_____

_____

As part of your anxiety-management program, what techniques will you use to alter distorted ways of thinking? (Some techniques are presented next, but try to create some of your own before reading on.)

_____

_____

_____

_____

_____

_____

Cognitive therapists employ various techiques designed to change faulty thinking patterns and encourage cognitive restructuring. These include questioning the validity of the client's hypotheses; decentering ("the process," according to Beck, "of prying the patient loose from the belief that he or she is the focal point of all events"); decatastrophizing (presenting "normal" or "usual" alternatives to the client's persistent worst-case scenarios); and helping the client acquire and practice "rational responses to dysfunctional thoughts." Other techniques include cognitive modeling, thought-stopping (see box, page 133), and stress inoculation.

The application of cognitive therapy to the treatment of performance anxiety has been studied quite a bit. In one study, fifty-three pianists were treated for performance anxiety either with behavior-rehearsal techniques or with cognitive therapy techniques (additionally, there were controls who received no treatment). Whereas the rehearsal techniques proved successful, the cognitive techniques proved even more successful.

Another study investigated the relative merits of treating performance anxiety with cognitive methods versus the anti-anxiety drug buspirone. The results again demonstrated the effectiveness of cognitive therapy.

COMMON TYPES OF COGNITIVE DISTORTIONS

1. *Selective abstraction:* focusing on a detail out of context.

2. *Arbitrary inference:* making conclusions on the basis of inadequate or improper information.

3. *Overgeneralization:* making blanket judgments or predictions based upon a single incident.

4. *Personalization:* overestimating the extent to which particular events are self-related.

5. *Polarized thinking:* sorting information into one of two dichotomous categories.

6. *Magnification and exaggeration:* overemphasizing the most unpleasant, negative consequences that can arise in any situation.

7. *Assuming excessive responsibility:* attributing negative events to one's supposed personal deficiencies.

8. *Incorrect assessment* regarding danger versus safety: overestimating the risk involved in situations.

9. *Dysfunctional attitudes* about pleasure versus pain: setting up prerequisites for true happiness or success—for example, "My value as a person depends on what others think of me."

10. *Automatic self-injunctions,* or "tyranny of the shoulds": unrealistically high standards for human conduct—for example, "I should know, understand, and foresee everything."

From "Principles of Cognitive Therapy," by Richard Bedrosian and Aaron Beck (Mahoney, M. J., ed., *Psychotherapy Process: Current Issues and Future Directions,* 1980)

It should be abundantly clear from the above discussion that cognitive work is a vital component of a performer's long-term anxiety-management program. If performing and making presentations are a part of your life, take steps to identify and record your negative self-statements and practice cognitive treatment methods like thought-stopping and thought substitution. Many books on this subject are available to you, and therapists who use this treatment mode may also be available in your area. There is magic in this method for those who can master it.

*How would you define "cognitive restructuring"?*_____
_____
_____
_____

*Are you aware of any techniques you can employ to alter your thought patterns, reduce negative self-talk, and so on?*_____
_____
_____
_____
_____

THOUGHT-STOPPING IN THERAPY

In this first phase of thought-stopping, the counselor assumes the responsibility for interrupting the thoughts. The interruption is overt, consisting of a loud *Stop!* that can be accompanied by a noise such as a hand clap, a ruler hitting a desk, or a whistle.

1. The counselor instructs the client to sit back and let any thoughts come to mind.

2. The counselor instructs the client to verbalize aloud these thoughts or images as they occur.

3. At the point where the client verbalizes a self-defeating thought or image, the counselor interrupts with a loud Stop! Sometimes, in addition, a loud noise stimulus such as a hand clap, a whistle, or a ruler hitting the desk is used.

4. The counselor determines whether the unexpected interruption was effective in terminating the client's negative thoughts or images.

From *Interviewing Strategies for Helpers*, by Cormier and Cormier

Describe how you will incorporate one or more of these techniques into your long-term anxiety-management program. _____

_____

_____

_____

_____

If you are not aware of any such techniques, what will you do to acquire them? _____

_____

_____

_____

Stress Reduction

It's an open question how well cognitive restructuring or any other therapeutic technique can work if a person remains beseiged by too many life stressors. It's a feat of nearly superhuman proportions to be able to effectively block thoughts, substitute thoughts, or positively reframe situations if the pressures of work, relationships, and the world remain too severe.

The typical performer's life is anything but serene and rather more resembles a wild rollercoaster ride. After the run of each play, actors are unemployed again (even if they still work at day jobs). One moment they are "up" because they are performing and energized, the next they are "down" because they are unemployed and auditioning again; they are up when called back for a role in a television series, then down when they don't land it. And so it goes. Ruby, musical-comedy actress, works a day job which itself is tiring and stressful. She takes a voice class one night a week, a dance class another night. Periodically her twelve-year-old car

breaks down and she is sometimes ill because of fatigue and stress. In a tumultuous relationship with another actor, one Monday she gets a call from her agent, who tells her she's being considered for a spot in a touring company of a popular musical. The director wants her to come in for an audition—not a cattle call, but one in which Ruby is one of a handful of actresses the director is considering. Her agent adds that the company will be on the road for a demanding eight months. Many thoughts run through her mind, and of the negative ones only some are related to performance anxiety. More are related to the everyday stressors in her life. Can she be separated from her boyfriend for eight months? Will there be a relationship to return to? Is she physically up to the demands of touring? Has stress worn her down so much that she's incapable of performing adequately? Will she take time off from her job the day before the call, in order to prepare? Will her job still be there for her if she goes on tour, and is the job too good to quit, if need be, for the sake of this tour?

Ruby is excited about the prospect of landing this role, but she feels her anxiety mounting. All these worries distract her and will perhaps prevent her from adequately preparing for the audition. She may feel the need to take tranquilizers. She may feel the need to call her friends and try to learn about this director, in order to eliminate some of her anxiety by making him a more known quantity. (Some of her friends will say the director is nice to work with, and some will have reports that will put another knot in her stomach.)

STRESS REDUCTION NOW

Take at least one active step now toward reducing the stress in your life. You might:

- Check with your health plan to see if they offer stress reduction workshops, biofeedback classes, yoga or meditation classes, and so on.

- In a bookstore, locate books on stress reduction. Look through them and select the one that makes the most sense to you. Begin to put into effect some of the stress-management strategies offered in that book.

- Begin to do that one thing you *know* helps to reduce your experience of stress. Is it walking three miles a day? Getting to the beach on the weekend? Talking with a certain friend?

- Learn one meditation technique and begin to use it.

- Learn one self-massage technique and begin to use it.

- Change one thing in your life that you know you need to change to reduce stress. Is it not talking to your mother so often (and then not feeling guilty about it)? Is it finding different day-care, changing your day job, making a new friend, somehow getting out of debt?

Start by doing just *one thing* that supports your intention of reducing the stress in your life.

She may try to put the audition out of her thoughts, trusting that she'll come through in the last minute. Thus Ruby may be prevented from giving her strongest audition, not because the part intimidates her or because audition situations frighten her, but because, under too much stress and negatively affected by it, she is unable to adequately prepare herself for the moment.

Everyone needs to manage stress on an ongoing basis. Some stressors can be eliminated, but others can only be managed.

The simple but effective stress-reduction techniques already known to you—a hot shower, a stroll by the ocean, a hot meal, an evening with a mystery novel—probably must be supplemented by other relaxation techniques. The use of biofeedback, guided visualizations, a meditation practice, or yoga; a regimen of regular exercise, decent diet, and sufficient rest; and contact with other living creatures—pets as well as people—can all help reduce the stress in one's life.

What stressors, quite apart from performing, currently affect you? _____
_____
_____
_____
_____

Which seem the most important to attempt to eliminate or reduce? _____
_____
_____
_____
_____

Can you devise a detailed plan for eliminating or reducing one of these significant stressors? _____
_____
_____
_____
_____
_____

What stress-reduction technique or strategy will you employ on an ongoing basis as part of your long-term anxiety-management program? _____
_____
_____
_____
_____
_____

Interpersonal Analysis

Performance anxiety is a problem embedded in a social context. Whether you have an audience of millions or of one, an audience real or imagined, seen or unseen—or just your own introjected critic—it is with respect to some audience or observer that you grow anxious. Therefore it helps to analyze your social and interpersonal interactions.

- What do you really have to be nervous about in the company of others?

- Are you really threatened at such times?

- Is your "paranoid quotient" appropriate or inappropriately high?

- Do you really have anything to fear from others in presentation situations?

Rather than having anything real to fear, isn't it more likely that you are simply made uncomfortable by the pressure to perform, by the pressure to hold up your end of a conversation, by your inability to remain calm in a charged social atmosphere, by a worry about how you'll look if you flub some of your lines or play the wrong notes?

Probably the best way to study the exact nature of one's relationship to others is in formal group work. The group can be a psychotherapy group formed for that purpose, a group formed by an acting, music, dance, or speech teacher (see box), groups like AA or Toastmasters, or a leaderless group formed by peers who are willing to work together to support and learn from each other. Not all such groups are successful, and not all such learning experiences are positive ones, but when they do work they provide information that can be obtained in no other way.

While you're working to gain confidence in interpersonal and group situations, you'll also want to work to identify those interactions that increase your performance anxiety.

PERFORMANCE ANXIETY SUPPORT GROUPS

The process begins with a support team of three to six who want to be more effective in front of groups.

1. Each person in turn takes three minutes in front of the group to take in total support and to see what comes up to say, or not to say.

2. The person maintains eye contact with the audience one at a time rather than scanning the group.

3. Dare to be boring rather than chattering to cover anxiety. Be willing to feel the anxiety.

4. Try to let the speech come from the relationship with the audience at that moment rather than from memory or ideas.

5. [In the second round] each person gets up for five minutes.

6. After each five-minute talk, the group gives the speakers the opportunity to quickly report on their experiences. The rest of the group gives brief, rapid-fire and supportive feedback.

From "Group Work and Stage Fright Recovery,"
by Lee Glickstein (*Recovering,* no. 54, June 1993)

Do you and your department manager need to iron something out that you've been afraid to talk about so far? Is something going on between you and other members of the cast that needs to be aired? Your goal of anxiety management is served by your increased ability to engage in direct talk when direct talk is necessary and to weather such interactions without guilt or other psychic distress.

Can you evaluate which aspects of your interpersonal relationships provoke performance anxiety? _____

_____

_____

_____

Do you tend to feel that your audience is sitting in judgment of you, or do you consider them friendly or at least neutral?

_____

_____

Are you overly concerned about the opinions of others? _____

_____

Do people in authority — directors, gallery owners, conductors, and bosses — tend to make you nervous? _____

_____

_____

Do your peers tend to make you anxious? ___

_____

_____

What one thing would you like to change about your interpersonal relationships? _____

_____

_____

_____

_____

What activities would you like to incorporate into your anxiety-management program to help you feel less anxious about your interpersonal relationships? _____

_____

_____

_____

Counseling and Therapy

That a person experiences butterflies before giving a speech or going on stage is not a reason to begin counseling. In a performer's life even a severe case of performance anxiety may occur as a "perfectly normal" event because a great deal rides on a given performance or because it is more difficult than anything he or she has undertaken before.

An actress with many roles under her belt may suddenly experience severe anxiety when auditioning for the lead in a TV sitcom. She can't help but realize that a hit series, one that is picked up by the net-

works, renewed, and eventually syndicated, will lead to her full financial independence. No more day job! A car that runs! Yes, fifty thousand members of the Screen Actors Guild earn less than $1000 a year, but a thousand earn more than $100,000 a year — so the results of today's audition could leapfrog her from the bottom of the pay ladder to the very top. Is there any wonder that she feels dizzy, has trouble breathing, or feels ready to die?

Regular bouts of mild performance anxiety and occasional bouts of severe performance anxiety can be handled in ways suggested in this book, by long-term anxiety-management and by techniques you can use before and during presentations. What, then, are good reasons to engage in counseling or psychotherapy? Recounting the experience of one well-known performer, Spalding Gray, interviewer Belinda Taylor wrote in *The San Francisco Chronicle*:

> Gray's autobiographical novel, *The Impossible Vacation* is a compelling page-turner, simultaneously quirky and jarring, about his mother's suicide some years ago when Gray was a young twenty-something and she was in the grip of a clinical depression. As we talked, Gray opened a prescription vial, took out a pill, and swallowed it. I asked what he'd just taken. "Klonopin," he said, unhesitatingly. "It's an anti-anxiety drug. I take lithium, too. I'm bipolar depressive." Back to his mother. Gray said she was 52 when she

killed herself, the age he is now. He said if he survives this year he will have outlived his mother, a milestone that carries more than casual significance for him, especially in light of his revelation that in recent months both his father and his therapist have died.

Gray's circumstances suggest that psychotherapy has been and may continue to be of value to him. Both his severe mood swings and the wounds left by his mother's suicide are the sorts of human problems that can be effectively addressed in therapy.

Some past experience may have been particularly harmful to you also. A client of mine who played the trumpet still felt, in his early fifties, the sting of his high school band conductor's withering criticisms. Served up by parents, friends, peers, teachers, critics, agents, directors, or conductors, critical remarks may so profoundly get under a performer's skin that, like little murders, they kill the performer's desire to perform and ability to do so without anxiety. The detective work of therapy may help to solve these little murders.

A particular experience of failure may likewise prove difficult to forget. Did you do poorly giving a vitally important talk in your first job? Did you bomb in a college play? The cutting remarks of others and the knowledge of our own unfortunate failures are often secrets that we carry around with us. As secrets, they have the power to wound us over and over again. Letting them out in therapy may remove their sting for all time.

But what if your performance anxiety is rooted more in your formed personality than in an event or secret? Can you gain insight into the system when *you* are the system, when you are both the observer and the observed? Psychotherapists argue that, with their help, people can indeed gain insight into their own personalities. Formerly blind to the ways they hurt or hinder themselves, clients learn in therapy to become more psychologically-minded and aware of their motivations and behavior. Even as their defenses remain intact, protecting them from the therapist's comments (which can feel accusatory), they can, in a good therapeutic relationship, let down their guard enough to learn about themselves. What sort of treatment might then occur? From our earlier discussion of cognitive restructuring you have an idea how a cognitive-behavioral therapist might work, by identifying negative self-talk, teaching thought-stopping and thought substitution techniques, and so on. A psychodynamic approach (see box, page 140) might work equally well.

A given therapist may specialize in working with phobias, panic attacks, and other anxiety disorders or may pursue anxiety-reduction from some specific theoretical orientation—existential, gestalt, humanistic, transpersonal, self-psychological, and so on. Sometimes even a single session with the right practitioner can produce important and even remarkable results. Stephanie Judy writes, in *Making Music for the Joy of It*:

> I was treated for stage fright on a stage, in front of fifty people. The therapist was a Neurolinguistic

Programming (NLP) practitioner, doing a demonstration for a group of students. The improvement was immediate and it has lasted. On a scale of 10, my nervousness has gone from a paralyzing 9.9 to an acceptably anxious 3, though I still have to work at it.

PSYCHODYNAMIC TREATMENT OF A CELLIST'S ANXIETY

In therapy, the patient, a talented cellist with severe performance anxiety issues, quickly developed a dependent transference on me, yearning for my approval and not wanting to leave my office after sessions were over. He longed for my words of approval. He recalled experiences of childhood where he felt especially close to his mother, since his father frequently traveled out of town on business trips. During the early stages of his therapy he took several auditions, always experiencing such severe stage fright that he knew his chances were eliminated before he left the audition. Also, his tendinitis often flared after lengthy hours of intense practice prior to these auditions. It became evident during his therapy that each time he traveled to a new city to audition, he became angry at me for "allowing" him to leave. It felt as though I was sending him away (just as it felt that his teacher was sending him away when therapy was suggested). The only way he could express this anger (and guilt for feeling angry) was indirectly, by unconsciously sabotaging his audition. . . .

As we worked through unconscious issues and the feelings they engendered, the patient gradually began to realize how he was re-experiencing and re-enacting his past in the present. Conductors and I had become parent substitutes and authority figures whom he had to please in order to be nurtured and loved. His failure at auditions had an unconscious protective meaning for him—he could stay at "home." Also, by not winning auditions, he was punished for his perceived transgressions, such as his rivalry with his father for the favor of his mother. Before treatment, his conflict sabotaged his quest for independence and adult autonomy. After treatment, he was successful in winning a chair in a good orchestra and currently is enjoying his life without debilitating anxiety and self-doubts.

From "When Good Teaching Isn't Enough," by Julie Nagel (*American Music Teacher*, Feb.–Mar. 1991)

When, then, should a person include psychotherapy or counseling as part of a long-term anxiety-management program? Answer: In any one of the following cases.

1. If your symptoms or experience of distress are severe.

2. If a family history of disturbances is burdensome to you or suggests to you that there may be hereditary links to your present state of distress.

   If you are the child of an alcoholic parent, if one of your parents committed suicide, if there is a history of severe depression in your family, you may be more susceptible to these problems than the next person.

3. If you have identified certain specific issues you want to work on with a therapist.

   A study conducted by Farley and Lealien in 1981 concluded that while there were no gender differences as to the amount of performance anxiety experienced by their subjects, males and females differed in their self-reports about the causes of their performance anxiety. Both males and females listed "loss of control" as their chief anxiety, but fear of failure ranked second with males and fourth with females, while the opposite held true for rejection, which was number two among females and number four among males. Thus a woman might come into therapy with a clear idea that she wanted to work on "rejection issues" while a man might come in wanting to work on "fear of failure" issues.

4. If medication, including anti-anxiety medication, is desired or required.

   It is possible to use medications without also engaging in psychotherapy, but it is generally wiser to use medications in conjunction with "talk" therapy.

5. If you have the desire to work on performance anxiety issues with someone who specializes in that sort of work.

   You might check with people who perform regularly for a word-of-mouth recommendation—ask a voice, music, or acting teacher for suggestions—or contact a local medical or university counseling clinic. Or simply look for a clinic or therapist who specializes in anxiety work (in working with phobias, panic attacks, and so on).

Counseling can prove valuable to you, but only if you actively take part in the process by bringing up the issues that concern you and by then working to make changes in your life. Although counseling may not turn out to be a necessary component of your long-term anxiety-management program, it is a possibility worth considering.

If you've previously engaged in counseling, what did you find to be its strong points?

_____
_____
_____
_____
_____

*Its weak points?*_____
_____
_____
_____
_____

*What would you look for in your next
counselor or psychotherapist?* _____

_____

_____

_____

_____

*If you haven't engaged in psychotherapy
before, have you felt the need or desire to do
so but found yourself resistant? If so, can you
analyze that resistance?* _____

_____

_____

_____

_____

*What do you think a good therapeutic
relationship would be like?* _____

_____

_____

_____

_____

Discipline Practice

Pianist and conductor Vladimir Ashkenazy
reflected on the management of anxiety
within his performing discipline:

> Working hard at practice is also the
> best defense I know against pre-
> concert nervousness. It can never
> be entirely eliminated but can be
> psychologically prepared for by
> convincing oneself that one has
> done all the homework necessary
> for a solid performance and that
> everything will work out all right.

Or, as Spencer Tracy succinctly put it,
"First of all, learn your lines."

This advice can't be underlined enough.
But practice means considerably more than
repetitive playing of one's repertoire, hon-
ing of one's audition pieces, and rehearsing
of responses to interview questions. It also
means practicing those techniques and
strategies that help you present yourself
more confidently and fearlessly.

Kato Havas, in *Stage Fright: Its Causes
and Cures,* analyzes the fears that violinists
typically encounter. Among these are a fear
of dropping the violin, of a trembling bowing arm, of being out of tune, of high positions and shifts, of not being loud enough,
and of not being fast enough. To combat
each fear Havas suggests certain exercises
and "cures," as for instance with respect to
the fear of a memory lapse (see box).

The procedures Havas describes help
the performers *learn* music, not merely
repeat it or memorize it. Similar procedures
can help actors learn a script (see box, page
144), speechmakers learn a speech, or test-
takers learn test material.

Every performer benefits from "deep-
learning" material as part of his or her
practice regimen, for, apart from its other
benefits, deep learning is an anxiety-
reducer. We recognize the truth of this if
we remember Suzuki's definition of anxiety as essentially an incomplete knowledge
of a given situation. The more we know
about the material we must present, the
more complete our knowledge, the less
anxious we feel.

Similarly, it helps to identify anything you
fear about your material, discipline, instrument, and so on. You then need to create

FEAR OF MEMORY LAPSE

Many players memorize only through their fingertips. This works—while playing at home. But the moment the player is exposed to any stresses and strains, i.e. an examination, audition or public performance, the fingertips do not have the necessary physiologic authority to carry him through. Cures:

1. A release from physical blockages.

2. The division of each piece into sections.

3. The identification of the notes within each section through singing, and miming with the rhythmic pulse before playing it on the violin.

4. The alive *lead* of the left-hand control with the bowing arm responding.

5. The elimination of the "self" through a systematic training of the mind.

The learning of a piece through the total coordination of mind and body not only helps the player release physical tensions when on stage, but also enables him to give full vent to his musical imagination.

From *Stage Fright: Its Cause and Cures*, by Kato Havas

exercises to combat or exorcise those fears, practicing the exercises as part of your practice regimen. For instance, if you must make an oral presentation, do you fear that the quality of your voice or something about your posture is reducing the effectiveness of your speeches? If you are an actor, do you fear dialects or fear that your own regional accent is losing you roles? If you are a singer, do you fear that, while you can sing opera, you can't act opera? *Each of these challenges can be met, but only if you include meeting them as part of your practice regimen.*

How will you go about learning your material in a deeper way? Can you map out a plan? __

_____

_____

_____

What about your discipline, material, or instrument scares you the most (fast passages, long speeches, your reed failing)? Being specific and creative, how can you better handle these problem areas? _____

_____

_____

_____

ABSORBING A SCRIPT

I opened the workshop by saying, "I think I have found a way to learn a script in one reading." Then I gave these instructions: "Read the script through slowly on as deep a level as possible, seeing and feeling everything that takes place. If it is in a restaurant, be in that restaurant. See and feel and hear and smell what it is like. Create your own version of the restaurant. If you are aware that you're thinking, 'That's a long speech,' or if you find yourself wondering what happens next, then you have stopped feeling and started thinking. Stop reading, breathe deeply, and go back to feeling the script again." By the end of the scene everyone was joining in and even correcting small details. There was tremendous certainty and enthusiasm, and I began to get excited about our success.

From *Setting Free the Actor,* by Ann Brebner

Have you noticed a clear relationship between a lack of practice and performance anxiety? Can you describe that relationship?

_____
_____
_____
_____

What sort of ideal practice routine would you like to set up for yourself? _____

_____
_____
_____
_____

Discipline Understanding

The processes that Kato Havas and Ann Brebner describe above facilitate not only your deep learning of your material but also a more thorough understanding of the particular discipline you are engaged in. In such ways you come to really absorb the intent of the firm's top sales strategist, the playwright, or the choreographer, and that absorption both enriches your creativity and reduces your anxiety.

You begin to understand the music you're playing in multiple ways. You learn not only how the notes go but about its structure and design, about the story the music is telling, about the emotional resonances of the piece. You learn not only the words of your presentation, but where to pause for effect, which ideas you really want to sell, and how you mean to build to a powerful finish. You begin to understand the play in multiple ways, not only learning speeches but really experiencing the conflagrations in Sophocles' *Antigone* or the dynamic tension between upholding tradition and achieving personal liberty in a play by the contemporary Chinese dramatist Bai Fengxi.

Deeply understanding your discipline will reduce your anxiety, but in order to attain that you must approach your encounters with the material more openly, expansively, and calmly than perhaps you do currently. To do this you may want to change the cognitive instructions you give yourself, in order to enter into a new relationship with the company plan, the score, the script, and so on (see box).

Prodigious and even amazing feats of mind and memory are the fruits of a richer relationship with the discipline in which you are working. Like novelists who carry everything they need to know about their characters around in their minds and never worry about losing track of them, or like Mozart, composing different pieces simultaneously, you can, if deeply connected to your discipline and material, produce miracles of memory.

"DO THIS" VS. AWARENESS INSTRUCTIONS

The way to change a "do this" instruction into an awareness instruction is simply to rephrase it so that the focus of attention is on the experience. Here are some examples.

"Do This" Instruction	*Awareness Instruction*
Draw the bow perpendicular to the bow string.	Notice the angle of the bow when the resistance is steady.
Don't clip your consonants at the ends of the phrases.	Listen to the sound of the consonants at the ends of your phrases. See if you can clearly hear the words.
You must play these bars forte, and you're too loud. Play with correct intonation.	Notice what forte level allows the piano still to be heard. Be aware of your intonation. Notice when or if you're playing sharp or flat. Notice how sharp or how flat.

From *The Inner Game of Music*, by Larry Green and Timothy Gallway

Michael Raucheisen, a pianist and accompanist to the violin virtuoso Fritz Kreisler, told the following story:

> When we arrived in Tokyo we found that the Japanese attached special importance to sonatas. During the eight performances at the Imperial Theatre of Tokyo, Kreisler was expected to perform virtually the entire existing sonata literature. Kreisler had, of course, not prepared for such an unusual situation. Imagine, eight different programs! And yet, one—I repeat —one rehearsal sufficed and Kreisler played the sonatas which he had not had on his repertoire for many years, by heart, without a single flaw of memory, before this select international public. "I never have any trouble remembering," Kreisler said. "I know the music so well that I do not even keep the violin part. I get it into my head with its accompaniment."

To learn *by heart* is the goal. Such a deep understanding has a warming, calming influence, counteracting the anxiety we all feel when we know things only shallowly and superficially.

Can you describe what "deepening your relationship" to your discipline might mean?

_____

_____

_____

_____

Does your description suggest some concrete actions you might take to foster that deepening? _____

_____

Is your relationship to your discipline a loving one? Describe the ways in which it is and/or is not.

_____

_____

_____

_____

How can you help yourself enter into a more open and loving relationship with your discipline? _____

_____

_____

_____

_____

Preparation

Everything we've discussed so far might be thought of as preparation. But even in the narrowest sense, "preparation" should include more than getting your clothes pressed, thinking about your character one last time, or organizing the note cards for your speech. It should also include all of the following:

- Taking care of the business end of the event, like mailing out announcements to your mailing list, creating interview opportunities, personally inviting the people you really want to come, and so on.

- Arriving at the point of feeling satisfied about (or accepting) the nature and quality of the material you will perform: the speech, the concert program, song set, play, and so forth.

- Arriving at the point of feeling satisfied about (or accepting) your readiness to make your presentation.

- Creating a mental-image rehearsal of the presentation. Part of the process of effectively preparing for such an event is picturing it in your imagination. Try rehearsing, detail by detail, the whole occasion— beginning prior to your arrival and including the time after your departure.

This last item is worth underlining. Apart from the other benefits this mental rehearsing affords, it serves to desensitize you to the "performance environment." As Ann Seagrave and Faison Covington explain in *Free from Fears*:

> Imagery desensitization gives us an opportunity to think or imagine a situation the way we would *like* it to occur. Instead of imagining that a catastrophe befalls you, imagine that you will feel comfortable and secure in the situation, filled with confidence about your skills. If, as you are doing this, anxiety creeps into your conscious thoughts, stop the imaginary event, use your relaxation technique, and then begin again. Depending on the event, it may take days to go all the way through the exercise free of anxiety, but rest assured that you *will* reach the point of being able to think through or imagine a

feared situation without having an anxiety reaction.

Studies by psychologist Donald Meichenbaum, who has developed a cognitive theory of behavior change, have shown how the use of mental imagery can become a technique of great power and versatility. (see box, page 148).

When you mentally rehearse you provide yourself with the chance to practice the coping skills and anxiety-management techniques you will have learned here and in the next chapter. You bring the presentation to mind, notice your own negative thoughts or anxiety reactions, and *stop everything* in order to try a technique out right then and there. Mental imaging provides you with the miraculous opportunity to work through the presentation in the privacy of your own mind.

Each performer will need to create a personal preparation plan. For example, Stephanie Judy recommends that musicians play their program "cold" at least once a day; arrange some "dry runs" that simulate the concert hall experience (maybe in front of a small audience of their friends); rehearse, if possible, in the hall where they'll be performing; and practice until they are satisfied with the program. These rehearsal preparations, including mental imaging of the presentation situation and the disciplined practice of anxiety-management techniques, reduce anxiety in the days and weeks leading up to the event and help ensure your readiness at curtain time.

Try mentally imaging an upcoming performance. When you've completed the

IMAGERY CONTRIBUTES TO BEHAVIOR CHANGE

. . . Meichenbaum uses three main psychological processes to explain why imagery-based therapies contribute to change. The first process is the sense of control that a client develops out of the monitoring and rehearsing of various images. This sense of control over images and inner thoughts in turn helps the client have a greater sense of control over his emotions and overt interpersonal behavior. The second process involves changing for the client the meaning of his maladaptive behavior. This changed meaning will be reflected in altered internal dialogue that is evident before, during, and after instances of the problem behavior. The third process is the mental rehearsal of behavioral alternatives that contribute to the development of coping skills. By engaging in this mental problem-solving the occurrence of the client's own symptoms will become a reminder to use the coping skills he has learned.

From "Imagery in Cognitive-Behavior Therapy: Research and Application," by Paul Crits-Chistoph and Jerome Singer (*Clinical Psychology Review*, vol. 1, 1981)

process, describe what you learned from the experience.

Apart from learning the material, how do you currently prepare for presentations? _____

_____

_____

_____

_____

What additional preparations would you like to begin to make? _____

_____

_____

_____

_____

Working Step by Step

Ten large areas of concern have been covered in this chapter. To put together a long-term anxiety-management program that addresses all these issues is a prodigious feat. But you can accomplish it by tackling the issues step by step.

Certain things you will want to do on a daily basis, like using your favorite stress reduction technique or mentally imaging your next presentation. Some will more naturally occur at longer intervals — psychotherapy, the maintenance of a performance journal, and so on. You will need to spend some real time with yourself in order to construct a program that suits you and takes into account the many aspects of personal growth and anxiety management discussed in this chapter.

Take some time now and begin to construct a robust, complete anxiety-management program for yourself. Describe the actions you will take and the techniques you will employ.

The purpose of this plan is as much about healing yourself as it is about reducing anxiety. The goals are greater self-confidence, fewer episodes of self-sabotage, and a real increase in self-love. Consider the words of one performer, the concert pianist, conservatory teacher, and career counselor Peggy Salkind. She writes:

> Musical performance is a celebration of aliveness and an existential challenge. Each time I sit down and play the piano I relive the most poignant emotions and experiences of my life. They are always present in the music. During those moments I also explore new avenues of feeling and deepen my philosophical perceptions. I remember as a ten-year-old child practicing the andante movement of Mozart's Sonata K. 545, and realizing that playing music was somehow connected to love. I know now that it is a reservoir of feelings containing the ultimate distillation of love. That awareness has guided my life. Music enables me to open my heart to my mortal brothers and sisters and to assimilate the beauty and terror of existence.
>
> Piano performance is not without nervousness and anxiety. Those aspects reflect the existential dilemma of being an artist and of being human. The horizon is never fixed. The player no sooner chooses how to execute a particular passage and then he or she is faced with the decision of how to follow up on that choice. And so it continues from second to second and phrase to phrase. The sense of risk-taking is tremendous. But so is the exhilarating sensation of aliveness. In confluence with the score, I create and recreate myself in each succeeding moment. I learn that to be human is not to be perfect but to persevere in giving myself over and over again to the dynamic energy of the universe of which music is an integral vibration. By daring to simultaneously discover and reveal myself in the presence of others, I keep faith with life. My humanity is reborn with every breath and every note.

6
Strategies and Techniques

Some readers will have turned to this chapter first, in order to arm themselves immediately with some anxiety-management techniques. Other readers will have read the preceding chapters and may even have put into place a long-term anxiety-management program. Both groups are confronted now by the challenge of selecting strategies to be rehearsed and then put into practice before and during their presentations. These strategies constellate into the following dozen categories:

1. Medication, Diet, and Diet Supplements

2. Relaxation Techniques

3. Breathing and Meditation Techniques

4. Reorienting Techniques

5. Guided Visualizations

6. Affirmations and Prayers

7. Disidentification Techniques

8. Symptom Confrontation Techniques

9. Discharge Techniques

10. Ceremonies and Rituals

11. Preparation Techniques

12. Cognitive Techniques

You may wonder if these strategies aren't too simple to work. But there's nothing simple about putting any new habit into place. Try your hand at thought-blocking as the audience filters in. Try it right now, with no pressure on you. Try your hand at constructing a calming visualization while the orchestra plays the overture. Try this, too, right now, in the safety of your living room. Even making use of something as simple as an affirmation—just being able to say to yourself "I can do this!" or "I'm glad to be here!" as butterflies dance in your stomach—turns out to be quite a feat.

Building an Arsenal of Techniques

Perhaps the first step in developing a ready arsenal of useful strategies is simply this reminder to the reader who has not read the preceding chapters: that your central tasks include finding inner peace and strength, on the one hand, and being very well-prepared for the presentation, on the other. These are tasks, already covered in the preceding pages, that cannot possibly be completed in the last minutes before going before your audience. In regard to the present material, consider these five steps:

Step 1. Read through all the techniques. Run through all the techniques before settling on any one. Which feel the most congenial? Which seem best-suited to managing your particular symptoms? Mentally give each technique a chance.

Step 2. Select a few and try them out. Practice them. See if you understand them. See if you can make them work. *To begin with, they may raise your anxiety.* This is natural. Do not discard a technique merely because you find it hard, unnatural, or anxiety-provoking. Give it a chance. Try to be patient.

Step 3. Imagine a presentation situation. Use your mental imagery skills and visualize yourself about to go on. See if you can make use of your new strategy in that visualization. Do you see how it might work? Is some fine- tuning needed? Change the strategy to fit what you learn from the visualization. Tinker with the words of your affirmation or try another breathing exercise if your first choice doesn't seem quite right.

Step 4. Create a harmless but potent presentation situation and try out your techniques. See if the strategy you plan to use really reduces your anxiety. See if you seem more present, less rushed, more capable. Learn from the experience.

Step 5. Try out your techniques before and during the presentations that matter. See if and how they work. See if you are practiced enough to actually use them, or if you revert to white-knuckling it. Continue practicing techniques between presentations and try out new ones.

As you read through the following techniques, imagine yourself in the wings a few minutes before a speech or performance, when your anxiety is at its greatest. The techniques you'll want to adopt are those that will provide relief at exactly such times.

Medication, Diet, and Diet Supplements

Many professional performers use both prescription and nonprescription drugs to manage their performance anxiety. This is a controversial subject, and no easy answers are available. Might a performer take anti-anxiety medication on a regular basis? Might he or she take it only before the most important performances? It's a fact of life that people take drugs to help them quell their anxieties, so much so that the psychiatrist Barry Blackwell predicted, "With the arrival of the millennium the whole of America will be taking tranquilizers."

The most commonly used anti-anxiety prescription drug among performers is propranolol, a beta-blocking drug sold under the trade name of Inderal. In the survey of 2,200 classical musicians mentioned previously (page 10), 27 percent said they used a beta blocker, and 70 percent of those said they used one without a prescription or medical supervision (that is, they borrowed or bought the drug from another performer).

Are beta blockers actually effective? According to Dr. Michael Liebowitz, director of the Anxiety Disorders Clinic at the New York State Psychiatric Institute, they are generally effective if the performer's symptoms are primarily physical ones like sweating, heart palpitations, and tremors. They appear significantly less effective if the symptoms are primarily psychological. In the study of 94 musicians referred to previously, 10 of the 15 who suffered from severe performance anxiety and who tried Inderal reported that the drug was not effective in reducing their feelings of anxiety.

Different performers have different experiences with beta blockers. The singer Anna Moffo explained, "My doctor gave me Inderal once for a rehearsal. I was slowed down. I still felt nervous but just weak, with no adrenaline. I thought, 'I couldn't possibly do a performance tonight.' So I never tried the drug for a performance."

But Elma Kanefield, coordinator of psychological services at the Juilliard School, noted that Inderal has seductive appeal for many performers: "The problem with Inderal is, it's so appealing. It can quiet the obsessive thinking—'God, I shouldn't be out here' or 'No sound is going to come out' or 'The audience will hate me.' It quells those thoughts by distancing the worries. What people don't realize is that they become psychologically dependent on it."

Klaus Neftel and his fellow authors of "Stage Fright in Musicians: A Model Illustrating the Effect of Beta Blockers" do not believe that psychological dependency is an issue. They concluded:

> It is our personal belief that beta blockade in stage fright should only be used under medical control and with well-balanced indications, e.g., a serious impairment of public performance in a professional musician. In our experience, psychological dependency on the beneficial effects of single-dose beta blockade in regularly performing musicians is not a relevant problem. In contrast, the sometimes striking results seem able to reinforce self-confidence for future performances. Therefore, a combination of beta blockade and psychological training may be a reasonable answer.

A different view with regard to singers is presented by Dr. George Gates in a letter to the *New England Journal of Medicine*:

> We tested the use of nadolol to control performance anxiety in students of singing and found that it did not enhance performance when given in low doses and that it actually detracted from performance in higher doses. In contrast to an instrumentalist, a singer is the musical instrument, and a tension-free performance may be perceived as lacking emotion, dull, or otherwise

uninteresting. The control of performance anxiety through maturation and behavior modification is preferable to pharmacologic shortcuts.

Paul Salmon and Robert Meyer argued, in *Notes from the Green Room*, that if performers found themselves in either one of two presentation situations, they might consider using beta blockers (see box).

Given the possible side effects of taking beta blockers, including lowered blood pressure, impaired memory, sleep disturbances, depression, fatigue, and even hallucinations, and considering that the use of drugs does not support your goals of achieving inner calm and emotional strength, you may well want to postpone using a beta blocker until

you've tried the other anxiety-reducing strategies available to you. The decision is ultimately yours—in consultation with a physician who is aware of the pros and cons of using anti-anxiety medications.

*What is your experience of using drugs (prescription, nonprescription, alcohol) to help manage performance anxiety?*_____
_____
_____
_____

*What have you learned from these experiences?*_____
_____
_____
_____

USING BETA BLOCKERS IN CERTAIN SITUATIONS

We believe that the use of drugs, such as beta-blockers, may be appropriate under certain conditions. First, when other measures have failed, performers with chronic, disabling anxiety in performance situations may benefit from the use of medications that help control the disturbing symptoms. Performers with histories of chronic anxiety may find that the abrupt cessation of some of the physiological symptoms of anxiety brings a tremendous sense of relief. This may give the performer a glimpse of what it is like to perform without disabling anxiety symptoms. The second situation in which one might consider using beta-blockers would be a performance that is absolutely critical to a performer's development or career. Under such circumstances, it might be argued that a performer should use any therapeutic agent that will result in or contribute to optimal performance.

From *Notes from the Green Room,*
by Paul Salmon and Robert Meyer

If you are a "pro-drug" sort of person, discuss the downside of employing drugs to handle performance anxiety _____

_____

_____

_____

*If you are an "anti-drug" sort of person, discuss the upside of using drugs to manage performance anxiety.*_____

_____

_____

_____

*Do you fear that if drugs worked to quell your anxious feelings, you would become psychologically dependent on them?*_____

_____

_____

Do you see a difference between "relying" on anti-anxiety medication and using such drugs "occasionally"? _____

_____

_____

It may also be helpful, through a journal-writing exercise, to hold a dialogue with yourself about the pros and cons of using prescription medication to reduce your experience of performance anxiety.

Taking care of what and when you eat can help in reducing anxiety before making your presentation. The right kinds of food can have a soothing effect, and the wrong kinds can cause upset. Bland food is recommended: A turkey sandwich and a glass of milk is one sort of traditional pre-performance meal. Some people prefer to eat nothing or next to nothing, to scrupulously avoid caffeine and alcohol, and in general to take the path of abstinence.

Dr. Douglas Hunt, who advocates treating all forms of anxiety with nutritional supplements, recommends a specific array of supplements for quelling performance anxiety (see box).

The relationship between the ingestion of a substance—whether beta blocker, vitamin supplement, nicotine, protein shake, or double espresso—and its increase or reduction of your anxiety is a personal matter. Carefully experiment with various pre-performance regimens, monitor your experiments, and make changes that seem appropriate and necessary.

Are you aware of a relationship between what you eat or drink and your experience of performance anxiety? _____

_____

_____

What is your experience with stimulants (like coffee) and performance anxiety? _____

_____

_____

_____

_____

*What is your experience with depressants (like alcohol) and performance anxiety?*_____

_____

_____

_____

_____

Do particular foods increase your experience of performance anxiety? _____

_____

*Do particular foods help reduce your
experience of performance anxiety?*_____
_____
_____

*What do you think is an ideal pre-
performance meal for you?*_____
_____
_____
_____
_____

Relaxation Techniques

Few of us relax very often or very well, and
many of the activities that do manage to
relax us—like gardening or bathing—are
hardly available to us as we wait in the
wings. Those techniques that are available,
like progressive relaxation exercises, self-
massage, self-hypnosis, the Sarnoff Squeeze,
or the Quieting Reflex, first must be learned
and practiced. These techniques are not
abstract ideas but are hands-on procedures
that require mastering.

Progressive relaxation exercises are
designed to work by relaxing different muscles groups in sequence. Renee Harmon
presents a short progressive relaxation exercise in her book *How to Audition for Movies
and TV*; she provides the following exercise, which takes about thirty seconds:

Relax your forehead.

Relax the area around your eyes.

Relax the corners of your mouth.

Listen to the sounds surrounding
you but do not concentrate on them.

NUTRITIONAL TREATMENT OF STAGE FRIGHT

Take the following nutritional supplements one hour before the performance:

Thiamine—500mg

Calcium lactate—1,000 mg

Choline—1,000 mg

Niacinamide—500 mg

Vitamin B6—50 mg

Biotin—2,000 mcg

Aspirin—5 grains

Pantothenic acid—1,000 mg

Folic acid—800 mcg (take four of
these tablets)

From *No More Fears*, by Douglas Hunt

*Note: Please consult Dr. Hunt's book before beginning this nutritional
program, and begin it only in consultation with your own physician.*

Feel your arms and legs become heavy. At the point of the most intense heaviness, imagine that all your tension flows out of your body. Your fingertips are the exit points.

Feel sunshine warm your stomach.

Lift your chin and smile.

Mental relaxation exercises can be supplemented with physical relaxation exercises like self-massage. Take the time to massage your hands, forearms, upper arms, shoulders, and neck. In doing so, give yourself real pleasure. Make the little sounds that express your satisfaction: Exhale, sigh, groan a little. Find the knot in your shoulder and work it hard. Lose yourself in the process.

Some people who perform find that *self-hypnosis* techniques, which they learn from a certified or licensed hypnotherapist, help them relax. The concert musician Robert Aitken, for one, explained,

It's a very useful thing. I think many of the great musicians always used it, maybe without knowing it. It can even be used for very specific purposes, like speeding up a trill.

The Sarnoff Squeeze is named after the actress Dorothy Sarnoff, who described the technique in *Never Be Nervous Again*. She learned this relaxation technique from watching Yul Brynner backstage before performances of *The King and I*. The technique worked as follows:

Sit down in a straight-backed chair. Carry your rib cage high, but not so high that you're in a ramrod straight military position. Incline slightly forward. Now put your hands together in front of you, your elbows akimbo, your fingertips pointing upward, and push so that you feel an isometric opposing force in the heels of your palms and under your arms. Say *sssssssss*, like a hiss. As you're exhaling the *s*, contract those muscles in the vital triangle (below the ribs, where they begin to splay) as though you were rowing a boat against a current, pulling the oars back and up. Relax the muscles at the end of your exhalation, then inhale gently. While you're waiting to go on, sit with your vital triangle contracting, your lips slightly parted, releasing your breath over your lower teeth on a silent *ssss*.

Dr. Charles Stroebel, in his book *Quieting Reflex Training for Adults*, advocates the following four-step Quieting Reflex as a primary relaxation technique:

1. Become aware of the stimulus you are responding to (say, the sounds of the audience arriving or a "what if" thought).

2. Give yourself the suggestion, "Alert mind, calm body."

3. Smile inwardly with your eyes and mouth to reverse their tendency to go into a grim set.

4. Inhale slowly and easily to a count of two, three, or four, imagining your breath

coming through the pores in your feet. A feeling of "flowing warmth and flowing heaviness coming up through the middle of your legs" may accompany this mental image. As you exhale, let your jaw, tongue, and shoulders go limp, feeling that wave of heaviness and warmth flowing to the toes.

Part of the work of relaxing before and during a performance is to gain permission from yourself to relax. You may currently believe that you are *supposed* to feel tense at such times, that that is natural or even desirable. But such a thought is worth blocking and replacing with a new one: *You can be as relaxed as you like.*

*Do you have permission from yourself to relax or are you "supposed" to be worried about something all the time?*_____

_____

_____

How might you gain permission from yourself to relax? What might you say to yourself or do for yourself to help gain that permission? _____

_____

_____

_____

*Try to think with a fresh mind about relaxation. What does the word mean to you?*_____

_____

_____

_____

What sorts of things help you relax? _____

_____

_____

_____

_____

_____

Which of these might be well-suited as pre-performance anxiety-management tools? ___

_____

_____

_____

Which is the very best? Describe how you might use it as your anxiety mounts "in the wings." _____

_____

_____

_____

_____

*Learn one progressive relaxation technique and describe how it works for you.*_____

_____

_____

_____

Try out the Sarnoff Squeeze. Does it seem potentially effective? _____

_____

Try out the Quieting Reflex. How does it seem to work? _____

_____

What relaxation technique or techniques will you add to your collection of anxiety-management tools? _____

_____

_____

_____

Breathing and Meditative Techniques

In *Managing Your Anxiety*, Christopher McCullough described several breathing exercises. The exercises have names like "Slow, complete breathing," "Slow, deep breathing with shoulder relaxation," "Counting breaths," "Following your breathing," and "Circling your breaths." "Circling your breaths," for instance, works as follows:

> As you start to inhale, you slowly bring your attention up the ventral centerline of your body from the groin to the navel, chest, throat, and face, until you reach the crown of your head. As you exhale, slowly move your attention down the back of the head, down the neck, and all the way down the spine.

Try McCullough's simple exercise. Even simpler is the breathing exercise described by Stephanie Judy, in *Making Music for the Joy of It*:

> Anxiety disrupts normal breathing patterns, producing either shallow breathing or air gulping in an attempt to conserve the body's supply of oxygen. The simplest immediate control measure is to *exhale*, blowing slowly and steadily through your lips until your lungs feel completely empty. Don't "breathe deeply." It's too easy to hyperventilate and make yourself dizzy. As long as you make a slow, full exhale, the inhaling will look after itself.

The person who has paid little attention to breathing is unlikely to understand how valuable breath attention can be. Consider this description of Zen practice from Philip Kapleau's *The Three Pillars of Zen*:

> Zazen practice for the student begins with his counting the inhalations and exhalations of his breath while he is in the motionless zazen posture. This is the first step in the process of stilling the bodily functions, quieting discursive thought, and strengthening concentration. It is given as the first step because in counting the in and out breaths, in natural rhythm and without strain, the mind has, as it were, scaffolding to support it.

It may seem odd to emphasize something as automatic and everyday as breathing. But both centuries of mindful meditation practice and the experiences of our contemporaries who heed their breathing confirm that breath attention is an anxiety-reduction tool of real value.

Spend a little time just paying attention to your breathing. What do you notice? _____

_____

_____

_____

Learn one breathing exercise, even one as simple as "consciously exhaling." Practice it until it actually serves to reduce your anxiety. To what extent does it seem to work?

_____

_____

_____

*Imagine yourself about to make a presentation. Picture yourself waiting to go on and using your breathing technique to reduce your anxiety. Get as detailed and visceral a picture as you can. Is your breathing technique working for you when it really matters?*_____

_____

_____

_____

Meditation is a discipline that includes breath, body, and mind awareness. Different meditation exercises have different goals. Some help you exercise thought control, while others are designed to allow thought free reign. Both skills are valuable to acquire.

An example of a simple meditative technique is the use of a mantra. As Stephanie Judy explains:

> A mantra is one kind of thought pattern you can use to block negative thoughts. Often taught in conjunction with meditative techniques, a mantra is a word or short phrase that is simply repeated quietly, over and over again, aloud or in thought. *Peace* can be a mantra, as well as *one* or *love.*

R. Reid Wilson wrote, in his book *Don't Panic*:

> Meditation is a form of relaxation training. You learn to sit in a comfortable position and breathe in a calm, effortless way. You learn to quiet your mind, to slow down racing thoughts, and to tune in to more subtle internal cues. You

acquire the ability to self-observe. You practice the skill of focusing your attention on one thing at a time and doing so in a relaxed, deliberate fashion. By reducing the number of thoughts and images that enter your mind during a brief period, you are able to think with greater clarity and simplicity about whatever task you wish to accomplish. By spending as little as thirty seconds meditating, you can interrupt your negative thoughts and create a bridge between one mindset, in which stress predominates, to one in which calmness predominates. In the blink of an eye, you can alter your sense of the situation and dramatically reduce your experience of anxiety.

Create several mantras for yourself and try them out. Next, select the most resonant one. Describing in some detail, how did you arrive at this particular mantra? _____

_____

_____

_____

_____

Create your own brief meditation, one that takes about thirty seconds or a minute to help release the grip of anxiety. This will take some practice, for you will first need to learn how to meditate and then create your personal meditation. After you've arrived at a workable personal meditation, describe the process of arriving at that meditation in a detailed journal-writing exercise.

Reorienting Techniques

What we focus on plays a large part in determining how we feel. If you focus for a few minutes on the picture of a new, deadly virus slipping under your door and climbing into bed with you, you can work yourself into a fine panic attack in no time at all. All that can save you is to interrupt your thoughts and to focus on something else.

As we have seen, cognitive theorists believe that much of the anxiety we experience is a product of *focusing on* or *orienting toward* our own negative self-talk. The problem isn't just that we possess that negative self-talk—for each of us will say negative things to ourselves and about ourselves at one time or another. It is only when we *focus* on that negative self-talk, rather than letting it slip by half-unheard, that we grow anxious. For instance, any one of us might notice a person leaving the auditorium as we're giving our speech and wonder for an instant, "Am I boring?" But the person who lets that thought slip by and reorients to the material and the task at hand will not grow anxious, while the person who focuses on the thought will.

Reorienting is an invaluable technique to learn. You learn to take your mind off the negative self-talk, doubt, and worry, off the stressor in the environment, and focus your mind upon something else, away from your presentation, or back onto it, *wherever you choose.*

Dr. Manuel Smith, in his book *Kicking the Fear Habit*, posits that each of us has a powerful "reorienting reflex" that we can effectively employ to manage our anxiety.

He explained that we naturally orient to five kinds of stimuli:

1. To stimuli with *novelty*: anything that is unexpected or new.

2. To stimuli with *biological significance*: anything that satisfies our biological hungers.

3. To stimuli with *innate signal value*: anything that we instinctually orient to, such as bodily sensations.

4. To stimuli with *learned or acquired signal value*: anything that we have learned to pay attention to by any means.

5. To stimuli with *instructed signal value*: anything that we have been told or instructed to pay attention to, either by others or ourselves.

Thus, while you're waiting backstage and growing anxious, you might orient to (1) an announcement on the backstage bulletin board; (2) the attractive person across the room; (3) your breathing; (4) the beginning of the piece you're playing or the first line of your speech; or (5) the last-minute instructions about your entrance routine that you've written out on an index card. Reorienting to that attractive person, Hunt argues, may be the best distractor of all.

The presenter's task is to learn where his or her eyes and mind can effectively turn when the tension mounts. Focusing on a serpentine crack in the wall may not be able to engross and distract one as the hall fills up—or it just might. If you practice reorienting to different kinds of stimuli, you will discover which distractors have the power to really capture your attention.

Have you ever reduced anxiety by reorienting away from an anxiety-provoking stimulus and toward a different stimulus? _____
_____
_____

What sorts of stimuli grab your attention? Stimuli of a sexual nature? _____
_____
_____

Instructions you create for yourself? _____
_____
_____

New, novel, or interesting visual stimuli (like paint peeling off a wall, clouds, the lastest model car)? _____
_____
_____

Your own breathing? _____
_____
_____

List the different sorts of stimuli that might reorient your mind from an impending presentation. How would you rank them? ____
_____
_____
_____
_____

Imagine yourself in a presentation situation. Picture yourself reorienting away from the performance and toward some neutral stimulus. Does it seem as if such a technique might work for you? _____
_____
_____

Guided Visualizations

Guided visualizations are mental pictures you create for yourself. You can imagine yourself in a tranquil spot—on the beach, in a garden, beside a secluded lake—and spend time there, in your mind's eye, relaxing and letting your worries slip away. For example, the pianist Andrea Bodo created, as part of a five-step routine to help her make her entrance onto the stage, a guided visualization in which she transported herself to a spot beside a pool filled with water lilies. Like meditative and reorienting techniques, guided imagery provides you with a powerful means of "leaving," even when you can't physically leave.

Guided imagery is a versatile technique limited only by your powers of imagination. Providing yourself with verbal *cues*, you can guide yourself step-by-step through a successful performance, picturing yourself acting or singing with confidence or presenting your message with great flair. You can visualize yourself on a mission or feel yourself protected in a bubble of your own creation. In each case the visualization proceeds similarly:

• Seat yourself comfortably, placing your feet squarely on the ground. Close your eyes.

• Using progressive relaxation and deep breathing techniques, quiet yourself. Your goal is to drift into the sort of receptive state where images flow.

• Slowly, clearly, and calmly, pronounce either silently or aloud the cues you give yourself to produce the desired images in your mind.

You'll need to practice the visualization cues you mean to use; you might tape record them and play them back before a performance instead of speaking them, letting your taped words guide you through the process.

Sometimes there's a person in your life whose presence calms you. It might be a current or former friend or teacher. It might be the one person who's always had great confidence in you and would say to you, "Why, of course, you can do that!" While you wait, create a visualization of that person. Picture her calm, confident smile, have a little conversation with her in which she assures you that everything will proceed splendidly.

While for many performers it isn't a good idea to focus on the audience or to imagine what they are thinking, you might, if it works for you, imagine making a friend with some member of the audience. You can visualize that new friend smiling, happy to be there, calm and uncritical, entirely on your side. Provide yourself with at least one sturdy visualization, whether it's making or bringing a friend, an image of tranquility, a vision of rehearsal and mastery of your material, or something else of your own creation.

What different "images" create in you a feeling of tranquility? _____
_____
_____
_____

Which one of these might you incorporate into a guided visualization with the power to reduce your anxiety? _____
_____

_____
_____
_____

Create your own guided visualization, one that you can picture reducing your anxiety before a presentation. What is it like? _____
_____
_____
_____

Imagine a presentation situation. Picture yourself using your guided visualization— see yourself with your eyes closed, listening to your prepared cues, conjuring up a soothing image. Do you have the sense that this technique might work for you? _____
_____
_____
_____

Affirmations and Prayers

An affirmation is a positive statement that you create and repeat as needed, in which you assert that you are capable and confident. To be most effective, affirmations should be short and simple and framed in the present tense. Examples of affirmations are "I'm perfectly able to perform today" or "I know the lyrics." Your affirmation can be as simple as the word "Yes," repeated with conviction.

Any one of the following might make for a useful affirmation:

"I'm equal to this."

"I'm a fine performer."

"I know my job."

"No problem."

"I have no doubt."

"I can do this."

"I love making presentations."

"I'm calm and capable."

"I am prepared."

"I want to do this."

The logic of affirmations should be familiar to you from our previous discussion of cognitive restructuring. There we noted that the essential feature of thought substitution was the replacement of negative self-talk with self-talk rooted in the *positive present*. Affirmations do just that. You affirm that *right now* you have no need to worry.

You acknowledge your strengths, not your weaknesses. You affirm yourself, rather than disparaging yourself. You affirm that the process is working, rather than that the process is derailing. You affirm that the "other" — audience, critics, whomever — is not your enemy. You say "Yes!" and not "No!" You make use of the power of positive suggestion to block negative thoughts, give yourself a boost, and remind yourself of the joy embedded in the moment.

PRAYER

Affirmations are not prayers, but prayers can serve as affirmations. If you pray, you might use one of the following Biblical passages as your pre-performance prayer:

> The Lord himself goes before you and will be with you; he will never leave you nor forsake you. Do not be afraid; do not be discouraged.
>
> > *Deuteronomy 31:8*
>
> The Lord is my light and my salvation; whom shall I fear? The Lord is the stronghold of my life; of whom shall I be afraid?
>
> > *Psalms 27:1*
>
> Strengthen the feeble hands, steady the knees that give way; say to those fearful hearts, Be strong, do not fear.
>
> > *Isaiah 41:10a*
>
> So do not fear, for I am with you; do not be dismayed, for I am your God. I will strengthen you and help you.
>
> > *Isaiah 35:3-4*

Affirmations serve a dual purpose. First, they positively reframe the moment, calming and encouraging you. Second, they serve to alter your self-image by providing you with new, positive self-talk that actually takes hold over time. One day you'll say "I feel fine" or "I can do this" and discover that you're speaking the literal truth, not uttering a hope or a prayer.

Try your hand at creating a variety of affirmations. Create at least a dozen. There are no rules involved: any phrase that feels affirming is a legitimate affirmation.

Which affirmation seems to have the most resonance? Why might that be so? _____

_____

_____

_____

Picture yourself in a presentation situation, using your affirmation. Do you have the sense that this is a technique that will work for you? _____

_____

_____

Disidentification Techniques

Disidentification is a concept elaborated by the Italian psychiatrist Roberto Assagioli as part of the therapeutic model he called psychosynthesis. Assagioli argued that people often become overly invested in and identified with transitory events and states of mind, and that the cure for that mistaken identification involved consciously *disidentifying*.

For you, as the person making a presentation, this means simply that you are not the equivalent of your speaking voice—you are

more than your voice. You are not the equivalent of a certain piece of music associated with you—you are more than any musical work. You are not the equivalent of any one of your weaknesses (or strengths)— you are more than, and different from, any of your subpersonalities, as Assagioli called them. And you are not the equivalent of one of your performances, you are more than any performance.

The process of disidentifying involves using guided visualizations of a certain sort. As Assagioli explained in his book *Psychosynthesis*:

> The first step is to affirm with conviction and to become *aware* of the fact: "I *have* a body, but *I am not* my body." For instance, we say, "I am tired," which is nothing less than a psychological heresy; the "I" cannot be tired; *the body* is tired. The second step is the realization: "I *have* an emotional life, but *I am not* my emotions or my feelings." To say "I am content" or "I am irritated" is to commit an error of psychological grammar. The third step consists in realizing: "I *have* an intellect, but *I am not* that intellect." Ordinarily we identify ourselves with our thoughts, but when we analyze them, when we observe ourselves while we think, we notice that the intellect works like an *instrument*. These facts give us evidence that the body, the feelings and the mind are *instruments* of experience, perception and action

which are deliberately used by the "I," while the nature of the "I" is something entirely different.

Making use of these ideas, we can create the following "disidentification affirmations":

"The presentation matters, and it also doesn't matter."

"I am not my performance."

"I can laugh at all my absurd investments!"

"I am not my situation. I can accept my situation."

"I have negative thoughts, but I am not my negative thoughts."

"I am more than the part of me that is afraid right now."

"I have fears, but I am essentially unafraid."

"I am more than any mistakes I might make."

"I am not this character or this play."

"My body is acting up, but I am all right."

"My emotions are acting up, but I am all right."

"My thoughts are acting up, but I am all right."

"Whatever happens, *I* will be fine."

Rather than wishing for the hall to burn down or for a flood to arrive and wash away the audience, you can detach, disidentify, and accept the situation. Say to yourself, "All right, I'm here. I came here of my own free will. I meant to be here, and I'm through squirming." Learn to step aside and detach. Learn to identify yourself as a whole person who also happens to get up

and make a presentation to other people, making use of disidentification affirmations that work for you.

How much do you identify with the presentations you make? Can you put that connection into words? _____
_____
_____
_____
_____

*Try dreaming up ways of disidentifying from your performances. What comes to mind?*____
_____
_____
_____
_____

Can you construct a few disidentification affirmations of your own? _____
_____
_____
_____
_____

*Picture yourself about to appear before an audience. Will disidentifying from your presentation help reduce your performance anxiety?*_____
_____
_____
_____
_____

Symptom Confrontation Techniques

Symptom confrontation is a technique associated with existential psychotherapy and with the therapists Milton Erickson and Viktor Frankl in particular. In therapy of this sort, a client is commanded, apparently paradoxically, to do *more* of the thing that he came into therapy wanting to do *less* of.

In her book *A Soprano on Her Head,* Eloise Ristad explains how she championed symptom confrontation in her workshops as a way to reduce performance anxiety:

> Take one of your own symptoms— clammy hands, shaky knees, or whatever—and apply the principle of pushing it to the point where it can go no further. Do *not* try to control it or make it go away; try only to increase the intensity and see how far you can carry this particular symptom. If you are like most people, you will find you can't push your symptom past a certain point, and that when you reach that point the symptom actually reverses. Your saliva begins to flow naturally again, your knees stop shaking, your hands get respectably dry. You may find that almost as soon as you *try* to intensify a symptom, it begins to disappear. The significance of this information impresses me each time I experience it again.

Not only can you confront the symptoms you have, you can create symptoms you don't have. Are you only suffering from butterflies in the stomach? Why not have your palms sweat too? Indeed, why not just worry about worrying?—an exercise known as the transcendental metaworry exercise. As Frankl put it, "A sense of humor is inherent in this technique. Humor helps man rise

above his own predicament by allowing him to look at himself in a more detached way." But Frankl is quick to point out that the "paradoxical intention" technique is not a superficial one, even if it employs humor. He added, "I am convinced that paradoxical intention . . . enables the patient to perform on a deeper level a radical change of attitude, and a wholesome one at that."

Trying to increase your symptoms in order to make them disappear is a technique that may or may not appeal to you. More queasiness! More woolly-headedness! More palpitations! What an idea! But if the idea intrigues you, do investigate it. Astounding results are possible for people, especially performing artists, who are able to add this technique to their repertoire.

*Does "confronting your symptoms" seem like a congenial technique to you?*_____

_____

_____

*Try in your mind's eye confronting a physical symptom, like sweaty palms or wobbly knees. Do you see how the technique might work?*_____

_____

_____

Try in your mind's eye confronting a mental symptom, like an inability to concentrate or a sense of impending doom. Can such symptoms be confronted? Does this confrontation technique work on them? _____

_____

_____

Practice "symptom confrontation" a little bit. Then imagine a presentation situation. Can

you envision using this technique while
*waiting to go on?*_____

_____

_____

_____

_____

Discharge Techniques

Presenters can discharge the tension building up in them by doing something active and dramatic. For example, before going on they can shake a fist or rail at the audience, softly shout a terrific battle cry, or silently scream. These emotional and physical discharge techniques are not quite as dramatic as the actions they stand in for, but they can prove effective nonetheless. A real ear-piercing "primal scream" would certainly discharge a lot of tension and might feel wonderful, but is rather impractical. For one thing, it could do serious damage to your voice. A silent scream, however, can feel almost as therapeutic as a real one. Practice a silent scream by noting how wide your mouth opens, how rapidly your head moves, exactly how your neck muscles flex. Practice getting the tension-discharging effect of a real scream without uttering a sound. Or imagine yourself preparing for combat, and discharge the tension by uttering a silent but fiery battle cry. Create your own cry, and treat the moment as if you were a bold, adventurous hero. Or imagine yourself as Don Quixote about to set off on a great, even foolish quest, jousting with windmills. Shout *"Charge!"* in as wild and playful a fashion as you dare.

In *Raise Your Right Hand Against Fear,*

Sheldon Kopp described the Buddhist symbolic gesture known as a *mudra*:

> Determined to destroy the Buddha, a dark and treacherous demon unleashed an elephant charging drunkenly. Just as the raging beast was about to trample him, the Buddha raised his right hand with fingers close together and open palm facing the oncoming animal. The fearless gesture stopped the elephant in its tracks and completely subdued the recklessly dangerous creature. The Sanskrit word for such ritually symbolic gestures is *mudra*. The Buddha's mudra allowed him to face the fears in his own momentarily uncontrolled imagination.

Simply moving about helps reduce anxiety. You can pace, jog in place, skip up and down, stretch, do a little walking meditation or yoga. If you can, go outside and walk around the block. Many performers find that just stepping outside for a few seconds works wonders in reducing their anxiety. This is true in part because stepping out gives you a feeling of control. You give yourself permission to leave the scene, without abandoning the presentation you are committed to making. It thus counteracts that sense of "inhibited flight" that for some performers is a prime source of performance anxiety.

Emotional discharge techniques come in every shape and size. You might make zany faces, laugh, or at least smile a little. Tell yourself a good joke. Imagine that the musicians around you have been transformed into animals out of a Dr. Seuss tale. How does your accompanist look now? Even if you can't smile a lot, try to smile a little. The very act of smiling counteracts the buildup of tension. Dream up some gesture or action—a wild dance, an amazing leap, a left jab followed by a right cross—that really works to release tension from your body and your mind.

Practice "silent screaming"—really get into it. Do you have the sense that this technique might work for you? _____

_____

_____

Let your imagination go and dream up several mudras, or symbolic physical gestures, that you might use. Does one in particular have some real resonance? _____

_____

_____

Imagine a presentation situation. Can you see your mudra working? _____

_____

_____

Does the idea of treating performances as battles seem like a congenial idea to you? ____

_____

_____

If so, what techniques might you develop based on the idea of "doing battle"? _____

_____

_____

_____

_____

What other discharge techniques come to mind? _____

_____

_____

_____

_____

Choose one of these techniques to practice. How does it seem to work? _____

_____

_____

_____

_____

Ceremonies and Rituals

The simplest and no doubt oldest sort of calming ritual involves the use of a good luck charm. The opera soprano Lily Pons, for instance, would cut off a piece of the curtain to hold onto before each performance. Luciano Pavarotti, severely plagued by performance anxiety, is said to look for a bent nail backstage and reputedly will not go on unless he finds one. In *No More Fears*, Dr. Douglas Hunt wrote:

> The simple faith that a good-luck charm will carry one through is a time-honored way to handle performance anxiety. Often faith in an object actually lowers anxiety and fear, and things consequently go better. Superstitions may seem out of place in modern society, but if not carried to extremes, they can be viable techniques for self-control.

Rituals that are repeated exactly the same way before every event can also have a soothing effect on one's nerves. In her book

The Bright Lights: A Theater Life, the actress Marian Seldes explained:

> There is a ritual in the dressing room, private for some, gregarious for others. The look of the room, the temperature, where each article of clothing is set—yours and the character's—mementos from other plays. A different robe for the theater. Special towels, soap, cologne. Brushes and combs. The actual tubes or sticks of makeup, the brushes.

Presenters can complement their use of good luck charms with rituals and ceremonies they consciously devise. A musical ensemble, a sales team, or an acting troupe can gather for a moment and enact a brief group ceremony. They can shout a battle cry together or honor as sacred the event about to begin. Initially such ceremonies may feel forced, false, and embarrassing, but over time they can acquire rich meaning and serve finally to reduce the group members' anxiety level.

Have you a good luck charm? Do you want to get one? _____

_____

_____

Invent a few pre-performance ceremonies or rituals that might work to calm you. Would you be willing to try one before making a presentation?

Pick out the one that feels the most resonant and useful. Picture yourself in a presentation situation. Try out your ceremony or ritual in

your mind's eye. How does it seem to work? _

_____

_____

_____

Preparation Techniques

Rehearsing your material and preparing to go on are activities you naturally engage in right up until curtain time. Repeating your entrance line like a mantra, humming the first measures of your piece, or glancing again at your note cards is likely a thing you already do, serving as it does to refresh your memory and block out negative thoughts. But bringing a certain calmness to these preparations is another matter entirely. There's a difference between frantically glancing at your note cards and not seeing a word versus reading them calmly, your breathing regular and your mind at ease. There's a difference between repeating your opening line to yourself over and over again in a panic, because you fear forgetting it, versus repeating it to yourself with assurance, working as you rehearse to put yourself into the role of presenter.

Certain special preparations may be important. Are you perhaps more worried about the post-recital reception than about the presentation itself? Use guided imagery to role-play that situation while you wait. What might people say about your performance? What have they said in the past? How would you like to respond? Do you need to create some simple answers to the questions you expect to be asked? If you're regularly unable to answer the question, "Now, what was that new music *about?*", this time prepare your answer: "Why, it was about love, death, infinity, and so much more!" The more you find yourself in the public eye, the more important it becomes to role-play situations like receptions and interviews beforehand. Just as your entrance, exit, and comportment may be mentally rehearsed beforehand, so too may these extra–presentation situations. You'll want to plan for your entrance as you wait in the wings. Do this planning calmly, affirming your readiness and willingness to go on. Stephanie Judy recommended the following five-step entrance ritual for musicians:

1. Acknowledge your audience.

2. Make contact with your instrument.

3. Make contact with the other musicians.

4. Think of a calming image.

5. Think about the music.

The singer and career counselor Reneé Hayes canvassed her performer friends and offers the following preparation advice:

- Know your personal ritual. I usually get very nervous the day before the gig and often have a nightmare that night. I'm often terribly nervous before I go on stage and spend time berating myself for choosing this form of torture. Then I go on stage, feel better after the first song, feel worse after the second number, and finally settle into being comfortable.

- Rehearse, rehearse, rehearse, rehearse. There is no such thing as being over-prepared.

- Give yourself plenty of time! Don't rush to the gig. Make sure you know how to get there and that you leave in plenty of time.

- Come to the venue early and take the time to stand on the stage (or the place you'll stand when you sing). Take a look around. Take in where the audience will be. "Own the joint." Tell yourself that it's yours and that when people come in the door they will be walking into your territory.

- Recognize that that awful feeling of "butterflies in the stomach" is just adrenaline. Adrenaline is energy. Terror is your friend. In other words, "reframe it."

- Minimize the goal. Remember that just getting there and opening your mouth is a triumph.

- Feel the fear and do it anyway.

- Concentrate on the song instead of the fact that you are the one performing, focus on the words you are singing, the message you are giving.

- Have fun.

- Please your own self.

Cognitive Work

As we have seen, people tend to talk to themselves in ways that are anything but encouraging. The anxious presenter is likely to predict that a catastrophe will happen. He or she will exaggerate the looming problems, magnify the danger, and in other ways engage in "mind tricks" that increase anxiety. The way to alter this self-sabotaging pattern is to stop the negative thought and substitute a new, positive one. For example, a common negative thought is that of being exposed to the audience's scrutiny: Everyone's going to be watching me! The new and alternative thoughts you might try substituting are:

I enjoy being watched.

I'm worth watching.

Naturally, the audience will watch me.

Here are a few more examples:

• *Negative thought:* I know they're going to judge me!

Alternatives: No one can judge me.

I expect I'll do a fine job.

Judging is *their* business, my job is presenting.

• *Negative thought:* I know I'm going to bore them.

Alternatives: If I bore someone, that's life.

If I really make music, no one will be bored.

I get bored myself sometimes.

• *Negative thought:* What if I suddenly have to scream?

Alternatives: I expect to have a good evening.

If I feel like screaming, I'll silently scream.

After the performance, I will enjoy a good scream.

• *Negative thought:* What if I goof and look stupid?

Alternatives: I'll survive whatever happens.

I can live with a little embarrassment.

I'm prepared and it will go smoothly.

• *Negative thought:* I won't perform as well as I did before!

Alternatives: Each presentation is unique.

Why shouldn't this time be better?

I don't compare one performance to another.

• *Negative thought:* What if I begin too fast?

Alternatives: I have my entrance routine down pat.

I know exactly how fast to start.

Everything's under control.

• *Negative thought:* What if I disappoint myself?

Alternatives: I'll learn from whatever happens.

I can disappoint myself sometimes.

I expect to make a wonderful presentation!

• *Negative thought:* What if I flub my lines?

Alternatives: I'm prepared and I don't anticipate any problems.

My job is to perform with passion—and to relax.

Such things happen. I'll get over it.

A great variety of cognitive techniques are available to you. The violinist and aikido expert Paul Hirata, for instance, teaches a technique he calls *Half-Half-Half*. The idea is to suggest to yourself that you release just half your anxiety, using the word "Half" as a kind of mantra. You exhale, relax, and quietly say, "Half." You inhale again, continuing to relax, and upon the exhale say "Half" again, continuing the process as necessary.

Another cognitive technique is reframing. Rather than believing one thing about a situation, you resolve to believe something else instead. The objective facts haven't changed, but your view of them has. For example, rather than feeling trapped, remind yourself that you have the freedom to leave *at any time*. Reframe the moment as one of free choice rather than of entrapment. You may find it surprisingly useful to picture yourself walking calmly out of the hall without a care or a backward glance.

The following is another powerful reframing technique. Normally we think of a presentation as the climax of long effort and the very reason for the effort. But there's an entirely different way to think of the process that begins when we first draft a speech, become acquainted with a piece of music, or read a play and ends with its formal presentation to an audience.

In this other way of thinking about the process, the exploration phase of rehearsing and practicing is held as the real work. You master the role or music so as to provide yourself with a joyful and fulfilling experience. Indeed, the experience may be more magical and revelatory in this phase than in the public performance. Film star Paul Newman explained it this way:

> My fantasy is that you get a marvelously inventive director, and you cast the play the way it ought to be cast, not because you have to cast it a certain way. You get together and you have four incredible weeks of rehearsal, and then you shut it down. No one ever sees it.

Try some of the cognitive techniques we've just discussed. Bring up a negative thought about yourself. Then try to stop the thought. Try shouting "Stop!" Create some other thought-stopping techniques that range from the very dramatic to the not-so-dramatic.

Do you find that you can successfully stop your own thoughts? _____
_____
_____

Can you substitute a more positive thought for a negative one? _____
_____
_____

Can you reframe a situation in an affirmative way? _____
_____
_____

Try to master thought substitution and describe the process of mastering it here. How does it work for you? _____
_____
_____
_____
_____
_____

Pick another cognitive technique that might help you. Picture yourself in a presentation situation and envision yourself using that technique. How does it suit your needs? ____

_____

_____

_____

_____

Conclusion

Having read along in this book is an excellent sign of your readiness and willingness to deal with performance anxiety in your life. The next step is doing the work: learning several anxiety-management techniques, practicing them, trying them out in the world and, finally, making presentations fearlessly.

I recommend that you outline a complete anxiety-management plan, including those things that you will do on an ongoing basis and those that you will do right before and during a presentation. If you do the work, the payoff will be tremendous: richer experiences in front of audiences, renewed joy in performing, and a career no longer hampered by unmanaged anxiety.

I wish you good luck—and may all your frights be little ones!

Index

About the Author

ERIC MAISEL, Ph.D. is a creativity consultant and licensed psychotherapist whose books include *Affirmations for Artists, Fearless Creating, A Life in the Arts,* and *Artists Speak.* He founded and wrote *Callboard Magazine*'s "Staying Sane in the Theater" column, and his articles have appeared in such magazines as *Writer's Digest, Intuition, Dramatics,* and *The California Therapist.*

   Dr. Maisel is available for consultations and workshops with businesses, organizations, and individuals on presentation matters, including sales presentations, performance anxiety issues, and creativity issues. He can be reached by fax or phone at (510) 689-0210, or by mail at the following address:

Dr. Eric Maisel
P.O. Box 613
Concord, CA 94522-0613